THE ROAD TO MUCKLE FLUGGA

'Superb' *CAR Magazine*

'This is the book I've been waiting for' *Top Gear*

'Motoring's own Bill Bryson' *Octane*

'Don't miss it' *Motor Sport*

'Irresistible' *Autocar*

'Llewellin has written a book that opens the gates of wonder and delight in a charming and telling fashion' *Cambridge Evening News*

'Whether he is charging around the D-Day beaches of Normandy or enjoying a Guinness in Ireland, the quality of the author's writing shines through' *The Herald*

'Hugely entertaining... vividly descriptive' *Worcester Evening News*

'Brilliantly written and crafted' *The Sentinel*

'A splendid travel writer' *Wrexham Evening Leader*

'The stories all add up to a terrific adventure' *Oswestry & Border Counties Advertizer*

'Travel writing as humorous and perceptive as Bill Bryson's' *TRUCK Magazine*

THE ROAD TO
MUCKLE
FLUGGA

Great drives in five continents

Phil Llewellin

'A masterpiece'
London Evening Standard

Haynes Publishing

First published hardback in May 2004
Reprinted September 2004

This paperback edition published in August 2010

A catalogue record for this book is available from the British Library

ISBN 978 08573 3003 1

Library of Congress catalog card no 2010924923

Published by Haynes Publishing,
Sparkford, Yeovil, Somerset BA22 7JJ, UK.
Tel: 01963 442030 Fax: 01963 440001
Int.tel: +44 1963 442030 Int.fax: +44 1963 440001
E-mail: sales@haynes.co.uk
Website: www.haynes.co.uk

Haynes North America Inc.,
861 Lawrence Drive, Newbury Park,
California 91320, USA.

Designed and typeset by Dominic Stickland
Printed and bound in the USA

Phil Llewellin was an award-winning writer whose adventures enthralled readers of leading magazines and newspapers worldwide. This book chronicles some of his most exciting journeys.

23 October 1940–1 July 2005

CONTENTS

Acknowledgements   8
Foreword by Jeremy Clarkson   9
Introduction   11

AMERICA
  1   Shropshire lad in Detroit – 1977   20
  2   The long weekend – 1978   24
  3   Big wheels rolling – 1985   31
  4   Meeting the legends – 1988   49
  5   Coast-to-coast on the Lincoln Highway – 1989   58
  6   Going for gold on Route 49 – 1990   62
  7   Laxative Ridge – 1993   66
  8   Inverness to Chester in seven minutes – 1997   72
  9   Hunting ghosts in Nevada – 1999   78
 10   Ticking them off in a Packard – 1999   83
 11   Going to extremes – 2001   87

CANADA
 12   Trucking across the big country – 1981   95
 13   Into the far north's freezer – 1982   115

AFRICA
 14   Long road to London – 1983   126
 15   A breezy tribute to the boy king – 1990   140
 16   High jinks in the Sahara – 1991   143

BRITISH ISLES
 17   Oysters and Guinness in Galway – 1986   150
 18   The little man with the big hat – 1987   157
 19   Wizards of ooze – 1988   165

20	The Colossus of Roads – 1989	171
21	The finest hour – 1990	180
22	Giraldus Cambrensis and the GT40 – 1993	187
23	The road to Muckle Flugga – 1994	191
24	All in good time – 1999	229
25	Great Britain's greatest drive – 2001	236

MIDDLE EAST

26	Cooke's tour to Abadan – 1976	242
27	Kamikazes and Kalashnikovs on the road to Pakistan – 1978	254

CARIBBEAN AND SOUTH AMERICA

28	Driving to the end of the world – 1998	277
29	Racing goats and scalp-lifting rum – 2003	283

FAR EAST

30	Battling through Borneo – 1985	287
31	China with western half-devil Clarkson – 1988	296
32	Old cars and good times on the equator – 1993	304

EUROPE

33	Back to the bloody beaches – 1984	310
34	The Bentley Boys – 1986	325
35	When the gates of hell opened – 1986	331
36	Strong beer and dainty dishes – 1989	339
37	France's spaceship on wheels – 1990	342
38	And the wall came tumbling down – 1990	350
39	Anthem for doomed youth – 1993	354
40	Taking the high road – 1997	360
41	A tribute to yesterday's heroes – 2002	365
42	The great quote – 2002	372

Appendix – Maps	375
Index	378

DEDICATION

This book is dedicated with love, thanks and respect to
my wife, Beth, and our children, Philippa, Magnus and
Howard; to my mother and stepfather, Muriel and Clenyg
Llewellin; and to the father I never knew,
Pilot Officer Philip Crush, RAF.

ACKNOWLEDGEMENTS

The Road to Muckle Flugga would not have happened had Ian Fraser, Mel Nichols, Steve Cropley, Gavin Green, Paul Barden, Clive Richardson, Mark Gillies, Jean Jennings, David E Davis Jr and other editors in Britain and America not pandered to my passion for travel. To quote just one example, it takes someone special to agree that an article about a Great War poet is suitable for publication in a motoring magazine. This book brings together stories that were written for *Car*, *Supercar Classics*, *The Audi Magazine*, *Truck*, *Supertruck*, *The Scotsman*, *Automobile Magazine* and *Car & Driver*. One of them, *China with western half-devil Clarkson*, has never been published before. They have all been revised, typically because the car that was hot news a couple of decades ago merits less space today.

Thanks are also due to four of the photographers with whom I have covered so many miles and who gave me permission to use their pictures – Ian Dawson, Martyn Goddard, Richard Newton and Tim Wren.

Finally, I am grateful to Mark Hughes, Flora Myer and the rest of the team at Haynes Publishing for their patience and understanding. Books are their business, but putting *The Road to Muckle Flugga* together was a completely new experience for me. They deserve medals for their unflagging patience, understanding, enthusiasm, humour and encouragement.

FOREWORD

BY JEREMY CLARKSON

When I was young and just starting out in the peculiar world of motoring journalism, Phil Llewellin was already very Welsh.

But despite this, he seemed to be by far and away the most talented of the hack pack. His column in the then prestigious magazine *Car* was a must-read event every month, partly because it was just so beautifully written and partly because Phil realised, even back then, that cars were dull. It was what you did with them that mattered.

What makes an engine go is irrelevant. Where it takes you is the important thing.

To this day I still remember a piece he wrote about spectating on what used to be called the RAC Rally. While everyone else was talking about stage times and tyre choices, Phil was writing about the weather. It was so cold, he said, that he didn't know whether to drink his mulligatawny soup, or pour it into his wellingtons.

Eventually, our paths crossed and I realised he was not only a phenomenal writer, but also a magnificent drinker. There was no bar stool he couldn't fall off and no hotel room lock that was manageable. Phil slept where he fell.

Our first adventure together was a trip to China. I'd never been that far abroad before, whereas Phil was already a seasoned traveller, so I thought he'd have a few choice pieces of advice about jet lag and so on. 'We need to get drunk,' he said. This made sense. I figured that if I'd got on the plane sozzled from a big night out, I'd sleep through the 14-hour flight.

It was, however, a rubbish idea. I got on the plane with a

monumental hangover and looked once again to Phil for advice. 'There's only one cure for a hangover,' he said. 'We need to get drunk again.' This was Phil's solution to pretty well everything.

The astonishing thing is though that I came back from China not really knowing where I'd been or what had happened there, whereas he came back and wrote a piece that was crammed full of detail and fact. You see this in everything he does, his trip to Detroit and the history of Henry Ford, and the mad dash across Afghanistan where a local tells him everything is upside down. For Phil, I guess, this would have been normal.

I love his ability to find something interesting in almost everything and, when he can't, to spice up the banal with his own take on things. I also love the fact he's a font of knowledge, especially on military history and the Welsh. Most of all though, I love the way he's just so damn funny.

As a result, so is this book.

INTRODUCTION

The great affair is to move

ROBERT LOUIS STEVENSON

Winston Churchill, Butch Cassidy, Isambard Kingdom Brunel, William K Vanderbilt, Robert Louis Stevenson, King Ludwig of Bavaria, Juan Manuel Fangio, Abraham Lincoln, Captain James Cook, Judy Garland, Adolf Hitler, Henry Ford and Calamity Jane are just a few of the people you will meet in this book. They have been with me in spirit for many years, because travelling to evocative places is the nearest we real-world mortals ever get to experiencing the sci-fi wonders of a time machine. I am fascinated by internal combustion engines, but what makes even the most powerful and beautiful of them work excites me far less than visions of using them to go places. Faced with the choice between attending a new Ferrari's launch in Italy or spending a few days driving a run-of-the-mill saloon car around the far north of Scotland, where wonderful roads unfurl across sensational scenery, I wouldn't hesitate for a nanosecond before heading north.

Reasons for regarding the car as a magic carpet stem from childhood. Born in 1940, I grew up when wartime restrictions ruled out private motoring. Dad's role as a Home Guard officer entitled him to a few gallons, so it was a great adventure to cover a few miles in his Morris Eight. I can still picture the little saloon's maroon and black paint, hear the engine, smell the musty leather and see a soldier cleaning his rifle as specks of dust dance in the sunbeam that lances over his left shoulder. What holidays there were involved public transport. In 1945, for instance, we went to Aberystwyth by train, down the coast to Cardigan by bus, then into Pembrokeshire aboard a taxi before walking the last half-mile to our destination.

I almost fainted with excitement in 1950, when my parents announced that petrol was no longer rationed, so we would be spending our summer holiday touring the West Country. Land's End was about 300 miles from our home in Shropshire, but that was twice as far as I had ever been before. Today, my 1996-vintage grandson thinks nothing of flying the Atlantic.

If there is wanderlust in my genes it must come from my mother, who loved to travel. She celebrated her 21st birthday with a Mediterranean cruise, way back in 1932, when a week in Llandudno was regarded as an adventure. Twenty years later she astonished her middle-aged, middle-class friends by hitch-hiking as far as Italy. Highlights included being given a lift in the Aga Khan's Cadillac. The trip was undertaken because my stepfather refused to go abroad, for the excellent reason that it in those days it was impossible to keep in touch with what was happening on the cricket field. When communications improved he became one of the world's greatest Francophiles.

My earliest declaration of intent came towards the end of an undistinguished school career at Wycliffe College, when four of us volunteered to attend an Air Training Corps camp in Gloucestershire. The hidden agenda was centred on the weekend coinciding with the Oxford-Cambridge boat race. There were visions of hitch-hiking to Oxford for a night of strong beer and nubile nymphomaniacs. We knew the race was staged in London, of course, but didn't realise that the university term had ended, which explained why the streets and pubs were not thronged with students.

The chances of four young men getting a lift after dark were remote, so we walked most of the way back to the camp, a distance of about 40 miles. I can still feel my blistered feet protesting a day later, when the drill sergeant had us marching up and down the parade ground.

Fast-forward to August 1957 and the Llewellins are sailing from Dover to Calais for a French holiday that includes a few days in Paris. The Austin A40 Somerset breaks down several times, and is towed through the City of Light at breakneck speed, but mechanical maladies are nothing to the thrill I get from being on foreign soil for the first time. Those were the days when 'GB' plates were as rare as snake feathers. I thought the initials stood not for 'Great Britain' but for 'Gone 'Broad'.

Like most of my generation, I was hugely influenced by Jack Kerouac's sublimely irresponsible beatnik odyssey, *On the Road*, with its inspirational accounts of wild journeys across the mind-boggling immensity of America. I loved the chapters about driving a '47 Cadillac from Denver to Chicago. It was 'a beautiful big car, the last of the old-style limousines, black, with a big elongated body and whitewall tyres and probably bulletproof windows'. Much of what Kerouac wrote was rubbish, but most of a lifetime later I still get a terrific kick out of such passages as:

> *In no time at all we were back on the main highway and that night I saw the entire state of Nebraska unroll before my eyes. A hundred and ten miles an hour straight through, an arrow road, sleeping towns, no traffic, and the Union Pacific streamliner falling behind us in the moonlight . . . It was a magnificent car: it could hold the road like a boat holds on water. Gradual curves were its singing dream.*

Travelling long distances by road didn't seem such a bright thing to do in April 1978, when my arrival in Afghanistan coincided with the bloody *coup d'état* that was destined to trigger more than two decades of strife. The long drive from London had already been enlivened by breakdowns, getting arrested in Yugoslavia and being hit by a truck in Turkey. Now, when the end of the road should have been in sight, a nervous young soldier was getting close to shoving his AK-47 Kalashnikov's bayonet up my nose. Tanks lined the road. Proceed at more than a walking pace and the troops with machine guns will start shooting, we were warned. That's a stiff speeding penalty in any language.

The extent to which Yugoslavia's political face has changed since that marathon is a reminder that several of the countries I have visited no longer exist as such. For instance, Germany has reunited while Czechoslovakia is now two nations. I have resisted the temptation to update my original stories, because each represents a snapshot taken at a precise moment in time.

My life as a freelance wordsmith had changed three years earlier, when a call from *Truck* magazine invited me to write and photograph a big rig's journey from Damascus to Kuwait. This really was the proverbial bolt from the blue, because what I knew about trucks could have been written on a gnat's kneecap. I remain convinced that the caller made a mistake, but that ride in a Volvo F89 established me as the magazine's 'Long Distance Diary' man for the next ten years. Concerns about being regarded as an ever so slightly posh outsider were soon discarded. That trip to Kuwait created the completely false impression of a veteran who could cap any story with yarns about dodging camels, crossing deserts and, on asking directions, being told: 'Straight on for 600 miles, then turn left at the crossroads.'

Trucking tales also took me all over America and Canada, where 18-wheelers with huge sleeper cabs, acres of chrome, mighty engines and dozens of gears lived up to expectations by covering immense distances at highly illegal speeds. Here again, my novelty value was a great asset, notably when English-English was heard on the CB radio. There were times and places when an alien stepping out of a flying saucer would not have attracted more attention.

'D'you know Prince Charles?' I was asked in a remote Texas town.

'Of course. He's in the pub with me most nights, knocking back pints of beer like there's no tomorrow,' I deadpanned.

Early visits also confirmed what I had been told about the average American's amusing yet alarming lack of knowledge about the rest of the world. Tales about places I had visited sparked several memorable questions.

One was: 'What kinda frontier is there between England and Spain? A river, or a range of mountains, or what?'

I said: 'Well, there's a stretch of water called the English Channel and a rather large country, called France.'

Another guy, enthralled by stories of Algeria, Egypt, Kenya and Sudan, said: 'How are things in Africa nowadays? That big black guy still in charge?'

Trucking assignments provided some of my most memorable journeys, such as the series of rides that took me across Canada from Newfoundland to Edmonton, then up the Alaska Highway to Whitehorse. That trek, the equivalent of driving from England to Pakistan, was undertaken in the summer of 1981. A few months later I returned to Whitehorse in winter and went up the Dempster Highway, which was then the only public road in North America to cross the Arctic Circle. Writers are often accused of exaggerating, and since then I have often wondered if I was guilty by claiming to have experienced temperatures as low as minus 50 degrees Centigrade. In fact, re-reading the story tells me that I actually survived minus 62 degrees – and that was before taking wind chill into account. In that fearsome cold it was a surreal experience to drive across broad, frozen rivers where the snow-covered ferries had been hauled high onto the banks to escape the yard-thick ice that would have crushed their hulls.

It has become fashionable to decry the car as one of the most dreadful menaces ever inflicted on the planet. At the other extreme it provides a freedom of movement that has liberated more people than all of democracy's great heroes put together. Planes and trains are fine, but nothing thrills me to quite the same extent as seeing new lands appearing through a car's windscreen. Pilots and train drivers don't take kindly to passengers who fancy unscheduled stops or lengthy detours, but the car provides that free-wheeling flexibility.

Four of the journeys were inspired by wars that ripped the world apart during the last century. They are reminders of how boyhood's vision of war as a game – 'Bang, bang! You're dead' – is replaced by the realisation that one of the few things politicians have done really well, generation after generation, is send young men to their death. School teaches us about great commanders and grand strategies, but those wars were all about ordinary people being pitchforked into extraordinary situations – the quiet bank clerk who closes the ledger, puts on a uniform and wins the Victoria Cross.

Ypres, Arras, Vimy, Le Cateau, Loos, Bapaume and Albert are among the place-names that sound in my ears like muffled drumbeats whenever I drive across Belgium and northern France. Amid the churning emotions I wonder how today's public, living in a world where one soldier's death attracts front-page headlines in every newspaper, would react to 60,000 casualties in a single day.

Far from home, I love the big skies and open spaces of America's Wild West. The cinema of the mind's eye often takes me back to a morning in North Dakota, when the rising sun combined with clear air to make the landscape seem almost unreal. We crossed into Montana, where the 'reasonable and prudent' speed limit freed our Jaguar XK8 to cruise at more than 100mph across a state not much smaller than Spain, where people are outnumbered by cattle. Running parallel to the Missouri for hour after hour prompted the thought that this part of the world must have seemed impossibly remote and empty to Meriwether Lewis and William Clark when their Corps of Discovery was heading westward, against the mighty river's current, in 1805.

My idea of a great holiday is what my wife refers to as 'another bloody endurance test'. That was one reason for not planning to drive too far while visiting Argentina in 1998. We decided to spend three nights in Puerto Madryn, where the first wave of settlers from Wales landed in 1865. It had become obvious that reasonably good roads and very little traffic enabled vast distances to be covered without too much effort, so I decided to be cunning. The ploy's first element involved spreading our map out on a table and suggesting we fly down to Tierra del Fuego. That would enable us to visit Ushuaia, the world's southernmost town, then hire a car and drive to the end of the world's southernmost road. My wife considered this proposition for a few seconds, then reacted by doing finger-and-thumb measurements of the distance covered since leaving Buenos

Aires. I held my breath, then: 'Why fly when we could drive it in two or three days?' she said.

We reached Ushuaia before I took a closer look at the map and realised that Patagonia's dirt roads would account for a significant part of our return journey up the western side of the country, overlooked by the Andes. Driving for hour after hour on those completely deserted ribbons of gravel was like crossing an ocean. We were very fortunate, because I had a heart attack shortly after returning home. I doubt if I would be writing this had the ticker decided to misbehave when we were hundreds of miles from nowhere, in a region where what appeared to be towns on the map could be nothing more than a battered sign used for target practice. We felt we were travelling, which is not the same as being on holiday.

Public transport provides better opportunities to meet people, as I discovered when a long weekend was an opportunity to do a long bus journey in the USA. That said, car and truck journeys have involved characters who made the stops memorable. One was Dicky Walsh, the jovial Irish lifeboat cox'n who wished there were eight nights in the week to drink Guinness. Another was Tomas Aksarlian, the Armenian who opened his Swiss-style hotel near Bariloche a day ahead of schedule when we were in Argentina. When we went down for dinner, and were told the menu hadn't been printed, he invited us into the kitchen to meet the chef and take our pick. What about wine? Down to the cellar. Back in the dining room he opened the piano's lid and asked if I liked the tango.

'Yes,' I said, 'but with the best will in the world I don't fancy dancing with you.'

He laughed, rattled off a few note-for-note-perfect bars, then treated us to a little Mozart followed by foot-tapping ragtime.

'Are you the manager or a professional entertainer?' my wife asked.

'Neither,' he said, 'I'm an orthopaedic surgeon from Buenos Aires. I'm one of a group of friends who decided to buy the hotel as an investment.'

A long delay in Damascus was enlivened by hours spent

awaiting news in a transport agent's tiny office. The one-man business was run by a jovial Palestinian who wore the same clothes day after day after day. He liked beer, despite his religion taking a dim view of alcohol. Drinking it was permitted as long as you didn't enjoy the stuff, he gurgled. He also enjoyed playing along with the British truck drivers whose sense of humour was as subtle as a sledgehammer.

'Mr Journalist, you are an intelligent man,' he said, handing me another beer. 'Please tell me if it true that when I visit England and meet your Prime Minister, the correct greeting is "Good morning, Sir, how are your bollocks today?" This is correct, yes?'

John and Lucy Hemsley earned my respect the hard way, driving a Range Rover at record-breaking speed from Cape Town to London. My role in that adventure was as chronicler rather than participant. I met them in Nairobi and Khartoum, then on the dock at Dover for the last-gasp dash to Marble Arch. Their feat, which received very little publicity at the time, epitomised that wonderful and quintessentially British character cocktail in which vision, courage and determination are blended with a great deal of humour and just a dash of eccentricity.

I enjoyed meeting the tough, resolute, independent, sincere, humorous people of northern Canada, where the pioneering spirit lives on. The news that a naturalist had been ripped apart by a grizzly underlined just how far I was from what passes for civilisation.

Best of all are the alliances forged with photographers, notably the four whose pictures appear in this book – Ian Dawson, Martyn Goddard, Richard Newton and Tim Wren. They are classic examples of colleagues who become friends.

'What's the best car in the world?' is a familiar question when I get cornered at a party. The simple and honest answer is another question – 'The best for what?' – because everything depends on the role it will have to play. The best car for taking Queen Elizabeth to Westminster Abbey will be less than ideal for crossing the Sahara, winning the Italian Grand Prix, bagging 'Best of Show' at Pebble Beach or sneaking into parking spaces little bigger than a matchbox.

The other predictable question – 'What's your favourite road?' – is easy to answer after motoring some two million miles on five continents. When returning from a trip, I still experience a literally spine-tingling thrill on catching my first glimpse of the Welsh hills that have watched over me since the day I was born. The best road of all is the road that takes me home.

1

AMERICA

Shropshire Lad
in Detroit

1977

I flew into Detroit with all the confidence of a skydiver who bales out only to realise he has left his parachute behind. With something in the region of 1,000 murders a year, and mugging a local speciality, Motor City is as good a place as any to get your torso ventilated or wake up in the gutter with an empty wallet and a skull resembling crazy paving.

But the metropolis is really a kid at heart, says the guidebook, breezily urging you to take 'Brunch with Bach' at the Institute of Arts, ride an antique trolley down Washington Boulevard, catch salmon from the wharves of Belle Isle Park and imbibe The Old Shillelagh bar's genuine Irish atmosphere. Singularly unimpressed by such propaganda, city-centre executives flee for the suburbs each evening, when the downtown streets look like sets for a film about the last man left alive in the world. Locals advise visitors to stick together, lock the car doors and keep the windows right up.

Inspired by the guidebook, I decided to take a look at Ford's plant on the Rouge River. Although a shadow of its former self, this vast complex still employs 28,000 people. You feel like a spectator in a subterranean zoo while filing past endless assembly lines. Hieronymus Bosch would have found dark inspiration in such a place.

'History is bunk,' said Henry Ford, realising when it was

too late that his words would make a less than flattering epitaph in the *Oxford Dictionary of Quotations*. And so, as they tell it in Detroit, he armed henchmen with suitcases of dollars and told them to buy anything and everything, as long as it was old. The result, known irreverently as Uncle Henry's Curiosity Shop, is the most astonishing and worthwhile experience the Detroit area has to offer. You need time, because Greenfield Village, Dearborn, covers 240 acres while the Henry Ford Museum is housed under one 14-acre roof.

Whatever grabs you is there. One showcase contains four violins – Henry liked fiddle music – made by Guarneri, Amati and Stradivari. Porcelain, telephones, stoves, cameras, silver, pewter, glass, old maps, newspapers, watches by the hundred – Henry used to repair them – aircraft dangling from the roof, fire engines, traction engines, Newcomen steam engines, dental instruments, furniture, boats, locomotives and, inevitably, regiments of cars. Fords ranging from Henry's first boneshaker to the Mark IV driven to victory at Le Mans in 1967 share space with models from Bugatti, Rolls-Royce, Kelsey, Oakland, Carter, Maxwell, Brush, Stoddard, Regal, Thomas, Tucker, Haynes-Apperson, Essex, Franklin, Hupmobile, Cord, Rope, String, Twine . . . After a while the mind starts reeling.

Several jumbo-sized estate cars are reminders that Henry liked to go camping with three of his closest friends. One afternoon, way out in the middle of nowhere, the car broke down and a straw-chewing yokel sauntered from the field to help. 'I'm Henry Ford,' said the leader of the expedition, 'and these are my buddies, Thomas Edison, the famous inventor, and Harvey Firestone, the man who makes the tyres.' At that point the fourth traveller – the long-bearded naturalist, John Burroughs – stuck his head out of the window. At last the wide-eyed, saggy-jawed rustic spoke: 'And if you try to tell me he's Santa Claus, I'll fetch you one with this spade,' he growled.

Greenfield Village, next door to the museum, enabled Henry to collect buildings. There's the little farmhouse where he was born in 1863, and the workshop where he built his first car. Elsewhere, you stroll into the shop where the Wright brothers constructed their epochal aeroplane, and visit the Menlo Park compound where Edison invented the phonograph and the electric light. The Owl hotdog stall is where Henry munched late-night snacks at the end of the 19th century.

'This,' said the lady guide to a cluster of stone buildings, 'is a farm from the Cotswolds, in Gloucestershire, England. It was originally the home of sheepherders and was built in 1602, during the time of King Arthur and his Knights of the Round Table. Over there' – pointing to the headgear of a Cromwellian trooper – 'is the sort of helmet the knights would have worn.'

Fascinated by such an unorthodox view of English history, I reluctantly made tracks for the city centre. Seen from afar, rising high above a wasteland of filling stations, hamburger joints and seedy dives with hopeful signs – 'Sam's World Famous Topless Go-Go Lounge' – the tight-packed downtown skyscrapers, their walls and windows caught by the westering sun, look like a golden fortress set in a stagnant, festering ocean. Above them tower the bronze cylinders of the new Renaissance Centre. Built to disprove the belief that downtown Detroit is only marginally more lively than a morgue, the centre is not short of gimmicks. One bar circles slowly and silently round a huge indoor pool, which is very confusing when you try to visit the gents' after a few extra-dry martinis. I tried to explore the more stratospheric levels, but was eventually turned back by a pert, smiling guide with 'Ask me, I know' inscribed on a bosom-bobbing button.

'I'm sorry sir. You can't go beyond this point wearing blue jeans.'

'What about red, green or black jeans?'

'Mmmmmm. I guess they might be OK.'

'What if I take my jeans off?'

'What if you what! I guess they never considered that possibility.'

Planned in the aftermath of the 1967 riots – 43 deaths,

3,000 arrests, damage costing $200 million – the Renaissance Centre is, to be honest, something of a sci-fi masterpiece, jeans or no jeans. But there are those who think the money could have been spent more usefully, that the building symbolises the gulf between the haves and the have-nots.

At night, my hotel room echoed to the music of urgent sirens and screaming tyres. Nerves twitched like bowstrings at Agincourt every time a fly farted in the corridor. Next morning, I noticed that the receptionist had recorded my surname as Leeuelling despite having had it spelled out slowly three times. You expect better treatment in a city filled with people called Quayhackx, Zyzzello, Czyzykiewicz, Xinderakos, Wyzywany and Kirejczyk.

2

The Long Weekend

1978

The bearded taxi driver who ran me to Trailways' depot on Jackson Street in downtown Dallas, Texas, was about as comforting as a punch in the teeth. 'You're going *all* the way to Seattle in one of *those*,' he drawled in disbelief. 'Well, I guess you're about to find out that all those adverts about luxury travel are just a pack of doggone lies!'

Why go by bus when I could have hopped on a jet and done the 2,000-mile trip in four hours instead of 60? There were several reasons. First, it was going to cost £38 instead of £85, and two full nights on the road would avoid a couple of hotel bills. Second, it was an ideal opportunity to take a look at the men and machines who transport people, the most valuable of all loads. Third, I was keen to see as much of the country as possible and had a long weekend available. If you've time to spare, why go by air?

Second only to Greyhound, Trailways spin their web over the entire USA and spill over the border into Canada. The waiting area in Dallas is like a small airport departure lounge. Rows of hard seats, people gazing vacantly into space, the inevitable kid who ignores his mother's yells and behaves like a nuclear war. I turn up 90 minutes early, because there's no way you can reserve a seat. Just perch near the sliding doors, poised for a granny-trampling sprint.

Greyhound and Trailways between them serve around 14,000 towns and cities scattered over a network of more than 100,000 miles. Each carry 50 million passengers a year and run about 4,000 buses. The typical bus weighs ten tons unladen and is wafted along by a Detroit Diesel V8 that does 7–8mpg. I made a dash for the rear when the 46-seater Silver Eagle arrived, having been tipped off that only a fifth of the pews are available for smokers. Looking out through the big, tinted windows, I see my case at the bottom of a mountain of luggage. The bus shudders as boxes marked 'FRAGILE' are hurled into the hold. Baggage handlers are the same the world over.

When the bus rolled out into the eyeball-searing sun, a good half-hour behind schedule, the seat next to me was the only one vacant as a result of my deliberate grimacing at the other passengers. We head west on Interstate 20, passing a sign that indicates 34 degrees C – downright chilly by the previous day's standard. Cool air oozes up from slots below the windows, but I would welcome the directional roof vents they have in aircraft. Some sort of stowage in the seatbacks would also make life more convenient.

This part of Texas is green and flat as far as the eye can see – an endless ocean of prairie with not even one fleeting glimpse of a cowboy. Nowadays they all drive Ford and Chevrolet pickups and use helicopters to herd their livestock. I had imagined that these buses ploughed down the interstates for hour after hour, cruising at the 55mph limit and making no more than three or four stops each day. But within 25 minutes of leaving Dallas we were in some dusty little Nowheresville and trying to cram in more passengers. The seat next to me is taken by a bronzed beauty whose long, shapely legs sprout spectacularly from shorts little bigger than a couple of postage stamps. Anti-social body language tends to be abandoned in such promising circumstances, but attempts to get a conversation going are thwarted by terse, monosyllabic replies. Perhaps she has been warned about strangers on buses heading into the night. So I doze instead, waking to see what appears to be an optical illusion sliding past the nearside windows. No train could possibly be that long. But it is. We were gradually passing a truly Texas-sized serpent of coal cars pulled by no fewer than seven big diesel locomotives.

Wichita Falls, seven o'clock. The first major stop and some

of our horde switch buses and head north for Oklahoma City. In the Trailways terminal I eat a gruesome meal of stone-cold chips and a cardboard hamburger. My leggy companion emerges from the loo, now clad in grope-defying denim dungarees. Out into the twilight, past scores of nodding donkeys that pump oil from the wells of northern Texas. Is this the way to Amarillo? Obviously so, because we reach the city at midnight. A strong breeze gusts in from the prairie, but it's still 28 degrees C on the street.

For reasons known only to herself, the denim dolly fled to another seat when we left Wichita Falls. But this time she is gracious enough to share the Llewellin pew again and chats like an old friend before we both slump into fitful sleep.

'Morning folks! We're now approaching Lamar, Colorado. We crossed the state line while you were all asleep back there and it's now five o'clock by Mountain Standard Time, so I suggest you all put your watches back an hour,' says the breezy driver. We must have changed chauffeurs in Amarillo, because the previous guy was not strong on the chat. I have a pre-breakfast snack of iced Coke and banana, then say farewell to Miss Longlegs as she changes for Colorado Springs. At last! Room to stretch for the first time in 14 hours. These buses have just about enough room for a short-legged six-footer until the character in front decides to recline and smash your kneecaps.

The land is as flat as a billiard table, but here at last you sense something of the Wild West. Big trucks sweep by pulling cattle-laden trailers. Huge stockyards sprawl at the outskirts of little towns with such evocative names as Kit Carson. At 7am in bleary-eyed Hugo, a cheery young couple serve excellent breakfasts with welcome efficiency. I pay £1.30 for bacon, scrambled eggs, hash browns, two rounds of hot toast and a couple of mugs of life-saving coffee, then hand over a few coins for a copy of the 124-page *Rocky Mountain News*. Back to sleep, suddenly awakening to the realisation that we are nearing Denver, known as Mile High City. The snow-clad Rocky Mountains provide a scenic uplift for the first time in 800 miles and 18 hours. Denver started as a gold-rush town in 1858, but

I'm more concerned about the rush for seats as we change buses. Wise to the game, I get straight into the Seattle queue instead of taking a break in the terminal. Strange words on the PA turn out to be Spanish, for many Mexicans pass this way. Denver gives me quite a buzz, because it features in Jack Kerouac's wonderful *On the Road* odyssey, which inspired me to do all manner of silly things when I was a young shaver. In those days, before long-haul flights became affordable, America seemed almost as distant as the far side of the moon.

Bang on time, the marathon's third driver heads out down Larimer Street. He's soon into the stump-hauling gears for a long, long climb into the heart of the Rockies, heading west on Interstate 70. We enter a spectacular world of lush pastures, pine forests, alpinesque houses, ski lifts, foaming rivers, abandoned mines and mighty peaks. Kenworths pulling trailers of Coors beer – 'Brewed from pure Rocky Mountain water' – are familiar sights. The interstate climbs to the tunnel at the head of the Loveland Pass, exactly 11,013 feet above sea level. My guidebook offers a sombre warning: 'Those with heart conditions or conditions that affect breathing should, if possible, avoid driving at altitudes over 10,000 feet.'

Down towards Glenwood Springs, entering a tremendous gorge carved by the rampaging Colorado River as a prelude to its Grand Canyon masterpiece in distant Arizona. For 18 breathtaking miles the bus is dwarfed by sheer cliffs rising to 1,000 feet, but the crags suddenly veer off to either side as we enter the 37-degree blast-furnace of Grand Junction in late afternoon. About 60 sweating bodies are somehow crammed into a coach designed for 46. We cross the state line into Utah, driven by a character whose infrequent announcements could easily have been ultra-brief bouts of severe indigestion. It is like being in a mobile Black Hole of Calcutta, but nothing can detract from the scenery. Desert and dusty creeks flank the road, rolling away to immense vistas of green canyons, snowy peaks and the Arches National Monument's amazing cliffs, which glow red and orange in the setting sun.

Utah is almost three times the size of Scotland, but has a smaller population than Birmingham. We stop briefly in the nearest thing I have ever seen to a ghost town, then cross the Green River whose surging rapids provide the theme for a rousing track on CW McCall's *Black Bear Road* album. Then on to Salt Lake City, where Brigham Young and his 148 followers started their Mormon world in 1847.

Changing buses involves a two-hour wait at dead of night. Apart from toilets and a solitary water fountain, Salt Lake City's terminal offers precisely nothing to comfort weary travellers. But outside, the illuminated towers of the Mormon Temple can be admired, spearing 212 feet into the inky canopy of star-twinkling sky.

Setting off for Idaho, the new driver warns us that Utah's state laws ban smoking on any part of the bus. The loo soon resembles the fume-filled crater of a volcano. Our latest chauffeur turns out to be a genial soul who takes the trouble to mention points of interest. Right now, for instance, we're running into Glenn's Ferry, so called because it's where the enterprising Mr Glenn built a boat to take 19th-century Oregon Trail pioneers safely over the Snake River. Vast farmlands backed by distant hills that could have been transplanted from Wales take us to Boise, Idaho's pleasant state capital. Then it's west again to Oregon, where watches go back an hour as we enter the Pacific time zone. During the lunch stop in Vale, just over the state line, I talk to the driver, Russel Stolhand. He joined Trailways 29 years ago, has logged about three million miles and is a regular on the 330-mile haul between Boise and Bend, in central Oregon. Long service tends to be the rule rather than the exception, he says. 'If a guy stays five years he's generally with the company for keeps. There's one driver working out of Boise who has been with Trailways since 1935. Another retired a couple of years ago and would have done 50 years if he could have gone on another six months.'

I ask about problems: 'Every now and then we get an awkward passenger. Mebbe a guy who likes to drink too much. And some of the older folks can get a little wishy-washy when they've been in the bus too long. Some just sit there and kinda drive all the way themselves, never relaxing.'

We are joined by Tom Turrentine, also Boise-based, who

works what they call the extras board. That means he's available to go when and where a driver's needed. When he was on the long haul between Phoenix and Long Beach he regularly clocked more than 400 miles a day and topped 100,000 in three consecutive years. He enjoys meeting so many different people. 'Say, do you know a guy called Raymond Baxter? Had him with me last summer. A real nice man. Guess he's some kinda TV celebrity in England.'

Oregon shares Utah's no-smoking rule on buses. I ask Tom if the police would stop him if they spotted an illegal cigarette. 'Oregon police'll stop you for anything!' he says.

Still bursting at the seams, the Silver Eagle forges steadily west through a memorable wilderness of hilly desert. As in Utah, you go for mile after mile after mile without seeing any life. 'This is real big-sky country, like where the closing scenes of *Close Encounters* were filmed,' says the burly young man from Cleveland who is now sharing my seat. He suddenly starts laughing: 'It's just so goddam ironic. You don't see anyone out there for hours, and here we are packed into this bus like a whole mess of beans in a can!'

In late afternoon the snowy peaks of Mount Hood and Mount Jefferson dominate the skyline as we head north then north-west. A few miles beyond Madras, an incredible and completely unexpected canyon is a mind-boggling gash in the land. This is classic cowboy country, lacking only a few smoke signals rising from the flat-topped, rock-rimmed hills. Then, after hundreds of virtually treeless miles, we climb into the vast pine forests of the Cascade Mountains where grey ghosts of rain-laden cloud drift through the dripping branches.

Portland and its skyscrapers come up just after nightfall – the first place of any real size since Salt Lake City. 'The only place you have to change is Denver,' the booking clerk in Dallas had assured me. He would have been absolutely right were it not for the additional changes in Salt Lake City, Bend and now Portland. Joined by a few newcomers, the few of us who have followed the same route all the way from Texas board yet another Silver Eagle and cross the Columbia River.

We reach Seattle just after 2am, motoring in past the

huge Boeing plant where Air Force One, the new presidential 747, is parked under bright lights. The journey ends as it had begun, with a not-so-funny taxi driver telling me something I didn't wish to know: 'You've come all the way from Dallas in *that*? Man, you sure must be a nut!'

3

BIG WHEELS ROLLING

1985

Paul Hughes of Oklahoma City is the only truck driver I
know who flies his own aircraft. But the neat little
Beechcraft Bonanza attracts considerably less attention than
his mile-eating, mind-blowing Peterbilt and its unique trailer.
That said, the £154,000 supertruck's value is almost invariably
exceeded by that of its load, because the 44-year-old owner-
driver whose CB handle is 'Western Flyer' hauls very
expensive cars for very rich people.

Paul once delivered five new Rolls-Royces to Bhagwan
Shree Rajneesh, a controversial Indian guru whose followers
have taken over a 100-square-mile tract of Oregon. The
quintet pushed his collection to within sight of the 50 mark.
Other star customers and cars have included Liberace and
Burt Reynolds, the 1949 Mercury driven by James Dean in
Rebel Without A Cause, a 1936 Duesenberg valued at £500,000
and a top-secret Chevrolet prototype. Ferraris, Porsches,
Mercedes, Bentleys, Aston Martins, Jaguars, Maseratis,
BMWs and custom-built limousines long enough to have a
bowling alley in the back are all in a day's work.

Paul started trucking when he left the United States Air Force
in 1965 and now has between two and three million miles to
his credit. One coast-to-coast operation with fresh flowers
accounted for 245,000 miles in 1972 alone. Paul and a friend
shared the driving. 'That truck was so fast we cruised with the
speedometer needle right off the clock,' he recalled. 'The guy in
the bunk used to ask the driver to keep it on the numbers,
because it was difficult to sleep doing more than 90mph.'

Paul favoured Caterpillar-powered cabover Kenworths

until the end of 1983, when Uncle Sam's liberalised length laws triggered a switch to the long-nosed 'conventional' Peterbilt. That was nearly three years after Paul became leased to Passport Transport of St Louis, who run the USA's biggest fleet of enclosed car transporters. No two runs are ever identical, but he generally shuttles between the sunshine states of California and Florida. That's why I flew into Miami. Unfortunately, my arrival there neatly coincided with Paul being diverted to Milwaukee, north of Chicago. In European terms, it was like jetting to Gibraltar for an appointment in Glasgow. But the 1,500-mile flight was a modest start to one of my life's longest hauls. Running from the Great Lakes to the Atlantic, the Gulf of Mexico and the Pacific, I was destined to cover more than 5,000 miles and cross 16 states before bidding farewell to Paul nearly a fortnight later in the smoggy atmosphere of Los Angeles.

Day One: Friends in California had told me to expect an exceptionally nice guy whose rig really had to be seen to be believed. They were right on both counts. Paul Hughes is nothing if not a hard-nosed professional, but with an easy-going exterior and a superb sense of humour. He's interested as well as interesting, so our conversations covered just about everything from trucks and aircraft to science-fiction, politics, the esoteric world of commodity broking – 'That's something I'd like to do when I finally quit trucking' – raising children, history, geography and flying hot-air balloons.

Paul was also good for my health. 'I can stand just about anything apart from smoking,' he grinned, indicating the cigarettes in my shirt pocket when we finally made contact at the Excalibur Automobile Corporation's factory in Milwaukee. Fair enough. Not one was lit in the truck, but I did a good impression of a hyper-active vacuum cleaner every time we stopped.

Information about the Peterbilt and its trailer filtered through while Paul added a vintage-styled Excalibur to the load's 308 GTB Ferrari and 6.9-litre Mercedes. Riding on a 250-inch wheelbase, the truck gets its prodigious performance from a 450bhp Caterpillar V8 driving through Fuller's

13-speed, double-overdrive gearbox. 'Get her into the last hole and 1,900rpm equals 104mph,' Paul smiled. 'That double-headed rat-killer of an engine's good for 2,350 revs, which would work out at 131mph if you could overcome the wind drag. Let's just say she cruises along pretty good.'

Details include Caterpillar's hydraulic brake-saver, Bendix cruise control, more dials and switches than the Beechcraft's cockpit, a 52-channel Bearcat scanner to supplement the Whistler radar detector, air conditioning, an auxiliary generator big enough to power a small car, and a Kysor warning system to monitor engine malfunctions. Double Eagle of Indiana built the huge, walk-in sleeper. Seven feet long, the home-from-home has a full-sized double bed, a wardrobe and several cupboards, stereo speakers, four fluorescent lights, its own door to the outside world, one of the truck's three digital alarm clocks and umpteen other features. What about the proverbial kitchen sink? That's not needed in a land where truckstops provide everything from diesel to DIY laundry facilities. The one-of-a-kind trailer has little more clearance than a rattlesnake's belly and its interior is as complex as a Chinese puzzle, to make maximum use of space. It can swallow eight small cars, although six or seven is a more typical load.

Trailer and tractor alike have air suspension, lightweight Alcoa wheels and low-profile Goodyear tyres. Lights total a modest 152 and are operated by no fewer than five switches. We must have heard literally hundreds of Citizens' Band radio remarks about a mobile Christmas tree and hating to have to pay that guy's electricity bill. Paul's pride and joy had just been featured in *Owner-Operator Magazine*, so we revelled in superstar status.

Kids crammed into a school bus pointed, beamed and waved as we headed southwards from Milwaukee towards the end of a crisp, clear afternoon. The peerless Pete, as smooth and sophisticated as a king-sized car, hummed along Interstate 94 at an effortless 60mph with an immense amount of muscle in reserve. Hydraulic ramps and a two-piece steel tailgate make it a heavy piece of equipment, even when empty, but high gearing helps the Cat to average a very creditable six miles per imperial gallon.

Paul left the interstate after a few minutes and headed through soft, rolling farmland on a tree-lined road with a six-ton weight limit. 'That sort of thing's an occupational hazard,' he shrugged. 'This sort of work takes you to all sorts of places where big trucks aren't really supposed to go. But what's the alternative when you're just trying to make a living? The cops can be quite reasonable about it if you treat them right. I've *always* made a point of *never* pretending I'm lost, because that's the oldest excuse in the book. Just tell them the truth. Tell them you're delivering or collecting a very expensive car and will be on your way as soon as possible.'

He had ventured down this rural by-way to load a 1936 two-door 20/25 Rolls-Royce – still complete with its original British registration plates – and the most pristine 1957 Porsche Speedster you ever did see. Getting them stowed away took a couple of hours, emphasising Paul's point that his work is to normal car hauling what chess is to checkers. 'Every load is different and every load is difficult to a greater or lesser extent,' he said. 'You have to contend with vehicles of every shape and size, from huge antiques to race cars little more than knee-high to a grasshopper.'

Juggling ramps and cars to win literally half-an-inch here and half-an-inch there adds up to a lot of dollars at the end of the year, but there must always be *just* enough clearance to eliminate any risk of damage. The cars are treated like precious pieces of fragile porcelain. Squeezing down from the top deck after the Porsche had been secured, bent almost double, I was reminded to make sure my belt buckle didn't touch the paintwork. The local sheriff wafted by and waved, just as Paul was raising the tailgate which extends the rig's overall length from 70 to 90ft. Then it was off into the twilight, across the state line through the skyscraper jungle of downtown Chicago and on to a Union 76 truckstop a few miles north of Indianapolis by one o'clock in the morning.

The middle-aged waitress was all smiles and jokes. 'That your fancy rig? The one with all the lights? Sure looks pretty.

Guess you've got red sheets on the bed and a mirror on the ceiling.' Paul took up the challenge. 'You suggesting I drive a cat house on wheels? Well, maybe I do. But the Cat's locked away there under the hood.'

Day Two: Gone are the days when Paul Hughes finished very late and started very early. Most folks had started earning their corn by the time we emerged from the sleeper – Llewellin having spent the first of several remarkably comfortable nights on the floor – washed, shaved and started tucking into breakfast. Mine was a typically American obesity special that combined scrambled eggs and bacon with pancakes drenched in syrup.

The next car lowered the tone for an entire day. It was a common-or-garden 1979 Pontiac Bonneville for a young executive who had moved from Indianapolis to the outskirts of Atlanta. It looked as big as an aircraft carrier as I started easing up the ramp. 'Don't worry about falling off,' Paul grinned. 'That old Rolls will prevent you falling too far.'

We were now a touch over the weight limit for the trailer axles, so Paul planned a brief dodge-the-weighbridge detour with information gleaned from the *National Truckers Scale and Inspection Station Atlas* and the *USA Truckers Guide*. Back on the interstate, heading for Kentucky in general and Louisville in particular, the Peterbilt was passed by a hard-charging Kenworth. 'There's my front door,' Paul muttered, easing the speedometer needle halfway round its 160mph scale. Nervous? No sir. I just sat back and enjoyed the smooth performance, completely confident in man and machine. 'It's not how fast you drive, it's how you drive fast,' said Paul, scanning the road ahead and cutting speed with the hydraulic retarder as a distant car started easing into the second lane. 'Over the years I've had some good equipment, but this truck really is the business, the whole nine yards. I may never buy another – unless they come up with an 800bhp turbine that runs on water.'

The flatlands of Wisconsin and Indiana gradually gave way to wooded hills as we sped eastwards from Louisville to Lexington, the capital of the Bluegrass Country and a city internationally famous for horses. Rain pelted down from thick, coal-black clouds as the Mercedes was delivered to its owner's home right across the road from a palatial country club. It was what Paul calls a high-dollar area where even the dogs wear mink coats in winter. Nearly 550 miles had passed beneath the wheels during the day by the time we stopped at Dalton – 'Carpet Capital of the USA' – after crossing Tennessee by way of Knoxville and Chattanooga, scene of one of the American Civil War's bloodiest battles.

Day Three: Averting our eyes from an enticing sign set back from the road – 'Nude Dancers For Lunch' – we made good time to the Pontiac's destination on a smart housing estate north-east of Atlanta. The owner, his family and neighbours all turned out to say nice things about the Peterbilt and to record its arrival on film. It was more of an event than a delivery. The grinning owner actually apologised for his tatty car travelling in such classy company.

On to lunch with Charlie Turner, an old friend of Paul's and a great character who swears his drive-in liquor store has closed since he gave up drinking gin. What Charlie doesn't know about Aston Martins could be written on a grain of rice. I liked the notice outside his office: 'Why do the English drink warm beer?' it asked. 'Because they have Lucas refrigerators.'

Charlie handed over a weary old 1958 Aston due to be restored by Bob Clark, a British engineer living down the road in Florida. Then we went out into the country to collect a 280 SL Mercedes before running due east through sudden rain to Augusta. That was where Paul parted company with the red Ferrari. The owner, a young enthusiast who had moved from California, was like a kid with a new toy as it inched down the ramp. His excitement was tinged with a modicum of distress. Rain was touching the four-year-old paintwork for the first time.

Day Four: A knock on the cab generally means either a hooker or a cop. This time it was a trucker who asked Paul to sign the cover of *Owner-Operator*. The day looked even brighter when Mr Hughes called Mission Control and was told that the Ferrari owner had phoned just to say how impressed he had been. So morale was high as we cruised into Florida, a state with all the scenic grandeur of a snooker table. Either swamp, forest or holiday resort, it makes you think the Flat Earth Society could be right. Paul hates the interminable, tree-lined highways. They provide good cover for lurking lawmen.

'What the *hail* you got under the hood of that thang, Mr Passport?' drawled a Deep South voice straight from *Gone With The Wind* as Paul passed a Kenworth whose driver grabbed his CB radio. 'You darned near blew mah pardner clean outta his doggone bunk. Thought the sun had come up kinda early when he saw all them lights. How many you got on that real fancy piece of eee-quipment, come on?'

Another crowd turned out to watch the superb little Porsche being delivered to its new owner in Daytona Beach, where it joined his 1962 fixed-head model, a Mercedes and a BMW. Later, the Union 76 truckstop at Vero Beach served me deep-fried alligator and chips. The waitress wondered what it tasted like: 'Very similar to crocodile,' I said, keeping a perfectly straight face, 'but with a faint hint of aardvark.'

It was nearly 2am on a wet Sunday when we reached El Cheapo Motel in Fort Lauderdale, a few miles up the coast from Miami. The seedy suite, complete with the remains of a wacky-baccy cigarette on the bathroom floor, had been offered free, gratis and for nothing when Paul called the Rolls-Royce man earlier in the day. He owned the place. Nearby attractions included a 24-hour, drive-through pawnbroker's shop called the Happy Hocker. Paul was more concerned about other aspects of local life. 'Watch out for three things in southern Florida,' he cautioned. 'A mugger with a switchblade, a Cuban with a driver's licence and a Yankee towing a U-Haul rental trailer. They can all endanger your health.'

Day Five: We slept like a brace of Rip Van Winkles before prising the eyelids apart at 10am. The bedroom had efficient air conditioning, but not the rest of the down-at-heel apartment. That's bad news when Florida's being pelted with what the local tourist board calls liquid sunshine. Torrential rain plus a temperature on the high side of 27 degrees C gives you a shrewd idea of what it must be like to flounder in a sea of hot, thick soup. Conditions were uncomfortable enough to warrant a cold shower while Paul called the car's new owner.

He arrived quicker than a bullet from an Armalite. The old Roller would have been off there and then had Paul not mentioned the fact that he and his sidekick worked better with something to keep the ribs apart. So we were ferried to a nearby restaurant while the man let us know just how important and successful he considered himself to be. He owned this, that and the other properties. His friend had just bought a cute little castle in England. As for the car: 'Let me tell you, that Rolls-Royce has actually been to Bucking-ham Palace, or whatever you call the place.'

Watched by the customary crowd – it takes more than rain to keep people way from the Peterbilt – Mr Big really got up Paul's nose by trying to mastermind the unloading operation. The final straw was a crafty attempt to snip nearly $50 off the bill.

The trailer was parked in the Zimmer factory at nearby Pompano Beach, where the ripe-for-restoration 1958 Aston Martin had been wheeled out before reaching Mr Big's motel. It was for Bob Clark, an Englishman who supervises the building of Zimmer's Ford-based, vintage-styled and definitely over-the-top cars. Paul checked into his regular motel, a few miles up the road. Spotless, spacious and well-equipped, it provided a Gideon Bible, a separate copy of the New Testament and a card announcing that the Rev Edward D Peachey of Coconut Creek was just a telephone call away should help be needed. All that religion swept away any thoughts of strolling out to sample 'Stylish Nude Entertainment for Ladies and Gentlemen' in the Cheetah Lounge, a few hundred yards away, so I immersed myself into a book about military history while Paul tackled his paperwork. Vital statistics included having covered 10,077 miles in just under three weeks, running from Florida to California and back with several collect-or-deliver detours along the way. That adds up to a lot of time on the road, but each trip generally provides the opportunity for at least a few hours at home with Diane, the lady he married 24 years ago.

Talking of ladies, the spare ribs eaten at the local branch of Bobby Rubino's restaurant chain were served by smiling, long-legged damsels whose uniform included a vestigial skirt and frilly white panties worthy of Little Miss Muffet. 'The food's good – and so is the scenery,' Paul chuckled, sipping a multi-coloured cocktail while I savoured the trip's first glass of Coors beer.

Day Six: Paul's telephone bills tot up to a small fortune, because every customer is contacted in advance, just to be on the safe side. Calls to regulars tend to be brief, but sorting out the details with one-off customers is frequently a lengthy process. Paul has to make them realise that he will be arriving in a *big* truck, not some rinky-dink transporter with space for just a couple of cars. The post-breakfast conversation with one lady went on for ever as she struggled to reconcile a 70-feet-long vehicle with local conditions. Paul was patient and polite. 'There's only two ways to do it,' he soothed. 'Either the truck gets to the car, or the car gets to the truck. Right?'

The 280 SL Mercedes and the neo-vintage Excalibur from Milwaukee went to a Fort Lauderdale dealer. 'Looks like Home Run City on this one,' said the salesman as he checked the latter. 'Know the only problem with these things? It's hell leaving them behind when you die.'

Paul contemplated the likely value of his westward load as we headed down I-95 towards Miami. Zimmer's two cars had been cancelled. So had a 308 GTB Ferrari. It looked like a classic wait-and-hope operation, followed by cutting and running with a half-empty trailer if nothing materialised to fill the gaps. He started carving his way into Miami's urban sprawl through the now-familiar picket line of Dunkin' Donuts, Kentucky Fried Chicken, filling stations, drive-in banks, Burger King, McDonald's, Arby's Roast Beef Sandwich, Radio Shack and dilapidated cinemas advertising triple-X movies. It had all the olde worlde charm of Los Angeles without the encircling mountains. Be that as it may, my morale was given the Cape Canaveral treatment when a blood-red Daytona Ferrari 365 GTB/4 was wheeled out of the

Vantage Motor Works. Nerves and sauna-like humidity soaked me with sweat as the 175mph supercar was winched right up to the front of the top deck. The winch stopped. 'Looks like you need to fire her up and slip her back *juuuuuust* two inches,' said Paul. 'More than that and we'll have a hole in the trailer.' No clutch and accelerator have ever been balanced with quite so much care. Fed by six twin-choke Weber carburettors, the 4.4-litre, 352bhp V12 bellowed like an enraged monster in the confined space. I could now claim to have driven one of the world's fastest and most exclusive cars, albeit backwards for only a couple of inches.

Next on the list, midway through the afternoon, was Fortune Imports of Fort Lauderdale, where Paul was due to load a hulking great 500 SEL Mercedes. It could not be handed over until the money was wired from California, three hours behind Florida, so the amiable salesman suggested we went across the road for a meal at The Mad Greek. The food was fine, but the dollars were still on the West Coast when the Peterbilt left at 6pm to collect a Porsche Turbo for Las Vegas. I accepted the owner's offer of a beer while Paul rocketed up a ramp so steep we had visions of the Porsche becoming West Germany's first spacecraft. 'A bad day, but it could have been worse,' was Paul's verdict when we returned to the motel.

Day Seven: Breakfast was shared with bright-and-breezy Bob Elliott, a Passport driver from Bagdad, Florida. 'Seven churches, one filling station and no bars,' he chuckled. Bob travels complete with a Honda Aero 80 scooter chained to his truck. Llewellin buzzed round like the poor man's Barry Sheene before Paul embarked on another telephonic marathon. It turned up a Ferrari in Palm Beach and the possibility of a Lamborghini Countach just 200 miles away in Tampa. Our return visit to Fortune Imports, where the money had materialised minutes after we left, was memorable for a young lady clad only in T-shirt and knickers being evicted from a rickety house on the opposite side of the street. 'You owe me five months' rent, you no-good whore,' a man bellowed as he slung a bundle of clothes across the pavement. The damsel didn't even glance over her shoulder. We also encountered a well-endowed cyclist who *appeared* to be stark naked apart from an incredibly long mane of blonde hair: 'Fort Lauderdale's answer to Lady Godiva,' said Paul, with a chuckle. Another laugh was provided by a battered old Chevrolet rumbling up I-95 in the general direction of Palm Beach. 'This is not an abandoned car,' a bumper sticker proclaimed.

Wayne Tucker Enterprises turned out to be run by a family from England. Stock included a blue Silver Shadow originally owned by Twiggy and the black Ferrari 308 GTS Paul was taking to Los Angeles. The two-piece tailgate had just been raised when up rolled the charming, middle-aged lady whose boss was having his beloved and beautifully original 1966 Mercedes 220S drophead shipped to Kellogg, Idaho. 'Guess that's up near Chicago,' she said. It was like describing Paris as being just down the road from Istanbul. She was just as vague about guiding the Peterbilt through her native city. 'Not sure which way we should go, but here's hoping we find Main Street,' were words that failed to fill Mr Hughes with confidence. Sure enough, she guided us straight to a posh promenade, all palm trees and high-rent buildings, whose attractions included a very clear sign about trucks being banned. Then came the bad news. We were heading for a bridge several inches lower than the trailer. That was when the lady finally came round to Paul's way of thinking. Bring the car to the truck. Everything looked better after sliced beef garnished with soy sauce and followed by a huge, all-the-trimmings ice cream which must have packed a million calories into a space the size of a football.

Paul ran northwards for an hour before pausing at Fort Pierce. He contacted a man about the Countach – 'Call me back in three hours,' was the message – while I studied a doom-laden tract published by one of several organisations who strive to save American truckers from sin. Smoking, drinking, dabbling with damsels, telling dirty jokes and playing around with fancy cars made you a candidate for the Lake of Fire, it warned.

We pushed on to Orlando, home of the 43-square-mile Walt

Disney World resort complex, and chatted over coffee until it was midnight and time to make yet another call about the Countach. Paul came out of the kiosk with his thumb pointing downwards. The plan was to run northwards for another hour, but Paul suddenly felt in a mile-eating mood as the Peterbilt slipped into its effortless air-sprung stride with the Bendix cruise-control system taking the strain off the leg muscles. It was just a little difficult to believe that Paul's dream on wheels was hauling a huge trailer. Its performance was marred only by that all-too-familiar chatter from the Fuller transmission. Three o'clock was within sight when Mr Hughes finally put the Cat out at Lake City.

Day Eight: Trucks that would cause a sensation on this side of the Atlantic Ocean are not exactly rare in the USA. Despite the competition, Paul's is sufficiently special to be deluged with attention. This lovely morning's first compliment came as we left the Double Eagle sleeper in search of breakfast. 'That really is something,' enthused a man in a battered straw stetson. 'When you drive a Ford it's nice to see a real truck.' Llewellin recalled the old joke about Ford being shorthand for 'Fix Or Repair Daily'. Paul, the proud owner of a Lincoln Continental made by FoMoCo, provided a loyal and charitable alternative: 'First On Race Day,' he laughed. 'Know what GMC means? Gotta Mechanic Coming.'

A call to Mission Control in St Louis brought news of a Rolls-Royce waiting in Austin, Texas, and the strong possibility of cars being switched in Oklahoma City. The mood changed within an hour when we stopped for diesel shortly after swinging westwards along I-10. Time to juggle the Porsche and the old Mercedes to make the weight on the trailer axles legal. No problem? Well, not if the electrics are working and the tailgate can be lowered. Getting that sorted out kept Paul busy with his circuit tester, soldering iron, pliers and insulating tape until it was late in the afternoon. Rolling once more, we reached the Central Time Zone near Tallahassee, dined a few miles later and then sped into the night with the rest of a clog-to-carpet convoy. The 64-miles-wide strip of Alabama went under the wheels in 54 minutes, despite slowing for traffic around Mobile. Little more than an hour later we had another state behind us and were in Louisiana, running hard for Baton Rouge where I-10 sweeps high above the mighty Mississippi as it meanders to New Orleans. By the time Paul reached the Union 76 truckstop at Lafayette he had covered 447 miles in well under seven hours since leaving the table in Florida.

Day Nine: Chances of reaching the West Coast before my time ran out appeared to vanish completely when Paul made his regular post-breakfast call to Passport Transport. A car being hauled from New York would not reach the Hughes home in Oklahoma City until Saturday, maybe even Sunday, and it was essential for yours truly to be in Los Angeles no later than Monday. The only way we could do it, Paul joked, was by abandoning the truck and taking to the air in his Beechcraft Bonanza. But would it haul a trailer?

Most of the 3,000-mile run had been across flat country. Today was much the same – mile after mile of scattered trees, and vast fields crossed here and there by sluggish, reed-choked waterways. Just before noon we entered Texas, where a roadside marker reminded us that I-10 spears across the state for 882 miles before reaching New Mexico. Paul told me about the pilot of a small aircraft who requested permission to land and told the control tower he had 42 passengers in his five-seater. Sure enough, out came 42 midgets: 'Texans who've had all the bullshit squeezed out of them,' the pilot explained.

Houston, home of the *real* Mission Control complex, loomed out of the endless plain an hour or so later. Paul dived into the city to collect a new BMW 633 CSi from the huge dealership owned by David Hobbs, a racing driver and a native of Warwickshire who has obviously done very well for himself in the New World. Next on the list was Austin, 164 miles west of Houston, where a Rolls-Royce destined for California was waiting. Battling through heavy, multi-lane traffic, Paul accounted for 35 of those miles before pausing for a late lunch. It was abandoned in favour of take-away sandwiches and drinks when a call to Passport Transport brought news that the Roller had just been cancelled. We had to go back to Houston for a Ferrari. Traffic conditions were now really bad, but the gentleman driving another Peterbilt made space for Paul to sneak across to the appropriate exit. 'Thought I'd better let y'in, because you were on the cover of that *Owner-Operator* magazine,' his voice drawled over the CB. Fame has its advantages.

Ferrari of Houston looked like a top-drawer villa on the French Riviera. The 1974 Dino 246 GTS was handed over by a *very* pukka English salesman from Ascot. 'This is a good life,' he said, 'but I love going home for the beer, the pub lunches and a sense of reality. Incidentally, old boy, I wonder if I might possibly scrounge one of those English cigarettes.' Old habits die hard. Thoughts sped even closer to my native heath when I noticed a sticker with the Welsh dragon on the rear window of a Chevrolet. By then we were cruising northwards towards the Corral Café at Madisonville, where I risked losing British citizenship by sinking a huge glass of iced tea. Americans think drinking the brew hot, with milk and sugar, is about as crazy as boiling beer. Dallas was just a million lights blurred by drizzle before Paul called a halt at the Union 76 in Denton. We had covered 600 miles since breakfast.

Day Ten: Murals depicting cowboys roping steers looked down on my orange juice, scrambled eggs, bacon and coffee. We were served by girls wearing fancy shirts, faded jeans and broad-brimmed hats. All they lacked were jingling spurs and Colt 45s. 'Yessir. You're in Texas and that's for sure,' Paul grinned.

Now, at long last, our road reeled into the distance across gentle hills whose modest crests were carved by rocky cuttings. We crossed the Red River and entered Oklahoma, where the greeting consisted of a sign detailing fixed penalties for speeding offences. 'You have to check your wallet to see how fast you can afford to go,' said Paul, easing off the loud pedal as a single-engined aircraft came into sight. 'Could be a cop, but it's probably just a guy flying down to Dallas by following the road. We call it navigating by the concrete compass.'

Paul's home on the western outskirts of Oklahoma City is a short drive from the Union 76 where he parks the truck. His wife, Diane, rolled up in her Oldsmobile Toronado a few minutes after news from St Louis plastered a big smile right across my face. There was no longer any need to await the car from New York, but the Peterbilt had to be in Los Angeles by Monday morning after dropping the Mercedes 220S convertible in Las Vegas. Paul would miss the all-too-rare luxury of a night at home, but his morale soared when Princess Di packed her bag.

Apart from lingering under a shower, the six hours spent in Okie City were not what you could call relaxing. Diane tackled Paul's laundry while he made a string of calls and tackled paperwork in a typically neat office lined with books about flying and how to run a successful business. We nipped to the bank, then visited Paul's accountant before launching into a tasty Mexican meal. Brimmed with fuel, the Pete pulled out of town at 8pm and wafted westwards into the cool, clear night.

Day Eleven: Paul had left Oklahoma, crossed the Texas panhandle and reached Tucumcari in New Mexico, before shutting her down at the Shell Truck Stop. There I spent another remarkably comfortable night on the Double Eagle's floor. Mine host had been very diffident about that aspect of the trip right from the start, but it appeared to do my back a power of good. Who needs physiotherapists and orthopaedic surgeons when you can have your spine sorted out by Dr Double Eagle?

Quail is not the sort of dish you associate with transport cafés, but it featured prominently on the Shell menu at Tucumcari. We settled for more conventional starts to the day while Mr Goodwrench and his associates changed the Cat's oil. Like most of his breed, Paul has routine maintenance work done out on the road where any truckstop worthy of the name has full, round-the-clock servicing facilities.

Hopes were high for spectacular sights later in the day, because an early-morning TV programme was coming live from the International Balloon Fiesta in Albuquerque.

Literally hundreds of intrepid aeronauts were drifting through the sky. Closer to hand, however, we were now running into the arid wilderness that would be a constant companion for most of the way to Los Angeles. Scattered tufts of coarse grass flanked the road while hardy little shrubs struggled to survive on the slopes of flat-topped hills. Far away to the north, where Wheeler Peak rises to just over 13,000 feet, snow glistened far above us like white fire.

'This is a road where you encounter lots of what we call dragonfly trucks. They drag up the hills, then fly down them,' Paul laughed. Despite the gradual climbs and long descents, or maybe because of them, you get the impression that your average altitude remains much the same. That's an illusion. What used to be Route 66, but is now I-40, takes you higher and higher as the hours slip by. Okie City is 1,200 feet above sea level, but by the time you reach Amarillo the altitude has trebled, with thin air to match the beer.

Despite being in a deep valley, carved by the Rio Grande and reached after plunging down through majestic mountains, Albuquerque – pronounced Alberkerky – is 5,000 feet above sea level. Unfortunately, we reached there around noon and hot-air balloons perform best in the cool of the morning. We saw a few, but they were tethered outside hotels flanking the interstate. The steep climb west of the sweltering city gave way to straights so long it was like crossing the most placid of oceans. They encouraged Paul to hoist even more sail and set the cruise control at . . . well, the rest of the westbound traffic appeared to be hammer-down in reverse. One mile, not the fastest of the day, went by in just 42.9 seconds.

Conditions changed as we ran towards Gallup – 'World's Largest Indian Trading Center' – through high, flat-topped mountains with cliffs the colour of raw steak. Forked lightning flickered from crag to crag as raindrops thudded into the windscreen like soft-nosed bullets. The storm was at its most violent when we stopped on the far side of town for a very late lunch. Your food's free if it's not served within 15 minutes of placing the order, notices announced. A glance at the restaurant's clock made me check my watch and realise it was an hour fast. We had crossed into the Mountain Time Zone on leaving Oklahoma last night. 'That's never any problem for me,' said Paul, 'because I always run on Okie City time, adding or subtracting where needs be. You also have to use "home" time in your logbook.'

Rain dwindled to drizzle and drizzle gave way to clear skies as the Peterbilt passed the Painted Cliffs which tower above the highway as it enters Arizona. The state is famous for the Grand Canyon, the Gunfight at the OK Corral, forests of giant cacti, the world's biggest meteor crater, Apaches – and cops who like nothing better than writing speeding tickets. Arizona covers nearly 50 per cent more square miles than Great Britain, but has a population half that of London. It seemed even emptier as night fell and we climbed past the 7,000-feet mark on the far side of Flagstaff. Paul was getting just a little weary, but really wanted to reach Kingman before hitting the hay. 'Time for a cup of battery acid,' he announced. The coffee did the trick. Kingman's lights, clear as crystal in the desert air, came into sight at 1am. Paul and Diane checked into a motel while I sampled Double Eagle's king-sized bed for the first time.

Day Twelve: 'Watch out for Santa Claus,' Paul said as we started up the road towards Las Vegas. Apart from the fact that Christmas was two months away, what the hell was the old boy doing out here in the desert? Maybe he had attracted sponsorship from a tobacco company and was switching from reindeer to camels, I said, winning a prize for the trip's corniest joke. Santa Claus turned out to be a community small enough to be missed if you blinked at the wrong time.

We cruised towards the Hoover Dam through a daunting landscape of barren mountains and creeks flowing with nothing more useful than sand. Over the dam and into Nevada, where we paused at the Gold Strike Inn Casino with its splendid collection of antique gambling machines. All brass, chrome, marble and oak, they are a far cry from today's poker-and-blackjack-playing video equipment. What's the secret of not losing a penny in Lost Wages, to use truckers' slang for Las Vegas? If your name's Paul Hughes, you just unload a couple of cars – the 1966 Mercedes and the Porsche Turbo – have your vehicle washed at the Magic Wand Truckstop, then get out of town without placing a single bet. By 6pm we were exchanging Nevada for California, where temptation is removed.

Los Angeles was now less than four hours away, but first we had to slog up a section of I-15 which climbs 3,000 feet in a handful of miles. It reduced even the mighty Peterbilt to 30mph as the sun slipped away behind saw-toothed mountains. Then it was down, down, down to Baker, Barstow, Victorville and the long, steep gradient which sweeps you into San Bernardino. Mr and Mrs Hughes secured a room at the Rodeway Inn, while I spent my last night in the truck, dreaming about the previous 5,000 miles.

Day Thirteen: What might charitably be described as singing filled the morning air:

> *Adios amigo,*
> *Adios my friend.*
> *The road we have travelled*
> *Has come to an end . . .*

Indeed it had. The western end of Santa Monica Boulevard, where the remaining cars were delivered to dealers within four or five blocks of each other, is also the western end of I-10. The highway runs right across the USA for 2,353 miles from Jacksonville, Florida. Paul smiled and held out his hand: 'That's it,' he said. 'There's nothing solid between here and Japan.'

4

MEETING THE LEGENDS

1988

The key to Chevrolet's blood-red Corvette convertible was no ordinary key. That two-inch strip of steel gave us the power to forge sharp-edged reality from childhood's misty dreams, to explore Mount Rushmore, Devil's Tower, Yellowstone, Bryce Canyon, Monument Valley, Dodge City and many other quintessentially American locations, where British accents stop locals dead in their tracks. It was the key to meeting, in the imagination, George Washington, Abraham Lincoln, Mark Twain, Colonel Custer, Crazy Horse, Wild Bill Hickok, Wyatt Earp and men whose obsession with speed lured them to the awesome immensity of dazzling salt named after Captain BL Bonneville.

We logged 5,439 top-down miles, plus a few more covered while dancing to guitar-and-fiddle music in Jackson Hole, Wyoming. Big distances were cut down to size by the automatic Corvette's 5.7-litre V8. The great wuffler's assets include 245bhp at 4,300rpm, 340lb-ft of torque at 3,200 revs and the ability to top 150mph after reaching 60 in less than six seconds. Our three-week odyssey started in Detroit.

Day One: Pan-Am's flight reaches Motown two hours late, having returned a critically ill passenger to London. Corvette looks superb in evening light, but we search in vain for the boot. One case travels on Mrs Llewellin's knees for drive to home of friends, where a welcoming party is in full swing beneath star-bright sky.

Day Two: Process of elimination finds Pan-Am's chicken guilty of devastating Mrs Llewellin's plumbing. Start long haul west, by way of Chicago. Speed limit on most interstates recently raised from 55 to 65mph. This equals 1,625rpm in the quiet, comfortable Corvette's top gear. Landscape flat as a steamrollered pancake. Cross the Mississippi, then stop for night in rural Minnesota.

Day Three: 'Must be one helluva job that gets you to drive a car like that,' marvels the guy in the filling station. Had expected ragtop Corvettes to be ten-a-penny over here, but are destined to hear many more comments of that nature. Beethoven tape sweeps us into South Dakota. Lunch at Al's Oasis – 'Coffee only five cents and the smiles are free' – where specialities include low-cholesterol buffalo burger. Black Hills of Dakota, our first real target, visible by mid-afternoon. Road to Rushmore View Motor Lodge is the first gradient in 1,200 miles that our Fiat Uno 60S couldn't have sailed up in fifth. Corvette shares car park with battered old Austin America, one of not more than a dozen British cars spotted during entire journey.

Day Four: Five-minute drive to granite cliff from which Gutzon Borglum and team carved heads of George Washington, Thomas Jefferson, Abraham Lincoln and Theodore Roosevelt between 1927 and 1941. The task involved blasting and chipping away 450,000 tons of rock. A few miles away, work on a three-dimensional sculpture that makes Mount Rushmore look small was started in 1948 by Korczak Ziolkowski. This tribute to the Indians will eventually depict Crazy Horse, one of their proudest warrior chiefs, stretching out an arm long enough to support 4,000 people. The statue will be three times higher than Nelson's Column. All four Rushmore heads could fit inside Crazy Horse's.

On through the warm, pine-scented afternoon to Custer, a small town named after the ill-fated cavalry commander. Custer's expedition of 1874 discovered gold in the Black Hills. Greed swept aside the treaty signed by President Grant, eight years before. 'As long as rivers run and grass grows and trees bear leaves, Paha Sapa – the Black Hills of Dakota – will forever be the sacred land of the Sioux Indians,' it promised.

Day Five: North to Deadwood, the gold rush town where Wild Bill Hickok – shot in the back while playing poker – is buried next to Martha 'Calamity Jane' Burke. Old photos reveal Miss Burke to have looked more like a buffalo's bum than the blonde, peaches-and-cream dazzler immortalised by Doris Day. Deadwood is now a tacky, down-at-heel place. Mrs Llewellin poses, hand on hip, outside the Green Door brothel. Leave I-90 for fast run to Devil's Tower, the astonishing stump of naked, volcanic rock where the alien spaceship landed in *Close Encounters of the Third Kind*. Climbers look no bigger than flies.

Loop north, then west, following virtually deserted roads on which the Corvette covers 200 miles in little more than two hours. Chevrolet's convertible feels rock-solid as its ghastly sci-fi speedo indicates 130mph at only 3,250rpm. Reach site of Custer's demise at 6pm, but lack of suitable accommodation nearby sends us down the interstate to Ranchester. This being empty country, distance is about same as that from London to Birmingham. Morale fully restored by drinking with cowboys in Silver Spur saloon – visitors from a distant planet couldn't have been regarded with more initial astonishment – then sinking huge, high-octane cocktails before relishing excellent steaks. Stroll back to Silver Spur for nightcap. 'When does this place close?' we ask. 'When the last person leaves.'

Day Six: Lieutenant-Colonel George Armstrong Custer and his men made their last stand on a small hill above the Little Bighorn River. This lonesome corner of Montana has changed only in slight detail since that June afternoon in 1876, when Sioux and Cheyenne – fighting under such chiefs as Crazy Horse, Crow King, Rain-in-the-Face, Gall and Two Moons – left not one of their foes alive. Why didn't the 7th Cavalry gallop to the rescue at the last minute? Custer and his troops *were* the 7th Cavalry. Relics in the first-class battlefield museum include Springfield carbines, Colt 45 revolvers, wonderfully evocative photographs and one of Custer's buckskin suits. A sombre postscript to the brief, bloody encounter notes: 'Under-trained and under-paid, the soldiers of the Indian Wars were pitted against a resourceful enemy in hostile country.'

Traffic isn't a word associated with Wild West states. Montana, three times the size of England, has a population far smaller than Devon's. The miles between Little Bighorn and Gardiner, the Yellowstone National Park's northern gateway, are ripped off like raffle tickets. Rocky Mountain peaks 10,000 snow-white feet high stand guard as sundowners are sipped in the Rusty Rail. Watney's Red Barrel – 'The aristocrat of British beers' – is an unexpected link with home. We drink tomato juice, diluted with vodka. When in Rome . . .

Day Seven: Yellowstone, the world's first national park, is renowned for geysers, hot springs, immense terraces of steaming calcium carbonate, mountains, waterfalls, grizzly bears and bison, to name just a few attractions. But the pilgrims who reach Mammoth Hot Springs just after we stop for breakfast snap each member of the family posed by our red Corvette. Drive through the forest to colonial-style hotel overlooking Yellowstone Lake, nearly 8,000 feet above sea level. Beautifully decorated and furnished room costs equivalent of about £55 per night. Expensive for rural America, but worth every cent for the view alone. Visit Old Faithful and other geysers before complementing succulent king-crab legs with a 1986 Vouvray.

Day Eight: Bubbling mud volcanoes and sulphur cauldrons make us wonder if the underworld spent last night feasting on red-hot vindaloo. Potter on to Grand Canyon of Yellowstone, notable for a waterfall higher than Niagara, then stop for lunch at Tower Fall. Snack served by a young American who admires Kipling. This is no more likely than encountering a cricket fan in Ulan Bator, but we chorus a verse that could well have been written for Custer:

> *When you're wounded and left on Afghanistan's plains,*
> *An' the women come out to cut up what remains,*
> *Jest roll to your rifle an' blow out your brains*
> *An' go to your Gawd like a soldier.*

Back at the lakeside hotel, cocktails slip down while a string quartet plays Mozart.

Day Nine: South to Grand Teton National Park. Mountains with splendid names – Rolling Thunder, Thor Peak – savage the sky above Jackson Hole. Consult guidebook: 'Early French-Canadian fur trappers gave the Tetons their name, French for big breasts. Perhaps they had been a long time on the trail, or their naming of the mountains represented wishful thinking, for there is nothing smooth, soft, or voluptuous about the jagged, irregular spires.'

Drop anchor in Jackson. Devote afternoon to lazing by Virginian Lodge's pool, then dine very well for less than £10 a head, including cocktails and bottle of Glen Ellen Cabernet Sauvignon from California. Virginian Lodge's dim-lit bar packed with big men wearing big boots and big cowboy hats, straight from a John Wayne movie. These guys drink from the bottle – so do their ladies – and dance the *Tennessee Waltz* at two o'clock in the morning. This is a far cry from Yellowstone's Vouvray and Mozart.

Day Ten: Over the mountains to Idaho Falls, then take I-15 to Pocatello and head south-west for Wendover. This route provides one of the great drives of a lifetime. Deserted roads spear and sweep along broad valleys flanked by high, barren mountains. Deserted roads? In three hours we encounter perhaps a dozen other vehicles – plus a puzzling posse of rusting wrecks daubed with anti-church rantings – while the Corvette cuts through the stifling afternoon air like a red arrow. The speedometer rarely indicates less than the ambient temperature readout, which hovers close to 100 degrees F. On roads such as this, and the western states have thousands of miles of them, the 55mph limit makes no more sense than would legislation restricting snowfalls to six inches at the South Pole.

Hot and dusty Wendover straddles the line where Nevada, home of round-the-clock gambling, cheap booze and legalised brothels, meets pious Utah of the Latterday Saints. We check into the Super 8 Motel, and fail to bankrupt the Red Garter Casino.

Day Eleven: Wendover's long main street passes the Bonneville Speedway Museum before joining I-80 on the western edge of the Great Salt Lake Desert. The collection lacks much in the way of record-breaking cars, but is packed with memories of Sir Malcolm and Donald Campbell, John Cobb, George Eyston, Donald Healey, Stirling Moss, Phil Hill, Art *Green Monster* Arfons, Craig *Spirit of America* Breedlove, Bob *Goldenrod* Summers, Gary *Blue Flame* Gabelich and Ab *Mormon Meteor* Jenkins, the local hero who eschewed a co-driver's help while hoisting the 24-hour record to 161mph in 1940.

Salt clouds whipped up by a strong wind no more soothing than a bunsen burner restrict eastward visibility as the Corvette rockets along the road whose end marks the start of the Bonneville Speedway's nine-mile straight. The temperature climbs to within a parched gasp of 49 degrees C. Shoes crunch into the soft, damp, sticky surface while we try to picture pioneers struggling to cross this brutal wilderness in covered wagons. Mrs Llewellin inches the Corvette off the black stuff while I click the Nikon. Seconds later, the Chevrolet is passed by a hell-for-leather Buick. When it returns, plastered with salt, we can almost hear the body corroding. 'Must be crazy,' we mutter, then notice the back bumper's Alamo Rent-A-Car sticker.

East to Salt Lake City – backed by craggy, snow-capped mountains – then south to Ranchester down a relatively soft, green valley, grazed by sheep, cattle and horses. This being Sunday in Utah, the law prevents anything more sinful than beer being served with dinner.

Day Twelve: Hit the road bright and early, pass the Big Rock Candy Mountain sung about by Burl Ives, then stop for fuel and food in Panguitch. The Flying M serves the trip's best breakfast. Menu states: 'Due to high altitude, no soft-boiled eggs.' Other possibilities include pigs-in-a-blanket – 'Savoury link sausages cuddled in a buttermilk pancake, served with whipped butter and a choice of syrups' – the wide-eyed strangers are told.

Corvette's next port of call is Bryce Canyon National Park. Mile after mind-boggling mile of white, pink and honey-gold limestone cliffs have been eroded to create a fantastic landscape of spires, pinnacles, spearheads, fortresses and cathedrals, bridges and ravines. One of the most memorable formations is an arch 54 feet wide and almost 100 feet high. The canyon is named after Ebenezer Bryce, a 19th-century Scottish farmer who said it was one helluva place to lose a cow.

Flat-topped cliffs the colour of rare steak dominate views for hour upon hour as we head for a night in Page, Arizona. Page, founded way back in 1957, grew up where the Colorado River was dammed to create a lake with an 1,800-mile shoreline. Sunset daubs desert and sky with ever-changing hues while one of the best Chinese meals we've ever tasted makes a change from conventional American fare.

Day Thirteen: Plans to delve deep into Monument Valley, another wonderland of eroded rock towers, are foiled by dirt roads incompatible with the Corvette's ground clearance. En route to Colorado, loping along at 100-plus does nothing to soften the sun's sledgehammer heat. Tiny riverside settlements with such names as Bluff, population 119, and Mexican Hat, account for what few people share this fissured immensity of sand, scrub and tumbleweed with rattlesnakes. Spend night in Durango.

Day Fourteen: Cruise eastward, climbing to almost 11,000 feet at Wolf Creek Pass and skirting a peak the height of Mont Blanc. But we're gradually leaving the Rocky Mountains behind. Relax by motel pool after reaching Walsenburg at 3pm.

Day Fifteen: Morning crisp and clear as drive fast for an hour without seeing another vehicle. Heat stifling when we reach Dodge City. What started as a frontier fort became the world's biggest cattle market when the Atchison, Topeka & Santa Fe railroad hit town in 1872. Pistol-packing lawmen included Bat Masterson and Wyatt Earp, who lived long enough to see himself immortalised by Hollywood. Dodge City's turbulent past is tastefully and vividly recalled in Boot Hill Museum, where the Main Street of the 1870s has been recreated. Press on to Salina, taking the Corvette across vast plains patchworked with rippling wheatfields and huge feed-yards where cattle are fattened.

Day Sixteen: Hannibal, Missouri, is reached eight hours after leaving Salina. Landscape now green and rolling. Day notable for lunch stop in Chillicothe, where the Corvette makes three young waitresses squeal with delight: 'How about letting us borrow it – just for a few weeks?' Hannibal, on the Mississippi's western bank, is where Samuel Langhorne Clemens spent his formative years. Who is he? Mark Twain, author of *Tom Sawyer* and *Huckleberry Finn*, coiner of such quips as 'The report of my death was an exaggeration' and 'What a man misses most in heaven is company'. Several buildings associated with the wordsmith, his family and his childhood friends have been preserved in a traffic-free street.

Reach sun-baked Springfield, Illinois, in time for a memorable dinner at Mountain Jack's on Stevenson Drive. This is voted the trip's best meal, by a wide margin. It's also the most expensive, but £25 a head includes cocktails, four courses, two bottles of wine, and a post-prandial snifter to help the coffee down.

Day Seventeen: Abraham Lincoln was a young lawyer when he moved to Springfield in 1837. Seven years later he bought the home that still stands on Eighth Street, and lived there before moving to the White House in 1861. The murdered president lies beneath a lofty granite monolith at Oak Ridge, north of the city centre. We buy copies of the great speech he made at Gettysburg in 1863, then drive across Illinois and Indiana to Fort Wayne. Corvette and crew are now just a two-hour drive from the friends' home where our journey started, but there's one more place to be ticked off the bingo card. Auburn is the home of the fabulous Auburn-Cord-Duesenberg Museum. Majestic Model J Duesies share the art deco entrance hall with rakish Auburn Speedsters and coffin-nose Cords. This not-to-be-missed collection's other treasures range from Packard, Cadillac, Mercedes-Benz, Bentley and Rolls-Royce to Kiblinger, Gasmobile and Economy Motor Buggy.

Day Eighteen: Final fill reveals lusty, long-striding Corvette to have averaged 26.6mpg. Cruise to Ann Arbor for laugh-a-minute farewell lunch with editor David E Davis Jr and other *Automobile Magazine* friends, then bid faithful Corvette farewell at Detroit airport. My co-driver on life's road says: 'Fifty-five hundred miles in three weeks. Know what I need now, Mr Llewellin? A holiday.'

5

COAST-TO-COAST ON
THE LINCOLN HIGHWAY

1989

Rampaging across Nevada at 165mph in Ferrari's snarling Testarossa was even more memorable than crossing Utah by Chevrolet Corvette, New Jersey by Ford Taurus, Pennsylvania by Mercedes 560 SEC, Ohio by Ford Mustang, Indiana by BMW 750iL, Iowa by Honda Civic, Nebraska by Lincoln Continental, Wyoming by Ford Probe and California by Range Rover. Invitations to drive right across the United States don't reach Castell Llewellin every day of the week. Invitations to drive right across the United States while sharing a bunch of really interesting cars with a posse of fun-loving friends are as far and few between as the lands where the Jumblies live. This most welcome of bolts from the blue took the form of a call from the *Automobile Magazine* office in Ann Arbor, Michigan, just a hoot and a holler from Detroit. Llewellin, ever the realist, assumed he would have to sing for his supper of Boston scrod and shoo-fly pie by writing an account of the 3,000-mile journey, but was told: 'All you have to do is drive, enjoy yourself . . . and make us laugh.'

We could have followed Interstate 80 every multi-lane inch of the way from New York to San Francisco, but that would have been significantly less stimulating than watching lichen grow. The erstwhile colonials decided that exploring the old Lincoln Highway, the first officially designated coast-to-coast route, would be far more entertaining. The road was the brainchild of Carl Graham Fisher, a gung-ho sportsman and property developer who gets the credit for the Indianapolis Motor Speedway and the blame for Miami Beach. His supporters included Packard's supremo, Henry B Joy, who became the president of the Lincoln Highway Association in 1912, when the name was officially adopted.

The first *Complete Official Road Guide of the Lincoln Highway* was published in 1915, but several years passed before many of the western miles were tamed. One of the most memorable photos in Drake Hokanson's splendid book *The Lincoln Highway – Main Street Across America* was taken in 1919.

It shows a Model T Ford literally axle-deep in Iowa mud. Coincidentally, that was the year when an army convoy spent 62 days battling from Washington to San Francisco. The strugglers included a 29-year-old officer who later inaugurated the National System of Interstate and Defence Highways. By then he was President Dwight D Eisenhower. The army convoy's guide had toured with Buffalo Bill's Wild West Show. This information is a reminder that the USA's folk heroes were doing their legendary stuff way back in the misty Celtic twilight of a week last Tuesday. No wonder the natives gaped when told that my idea of an old road was The Ridgeway, which had been busy for some 2,500 years before the Romans ticked Britain off their shopping list.

Our eight-day drive involved enough sights and escapades to fill a few books. But I'm limited to a few paragraphs, so please excuse the staccato shorthand.

Saturday: Clouds shroud tops of Manhattan's clustered skyscrapers as wagons roll. New Jersey's older towns look more English than many of England's. Eventually exchange urban sprawl for Pennsylvania's rolling, wooded hills. Hotel receptionist's accent sounds familiar. She's from Cardiff. Coincidentally, we carouse and sleep within staggering distance of such New World communities as North Wales, Gwynedd, Bryn Mawr, Bala Cynwyd, Radnor, Berwyn, Bethesda and St David's.

Sunday: A serious, 523-mile slog, but make time to visit Gettysburg, scene of Civil War's best-known battle. Road over mountains to Pittsburgh notable for last sequence of real corners for 2,000 miles. Snow and fog add interest.

Monday: Her Britannic Majesty's representative is 'mooned' from Mustang driven at 100mph by photographer Greg Jarem, one of the galaxy's greatest funsters. Naked backside believed to be property of John Phillips III, who runs him close. Store in Valparaiso, Indiana, sells everything from shoelaces at 50 cents to Uzi sub-machine guns at $2,000.

Tuesday: We're now in open, empty country, travelling fast, eyes supplemented by radar detectors. Nebraska is flat enough to make East Anglia look like the Himalayas.

Wednesday: Stop the 560 SEC to snap '1733 Ranch' sign while following old Pony Express route alongside River Platte. Ranch is exactly 1,733 miles from Boston and 'Frisco. Place called Lewellen on North Platte, but too far off course for detour to put them right about the spelling. Road climbs to 8,640 feet just before Laramie.

Thursday: Ferrari expires with knackered alternator before we leave Laramie. Lincoln Highway runs for ever across classic High Plains landscape of coarse sand, six blades of grass per acre, tumbleweed, distant mountains, eternal wind. Scourged by ferocious hailstorm as reach Salt Lake City. Temperature on flooded Bonneville Salt Flats is nine degrees C. It was 21 degrees higher when Mrs Llewellin and I checked in last year.

Friday: Ferrari rejoins party after covering 710 miles in nine hours. Nevada, three times size of Scotland, has fewer people than Glasgow. Drive at mind-blowing speeds for hour after hour, crossing dramatic mountains and shimmering deserts. Jarem clocks 158mph in BMW – 'I was just cruising along, listening to the radio' – then celebrates by handstanding through Merc's sunroof.

Saturday: Range Rover bowls me over Sierra Nevada to San Francisco and British Airways' flight to London. Asked what I'd choose if had to start back to New York right now? Heart says Ferrari, but vote goes to BMW. Fifteen drivers, five of them ladies, produce following order of merit: 750iL, 560SEC, Probe, Continental, CRX,

Taurus, Testarossa, Corvette, Range Rover, Mustang. Looking back, visiting Gettysburg – the jaunt's biggest bonus – was made all the more memorable by one of my colleagues, Kevin Smith, being the great-great-grandson of the rebel army's commander, General Robert E Lee. His scion made amends by driving a Lincoln along the Lincoln Highway to the spot where the Gettysburg Address was delivered . . . by Abraham Lincoln.

6

Going for gold on

Route 49

1990

'Boys, by God, I believe I have found a gold mine!' yelled James Wilson Marshall. The place was Sutter's Mill, a remote and tiny settlement in a valley on the thickly wooded western flank of the Sierra Nevada. The date was 24 January 1848. San Francisco, 140 miles to the southwest, was big enough to support five grocers, three doctors, two gunsmiths and a brewer.

Marshall, a carpenter by trade, had gradually wandered westward from his bucolic birthplace in New Jersey. He reached what was then the Mexican province of California on horseback in 1845. Two years later, he built a water-powered sawmill in partnership with the self-styled Captain John Sutter. A raffish and charming character by all accounts, Sutter had skedaddled from his native Switzerland when it became obvious that flight was the only alternative to being flung into jail for debt. The prospect of escaping from a nagging wife was an additional incentive.

The smooth-talking adventurer reached California by way of Hawaii and Alaska, was granted 50,000 acres of land and founded a settlement called New Helvetia. The first building, a simple adobe structure, combined rudimentary living quarters with a blacksmith's shop. This was the seed from which today's state capital, Sacramento, was destined to grow.

Gold! James Marshall's discovery on the American River

triggered the rush that turned California into El Dorado. What had been an almost mythical land, on the far side of a vast and daunting continent, now lured the good, the bad and the hopeful from all over the world. Gold! Dust and nuggets worth about $10 million had been accounted for by the end of 1848. As the late Irving Stone pointed out in *Men to Match My Mountains*, that represented two-thirds of what the United States had recently paid Mexico for California, Nevada, Utah, Colorado, Texas, Arizona, Wyoming and parts of New Mexico.

News being a slow traveller in those days, it was '49 before the real rush started. In that year alone, an estimated 40,000 prospectors, plus countless camp followers, flooded into what became known as the mother lode country. Men paid $100 for a blanket and $500 for a shovel while others made $7,000 – 15 times more than the average teacher earned in a year – on each barrel of rotgut whisky.

No fewer than 100,000 miners were working, fighting, praying, gambling, boozing and whoring in the mother lode region by 1852, when the manic quest for gold reached its $80 million peak. By then, more than 500 townships had sprung up in the wilderness.

Reading about that rip-roaring episode in America's brief but fascinating history was a highlight of my last year in school. The possibility of ever visiting the site of Marshall's epochal discovery never crossed my mind. I had never been more than 300 miles from my birthplace on the northern Welsh Marches. California, all of 5,000 miles away, was far beyond the reach of all but the most fortunate of British movie stars. Not a great deal of boodle was being staked on Llewellin's chances of becoming the next Stan Laurel, Cary Grant, Bob Hope or Laurence Olivier. In fact, I've been fortunate enough to visit the United States almost every year since 1969.

Few expeditions have been more interesting and enjoyable than the drive that has just taken the Llewellins and an eye-catching little Mazda RX-7 ragtop right through the mother lode on a road whose number could not be more appropriate.

State Route 49 runs for 325 miles, from Oakhurst in the south to Vinton in the north.

That stark, matter-of-fact sentence belies a route liberally blessed with the ingredients deemed essential by a connoisseur. First, all but a few of those are fun miles to drive, notably at the wheel of a compact and agile roadster whose twin-rotor engine spins out 160bhp at 7,000 rpm. Mazda's convertible also proved stylish enough to attract shouts of 'Hey! Love your car!' as we trickled along streets flanked by timber buildings that have survived since the 1850s.

Second, scenery that varies from rolling, oak-dappled pastures to deep, pine-clad canyons makes SR-49 a road that's equally rewarding when taken at a sedate pace. Third, attractive scenery is complemented by all manner of tangible links with the gold rush and its aftermath. Granted the time, which we lacked, serious students of the colourful past and tranquil present might spend a week or more ambling the length of SR-49. A good driver, determined to make the most of a mettlesome car, could do it all in maybe five or six exhilarating hours. We had two days to capture something of the atmosphere of places with such evocative names as Mount Bullion, Rough and Ready, Chinese Camp, Sutter Creek and Sonora – 'The biggest, richest, and wildest town in the southern mother lode,' according to one account. Auburn, with a population of about 8,000, was the biggest community we encountered. Homitos, reached on the first of several short detours, was far more typical. Here, according to the Automobile Club of Southern California's excellent *Mother Lode* guidebook, 150 people now live where 15,000 once toiled and roistered while Wells Fargo shipped out gold worth $40,000 a day.

Buildings that are virtually prehistoric by local standards, but only half the age of our home on England's border with Wales, please the eye and give an impression of what these places looked like in the good old, bad old days. Our favourites included Coulterville, population 130, where the Hotel Jeffery and its Magnolia Saloon were a 'cantina and fandango hall' in the 1840s.

Another short detour took us to the town of Murphys, where the Murphys Hotel served first-class steaks and reminded us of a cozy little *auberge* in rural France. This used to be *the* place to stay in a hell-raising town on an important stagecoach route. John Pierpoint Morgan, one of the world's richest men, slept in our room in 1869. Names painted on other doors recalled Ulysses S Grant and Mark Twain, to name but two. How much luggage did they travel with? Even our small-to-medium case was too big for the Mazda's boot, the lid of which had to be tied down with string.

On to Coloma, where James Marshall's statue looks down on a replica of Sutter's Mill. North of Nevada City, a gravel track swept us down to the Malakoff Diggins State Historic Park, the site of the world's biggest 'hydraulic' gold mine. Huge water cannons ripped a mountain apart, leaving a scar all of 7,000 feet long by 3,000 wide and 600 deep.

Last night, we slept like logs in Downieville, population 400, after smiling Sandra Dyer let us have a complete house for the price of a room in Dyer's Motel. We ate well in the Forks Restaurant, looked forward to taking the Mazda over the 6,701-foot-high Yuba Pass, and vowed to return to the mother lode. There's no longer gold in them thar hills. But we certainly found a lot to treasure in the Sierra Nevada.

7

LAXATIVE RIDGE

1993

Hellroaring Canyon, Poison Spider Mesa, Dead Horse Point, Devil's Pocket, Determination Tower, Paul Bunyan's Potty, Ruin Park, Coffee Pot Rock and Bagpipe Butte are just a few of the names encountered in Utah's spectacular Canyonlands. Laxative Ridge is my contribution. No less appropriate than Labyrinth Canyon or Delicate Arch, it identifies the most daunting sight I have ever studied through a windscreen.

'This has to be a joke,' was the gulped and gasped reaction when Tom Collins, the expedition's guide and mentor, took us to the rock formation whose official name is Lion's Back. Reaching the top of this great spine of sandstone involves climbing about 200 feet in approximately 200 yards. The gradient is awesome, but that's not what makes you concentrate *really* hard. What accounts for the exceptionally high rush of adrenalin through your bloodstream is that parts of Laxative Ridge measure no more than six or seven paces side to side, from vertical drop to vertical drop. It's like driving up the *outside* of the barrel of a colossal howitzer. Getting it wrong would certainly be the last of life's many mistakes.

'Would you like me to come with you?' Mrs Llewellin asked as I climbed aboard the Range Rover County LWB and wondered why this very expensive status symbol's specification didn't include a parachute and an escape hatch.

'No,' I said. 'You stay down here. I'd hate the kids to lose two parents in one accident.'

'Nervous? Or only pretending to be?' asked my wife.

'Let's say I'm just a little apprehensive,' I muttered, that being a very British euphemism for abso-bloody-lutely terrified.

'Who wants to go first?' asked Tom Collins.

Laxative Ridge would be famous if it stood in splendid isolation, but dramatic rock formations are commonplace in the Canyonlands of Utah. Nature's patient but powerful tools, notably water and wind, have spent tens of millions of years sculpting this vast plateau into all manner of weird and wonderful shapes. Two Spanish priests passed this way in 1776 –'Armed with brandy and cigars,' according to Tom Collins – but Major John Wesley Powell's expeditions of 1869 and 1871 were among the first to chronicle the astonishing blend of beauty and desolation, jagged lines and graceful curves, that makes this one of our planet's most mind-boggling and evocative landscapes.

'Wherever we look there is but a wilderness of rocks: deep gorges, where the rivers are lost below cliffs and towers and pinnacles: and ten thousand strangely carved forms in every direction: and beyond them, mountains blending with the clouds,' Major Powell wrote in his *Exploration of the Colorado River of the West and Its Tributaries*.

We are here to absorb a little of the region's unique magic while off-roading in three V8-powered four-wheel-drive vehicles that we came to know as two sputes and a splux. Spute is Mrs Llewellin's patented abbreviation for a sport-utility vehicle. It refers to the Jeep Grand Cherokee Laredo and the Chevrolet Blazer K1500 Silverado. She invented the word as a logical follow-up to the Range Rover's splux designation, saying: 'You can't stick a "utility" label on something that's no more utilitarian than Buckingham Palace. It has to be a sport-luxury. A splux.'

Mrs Llewellin was right, for only the 10,896,457th time since we tied the marital knot in 1963. Now powered by a stretched, 4.3-litre version of the long-serving, former General Motors aluminium V8, and riding on a new, electronically controlled air suspension system, Britain's standard-bearer out here in the Canyonlands offers a unique blend of attributes, from superb off-road performance to a

112mph top speed and a leather-and-walnut interior. The extended wheelbase makes the rear compartment ideal for species far more long-legged than *Homo sapiens*. This is impressive, of course, and very useful when passengers are rigid with terror, but extra luggage capacity would be more practical. The styling is as British as a tweed suit from Savile Row and the price is as steep as Laxative Ridge. We're talking about what it takes to buy a Blazer *and* a Grand Cherokee.

But this is not a head-to-head duel, because financial factors would make direct comparisons a pointless exercise. Big V8s are what these off-roaders have in common. Despite being uprated, the Range Rover's engine is no match for the Blazer's 5.7-litre or the much lighter and sleeker Jeep's 5.2-litre. The beefy Blazer has reminded us that there are times when there's just no substitute for cubic inches and old-fashioned corn-fed, pedal-to-the-metal grunt.

'I'm writing this while Jim Ramsey is driving the Range Rover along a sandy trail called Bartlett Wash!' is the notebook's first reference to off-road driving. The exclamation mark is a tribute to legibility and, therefore, to the County's standard-setting suspension. Replacing the old Jeep Cherokee's rear leaf springs with coils is one reason for the Grand Cherokee's ride also rating high marks, especially on the smooth sections of Interstate 70 and State Route 128 that snake from Grand Junction, Colorado, to the tourist town of Moab, Utah. This Jeep is an extremely attractive package, inside and out, but there were initial doubts about its ability to cope with the rough stuff. Gentleman Jim Ramsey said: 'I'm wondering if this is more of a suburban station wagon than a serious off-road contender.' Having convincingly conquered every terrifying inch of Laxative Ridge, the Jeep had him thinking otherwise.

On the road later that day, we were eating scrumptious sandwiches from Honest Ozzie's in Moab when our dauntless leader, David E Davis, Jr, shifted attention to the big-hearted Blazer. 'It's very trucklike but does what it has to do,' quoth he. Honest Ozzie's picnic lunch helped replace nervous energy lost while negotiating nail-biting slopes of smooth, steep rock

– 'They're fossilised sand-dunes,' Tom Collins told us – at the foot of a beaut of a butte called Merrimac. American Civil War buffs will guess, correctly, that its smaller neighbour is called Monitor. Their shapes make it easy to appreciate why the buttes were named, but there's something delightfully surreal about encountering two 19th-century warships in a bone-dry wilderness 5,000 feet above sea level and 400 miles from the nearest droplet of ocean. But that's typical of the most out-of-this-world terrain I've encountered while wandering as far afield as Yemen, Borneo, China, Iceland and Afghanistan.

The afternoon served up a sharp reminder that all things are relative. The fossilised dunes were relegated to off-roading's minor league when we reached what the Red Rock Four-Wheelers Club has named Wipeout Hill. An almost vertical drop of about four feet launched us into a rocky horror show of a gully where creeping along at 0.01mph in the lowest of low gears, inching left and right to avoid crevices and boulders, was the only alternative to jamming wheels, denting panels and bashing differentials. Rocks streaked and blotched with dusty, sun-baked oil were memorials to other wayfarers. Jeannie Davis had to be extra careful in the Jeep, because the diffs are not in line with each other, but its performance was indeed impressive.

Nobody was surprised by the Range Rover's confident performance on Wipeout Hill, where selecting the suspension's high-profile setting virtually eliminated the risk of crunching a sill. It lifted a rear wheel, as the Grand Cherokee had done, but the traction control system kicked in before Michelin's rubber started smoking. I was driving the Chevrolet. Longer, wider and heavier than even the British dreadnought – and width is another word for off-road vulnerability – the Blazer creaked and groaned like a weary old windjammer, while still retaining its reputation for doing the job with a minimum of finesse. Just about every facet of its character, from the way it aggressively responds to the throttle to the rear axle's leaf springs, is more medieval than modern.

The road from Moab to Poison Spider Mesa passes immense sandstone cliffs where crude petroglyphs depicting people and animals were carved hundreds of years before Columbus sailed to the New World. Nearby, we gazed in wonder at fossilised footprints left by a dinosaur that passed this way 140 million years ago, give or take a few weeks. Elsewhere, many of the trails that challenge today's off-roaders were first blazed as recently as the 1950s, when Moab suddenly became the focal point of a boom whose story is told by Raye C Ringholz in *Uranium Frenzy*.

It really started in 1952, when Charles 'Uranium Charlie' Steen, a destitute but determined geologist, discovered the ore that was to make him one of America's most colourful multi-millionaires. The clocks were always set at cocktail hour in his crag-perched home high above Moab. It's now the Mi Vida restaurant. Charlie Steen didn't mince his words. In 1958 he was invited to receive the Outstanding Student Award from Texas Western College in El Paso. Was he flattered and delighted? He was not. He was blazing mad, because Texas Western had replaced the famous Texas College of Mines and Metallurgy from which he had graduated. His speech suggested that the new college's scope should be extended to include courses in 'How to chug-a-lug beer out of a gallon pitcher without getting a permanent crease on the bridge of your nose' and 'How to chew tobacco and not dribble it on your chin'.

Aircraft were among the King of Uranium's favourite toys. Says Ringholz: 'Often his flights were frivolous. He flew to Salt Lake City for weekly rumba lessons. When there was a special television programme that he wanted to see, he would have his pilot circle the plane over Moab so that he could watch the tube where the reception was not hampered by mountains.'

Charlie Steen's never-say-die attitude was recalled on Poison Spider Mesa, where challenges included the ascent of a long, steep cleft filled with soft sand. Mr Davis went first, driving the Jeep whose off-road performance has made the sceptics eat their words. It failed to climb this one. So did the Range Rover, even with a driver as experienced as Tom Collins at the wheel. But the Chevrolet, blessed with aggressive tyres, oodles of torque – and a chauffeur so modest his name escapes me – blazed up at the fifth attempt. Contrary to expectations, the Blazer was the only vehicle that did *everything* it was asked to do.

All three climbed Laxative Ridge. Reaching the top in the Range Rover was the bravest thing I've done on four wheels while stone-cold sober. There were visions of another heart attack when the County slipped a few inches – it seemed like yards – at a point where nothing more solid than mountain air could be seen on either side. Gung-ho remarks belied the fact that hands were shaking when I reached the top while every muscle was rigid with fear. Having to pause for photographs was the really bad news, because that gave me time and enough to think about tumbling to my doom. I echoed Sir John Falstaff – 'The better part of valour is discretion' – and let Tom Collins drive me down to Eddie McStiff's bar for several gallons of brewed-on-the-premises beer. The only regret was being too traumatised, up there on Laxative Ridge, to realise that the descent would have been a piece of cake, because I could see where I was going.

Grappling with gravity had us on a pleasant high that evening, and our mood called to mind a racing adage from days gone by. After a race the sky is bluer, the women are prettier and the steaks are tastier. After risking life and limb on the red rocks, it was good to be alive.

8

INVERNESS TO CHESTER
IN SEVEN MINUTES

1997

God bless Montana! Thanks to the state's 'reasonable and prudent' speed limit, we whetted our appetites by clocking 215 miles in 240 minutes before breakfast, the day having started with coffee as dawn painted the Great Plains gold and purple. That glorious gallop set us up for one of the best driving days I can recall after trawling through memory banks that span 40 years and more than a million miles. Playing it by the book, I slowed to 25mph for tiny towns overlooked by vast grain elevators. Elsewhere, Jaguar's XK8 convertible wafted along one deserted and apparently endless straight at 135mph while Mrs Llewellin snoozed in the passenger's seat.

'Just how liberally the law's interpreted tends to depend on the cop's mood,' we were warned in Williston, North Dakota. 'Best keep a few five-dollar bills handy, in case his haemorrhoids are hurtin' or his wife's givin' him a bad time, or he can't resist stickin' one on a guy in a fancy foreign sports car.'

We experienced no such problems.

That exhilarating day was a terrific bonus, the real object of the exercise being to see how Jaguar's eye-catching ragtop fared on a seriously long haul. The plan involved linking two world-class gatherings of car enthusiasts by driving from Meadow Brook, north of Detroit, to Laguna Seca and Pebble

Beach, south of San Francisco. Rather than taking the logical route, we dog-legged via British Columbia, then cruised down the Pacific coast. This strategy gave the Jaguar 11 days to cover 4,000 miles, including a non-motoring weekend in Canada. The real challenge involved covering the 2,500 miles between Meadow Brook and Vancouver in four and a half days.

We had expected Michigan's answer to Pebble Beach's world-famous *concours d'élégance* to be a top-notch affair. We were right. Thanks to one of the organisers, Larry Smith, our base for the weekend was Meadow Brook Hall, where King Henry VIII would have felt at home. Built with Dodge millions in the Twenties, the fourth-largest residence in the United States is now part of Oakland University. As friends arrived for the eve-of-show black-tie party, I leaned out of our bedroom window, brandished a pre-cocktail cocktail and threatened to set the dogs on them. When asked what she thought of this Tudor-style palace, Mrs Llewellin said: 'Just like home . . . only smaller and with fewer servants.'

Oldsmobiles and Ferraris were thick on the ground, because both marques were celebrating major birthdays, but what impressed us most was the overall quality of Sunday's lineup, which totalled just over 300 cars. We admired such extremes as the cute little Bantam – America's version of the Austin Seven – and the Maybach Zeppelin that featured an 8-litre V12 engine and a transmission with eight forward gears. At day's end we dashed down from our room to admire and briefly ride in the Model J Duesenbergs that were being photographed for the Blackhawk Collection's ever-smiling Tim McGrane. It was a moment that epitomised the weekend's magic.

Our main pre-departure concern had involved the XK8's boot. In 1988 we explored a huge chunk of America's heartland in a Chevrolet Corvette convertible. Despite packing carefully, knowing stowage space to be at a premium, we had to leave one of two bags with friends in Michigan. This time, the Jaguar swallowed everything required for our three-week trip, including attire essential to look smart at the Meadow Brook weekend's most formal function.

Grey skies gave way to sunshine while heading north to the mighty Mackinac Bridge. Later, views of Lake Superior, the world's largest expanse of fresh water, punctuated a zillion square miles of forest. At day's end, we admired the great lake from our hotel in Ashland, Wisconsin. We could sail a small boat from here to within a five-minute walk of our home on the Welsh Marches. The day's best bumper sticker urged us to 'Eat potatoes and love longer'.

Eighty-six thousand people make Duluth, Minnesota, the biggest place we will encounter before Vancouver. We skirt it after crossing the bridge that commemorates Richard Bong, America's top-scoring fighter ace in the Second World War. He died back home in the United States while testing a Lockheed Shooting Star on the day the bomb was dropped on Hiroshima. Frances Gumm is remembered in her birthplace, Grand Rapids, Minnesota. She changed her name to Judy Garland.

Cruising speed increased as pine gave way to an eternity of prairie, which offers less cover for radar-toting lawmen. By mid-afternoon we are still in Flat Earth Society country and determined to keep the top down while skirting thunder storms. A monument in Rugby, North Dakota, marks the North American continent's geographical centre.

Next morning a jubilant 'Yeeee-hah!' greets the 'reasonable and prudent' speed-limit sign as the XK8 crosses into Montana. Entering another time zone enables us to joke about covering 120 miles in two minutes, running close to the broad Missouri, which should be regarded as America's greatest river. When we crossed the Mississippi, way back down the road, it was little more than a trickle. The juxtaposition of familiar British place-names in the United States is invariably amusing. The original Inverness and Chester are 450 miles apart. We can now boast about driving between them in seven minutes, the distance in Montana being a dozen miles.

Mountains eventually studded the horizon, so we looped northward and climbed to 6,649 feet in Glacier National Park. We were miles from nowhere when the XK8's engine-coolant warning came on. At the risk of being mugged by bears, I opened the bonnet and convinced myself that everything was working properly. Apart from a sensor, of course.

A good night's sleep, then a beautiful valley took us to Canada. Officials on both sides of this remote frontier crossing regarded the Brits and the XK8 as if we were friendly aliens aboard a flying saucer. 'Going to the post office' and 'Going for gas' were reasons given when travellers heading south were asked why they were visiting the United States. Hour after hour of stupendous Rocky Mountain scenery took us to an overnight stop in Keremeos, British Columbia, where the motel's owner greeted us with open arms. He used to drive a Jaguar XJS and lamented the passing of the V12 engine. He also warned that restaurants close at 8pm. Sure enough, hovering staff waited to snatch plates if we paused for breath. Is this Canada's ulcer-and-indigestion capital? I scrawl 'In haste!' in the visitors' book.

We love the way that obscure North American places claim international fame. 'Home of the world famous magic muffins' encouraged us to eat breakfast in Princeton, British Columbia. One of the many Jaguar fans encountered along the way chatted when we stop near Hope, where a landslide that thundered down a 6,500-feet-high ridge dumped 60 million cubic yards of rock on and near the highway in 1965.

Big hugs in Vancouver, then north for a convivial weekend in Whistler, a fashionable resort where Mrs Llewellin's cousin and her husband, the doctors Heather and Pat Fay, have an apartment. We will never forget relaxing over a gourmet picnic before the Vancouver Symphony orchestra's open-air concert, all of 7,000 feet up Whistler Mountain.

If it's Monday we're back on the road again, overlooked by Mount Baker, Mount Rainier and Mount Saint Helens as we cruised south along busy I-5. Life was quieter after crossing the Columbia River and heading for the Oregon coast. Enchanted by great cliffs and vast beaches, we pushed on to Manzanita and found an inexpensive motel with an inspirational view of the Pacific and an excellent restaurant nearby.

Only 156 miles unfurled beneath Pirelli's tyres on Tuesday,

the trip's shortest day. Reasons included visiting the air museum in Tillamook, Oregon, where warbirds and other flying machines are housed in what is claimed to be the world's biggest open-span timber building, which started life as a hangar for submarine-hunting airships during the Second World War. Cape Foulweather will be remembered for the sight of a whale. We spotted another little more than a stone's throw from our room at the Adobe Resort in Yachats.

Mist conceals the seascapes we've been hoping for as Oregon gives way to California. Ferndale more than compensates, being a miraculously preserved little gem of a Victorian town. The decision to overnight here is made when we spot the amazingly ornate Gingerbread Mansion Inn.

Thursday's 326-mile drive flings the XK8 through more corners than we have negotiated in total since our trip began. South of Eureka, a lonesome scenic byway loops to the so-called Lost Coast and the Avenue of the Giants, where immense redwoods flank the road. One is believed to have been more than 800 years old when it fell in 1987. At nearby Myers Flat, another has split to such an extent that Mrs Llewellin drives the Jaguar through the crack.

The town of Leggett marks the northern end of Highway 1, which serpents and zigzags over wooded mountains before reaching the misty ocean. The temperature drops 35 degrees F in as many miles as the XK8 provides a typically Jaguar blend of grip, handling and ride comfort. My tattered Rand McNally road atlas is deceptive in the sense that many of the coast's supposed towns are little more than names on the map. And this great driving road is less than ideal if your partner's stomach is upset.

Late in the day, the atmosphere becomes a little tense when my confident talk of San Francisco being around the next corner coincides with the road writhing over yet another mountain. Fortunately, there's a Holiday Inn and a surprisingly good restaurant in Mill Valley, a short drive from the Golden Gate Bridge.

And now for one of the world's greatest gatherings of the Clan MacPetrolhead. We start by visiting the Concours Italiano before checking in at the Monterey Plaza, at which point 4,013 miles have been covered since leaving Meadow Brook Hall. Saturday is spent at Laguna Seca, where we cheer our pal Mark Gillies to victory at the wheel of the only ERA in the United States. My American editor and his wife, David and Jeannie Davis, are ready with breakfast when we reach Pebble Beach at 7am on Sunday for a long day with the world's finest assembly of classic automobiles, from microcars and steamers to Duesenbergs and Aston Martins. We love the outrageously rakish Alfa 8C-2900B with coachwork by Touring of Milan, but 'Best of Show' goes to a gorgeous Talbot-Lago coupé with Figoni & Falaschi bodywork.

The trip total is 4,188 miles, every one with the top down, when the XK8 is left in San Francisco. It's like abandoning a faithful friend, because there are very few complaints, apart from the engine-coolant warning light, which has continued to malfunction.

As for the great intangibles, style and class, five dollars for every 'Love your car!' and 'Wow! Is this the new Jag-wah?' would have enabled us to pay for the trip *and* buy an XK8 with the change.

9

HUNTING GHOSTS
IN NEVADA

1999

A cool breeze whispered through the sagebrush while the setting sun turned Nevada's sky into a psychedelic glory of colour, from silvery gold to high heaven's deepest, darkest purple. There was just enough light for us to read names on the sculpted stones and weathered boards that mark graves in the dusty cemetery where Tonopah's dead were buried from 1901 until 1911. They recall the miners and others who lived and died here after Jim Butler discovered silver while searching for a lost burro. Anders Antony Hoffsted was killed while being hoisted to the surface; Manuel Cordoza and Clarence H David were among the 14 men who perished when fire raged through a mine in 1911; a runaway ore car accounted for Felemir and George Marojevich. Elsewhere amid these sparse and poignant glimpses of the past, I breathed a prayer for Baby Harrington – 'Our little flower' – and wondered who gunned Sheriff Tom Logan down in 1906. He left a widow and eight children.

Photographer Martyn Goddard and I sensed the presence of Tonopah's ghosts during the remainder of our 1,000-mile journey in the scenically spectacular Silver State, where exploring ghost towns in a Suzuki Grand Vitara was the name of the game. Serious fortunes in silver, gold and copper have been mined in Nevada since 1859, when the Comstock Lode was discovered near Reno. Four years later, the miners' camp on that remote mountainside had become Virginia City. Nevada's second great silver boom started in Tonopah, almost a century ago.

Although we failed to win a fortune, or even a cent, morale was sky-high when the Grand Vitara left Las Vegas. First and foremost, we had struck gold in the shape of Mickey Goodweiler. A leading light in the Nevada United Four Wheelers Association, he volunteered to play the native guide's role in the mountains west of Ely. He also enlisted Mac McCarty, a local expert whose white beard reminded me of Gandalf, the wizard in *The Lord of the Rings*. On the nuts-and-bolts front, it was illuminating to see how enthusiastically the valet parkers at our hotel, Circus Circus, reacted to the cute little Suzuki whose silver paint was the most appropriate of colours. But only the more dimensionally challenged of them would have enjoyed more than a few miles in the back seat, even before it was filled with stuff. The boot was not compatible with Goddard's cameras and personal effects plus my luggage.

Although the Grand Vitara earned points for being a refined cruiser, its 2.5-litre V6 worked hard en route to Ely, for reasons that included power-sapping altitude. Internal combustion engines need air and this adventure involved several climbs to more than 7,000 feet.

A wind sharp with the threat of snow was slicing along Aultman Street when we reached Ely – the focal point of a county where silver, gold and copper have been mined since the 1860s – but Bert Woywod's staff radiated warmth as we checked in at the six-storey Hotel Nevada, which used to be the state's tallest building. I like Ely for being a friendly, unpretentious and independent little town with a Fifties atmosphere to complement attractions that range from the Hotel Nevada's cheap drinks to the railroad museum's 1910-vintage steam locomotive.

Ely has been White Pine County's seat since 1887. To find its predecessor, Hamilton, we drove along a dirt road for ten miles before dropping into a valley where skeletal ruins were scattered among the fragrant sagebrush. Two arches of brick caught the eye – 'That was the opera house,' said McCarty.

While this was akin to discovering a haystack in the middle of New York, it would not have been incongruous when Hamilton was a rip-roaring town of 20,000 people. But the boom was brief. The population started dwindling within a year or two and fell even faster in 1873, when the owner of a cigar store torched his premises in an attempted insurance scam. The fire exceeded his expectations by raging through the town.

Treasure City is as good a name as even the most romantic and optimistic explorer could hope to encounter while searching for ghost towns. Almost 9,000 feet above sea level, what used to be its mile-long main street is still flanked by the substantial remains of stone buildings, including the Wells Fargo office that served a community of 6,000 hardy souls. Silver worth about $20 million was mined here between 1867 and 1880.

A three-mile aerial tramway linked Treasure Hill to the stamping mill at Eberhardt, where a typical ton of ore yielded silver worth $1,000. The more conventional route into the valley confirmed the Grand Vitara's ability to soak up punishment despite its short wheelbase, but its engine braking left a lot to be desired. In theory, the lowest of low gears should let you inch down a very steep slope without touching the brakes, because that risks locking the wheels and slithering out of control. We would have ended the day in a hospital or mortuary had I relied on that technique down gradients that would be a real challenge only to the most inexperienced off-road driver.

The afternoon's highlights included mind-blowing views from Babylon Ridge and a visit to the Belmont mine, where remains include a building crammed with massive machinery and deserted homes complete with abandoned cars. We also walked to a rickety log cabin that encapsulated three decades. Taking care not to disturb anything, I found clothes hanging from a rail, timesheets dated January 1944, the Rigid Tool Company's September 1961 calendar, and a *Reader's Digest* from 1974.

Next morning we lingered awhile in Eureka, where about 1,500 people now live in what was Nevada's second biggest city in 1878. Today's attractions include a museum in the building where the *Eureka Sentinel* was published for many years. Another crisp canter westward along US-50 set us up for a gravel-road drive on which the Grand Vitara encountered only one other vehicle in 70 miles before rejoining the pavement at Belmont. Snugged into the head of a valley overlooked by outcrops of fissured, wind-sculpted rock, Belmont produced silver worth about $15 million before the boom ended, just over a century ago. Tangible links with the town's heyday include a handsome brick courthouse. The chimney of the brickworks is the first and somewhat surreal thing you spot on approaching this ghost town from the north. The Monitor Inn, Dirty Dick's Saloon and several other buildings were evidence that Belmont is still inhabited, but we saw no other people. The only sounds louder than Goddard's camera were boots crunching on gravel and the breeze whispering secrets to the sagebrush.

When is a ghost town not a ghost town? The question asked and answered at Ely and Eureka was repeated in Tonopah – a Shoshone word meaning 'little spring' – which used to be one of the world's greatest sources of silver. The mines closed long ago, but Jim Butler's town soldiers on as a 2,000-strong community notable for hyperactive cops who have turned US-95's interminable 25mph speed limit zone into the biggest source of revenue since the silver ran out. We saw more uniforms in Tonopah than on the rest of the trip put together, Las Vegas not excluded.

Fifteen minutes were spent watching the Tonopah Historic Mining Park's excellent video before we explored old buildings filled with king-sized machinery. Miners who dug almost 500 miles of tunnels between 1900 and 1948 went down these and other shafts. Interesting in itself, this 70-acre site also has views across the town where Jack Dempsey worked as a bartender before becoming the world champion heavyweight boxer. Wyatt Earp ran a saloon here after moving on from Tombstone, Arizona.

There are no prizes for guessing what made Goldfield one of the richest places on the planet and Nevada's biggest city for a few years at the start of this century. This main-road community of 20,000 people had just about everything from a stock exchange to banks, breweries and brothels. Folks still live in Goldfield, but most of the big buildings are derelict, including the 150-bedroom Goldfield Hotel. This was one of the fanciest establishments between the Mississippi and the Pacific when it opened in 1908 amid a great popping of champagne corks. It closed in 1936.

Las Vegas was calling, but the Suzuki looped west of US-95 to lonely Gold Point, which dates from just after the American Civil War. The detour was richly rewarded when we met Coleen Garland, a remarkable, silver-haired lady who has turned Mitchell's Mercantile into a beguiling blend of general store and museum. Cases of Old Bushmills Irish Whiskey and colourful tins of Prince Albert Tobacco were among items that caught the eye. We bought cans of soda and joked about this seething metropolis of 27 people boasting no fewer than three fire-engines – none of them in working order – whose combined age must be at least a century. Garland, a teacher in Las Vegas for 33 years, 'adopted' Gold Point in 1974. 'Coming up here from Vegas was a classic example of going from the ridiculous to the sublime,' she laughed as we admired the view before taking a dirt-road detour back down the mountain to US-95.

Prospectors discovered gold a few miles west of Beatty in 1904. Four years later, what had become the boom town of Rhyolite was big enough to attract Barnum & Bailey's famed circus, complete with elephants. The high walls of several buildings still stand on Golden Street where their beautifully dressed stonework contrasts with the arid, untamed landscape, but a fence surrounds the Las Vegas & Tonopah Railroad's picturesque station.

There was a lot to talk about over a few cold and therapeutic beers when we returned to the real world, if Las Vegas can be described as such, but the most haunting memory was of those miners' graves catching the last of the day's light in the old cemetery at Tonopah. We had found our ghosts.

10

TICKING THEM OFF
IN A PACKARD

1999

A triumphant 'Bingo!' was appropriate as we left Connecticut and entered Rhode Island. Thirty years after going to America for the first time, your travel-stained reporter achieved an ambition by visiting each and every one of Uncle Sam's mainland states, from Alaska to Florida, from Maine to California. I completed the set in style at the wheel of a 1938 Packard Twelve Club Sedan some two feet longer and infinitely more eye-catching than a Rolls-Royce Silver Seraph. Packard built only 566 of its V12-engined flagships in 1938, when the Club Sedan cost $4,255 while cheapskates could buy a Cadillac for as little as $2,285 and Ford's V-8 was listed at $625.

Our four-day safari coincided with Packard's centenary year. The story of the marque whose admirers included Enzo Ferrari – this helps explain the old rascal's penchant for V12 engines – starts in Warren, Ohio, where James Ward Packard paid $1,000 for a Winton. Unimpressed by the single-cylinder boneshaker, and by Mr Winton's dismissive reaction to complaints, James and his brother built their first car in 1899. Four years later, the company's reputation was boosted after a Packard scampered from San Francisco to New York in only 61 days. Packard put down a technological marker in 1915, unveiling the world's first series-produced 12-cylinder car engine. Prestige soared even higher in 1921, when Warren

Harding stepped into a Packard and became the first American president to be driven to his inauguration. Hydraulic brakes and independent front suspension were standardised in 1937 and swanky air conditioning became an option in 1940. During the war, Packard built under licence the 27-litre Rolls-Royce Merlin that helped make the P-51 Mustang one of the greatest of all fighter aircraft. Despite its enhanced reputation for engineering excellence, Packard never got back into top gear when peace returned and car production recommenced. The curtain came down in 1958.

Celebrating the 100th birthday aboard the Club Sedan was a fun thing that just happened. The seeds were planted in New Hampshire in 1997, when Mrs Llewellin and I were staying with our great friends, Bud and Thelma Lyon, whose classic automobiles include two V16 Cadillacs, an Auburn Speedster, umpteen Porsches and Ferraris, a Bentley R-type Continental, a D-type Jaguar and a Mercedes 540K Special Roadster. My determination to complete the set of mainland states was being discussed over breakfast when Thelma said: 'One of those old Packards would look really neat among all those mansions in Newport, Rhode Island.'

Her husband's response – 'The only problem is that we don't have an old Packard' – was delivered with a hint of an impish smile. Sure enough, he eventually called to say that a suitably spacious model had been acquired and was about to be fettled. Dr Lyon is nothing if not a class act.

The Packard must have tipped the scales at almost three tons when laden with four adults and our luggage. This was not a problem, because the 7.7-litre engine's torque reminded me of the day, back home in Britain, when I drove a steam-powered locomotive that used to haul the Great Western Railway's express trains. In the Packard, prodigious pulling power from absurdly low revs almost eliminated the need to change gear after easing the three-speed transmission's yard-long lever into top. Although less than twinkle-toed for close-quarter combat on New England's rural roads, the Club Sedan cruised at 60–65mph when conditions were appropriate, wafting along like a galleon under full sail. The extent to which it blended refinement, luxury and jaw-dropping presence explained why many pundits consider a Packard Twelve to be every inch and ounce as good as a Rolls-Royce Phantom III, despite the American car costing much less than its British contemporary.

The Great Statebagging Expedition notched-up its first trophy after crossing the Connecticut River and entering Vermont, the penultimate name on my list, in time for a picnic lunch on Brattleboro Common. I tend to think of the north-eastern USA as being shoulder-to-shoulder with people, but the fact that 12,500 citizens make Brattleboro the third biggest town in Vermont proves how wrong a boy can be. New England provided a link with old England, because Brattleboro is where Rudyard Kipling lived for a few years in the 1890s, and wrote *The Jungle Book*. His home is now owned by the Landmark Trust, which rescues and restores interesting buildings, then rents them for holidays.

Fed and watered, we bowled southward to enchanting Deerfield, Massachusetts, where buildings from as long ago as the 1720s flank tree-lined streets. Today's tranquillity belies a hair-raising history, because in 1704 the little town was attacked by French and Indians who stormed the stockade, killed 47 people and marched 112 survivors off to captivity in Canada. We spent a comfortable night in the Deerfield Inn, where the Veuve Clicquot champagne that whetted appetites for dinner was also quaffed to toast the Packard for exceeding expectations. The virtually silent engine was complemented by suspension that absorbed all but the nastiest bumps, and by steering that was not heavy enough to merit gasped and hernia-popping jokes about sending for Superman. Pre-war brakes are often less efficient than throwing out a boulder lashed to a rope, but the Packard's drums inspired confidence.

The real delight was doing a genuine journey in such a rare and capable old car, and giving so much pleasure to others, from the little girl who squealed with delight in the passenger seat of a battered Chevrolet pickup to the senior citizen who hailed us in Newport, Rhode Island, and said, with justifiable pride, that his father *always* had Packards, back in the good old days.

Newport was indeed the perfect setting for such a distinguished car, because this is where the East Coast's platinum-plated plutocrats built astonishingly palatial summer residences – several of which are now open to visitors – around the end of the 19th century. We visited The Breakers, on which the second Cornelius Vanderbilt lavished the equivalent of about $400 million in today's money – he was wealthier than Microsoft's Bill Gates is now – then toured Marble House, which was built by his younger brother, William K Vanderbilt. We discovered a strong motoring link here, because William K Vanderbilt Jr was a pioneer car guy who inaugurated the Vanderbilt Cup races, staged between 1904 and 1937, and hoisted the world land speed record to 76.08mph in 1902, driving a four-cylinder, 9.2-litre Mors on a road near the French city of Chartres. It was the first time the LSR had been held by a car running on petrol.

Our imperious Packard quaffed a gallon of the stuff every few minutes, but the Yankee Candle Company's exceptionally interesting car museum in South Deerfield, Massachusetts, reminded us that all things are relative as we contemplated a Pierce-Arrow 66-A powered by a 13.5-litre straight-six. The old monster's thirst must be expressed in gallons per mile, not miles per gallon. However, what concerns me far more than fuel bills is finding a reason to visit Hawaii, which joined the union in 1959. Granting statehood to islands that are separated from the rest of the nation by 2,000 miles of ocean is about as logical as establishing a drive-in cinema at the South Pole, but reaching that remote cluster of volcanic peaks has become a priority. The governor's invitation is awaited as eagerly as the flowers that bloom in the spring, tra-la, and I look forward to cruising through Honolulu in something every inch as classy as the Lyons' peerless Packard.

11

Going to Extremes

2001

'Look after yourself and respect the mountain, because medical problems caused by altitude can make you anything from uncomfortable to very sick to well and truly dead,' I had been warned by Dr Kate Keohane. 'The amount of oxygen available will be much less than you're accustomed to breathing, because the atmospheric pressure is a lot lower up there, so there's a very real risk of suffering from headaches and nausea, and so forth. Even poorer judgement than usual is another potential problem. And if your luck's really out to lunch, the coroner's verdict will probably be that you died from pulmonary oedema or cerebral oedema. In layman's language, that's fluid on the lungs or the brain.'

Doc Kate is a friend whose idea of fun is gasping for breath very high up in the Andes and the Himalayas. She once shared a small, freezing, wind-blasted tent with a woman who had fluid on the brain, then suffered a massive stroke. This happened in a region so remote that there was no radio contact with the outside world. I sought Keohane's advice before attempting to fly the *Automobile Magazine* flag from the top of the world's highest mountain.

The gods were in a good mood, because I have proved that a 60-year-old hack with a dodgy heart can romp up that lofty landmark without ropes, crampons, ice-axes, oxygen cylinders, thermal underwear, bivouacs and a posse of porters. But don't hold your breath waiting for the *National Geographic* magazine to publish a feature about the exploit, because the ascent involved about as much physical effort as peeling a banana. Whatever else it may have achieved, this expedition proved that mountaineering is much easier when you drive a luxurious Mercedes ML430.

Aware that this makes me sound like a latterday Baron Karl Friedrich Hieronymus von Münchhausen, the 18th-century soldier and traveller whose wondrously embellished stories were as remarkable as his name, I hasten to add that the adventure did *not* involve Mount Everest. While this appears to reveal a shameful lack of knowledge about our planet's most salient features, it actually makes the point that everything depends on how you measure a mountain.

Published before large photographs of Shania Twain, Claudia Schiffer and Madonna flaunting one of her 'distinctive studded bras' were regarded as more important than really useful facts, my 1990-vintage *Guinness Book Of Records* states that the world's tallest mountain is Mauna Kea, which tops out at 13,796 feet above sea level. How can that be true when anyone with enough brain to keep their ears apart knows that Colonel Sir George Everest's namesake towers just over 29,000 feet into the sky?

Well, Mauna Kea's height is calculated from its base, all of 19,680 feet below the Pacific in what oceanographers call the Hawaiian Trough. That gives a total of 33,476 feet from basement to penthouse, which the ML430 and its crew shared with a cluster of observatories. Thin, cold air and other factors combine to make this one of the world's finest locations for studying the universe with optical and infrared telescopes.

Not satisfied with driving up Mauna Kea, and not inclined to waste time lazing on a beach, I had concocted a going-to-extremes theme for this frustratingly brief visit to Hawaii. The other extreme involved going under the island, as you will discover in due course.

This journey really started in 1969, when an opportunity to visit America for the first time came out of the blue. Florida and other destinations have become so popular with British holidaymakers that it is difficult to appreciate how remote the USA seemed to be in those days. Years later, I was having a beer in Skagway, Alaska, when I realised that most of the states had been ticked off the bingo card. By mid-1999 the only one left was far-flung Hawaii.

Completing the set having become an obsession, everything in the diary was flung overboard when an opportunity to visit the islands arrived as unexpectedly as the original invitation had done. I had pictured the state as one island dominated by big, brash, Honolulu, but a little research revealed a volcanic archipelago strung out over about 300 miles. The first inhabitants are believed to have arrived some 1,500 years ago. Their descendants speak English, of course, but Hawaiian is still used. The alphabet has only twelve letters, so visitors' vocal chords have to cope with such place-names as Kealakekua and Waiananpanapa. The waiter will think you're drunk or choking, or both, if you trying ordering a fish called the humuhmunukunukuapua'a.

Mountaineers keen enough to rely on their own bodies train hard before tackling the big peaks. I limbered up by watching Tiger Woods play golf on Maui, where the American PGA Tour's annual Mercedes Championships were staged on a course overlooking the Pacific. The sight of whales doing low-level aerobatics puts even the most focused professional off his stroke. Woods finished several shots behind the winner, Jim Furyk, who went home with $576,000 and an SL500 Mercedes, but just watching the world's greatest golfer in action was a pleasure and a privilege.

Photographer Scott Dahlquist and I also motored briskly around Maui. Nervous drivers should circumnavigate the island clockwise, which places you a car's width away from the precipices that flank many miles of exceedingly narrow, tortuous coastal road. And don't trust the maps. I failed to find what appeared to be a major highway, then asked a local for help. She looked at the map and laughed: 'They did *think* about building it,' she said.

Next day we hopped to the Big Island on a flight so brief there was little point in closing the door. The name is even more appropriate than you may imagine, because the Big Island gets bigger all the time, thanks to the world's most active volcano oozing molten rock into the Pacific. Acres of solidified lava flanked the Queen Ka'ahumanu Highway as our silver ML430 cruised up the coast from Keohole-Kona airport. The smooth highway ran virtually straight, so there was no need for such goodies as permanent four-wheel drive, traction control and stability control.

It was early afternoon when we met Steve Martin, who was playing the native guide's role. Steve hails from Cleveland, Ohio, but has lived on the islands since he 'just blew in and kinda took root' as a teenager. Surfer, traveller, writer, philosopher and all-round good guy, Steve has visited outlandish places – Tibet, China, Australia, Morocco, Ecuador, you name it – and is the only person I know who has crossed the Gobi Desert *and* skateboarded along the Great Wall of China. Years ago he worked as a cook in the camp that provides basic essentials for the astronomers on Mauna Kea. What he doesn't know about the mountain could be written on a flea's eyelash.

One of the Merc's many useful features revealed the outside temperature at sea level to be 30 degrees C. Soon after turning inland we fuelled-up in prim and prosperous Waimea, which barely existed when Steve first came to the island, crossed part of the 225,000-acre Parker Ranch – said to be the biggest privately owned cattle farm anywhere in the United States – and turned onto Saddle Road. A little trepidation was appropriate here, because many rental car agreements prohibit driving on this narrow, 53-mile-long ribbon of blacktop that flicks and switchbacks between the great massifs of Mauna Kea and Mauna Loa. But the going is due to be made much easier, according to our guidebook. Tongue firmly in cheek, it states: 'The government is thinking about straightening Saddle Road. This study might be completed by the year 2160 and work should commence shortly thereafter.'

Although reality revealed 'The Saddle' to be much better than many roads near my home on the Welsh Marches, its poor surface and sharp corners could have been created to flatter the ML430. Some truck-based sport-utes ride and handle like prairie schooners on anything other than good surfaces. Realising that few of those who buy four-wheel-drive vehicles ever venture off-pavement, but like to know they could keep going across something more challenging than Wal-Mart's parking lot, Mercedes wisely pitched the M-class compromise in favour of conventional motoring. Saddle Road also proved the brakes to be more than a match for the 4.3-litre V8 engine, which delivers 268bhp and 288lb-ft of torque.

Immense areas of lava and countless 'cinder cones' characterised the volcanic landscape as we approached the unsigned turn-off for Mauna Kea. By then we had climbed to 6,500 feet and the temperature had dropped to 15 degrees. A notice in the hotel room warned about such local specialities as earthquakes, hurricanes and tsunami – 'Close your balcony door if you see an immense wave racing towards the shore,' it advised – but the sign at the start of the real slog to Mauna Kea's summit was even more daunting. The way ahead being rough, narrow and laced with sharp corners, we had to be prepared for sudden changes in weather conditions, storms, high winds, fog, rain, hail, snow, freezing temperatures and altitude sickness. If the *wurst* came to the *wurst*, as they say in Germany, we should not expect to find water, food, fuel, shelter or medical facilities.

Another stark warning – 'Hazardous road . . . Travel at your own risk beyond this point' – greeted us at 9,200 feet, where the black stuff gave way to a gravel track bulldozed through the now-dormant volcano's vomit. This was by the Onizuka Center for International Astronomy's information centre. Named to commemorate Ellison Onizuka, the Hawaiian astronaut who died when the space shuttle *Challenger* exploded in 1986, the centre has a small telescope and hosts star-gazing sessions. Just strolling around, looking at the exhibits, made me realise how much thinner the air had become. Because we had already passed the rule-of-thumb threshold for altitude sickness, at around 8,000 feet, what should have been deep, lung-filling, energy-giving breaths were already more like dry, rasping gasps.

According to one of Doc Kate's books on mountain medicine, it would have been extremely foolish to have relied on our own strength to climb Mauna Kea so soon after reaching the Big Island. It warned: 'Prior to climbing and sleeping at altitudes of 10,000 to 14,000 feet, gradually increasing exercise should be carried out at an intermediate altitude of 6,000 to 8,000 feet for three or four days.'

The fact that *sleeping* can make you sick speaks for itself.

Five steep miles on gravel enabled Mercedes' four-wheel drive to prove its worth. I also blessed the traction control system, because the ML would have been a handful without it in conditions where I had to keep my right foot down on a surface that was always loose and, in places, brutally corrugated. Conventional vehicles can reach the top of Mauna Kea, granted good conditions, but two wheels scrabbling for traction do a lot of damage to the track's surface. Although it was difficult to imagine anyone being brave or foolish enough to exceed the 25mph speed limit, Steve Martin told tales about visitors who had paid with their lives for failing to take the mountain seriously. This was quite easy to believe. The drops are so huge that you could recite William Wordsworth's ode, *Intimations of Immortality*, before reaching the bottom.

Gravel gave way to paved road as we approached the summit, where a dozen multi-national observatories, the oldest of which has been operational since 1968, make Mauna Kea look like a *Stars Wars* set. The temperature was now just a gnat's whisker above freezing and the amount of air available for breathing was 40 per cent lower than it had been on the coast, a couple of hours earlier. The extent to which the V8's power was being sapped had become increasingly apparent as we zig-zagged higher and higher. The engine was running hotter than at sea level, despite the ambient temperature being much lower, and a startling backfire emphasised how hard the remaining horses were working.

Fred Heiler, one of Mercedes-Benz USA's top technical men, later told me what happens to naturally aspirated internal combustion engines. 'Altitude translates to air density, which results in less power for engines and people,' he explained. 'As an aside, that's the original reason why supercharging was developed – to enable airplanes to fly higher. Carburettor systems could never compensate for the reduced air density, so those engines would run super-rich at high altitude and belch black smoke. Modern fuel injection systems measure air density and meter fuel pretty well at altitude, but they still can't restore the horsepower that's lost simply because of fewer oxygen molecules per stroke.'

Like its occupants, the Mercedes had lost about 40 per cent of its power en route from the coast to the summit.

This was far and away the highest I had ever been except in a machine with wings, jet engines and a well-stocked bar. Here on Hawaii, the view I had travelled so far to see was literally breathtaking, because we were way above the thick, white, fleecy cloak of cloud that extended westward from mighty Mauna Loa's western shoulder. Mauna Kea's 13,677-feet-high neighbour is reckoned to be the world's most massive mountain, because people clever enough to make such arcane calculations credit it with 10,000 cubic miles of rock. We gasped for breath and shivered with cold, but a little discomfort was nothing to the sense of holy wonder that filled me as dusk painted the sky every colour from silver to pink to gold to blue to black. The view became increasingly magical, and the feeling of being close to heaven even stronger, when diamond-bright stars began to stud the sky.

There was almost total silence as the sun set, just after 6pm, then faint whirring and humming sounds made us realise that the observatories, most of which are operated by remote control from more congenial locations, started probing the heavens. The biggest have mirrors ten metres in diameter. Operated by Japanese astronomers, the newest telescope's 23-ton mirror is supported by 261 computer-controlled actuators which maintain its shape to one part in a billion. Called the Subaru telescope, Subaru being Japanese for the Pleiades star cluster, it has photographed a quasar all of 15 billion light years away. If the scientists are right, this is like looking back to almost the beginning of time. I recalled a quote along the lines of: 'The universe isn't stranger than we think. It is stranger than we *can* think.'

Just about anything should have been an anti-climax after watching the sunset from Mauna Kea, but the following day we visited two spectacular beaches, one of which involved negotiating the steepest, narrowest road I have ever clapped eyes on, before meeting Kurt Bell at Sea Quest's base on Keauhou Bay. Kurt is a mine of information and an incredibly skilful sailor who operates one of Sea Quest's agile, six-passenger, rigid-hull inflatables. Powered by two snarling Yamaha outboards, this exhilarating little craft whisked us southward like a wave-skimming rocket. Several humpback whales spouted, jumped and flipped their mighty tails close to the inflatable before we went 'under' the island as Kurt nosed into caves of multi-coloured volcanic rock where the Pacific churned and foamed.

The first glimpse of a small, white monument on the palm-fringed shore of Kealakekua Bay told me it was time to fly the Union Jack while singing *Rule, Britannia!* and dancing the hornpipe. The obelisk commemorates Captain James Cook, the son of a Yorkshire labourer who became perhaps the greatest of all sea-going explorers and is credited with being the first European to visit Hawaii. He was killed here in 1779, after going ashore to remonstrate with natives who had stolen one of his ship's boats. Cook's three great voyages in ships intended for nothing more ambitious than coastal waters took him as far afield as Antarctica and Alaska. Cook is one of my heroes, so I growled 'Never make fun of the Royal Navy' when an American couple joked about 'Captain Cook RN' giving the impression that the great navigator was a Registered Nurse.

I have already vowed to return to the Big Island for a full-scale holiday rather than an absurdly short visit. Steve Martin suggested waiting until Mauna Kea lives up to the meaning of its name – White Mountain – then driving to the summit in a four-wheel-drive pickup, filling the bed with snow, dashing back to sea level and building a snowman on one of those tropical, palm-fringed beaches. That really would be going to extremes.

12

CANADA

TRUCKING ACROSS

THE BIG COUNTRY

1981

The awe-inspiring truth about Canada really hit me like a kick from a bucking bronco when Richard Dubé's magnificent Kenworth, cruising westwards through the afternoon at a relaxed 75mph or so, passed a large sign a few miles from Winnipeg. It marked the exact centre of the country in coast-to-coast terms. But at that point I had already been travelling for nearly a week and had logged just over 3,000 miles. That's roughly the distance from London to Turkey's border with Iran and longer than the haul from New York to Los Angeles.

It hammered home the message that Canada is not a *big* country. You can use that word to describe the likes of Australia or Brazil, but Canada demands such adjectives as huge, vast, enormous and immense. It covers 3,850,980 square miles and is considerably bigger than the USA, even when Alaska and Hawaii are taken into account. Texas may sprawl over 267,339 square miles, but the province of Ontario boasts 412,582 while its neighbour, Quebec, extends over 594,371. But even Quebec, six times the size of the United Kingdom, seems little more than a cabbage patch when you consider the Northwest Territories' 1,304,903 square miles.

All that land must also be related to a population of only 24 million, most of whom live within a stone's throw of the US border. For all its vastness, the Northwest Territories can claim only 46,000 residents. In trucking terms, Canada is obviously a country where big engines, lots of gears, long hours and high average speeds are essential if men like Richard Dubé are not going to be within sight of an old-age pension by the time they finish a run. Richard's 400bhp Cummins seemed impressive enough as it covered the 1,500 miles from Montreal to Winnipeg in 48 hours, but I was destined to experience much more power before the end of the road was reached.

This is the story of a two-week journey that covered 5,200 miles – like driving from England to Pakistan – without crossing a single international frontier. It started in Newfoundland, followed the Trans-Canada Highway for many days and finished with a dusty, sun-baked haul up the Alaska Highway to Whitehorse, the pint-sized capital of the Yukon. The first 3,900 miles were by courtesy of Winnipeg-based Arnold Brothers Transport, one of the few firms with the paperwork needed to operate throughout Canada and the USA. The fifth and final stage of the marathon saw me in the capable hands of White Pass Transportation, a company whose roots go back to the Klondike goldrush days at the tail end of the 19th century.

My sincere thanks must also go to Fred Billings, communications manager for International Harvester's Canadian operation, who got the show on the road in the first place. I had expressed interest in the Alaska Highway, but Fred suggested going the whole hog and put me in touch with Arnold Brothers. All of which explains how I found myself flying from New York to Newfoundland one sunny Sunday afternoon in July.

Day One: A busy port, founded way back in the 16th century, St John's is as far east as you can go on the North American continent without falling into the Atlantic. Brent Richardson, manager of the terminal that covers the eastern provinces, had obviously taken my talk of going right across Canada at face value. I was awake at 5am, worried about the risk of missing my transport out of such an isolated place, but everything went to plan. It was exactly 9am when Bill Hamilton's Mack kicked up dust outside Dowell Chemical with a $150,000 high-pressure pumping unit for the offshore oil industry chained to its low-loader. An exceptionally fascinating character who collects old books and breeds African violets, Bill is one of the many owner-operators whose trucks supplement the 400 or so in Arnold Brothers' own fleet.

'It's not a fancy truck by any stretch of the imagination, but it does almost eight to the gallon and earns the sort of money that makes sense,' he grinned, reminding me that Canada uses true-blue imperial gallons, despite a swing towards the dreaded metric system, rather than the somewhat smaller US measure. He had never been to Newfoundland before and chuckled as he recalled the reaction of his insurance company, way out west in land-locked Manitoba, when he asked about cover for the ferry. 'Fairies? Ferries? Ferries! Hell, they thought I was talking about Hans Christian Andersen, or nice boys, or something.'

A crane arrived to remove the load, freeing the Mack to collect a tarmac recycling machine and a Ford 350 van destined for Cap-de-la-Madeleine, some 1,400 miles away to the south-west of Quebec city. Bill did a good impression of Marley's ghost in *A Christmas Carol*, clanking around with chains and binders to defy even the roughest sections of road. 'Variety's one of the things I like about this job,' he said. 'I've never carried one of these machines before, so it's a case of working out the best way to keep it secure. You can spend half a day chaining some loads down, but they still walk all over the place.'

I had always thought of Newfoundland as little more than a small hunk of far-flung rock, but the only road from St John's to Port-aux-Basques and the ferry twists and turns to such an extent that the distance is just over 550 miles. It traverses a wild, wooded island with lakes by the thousand, a spectacular coastline and distant mountains shimmering in the summer heat. The population is spread thinner than butter on a motorway sandwich and you are almost as likely to see a moose as another human being. A superbly entertaining talker, Bill wasted no time telling me that mainland Canadians delight in Newfie jokes which, I soon discovered, are exactly the same as the jokes we tell about the Irish, the Swedes tell about the Norwegians and the Americans tell about the Poles. The locals also drink Newfie Screech, a rum allegedly strong enough to put the top of your head into orbit if you so much as sniff the cork.

Delivering about 285bhp to the wheels, the Mack's engine hauled us steadily through the afternoon to Gander, where airliners touched down before they could span the Atlantic in one long hop. Night had fallen and rain was beating down over the endless forests when we paused for a meal beyond Grand Falls, patronising one of the Irving truckstops that proliferate on the highways of eastern Canada. The food was fine, but the service prompted jokes suggesting we should start thinking in terms of breakfast rather than supper. 'They're lovely, friendly people, but they just don't know how to hurry', Bill sighed, highlighting characteristics that I was going to note in similar establishments right across the country. He had put 440 miles under the wheels by the time we stopped for a head-to-toe sleep.

Day Two: Mountains shrouded in grey cloud, and rain sweeping across the inevitable lake, made Newfoundland look more like Scotland than ever. I was eagerly anticipating breakfast, but the smiling young lady behind the counter, built like a haystack, said there was no food available because the cook had failed to arrive. So she served us coffee, then sat down to devour a fried fish big enough to be Moby Dick's twin brother. Local dishes, incidentally, include moose chop suey, seal and rice casserole, bear stew and barbecued caribou ribs.

The early morning had been stormy enough to provoke thoughts of *mal de mer* on the six-hour crossing, but the weather improved dramatically as we neared Port-aux-Basques on the south-west tip of the island. The clouds lifted like a theatre curtain and the sun came out to warm a memorable tract of country where the first real farmland seen in 500 miles was overlooked by mountains streaked white by waterfalls. Down at the port, disinfectant sprays made the point that Newfoundland is the only part of Canada with potato wart – and the rest of the country wants to keep it that way. The waiting boat was full, so we were forced to kick our heels for six hours until the *Stena Nordica* arrived. She really foxed me by being registered in Sweden and a sister ship to the one in which I crossed between Fishguard and Rosslare in 1980.

Day Three: 'Twenty minutes to docking,' yelled a voice as a fist thundered on the cabin door just after midnight. I was sufficiently alert, after a big coffee, to remember to change my watch, setting it back 30 minutes. 'Be doing that a few more times before you've finished. Time zones are one thing Canada doesn't lack, and that's for sure,' said Bill.

We were all set to leave the ship at North Sydney, on Cape Breton Island, when he cussed, pumped the clutch pedal and announced a problem. A little high-technology treatment with a hammer did the trick, however, and off we roared into the inky darkness. 'This is great country if you could only see it,' the voice behind the wheel enthused as the Mack surged up Kelly Mountain. It could have been one of those eye-drooping drives into the dawn, but the cab kept buzzing with lively conversation. One topic was military history. It prompted Bill to regale me with a few lines from *The Burial of Sir John Moore at Corunna* – a poem remembered from my own schooldays – and he launched into Thomas Gray's wonderfully evocative *Elegy Written in a Country Churchyard* when I mentioned that General James Wolfe had recited it to his men before capturing Quebec from the French in 1759.

We crossed Canso Causeway, the link between Cape Breton Island and the true mainland of Canada, and stopped for an early breakfast at the Trail Blazer Pioneer in Lower Debert. It calls itself the best truckstop in the east. That could well be true, if not exactly modest. Bill gave the facilities full marks – they include showers and a TV room for truckers – and the food was excellent as well as inexpensive.

Nova Scotia's border is dubbed the Iron Curtain, because the province is notoriously strict where trucks are concerned. Although we slipped out into New Brunswick without any hassles, there was just one small cloud on the Hamilton horizon. Canada's haulage industry is bedevilled with regulations and you need permits to move this and that type of freight from province to province. The big tarmac recycler was perfectly legal for New Brunswick, Bill explained, but he had no authority to cart the Ford van. How come? Because officialdom draws a line between machinery and road-going vehicles, and you must have a local permit for each. 'But that's no big problem,' Bill grinned, sipping coffee in the Irving on Lutes Mountain. 'We'll just take the scenic route and avoid the only scales.'

Sure enough, we had a trouble-free run to his home town and reached it around 1pm. First stop was at Mack Maritime, where Bill arranged to have his clutch cable fixed. Then it was down to the Arnold Brothers' terminal to meet Brent Richardson. Tall, slim and friendly, a former officer in the Royal Canadian Mounted Police, he greeted me with the welcome news that an International Transtar driven by Fred Brewer would be taking Bill's load straight through to Montreal, leaving in the morning.

Day Four: Bill's wife, Ann, produced a belt-busting breakfast before the Mack bobtailed me down to the terminal to meet Fred and '309'. Its fleet number reminded me of an old trucking favourite, *Phantom 309*, but the immaculate 'Cornbinder' and its driver were anything but ghosts. Fred checked the chains on his load while I chuckled over a notice in the office. It listed the main characteristics of company personnel, starting with the president: 'Leaps tall buildings in a single bound, is more powerful than a locomotive, is faster than a speeding bullet, walks on water, gives policy to God.' As for the trucker: 'Lifts buildings and walks under them, kicks locomotives off the track, catches speeding bullets in teeth and eats them, freezes water with a single glance. HE IS GOD.'

The haul from Fredericton to Montreal by way of Cap-de-la-Madeleine involves about 570 miles, but Fred had every intention of covering it in the day and then chewing off a bit of the homeward chunk before getting his head down. The 350bhp Cummins working in cahoots with a 15-speed Fuller transmission made light work of the highway as we headed almost due north, skirted the US border, crossed into Quebec province and gained an hour. It was so like entering a different country that I half-expected to be asked for my passport. Bilingual signs and notices are commonplace all over Canada, but Quebec makes no concessions to English. Indeed, many locals have never learned to speak anything other than French, albeit with an accent that makes genuine Frogs fall over laughing, and there are others who *can* speak English, but refuse to do so for reasons of provincial and cultural pride. 'If there's one thing in this life I *hate* it's delivering in Quebec, because I can't understand a word they say,' Fred growled.

I had my first view of the St Lawrence when the International reached Rivière-du-Loup and started heading south-westwards at last. The river is barely 15 miles wide at that point and gets much more impressive as it nears the Atlantic. We're talking about a serious amount of water. Fred cruised through the hot afternoon at a steady 60–65mph before pausing to call the terminal in Montreal. The news was good, he reported. An owner-operated White Western Star was waiting to take me on to Winnipeg. But there was no sign of the truck when we arrived, about an hour later than expected. I decided to sit it out, just in case the guy had gone for a meal, and parked myself on an upturned wastepaper bin sheltered by the office's rear porch. Fred wished me luck and started pedalling the metal back home.

All hope had vanished by midnight, but the presence of luggage and the absence of a taxi-calling telephone combined with the terminal's location, out on an industrial estate, to leave me with no viable alternative for the rest of the night. So I watched a spider spinning its web, talked to the ants, smoked a million miserable cigarettes and waited for the place to get back into gear at 8am. Morale went right down during the chilly pre-dawn hour, but I recalled the words of Bill Hamilton: 'You'll probably get in with one of those hard-trucking Frenchmen who runs a real fancy rig and covers the miles like there's no tomorrow,' he had chuckled.

Day Five: Morale on any long journey tends to shoot up and down like a seismograph needle in an earthquake. Soaring peaks of elation swiftly collapse into great troughs of black depression when all you want to do is pull the pin and head for home. I was very depressed until terminal manager Gilles Chartier arrived. Gilles is one of the many natives of Quebec province who speak French as a first language, but the words were definitely basic, paint-blistering Anglo-Saxon when he realised that the fickle finger of fate had poked yours truly straight in the eye. The owner-driver with the Western Star had been waiting two days for a load, he apologised, and was obviously not inclined to waste any more time. I could appreciate that. 'Don't worry, we should have a real nice Kenworth – the smartest truck that operates out of here – starting for Winnipeg later in the day,' he went on, handing over the keys to his car and pointing me in the general direction of breakfast. An hour later, showered, shaved and inside a clean shirt, I was ready to apply to rejoin the human race.

'Your taxi's arrived,' Gilles announced midway through the afternoon. Out there in the yard was a new, long-nosed Kenworth whose glittering chrome and aluminium, immaculate paintwork and double sleeper made the morale graph do a vertical climb. It was owned and operated by Richard Dubé – pronounced Doobay – whose big smile, firm handshake and eyes bright with humour immediately made it obvious that we were destined to get on well.

The only possible snag, I thought, is that he speaks very little English and I have only a few hundred words of schoolboy French. But we were to talk virtually non-stop all the way to Winnipeg, switching from one language to the other and often roaring with laughter at ridiculous mistakes. You have to take your hat off to a guy who can crack jokes in a strange tongue. 'No problem, I just buy another truck,' said Richard when the ashtray overflowed.

Heading out of Montreal, hauling a load of International Harvester machinery and grossing about 34 tons, I soon realised that the Kenworth had plenty of go to match its classy show. Out there in front was a Cummins 400 that gives between 5.8 and 6.8 miles per imperial gallon. Next in line was Mr Fuller's RTO-12515 transmission and she was geared for a top speed of 85mph. That sort of performance, allied to air-ride suspension and air-ride seats, added to the delightful illusion of travelling in a big, smooth, sophisticated car. What seemed like a modest 50–55mph invariably turned out to be more like 70–75, just as 85mph came along with little drama on the few occasions when Richard turned the wick right up.

He looked more like an Olympic swimmer than a big-bellied trucker, despite eating at least three good meals a day, but had been driving since he left school. Shooting through Ottawa like the proverbial dose of salts, he recalled the time spent on loggers in the forests of northern Quebec where rigs grossing more than 70 tons are commonplace. 'Big loads and bad roads,' he grinned as we left the Canadian capital behind and headed into a landscape of rolling hills, broad rivers, lakes dotted with floatplanes, and trees shooting up by the billion. Slender pines and silver birch had flanked the Trans-Canada Highway virtually all the way from St John's and were to be constant companions, apart from a few miles of farming country, until we reached the Manitoba border. I never imagined there were so many trees in the entire world.

'Just like New York!' Richard laughed as he switched the lights on, illuminating no fewer than 17 dials and a regiment of neat switches. Sunset was painting the lakes a magical shade of romantic pink, but the man behind the wheel was more concerned about the possibility of moose, or even bears, wandering out of the forest. An adult bull moose, tipping the scale at well over half a ton, is big and solid enough to remove even a Kenworth's front axle.

We stopped to eat near Mattawa. The break was made memorable by the arrival of a young lady whose tanned legs seemed to go right up to her shoulders and whose shorts were about the size of a dormouse's ears. Dubé and Llewellin joined in a spontaneous duet of delirious groans as the lithe vision leaned across the counter. 'I think we go,' Richard urged. 'You have been away from home too long, *mon ami*, to see sights like that.'

So the KW sped on to North Bay before he switched the mighty Cummins off for the night. The sleeper was every padded, insulated inch as impressive as the rest of the truck with a big bunk, wardrobe, shelves, air conditioning, stereo and TV. Thick carpets made even the floor more comfortable than some hotel beds I've experienced.

Day Six: The sight of a logging truck with more wheels and axles than a stray dog has fleas helped prise my eyes open as we patronised Norm's Roadrunner truckstop for coffee at 5am. We were on The King's Highway, one of only two major roads running westwards across Canada, but 45 minutes passed before the Kenworth encountered another vehicle going the same way. It was one more reminder that Canada is a vast country with very few people and no traffic whatsoever by British standards. We stopped for a relaxed, 90-minute breakfast at New Liskeard, then soon passed a sign marking the Arctic watershed, the point from which all rivers flow northwards towards the great polar basin. It made the end of the road seem just that little bit closer. Huge piles of logs and the sickly stench of pulp-mills characterised the few small towns encountered along the way as Richard marched on through Ontario at a steady 70–75mph. Midway through the afternoon he pulled into the Husky truckstop at Hearst, gave the brightwork a good polish and then took a free shower – soap and towel included – before we sat down to a belated lunch that went on for two hours. The food may not have been French, but the attitude definitely was.

A strong, hot wind was making the dust swirl viciously when we finally hit the road again. Blowing hard on the port bow, it reminded me of Gilles Chartier's story about battling with the elements in a low-powered truck, years ago. 'Those headwinds! They used to pull me right down from 70 to more like 45mph. The first time I ran into one it was so bad I got out to see if the brakes were binding. Real bad news. But it is *fantastique* with that same wind behind you.'

Abundant horsepower allowed Richard to maintain a crisp cruising speed, but the great increase in wind noise somehow made the forest-flanked straights beyond Hearst seem endless rather than just incredibly long. He stopped at Longlac to let his tyres cool down, then pushed on to Beardmore where the wooded plain suddenly gave way to spectacular cliffs daubed pink and gold by the setting sun. It made a welcome change of scenic diet after that interminable 'trench' of tight-packed pines. In the mighty metropolis of

Nipigon he ordered a black coffee with a teabag in it – 'Is good for the eyes open' – before averaging 65mph through the night to Thunder Bay, on the shore of Lake Superior.

High above the city – the first place of any real size encountered since Ottawa – the KW passed a viewpoint dedicated to Terry Fox, a young man who had his right leg amputated in the hope that such drastic surgery would prevent cancer spreading. He battled against his handicap and eventually became determined to run right across Canada for charity. Starting in St John's, Newfoundland, Terry Fox did a 26-mile marathon, day after day after day, and had covered 3,339 miles by the time he reached Thunder Bay. Then he was forced to give up, tortured by a terrible cough. Cancer had spread to his lungs, and proved fatal, but the 'Marathon of Hope' raised more than $16 million for cancer research. My journey with Richard was nothing if not light-hearted, but we fell silent as we passed that point and eased through Thunder Bay's ocean of twinkling lights before stopping for the night.

Day Seven: Five o'clock. Not the best time to be greeting a Sunday morning, but I was sufficiently alert to realise that we had parked alongside several other Arnold Brothers' trucks, including a brace of magnificent B61 Mack Theodynes that could almost have been older than their drivers. As usual, Richard warmed his engine with all the care of a mother preparing baby's bath, before tackling the last 440 miles to Winnipeg. The Johnny Cash tape he bought at the breakfast stop in Dryden put a lump to my throat when it played that *Sunday Morning* track about wishing you were home. What with one thing and another I had been on the road for almost a month.

'Sheet!' Richard's expletive shattered my thoughts as we charged up a hill in a rocky tract of country whose trees had recently been devoured by fire. At the side of the road was a young, ginger-haired cop whose radar had clocked the Kenworth at 69.5mph in a 55mph limit. Richard was philosophical about the fine. 'Good for tax. First ticket since two years and maybe 200,000 miles,' he shrugged, reaching for the CB radio to warn others about the skulking smokey. 'And now you have official proof that this really is a fast truck.'

It was nearly 2pm when we finally said farewell to Ontario and started rolling along the dual-carriageway towards Winnipeg at 75mph. Flanked by open prairie, the road was as flat as a sheet of glass and so straight it could have been the barrel of a gun. It vanished into a heat-shimmering point of perspective before Winnipeg's cluster of tower blocks rose up to form the only landmarks. Richard dropped his trailer in the huge Arnold Brothers Transport terminal – Winnipeg is also the company's headquarters – and we relaxed over big steaks before checking into a motel.

Just on 1,500 miles had been covered in 49 hours, including many stops and two good sleeps, but prospects for the immediate future were not too good. Monday was a public holiday and, according to other truckers in the terminal, there was not much freight moving westwards for that reason.

Day Eight: Richard got a load that would take him back towards Montreal, his wife and baby daughter, but I seemed doomed to twiddle my thumbs for at least another 24 hours. So I checked back into the motel for another night and was settling down to a mid-afternoon read when the phone rang. 'There's a truck leaving for Edmonton *right now* if you're interested,' said Arnold's dispatcher. Was I interested! Nine minutes later, Llewellin was clambering into the cab of an International Transtar and shaking hands with Joe Thomas.

'I guess this could be an interesting trip, because the fuel pedal's been sticking and the radiator's leaking,' Joe said, revving the 350 Cummins and easing up through the Fuller RT-1110's gears. He brimmed the rad' when we stopped for fuel on the far side of holiday-quiet Winnipeg, then told me something about himself over a meal. 'I was born in Ontario,' he said, 'but live in Calgary nowadays. It doesn't really matter where I live, I guess, because I'm rarely home for longer than it takes to get my clothes washed through. Trucked 12,000 miles last month,' he added, confirming rumours that 3,000 miles a week is not unusual.

Although it is 825 miles across the prairie from Winnipeg to Edmonton, Joe was talking in terms of a 17-hour run. He had covered 841 miles in the previous 24 hours when midnight arrived shortly after we left Manitoba and entered Saskatchewan. But thoughts of punching it straight through were understandably and mercifully abandoned when fatigue started taking its inevitable toll.

Day Nine: Joe slept for an hour, slumped over the wheel, moved the truck forward maybe 50 yards, then stopped again for another 30 minutes of shut-eye. Then we drove 20 miles down the road before another sleep, this time for several hours. Then it was on to the Husky truckstop in Saskatoon for buckets of black coffee and the boost provided by a big breakfast.

Joe had now revised his plans to such an extent that he was thinking about *maybe* reaching Edmonton, still 500 miles away, before the terminal closed for the night. But even that seemed wildly optimistic a few minutes later when we trickled to a halt on the Yellowhead Highway, named after a fair-haired half-breed who guided pioneers across the country before being killed by Indians in 1827. The problem involved a temperature-sensitive cutout for the fuel pump, so we were eventually able to limp into Langham at 15mph, brim the radiator and press on at a sedate 50–55mph. At least the terrain was flat. So flat, for most of the way, that it could have been East Anglia, albeit with lofty grain elevators rather than the towers of medieval churches rising above the patchwork of wheat-gold fields. Joe nursed the truck through Lloydminster – a booming oilfield town, right on the Alberta border – but the engine died again, about 100 miles from Edmonton, even though the temperature gauge was registering normal. Joe finally traced the source of the problem. It was 100 per cent electrical – the leaking radiator was nothing more than a coincidence – and a little DIY work had us in the terminal shortly after 5pm. Joe then headed back east and I wondered what Dame Fortune would deliver in the morning.

Day Ten: 'Guess you've reached something of a dead-end here,' said the dispatcher when I fell through the Arnold door at 8am. 'We've only got two trucks licensed to run the Yukon. One's already heading north and the other's almost certainly due to go to Winnipeg when it gets back. Sorry, but that's just the way it is.'

Morale crashed to an all-time low. I was thinking about combing the *Yellow Pages*, in the hope of finding a company with trucks heading in the right direction, when John Andrews, the cheerful local supremo, emerged from his office. He had just had a message about me from HQ in Winnipeg and was confident that a few phone calls would sort things out. Sure enough, I was back on top of the world within a couple of hours. 'I've been in touch with White Pass Transportation,' he said, 'and they've got a really nice owner-operated Kenworth that leaves every Friday night for Whitehorse.'

Day Eleven: Kicking my heels in Edmonton should have been frustrating, but it was great to be in the same place for more than a few hours. I have now clocked about 15,000 road and air miles since leaving home. John Andrews put me in touch with Michelle Desjarlais. She runs the Edmonton terminal for White Pass – a company whose interests include ships and the White Pass railway that links Whitehorse to the Pacific at Skagway – and she turned out to be nothing less than pure gold. It was just a case of being at the terminal on the Friday night.

Day Twelve: The well-groomed hair, neat moustache, glasses, smart shirt and spotless jeans made Ken Jones look more like a bright young accountant, casually dressed for the weekend, than a hard-hauling trucker. Thanks to the Alaska Highway's reputation I had expected something closer to a grizzly bear than a member of the human race. But his praises had been sung long and loud by Michelle before the customised Kenworth appeared. 'Ken's been with us about two years and he's good, believe me. Last year he did 50 runs to Whitehorse and back – that's a round trip of about 2,500 miles – but was never late and never had an accident. That's quite some record.'

Ken's immaculate truck, known as *Bad News* because of early problems, was just as impressive as its owner's reputation. The huge, padded doghouse between the seats can be forgiven for taking up so much space because it conceals nothing less than a Cummins 600. Hitched to what amounts to a 24-speed Spicer transmission – there's a six-speed main box with a four-speed auxiliary, both worked from the same lever – it delivers no less than 535bhp to the eight Michelin-shod rear wheels. That sort of power, together with a prodigious 1,660lb-ft of torque at 1600rpm, makes a whole heap of sense when you earn your keep pulling a twin-trailer 'B-train' all of 75 feet long and grossing out at around 54 tons.

This run involved the usual mixed load and we tipped the scales at a mere 46 tons. 'We only run *real* heavy in the winter, when the ground freezes solid and the road's strong enough to take the extra weight,' Ken explained as we rolled out of Edmonton an hour or so after sunset. That mighty engine and all those smooth-shifting gears seemed to reduce every mile to an effortless 880 yards as Jones the Power cruised into the night. Gradients that should have pulled a 46-ton combination down to the pace of a three-legged mule were treated as if the slope went the other way. Ken chuckled over the tale of a Cadillac that had been bugging him for miles on one trip when he was running empty from Whitehorse. He eventually felt obliged to drop a gear or two, put the pedal to the metal and leave the car standing: 'You should have *heard* that sucker when he called me on the CB! He just couldn't *believe* a great big old B-train could do that kinda thing. I told him that was the difference between my $110,000 Kenworth and his $22,000 Cadillac. Fuel mileage? I get around 4.8 in summer and more like 4.0 in winter, when the engine never stops running because it's so doggone *cold* up there. I've been in Watson Lake when it was minus 68 degrees F, but it gets much colder than that in places. You have to be kinda tough to live up there. I tell you, those people have still got the bark on them.'

Among those who paused for coffee and a snack at Valleyview was Al Kettle, a veteran who first ran the Alaska Highway – 'Only newcomers and tourists call it the Alcan' – 13 years ago, as a kid of 18. He now operates his own International 4300, powered by the KTA-525 Cummalong, and was destined to keep us company for most of the way to Whitehorse. Ken, an old friend from way back, delighted in calling the International 'that piece of *farm* equipment' whenever an opportunity presented itself. It was 5am when the two trucks stopped at

Grande Prairie, the last place of any size before Dawson Creek, for a rest before the tough stuff started. 'Guess we should have a couple of hours,' said Ken, making me realise how he once covered 156,000 miles in nine months.

Day Thirteen: Perfect weather emphasised the feeling that I should really be tackling the road in winter. Ken shook his head: 'You sometimes have to chain your front tyres to be able to steer in freezing rain, but spring and fall are the most dangerous periods, if that's what you mean, because conditions are so unpredictable. I've only been doing this since the fall of '77, but I've known the temperature to go from plus 18 to minus 37 in just five miles.' It may not be much by local standards, but minus 37 degrees is about ten per cent below the coldest temperature ever recorded in Britain.

'You get these newcomers who run up here a couple of times in summer and think that makes them *reeeeal pro-fessionals*,' Ken snorted, recalling one firm that lost five tankers in a single week. 'But you don't have to be a bad driver to get yourself killed. I've lost several good friends up here and they were guys who knew what trucking was all about.'

It was 8am when we reached Dawson Creek – 'Mile Zero City' – and swept round the king-sized sign marking the start of the Alaska Highway. After that, I can pin-point the spot as precisely as the newest and most sophisticated guided missile. Mile 55 is where the spine tingled, the heart beat a little faster and a smile blending delight with triumph spread across my face. Trees, wheatfields and lofty grain elevators – familiar sights after some 1,500 miles of trucking across the prairie – suddenly gave way to the Peace River's dramatic gorge. Beyond, rolling away into the wild north-west of Canada, was an infinity of forest where people are outnumbered by moose, caribou and bears. In the far distance, almost sensed rather than seen, the Rocky Mountains shimmered like smoke-blue ghosts in the heat of a summer morning. Mile Zero may have been an hour back down the road in Dawson Creek, but that first, emotion-stirring glimpse of the river and the great green wilderness beyond was for me the moment when the Alaska Highway really started.

'Don't need to say a word. I know *exactly* how you feel,' said Ken, easing *Bad News* down the long, steep hill to Taylor Landing with the engine brake snarling like some angry monster from the realms of mythology. I grinned and nodded, although my senses were additionally charged by the elation that surges through you on the last leg of a long journey.

Not so much a road as a linear legend, the Alaska Highway runs for 1,520 miles from Dawson Creek to Fairbanks. Despite the terrain, the almost total lack of habitation and one of the world's most extreme freeze-or-fry climates; despite the howling blizzards, the deadly ice storms and the raging rivers; despite the mud and dust; despite the fatal accidents, the plagues of mosquitoes and the deaths from pneumonia; despite the landslides and the fact that much of the road had to be built on sponge-like muskeg; despite just about every sling and arrow in Mother Nature's arsenal when she is in her most bitchy mood; despite all that, and a great deal more, the men of Canada and the USA created the Alaska Highway in just nine incredible months of toil in 1942.

Work started shortly after Japan's attack on Pearl Harbor underlined the ugly fact that Alaska and north-west Canada were dangerously isolated from the rest of the continent. Peacetime planners would doubtless have spent years just discussing the project, but there is nothing quite like the threat of a full-scale invasion to oil the wheels.

Mile 86 gave me my first glimpse of a moose, but Ken had other things on his mind. 'Get ready to kiss the pavement goodbye,' he warned, 'because there's more than 100 miles of loose gravel up ahead, starting at Mile 93. After that there's a few stretches of blacktop, but it's mainly oiled gravel and what we call Japanese pavement – fine gravel that's treated to make it pretty good – all the way to Whitehorse. And that's more than 800 miles from where the loose stuff starts. On a day like this, when it's hot *and* dusty, you just pray the air conditioner keeps working.'

The highway does not scale any great heights, although Dawson Creek gets you started at 2,186 feet above sea level, but there are lots of wicked gradients liberally laced with the sort of corners that can easily spell disaster. Your first mistake may well be your last, even on the flat, because much of the road is virtually a steep-sided causeway built high above the peat-like muskeg that would otherwise swallow it. The surface bounces like a trampoline under a truck's weight. Ken took things very carefully as we switchbacked through the Trutch Mountains before stopping at the 4,134-feet-high summit. The food was good in the restaurant, its entrance decorated with antlers, and the view westwards to the snow-flecked Rockies was a sample of what lay ahead.

A long, straight stretch of blacktop swept us into Fort Nelson and was a reminder that Canada's section of the road is slowly being tamed. Regulars joke about the job going soft, but running the Alaska Highway will never be anything a million miles this side of easy. Be that as it may, men like Ken and Al tell you that tourists are the greatest hazard. The words used to describe them merit a 'Fire Hazard' label. Talking of fire, vast clouds of smoke away to the west had Jones the Power crossing his fingers as we left Fort Nelson after brimming the trio of 100-gallon tanks. 'If that's near the road, and the wind's blowing in the wrong direction, we could find ourselves being stopped. They halt traffic because of the smoke and you get yourself "volunteered" to help fight the fire', he worried, although the possibilities were expressed in considerably more colourful terms. But we were lucky.

Scenery that had previously been nothing more than spectacular became breathtakingly majestic as the huge engine laboured long and hard to haul us up Steamboat Mountain on the fringe of the Rockies. Blasted into the rock, with an awe-inspiring drop on the left, the road must be a 10-mile nightmare in bad weather and can turn your hair grey even when it's fine. I loved the Steamboat sign – 'Population: four people, two dogs. Home-made pies. Welding. Diesel' – and was soon spellbound by the barren, brutal grandeur of Stone Mountain. Bathed by the setting sun, it towered high above Summit Lake, the loftiest point on the entire road at 4,250 feet. He may not be as big as Stone Mountain, but Bob Price can claim to be almost as tough. A tremendous character, he runs the Toad River Lodge and, early in 1981, survived being run over by a Kenworth. 'How're you doing Jonesy, you old sonofabitch,' he laughed as we sat down to bowls of delicious chili.

Talk soon focused on the naturalist who had been camping out near the hot springs at Liard, 70 miles on up the road. A few days earlier, not having seen the man for some time, investigating locals found just his head and an arm. Now the forest was being combed for the killer grizzly. But even the relatively small black 'garbage bears', weighing upwards of 500lb, pose problems when they start raiding the rubbish. 'We had to shoot nine around here last year,' said Bob. 'A couple of years ago one got an Italian cyclist a few miles down the road. He needed 360 stitches, but was lucky not to be just so much spaghetti and meatballs.'

Day Fourteen: We were up at 4.45am, just as dawn's soft touch started caressing scenery every bit as magnificent as the previous evening's. Bob Price greeted Ken with a cordial 'Good morning, you mangy old bastard' as we helped ourselves to coffee before those 26 wheels started rolling. Mountains, rivers, lakes and the endless ocean of trees made it easy to forget the bumps and dust as *Bad News* crossed Contact Creek – the point where the Canadian and American engineers met in 1942 – and at last entered the Yukon. 'I'm hungry enough to eat the ass out of a skunk walking backwards, as they say in these parts,' Ken announced as we pulled into Iron Creek Lodge for a late breakfast. He produced a pair of boots for mine host, Steve Kerik. 'They've been all the way to Edmonton and back. I wonder if 1,900 miles is a record for a repair job?'

It was noon when we entered Watson Lake, where a sizzling 98 degrees F contrasted vividly with the minus 68 degrees once experienced by the man behind the Kenworth's wheel. The little township's most remarkable feature is a forest of place-name signs started by a homesick American soldier when the highway was being built. Nearly five hours later we ate at the Yukon Motel, overlooking the 78-mile length of Teslin Lake, and were made to feel like members of the family by the owners, Gordon and Adele. They gave me a

'Yukon Motel' belt buckle as a souvenir. 'Thought you were dead,' Ken called to a trucker he hadn't seen for some time. 'Nope. Just *smell* that way, Jonesy!'

Immense crags reared above the last stretch of gravel before the first genuine blacktop since Fort Nelson paved the way to Whitehorse. Ken fed most of the KTA's 535 prancing ponies through to the road and devoured the last 50 or so miles at an effortless 70mph. At precisely 7.50pm we reached the 'Welcome to Whitehorse' sign. Ken had covered 1,261 anything-but-easy miles in just under 48 hours.

'Why do I run this road?' he mused over a big rum and Coke. 'It just gets into your blood. It's a real *driver's* job, not like spending your life cruising dead straight and dead flat over that prairie pavement. I just love this country, the money's good – very good – and the people up here are fantastic. So what more do you need?' Then he leaned back, ordered another round and quoted a couple of lines from Robert Service, the English poet who immortalised the Yukon during the hell-raising, claim-jumping, hard-drinking days of the Klondike gold-rush, way back in 1898:

> *This is the Law of the Yukon,*
> *That only the Strong shall thrive;*
> *That surely the Weak shall perish,*
> *And only the Fit survive.*

13

INTO THE FAR NORTH'S FREEZER

1982

Spare a thought for Diamond Tooth Gertie, Swiftwater Bill, Klondike Kate, Nellie the Pig, Arizona Charlie and the Oregon Mare; for the girls who plied their trade in the redlight settlement of Lousetown; for the sourdoughs who were lost for ever amid the pitiless ice and snow; for the miners who trampled gold dust into the floors of honky-tonk saloons, swigged champagne at $40 a pint, gambled hard-won fortunes away in a single night and helped make Dawson City a hell-raising, hair-raising legend. Salute the memory of George Washington Carmack, Skookum Jim and Tagish Charlie, for it was they who started it all by discovering gold in the Klondike Valley on 17 August, 1896.

It was thanks to them, albeit at a distance of 86 years, that I found myself riding through the awesome cold of a Yukon winter with Ken Kirby and his Kenworth. My main reason for visiting the Yukon in February was to sample the Dempster Highway, the only public road in North America that crosses the Arctic Circle. Opened four years ago, it is a lifeline for Inuvik – 'The Place of Man' – where a population of just over 3,000 constitutes the largest community in the far north of Canada. *The Milepost* guidebook for travellers on the edge of civilisation does not beat about the bush: 'Although the highway is expected to be maintained in winter, limited facilities, inclement weather, river crossings and maintenance problems make driving the Dempster extremely hazardous. DO NOT start out without checking with the RCMP in Dawson City or Fort McPherson.'

The idea of discovering how trucks and truckers cope with some of the world's most ferocious weather had been born six months earlier, when I reached Whitehorse after a 5,200-mile journey from Newfoundland. More than a little complicated by an air traffic controllers' dispute, my long haul home had started with White Pass Transportation's Don Frizzell running me to Skagway, where I managed to escape in a six-seater Piper. We said farewell on the tiny airfield in conditions worthy of an English heatwave. 'We have two seasons here,' said Don. 'Winter and August. This is August. Come back in the winter. That's a very different story.'

Six months later I returned to Whitehorse after spending the previous night with my wife's cousin and her husband in Vancouver. They whisked me straight to a party, dominated by Scots and Irish, where any thoughts of sleeping after the long flight from England were washed away in high-spirited company. Next morning, pole-axed by a deadly cocktail of jetlag and hangover, I collapsed onto Canadian Pacific's flight for Whitehorse, fell into conversation with my neighbour and was given the glad tidings that conditions up there were the coldest for many a frostbiting year. The temperature had been down to minus 40 degrees C or lower for 30 days spanning Christmas and New Year. It was a relatively benign minus 26 when we landed, but that failed to take a 20–25mph north wind into account.

Later, rendered almost human again after Don Frizzell's welcome and a fine meal with his family, we drove through the darkness to the hot springs at nearby Takhini. A good swim would complete the treatment, Don reckoned, but the heart skipped several beats when I realised that the pool was completely open to the elements and the temperature had sunk to minus 40. The water was as warm and soothing as a bath, although every minute or so you had to duck right under to melt the ice encrusting your hair. Don roared with laughter at my incredulity and quoted a couple of lines from

The Cremation of Sam McGee by Robert Service. His poems about the Yukon and the 1898 goldrush are fed to the locals with their mother's milk:

> *The Northern Lights have seen queer sights,*
> *But the queerest they ever did see . . .*

Breakfast, then a 9am call to Don produced the right news. Owner-operator Ken Kirby, hauling for Points North Transportation, would be leaving town in the afternoon, en route for Inuvik at the far end of the Dempster. A few hours later I was sharing a table at the Klondike Inn with Don and Larry Haddon, manager of Points North's terminal in Whitehorse, and hearing horror stories about the Dempster. Trucks blasted off the road by 80mph winds raging down off the pole, people trapped for days by blizzards, trucks being lost when the 'ice bridges' over the Peel River and Arctic Red River collapsed. They made such hazards sound no more remarkable than Friday-night traffic jams on the M1, but a host of butterflies were churning my stomach round like a cement mixer. The prospect of covering just over 1,500 miles through virtually uninhabited country in conditions that can freeze your skin solid in less than 30 seconds made all previous trips seem only marginally more formidable than being pushed along Bournemouth's promenade in a wheelchair.

Nervous tension increased back at Points North when I studied a petition signed by dozens of truckers. It complained about the 'extremely icy and hazardous' conditions between Whitehorse and Carmacks, drew attention to the fact that 'there have been too many accidents' on that section of road and called for the local Minister of Highways to resign. Ken provided a crumb of comfort. Unshaven, clad in a black, heavily-insulated skidoo suit, eyes bright beneath the peak of a battered, gold-braided Kenworth cap, he looked tough and exuded quiet confidence. But one side of his face was blotched with dark, dead, peeling skin. 'Frostbite,' he explained. 'Got stuck in the snow for 13 hours last week, up there on the Dempster, and collected this when I helped them get me out.'

Clad in the ankle-length thermal underpants and a matching vest bought earlier in the day, I followed Ken and Larry out into the yard where almost 20 tons of steel and a beefy GMC Suburban station wagon were loaded onto a flatbed. It was mid-afternoon when the Kenworth climbed out of Whitehorse to join the Alaska Highway, hauled by its KTA-450 Cummins, drinking the special blend of 'low pour' diesel formulated to flow in hellish cold, and protected by all manner of special lubricants and greases. The engine works night and day on winter trips, granted freedom from mechanical maladies. Ken had been running the daunting Dempster since the summer, when he started driving after a nine-year break following a bad accident. He worked his way up through the 15-speed Fuller gearbox, craning forward to listen to the engine. 'Keep your fingers crossed,' he said. 'I've been having trouble with head gaskets and it sounds like I've still got trouble. It sounds OK when the engine's good and hot, but keeping it that way's not easy in these temperatures.'

Ten minutes out of Whitehorse we paused at the Trails North truckstop for coffee, burgers and a brief chat with others in the same line of business. The main news concerned a hero who had been fined for speeding, which sounded an unlikely offence in view of the conditions. 'You better believe it,' I was assured. 'Speeding sideways through the gatehouse up there at the Anvil Mine! Sure did make those guys jump.'

Darkness was drifting over the snow-covered mountains and endless forests as Ken made good time along the Klondike Loop road, which runs north-westwards towards Dawson City. The surface was packed snow, but conditions have to get *really* bad before any trucker worth his salt resorts to chains. Ken shook his head when I asked about studded tyres: 'Never even think about them. They give you a feeling of false confidence. I run Bridgestones on the front, because their firm sidewalls give you plenty of feel, and Michelins on the drivers. Traction actually improves as it gets colder, and we very rarely get the sort of damp cold you have in England. Up here it's second nature to be real smooth with the steering, brakes and clutch, and there's very little traffic to worry about. I reckon these conditions give you about 40 per cent of the traction you'd get running on dry pavement, and if you can maintain that traction you're OK. But it's a bit like walking a tightrope. If you lose *any* traction you've lost the lot.'

He stopped to check the tyres just outside Carmacks, a settlement named after the man who discovered gold in the Klondike Valley in '98. With a population of about 400 it is easily the biggest place encountered between Whitehorse and the start of the Dempster Highway, 26 miles before Dawson City, and the biggest before Inuvik unless you take a brief detour into Fort McPherson. The closest contender for metropolitan status is Pelly Crossing with what Ken described as 'one cop, 45 Indians and 75 dogs'.

The big diesel engine pumps out a lot of heat, but ice started forming on the truck's side windows as we headed into the night. I slipped my anorak over my shoulders, scraped the stuff away a few times, then abandoned the struggle. Ken cursed as Kenworth suspension battled with a few miles of denture-dislodging ruts. We saw perhaps six other vehicles in three hours, one being a Toyota pickup parked miles from nowhere. Ken checked that all was well before driving on. 'That's the Law of the North. You *never* pass a stopped vehicle,' he explained. At 11pm, with the thermometer registering minus 40 degrees C, we halted for coffee and a meal in the Klondike River Lodge – 'Gateway to the Arctic Circle' – and shared a table with the local Mountie, Pat McKay. Canada being officially bilingual, the Royal Canadian Mounted Police badge on his tunic was matched by its French equivalent with the initials GRP. That, I was told, stands for Gravel Road Cops in this isolated neck of the woods. Pat had news for us. It had been down to minus 52 degrees at Inuvik during the day.

I sipped the steaming coffee and thought back to *The Milepost* guide to the roads of northern Canada and Alaska that had been purchased in Edmonton, six months earlier. It related how the Dempster had been started in 1958, finished 20 years later and named after Corporal W J D Dempster of the Royal North-West Mounted Police. In the winter of 1910, Dempster and three others left Fort McPherson to search for a lost patrol whose frozen bodies were found three months later. The book said that the Dempster Highway consisted of gravel banks built above the permafrost – a typical Yukon road, in other words – and was 'extremely hazardous' in winter. We left Mile Zero at midnight.

Traffic during the next six hours added up to a solitary Kenworth, which came towards us just after the start, and a couple of Freightliners parked for the night near Tombstone Mountain, some 45 miles up the road. The temperature dropped lower and lower. Even that big engine, working hard to haul us to 4,000 moonlit feet in the Ogilvie Mountains, was running cold despite its closed radiator cover and a 'belly wrap' of stout canvas to shield the sump. Ice crept over the inside of the windscreen and demanded a non-stop assault with a scraper. Minus 55 degrees. Minus 62 in a river-carved valley – warm air rises, letting the cold flow in – then a few degrees warmer as we climbed again. Ken took a break at one of several places where the Dempster widens to form an emergency airstrip, delved into the box between the seats and produced a flask of tea. He always carries supplies, just in case. 'I don't want to sound dramatic in anyway,' he said, 'but this job's all about working on the basis that you may find yourself in real trouble. You *must* assume that, just as you *must* check *everything* before you start out. Careful preparation can quite literally be the difference between life and death if you run short of luck.' He puffed away at his pipe, yawned and rubbed his eyes. 'I'd like to get out and stretch, but I'm scared I'd freeze solid with my arms and legs extended.'

We rolled on under the dancing Northern Lights, hoping to reach Eagle Plains, but Ken stopped for a sleep at 6am parking at the end of the Mile 200 airstrip. 'No sense in being a hero and putting her off the road,' he announced, clambering into the single sleeper while I angled six feet of humanity across the seats.

He was back at the wheel in less than two hours and wasted no time covering the 31 miles to Eagle Plains where a $3.5-million complex, way out in the wilderness, provides motel, restaurant and other facilities. I was zapped back to life by a spectacular electric shock – cold, bone-dry air and carpets of man-made fibre charge the body with awesome amounts of static – as we hurried in to wash, shave and swill breakfast down with serve-yourself coffee. The sky was as clear as a saint's conscience and it was a mild minus 33 degrees when we left at sunrise. It suddenly became a lot colder a few miles later, down in the Eagle River's valley, but we passed a trapper and his family living in a tent.

Crossing the Arctic Circle for the first time was a major milestone in my travelling life, although Ken sometimes does it four times a week, and we were soon in the Richardson Mountains where traffic became hyper-hectic by local standards. Eight or nine cars and pickups came towards us in less than an hour, all heading for the Sourdough Rendezvous celebrations in Whitehorse. Four of the vehicles, running within a few miles of each other, brought the CB radio to life. 'Jeeeeezus! Next time I'll remember to bring a box of diapers,' a voice gasped from a Chevvy as it vanished into a great swirl of snow from the Kenworth's wheels.

Midway through the morning we crested the Richardsons, crossed into the Northwest Territories and ran down to the 'ice bridge' over the Peel River. The sight of the ferry hauled up on the far bank was a sharp reminder that winter closes the Dempster for a month or two in the spring and autumn. You reach a stage where the ice is too thick for the boats to operate, but not thick enough to be crossed in safety. A stiff breeze was blowing upstream when I walked ahead to take some pictures. Just five minutes radically altered all previous concepts about the cold. Contrary to expectations, truly Arctic cold does not make you feel as if you have been run through with an icicle. For the first few seconds, in desert-dry air under a clear blue sky, you recall damp winter days in

Britain that seemed a lot colder. But the chill factor has stunned your senses, just as a heavy blow knocks you straight out while a much lighter one causes pain. In less than a minute you realise that every square inch of exposed flesh is starting to freeze. By the time I reached the far bank my face was feeling like an ill-fitting mask. I removed the outer mittens. Underneath were gloves which left my fingertips exposed. I waved to Ken and started snapping, horribly aware that my Nikon's super-fine lubricants were already making adjustments difficult. Components that normally move as freely as water on tilted glass were demanding genuine effort. All feeling went from the fingers. Other senses told me that the shutter release was being pressed. I could hear it, but that was all. Back in the truck, my fingertips soon felt as if they had been run over by a tank. A few days later several layers of dead skin peeled off each one. I had been out of the cab for no more than 300 seconds.

We skirted Fort McPherson – 'Just a street of skidoos and dog teams' – crossed the Arctic Red River on an ice bridge much longer than the Peel's, then followed the Mackenzie River's estuary towards Inuvik on long straights flanked by growths which looked more like discarded pipe-cleaners than pathetically stunted spruce and tamarack trees. Just before the Points North terminal, a mile or two before Inuvik, the engine started suffering from fuel starvation. Ken donned his skidoo suit and diagnosed a blockage between the auxiliary and main diesel tanks. The cold had brought us to a halt and the Cummins stopped for the first time in 750 miles, but he sorted it out with doses of pure alcohol and the heat of a propane torch.

I had expected each leg of the trip to take at least two days, but Ken was unloading less than 24 hours after leaving Whitehorse and we started straight back. Although I never got to see Inuvik, which is basically a supply base for oilfield exploration in the Beaufort Sea, I had completed the final stage of a 6,000-mile trip across Canada. As we roared southward the local radio had news of yet another drive to curb Inuvik's horrific booze problem. Rationing was being introduced and the locals were being cut down to just 12 cans of beer or one bottle of the hard stuff . . . per day. We stopped to admire the sunset, drink tea and devour DIY sandwiches of tinned meat, then crossed the ice bridges and were back at Eagle Plains by 10pm. A couple of swifties in the bar should have knocked me out after such a meagre ration of sleep, but too little space and too much heat from the engine made for a restless night.

The Cummins idled its way through about 20 gallons during our overnight stop. I was sufficiently dehydrated to drink about as much coffee with my breakfast before Ken guided the KW down the snow-banked mountains like an expert tackling the Cresta Run, reeling in the miles as sunrise painted the land with soft shades of pink and gold. The only truck that came towards us all morning was a Mack from Yukon Freight Lines which popped up from a sharp undulation and forced Ken to swerve into hub-deep snow. But by then we were just over the crest and the other guy reversed a few yards to push us out with the tail of his trailer.

A little later, Ken eased the Kenworth to a halt, checked its instruments, filled his pipe with Old Chum and peered silently out through the ice-framed windscreen, contemplating the conditions through a cloud of fragrant smoke. The scenery was majestic, up there in the Ogilvie Mountains, and the noonday sun poured liquid gold from the clearest of blue skies as a sharp breeze, knifing down from the north, sent flurries of powdered snow swirling and snaking down the Dempster. It was like being in the middle of a Christmas card, but Ken's voice had the stern, measured ring of a High Court judge passing sentence. 'OK. It looks real pretty from where we're sitting, but don't let that fool you,' he warned. 'Put the jacket on and zip it right up. Put your hat on, then cover it with your hood. Put both pairs of mittens on and don't remove the outers until it's absolutely necessary. Don't stay out for more than just a few minutes, because you're about to discover what it's like to be *really* cold.'

Although it produced a string of bone-chilling temperatures that made headlines day after day, Britain's record-breaking winter of 1981–82 seemed almost tropical by comparison. The big freeze produced an unofficial all-time low of minus 29.8 degrees C from an amateur weatherman in Shropshire, less than 20 miles from my front door, but the temperature rarely crept more than a degree or two above that during my winter week in northern Canada. The still-air temperature was minus 62C or about minus 80F when I climbed down from the KW to snatch a few photographs in the mountains. But the air was not still. A wicked wind was blowing down the valley, adding a significant chill factor to the equation and creating conditions as potentially lethal as a short-fused time bomb. Taking that all-important chill factor into account, the temperature was hovering around minus 90C or way below minus 120 on Mr Fahrenheit's scale. During the previous few days, when the thermometer was often registering in the region of minus 40C, I had become used to every intake of nostril-freezing air giving the impression that two tiny hedgehogs were flexing spines of ice in my nose. But this was cold beyond the bounds of belief. Cold enough to freeze the soul. Cold enough to make a man tremble with fear.

I took a few pictures before the camera started to freeze solid, then we were back at Mile Zero soon after 1pm. Checking through my notes, I realised that we had seen only 29 other vehicles in 900 miles. It was much the same after our meal – one truck, one car and five pickups in about 150 miles – and thoughts raced ahead to the prospect of a good night's sleep in a proper bed when we reached Ken's home just outside Whitehorse. The trip was completed in a little more than 52 hours, but it certainly made me appreciate the sentiments of that Sam McGee character in the poem quoted by Don Frizzell. Robert Service's yarn tells how Sam, out seeking gold, reaches the end of his tether on the shore of Lake Laberge, whose shore we traced, and makes his companion promise to cremate his body. The other guy places the corpse in a derelict cabin, sets it on fire and returns an hour or two later, expecting to find nothing but smouldering ashes. But the fire's still blazing when he opens the door:

And there sat Sam, looking cool and calm, in the heart of the furnace roar; And he wore a smile you could see a mile, and he said: 'Please close that door. It's fine in here, but I greatly fear you'll let in the cold and storm – Since I left Plumtree, down in Tennessee, it's the first time I've been warm.'

14

AFRICA

LONG ROAD TO LONDON

1983

Davinder Singh checked his watch and peered down the road which runs southwards from Nairobi towards Mount Kilimanjaro and Kenya's troubled border with Tanzania. We had been waiting at the junction since a chilly 5am, sipping coffee and worried that the VW might attract bandits lurking in the bush. Now it was light up there on the dusty plateau, 5,500ft above sea level, and the danger of attack had passed. Huge birds of prey patrolled the sky, wheeling above battered, diesel-belching trucks lumbering towards the city. The Sikh's eyes suddenly blazed beneath his spotless white turban – 'Here they come!' – and he waved a red shirt to greet the couple whose muddy Range Rover had covered the 3,500 miles from Cape Town in just 70 hours.

'Jolly decent of you to turn out and meet us. Hope we've not kept you waiting too long,' said 47-year-old Brigadier John Hemsley, Commanding Officer of the 24th Infantry Brigade. Out of the co-driver's seat bounced his wife, Lucy, whose slim figure and girlish face belie a core of steel. Born in Sydney, Australia, she looks closer to 17 than 37 – even after being strapped into a Recaro seat for three days and nights.

John Hemsley's background includes such long-distance epics as the 1968 London to Sydney Marathon and the 1970 World Cup Rally from London to Mexico City. But his dash from Cape Town to Nairobi represented little more than the start of the toughest challenge of all. International rallies involve hundreds of organisers, mobile service crews and border officials who know exactly what to expect and when to expect it. That sort of thing is a far cry from a man and his wife trying to clock the fastest possible time between Cape Town and London. They planned a route of nearly 12,000 miles that involved crossing 17 frontiers – including the one between Israel and Jordan – traversed vast, trackless deserts and climbed mountains certain to be swathed in snow. There were also areas where safety depends on who happens to have his finger on the Kalashnikov's trigger. John and Lucy hoped to complete the journey to Marble Arch in a dozen days . . .

The attempt was conceived and backed by Ben Hogan, a British businessman whose activities include selling Sodastream products in West Germany. He also holds the Subaru franchise, but the Japanese came down very heavily against any involvement in the adventure. The next candidate was a Mercedes G-wagen, but John felt that a British officer should really be driving a British vehicle. His close and long-standing links with BL resulted in Land Rover joining forces with Sodastream to fund the preparation and running costs of a 1981 four-door Range Rover, an ex-works model with nearly 19,000 miles on the clock.

Tom Walkinshaw Racing handled the preparation. The 3.5-litre V8 was fitted with electronic ignition, modified to run on low-grade petrol and tuned to deliver 173bhp and 207lb-ft of torque. Other changes included fitting a roll cage, uprating the suspension and replacing the back seat with three extra fuel tanks which boosted capacity to 90 gallons. There were still worries about running dry in the more remote parts of Africa. All that petrol, plus essential spares, tools, gear to extricate TKV 639W from sand or mud, drinking water, food and a few personal belongings pushed the weight up to around three tons. John opted for Michelin tyres and carried four spares, two of them complete with wheels.

Just what did the Hemsleys set out to achieve? John admits that the whole subject of high-speed runs between South Africa and England is a mire of confusion. In 1967, for instance, Eric Jackson and Ken Chambers charged from Cape Town to Southampton in a Ford Corsair 2000E, racing a Union Castle liner. They crossed the Mediterranean by ship, logged just under 10,000 miles and finished in 11.5 days. The route plotted by John and Lucy was nearly 20 per cent longer, because their study of international sporting regulations made it clear that a vehicle on a pukka endurance run – the powers that be decline to sanction *record* attempts on public roads – had to go by land wherever possible. That clearly restricted the seafaring to the English Channel only, and obliged them to tackle Sudan, Egypt, Israel, Jordan, Syria, Turkey and eastern Europe. All previous attempts had involved the *relatively* soft option of swinging north-westwards across the Sahara.

John arranged for their departure from Cape Town to be recorded by the local Federation Internationale de l'Automobile representative. His British counterpart, Neil Eason-Gibson of the RAC, promised to authenticate the Range Rover's arrival at Marble Arch in London. A special book was carried to be stamped, signed and timed at every frontier. In other words, the object of the exercise was to establish an 'unofficially official' record under conditions laid down by the FIA. Those conditions, incidentally, also stipulate a crew of not more than two people.

Time was critical in more ways than one. John had served in Africa and was keenly aware that the attempt had to be made right at the start of the year, before tropical rains effectively closed many miles of so-called road in parts of Tanzania, Kenya and southern Sudan. Getting the Range Rover organised was almost incidental to cutting a path through the jungle of diplomatic problems. Lucy trekked from embassy to embassy while John used the Old Pals Act to solicit help from defence attachés and other military contacts along the way. Special permission was essential to cross the closed border between Tanzania and Kenya. Driving from Israel into Jordan promised to be only marginally easier than getting the Red Sea to part: 'Sorting out the paperwork involved ten months of *very* hard admin' work,' said John. 'We came to the conclusion that driving 12,000 miles was going to be a lot easier than all the hassling for visas, special clearances and fuel supplies.'

It was 8am on a Saturday in January when the Range Rover left central Cape Town, climbed spectacular mountains and started running hard across the endless Great Karroo plain. Temperatures in the region of 49°C – the hottest the locals had ever known – combined with shimmering gum trees to remind Lucy of Australia. She smiled and waved at policemen as the Range Rover stormed north-eastwards. The schedule predicted averaging 72mph over the 898 miles to Johannesburg, but 82mph was nearer the mark. Their fuel stop south of the city coincided with a sudden storm whose titanic ferocity suggested a full-scale dress rehearsal for Armageddon. Rain pounded into the baked ground while immense bolts of lightning seared the maelstrom of coal-black clouds. It was there that John and Lucy were met by Fred Ferrari, Land Rover's local sales manager and the first of many stalwarts who provided help and hospitality. He took them home for a meal and a bath, then guided the Range Rover out of Johannesburg, around Pretoria and onto the right road for the overnight haul to Zimbabwe. The only incident involved a zebra hellbent on suicide. John's sleep was shattered as Lucy swerved to avoid the animal. 'I opened my eyes to find us going sideways down a hill.'

At 4am they reached the point where Beit Bridge spans the Limpopo and marks South Africa's frontier with Zimbabwe. The border was not due to open for another two hours, but they had averaged a crisp 62mph since leaving Cape Town. Fuel consumption, aided by a strong tailwind, was about 12mpg despite many miles of high-speed cruising. Two worries occupied their minds as the frontier formalities were completed. The ignition system was not 100 per cent right and there was also a risk of being ambushed by guerillas from neighbouring Mozambique.

Friends greeted them at the Jameson Hotel in Harare where John worked on the ignition. One hour later the Range Rover was back on the road, passing mile-long petrol queues as it dog-legged north-westwards towards the third frontier in less than 36 hours. There were elephants amid the roadside trees. The temperature climbed higher and higher as TKV

639W hurried down the potholed highway to the Zambezi valley below Lake Kariba. The route to Lusaka was rough and littered with meandering trucks, but the Hemsleys arrived three hours ahead of schedule.

'Our sleep patterns dovetailed very neatly,' John recalled later. 'I start feeling tired at about 3am, but that's the time when Lucy wakes up feeling full of beans after zizzing since about 11pm. On a run like this it's vital to recognise the symptoms of fatigue, to be *absolutely* honest when they hit you and to hand over the wheel even if you've been driving for only an hour or two. Nodding off for literally one second can be fatal. Lucy was magnificent, but there was one stage where her eyes just gave up the battle. She said "There's a bloody great Chinese dragon out there" and had to stop. It was actually a thorn tree.'

They reached the Tanzanian border 90 minutes before opening time. Ben Hogan had thoughtfully provided a supply of digital watches to overcome such problems, but the modest bribe was declined. The inevitable delay, far from serious in itself, proved to be an omen for bad times ahead. The local Land Rover man was waiting a few miles up the road in Mbeya, but John's request for 360 litres of petrol was greeted with a sad shake of the head. 'I don't think we can get you six litres.'

John eventually found the only service station in town that had any fuel, but less than 20 gallons had been pumped when a trio of heavies stopped the operation. They turned out to be the local committee of communists responsible for deciding who could and could not buy petrol. Helped by a friendly Sikh, John finally managed to get a host of helpers running all over the place and ferrying cans to the garage. Nearly six hours were lost before the Range Rover was ready to roll again.

'The fuel was real 32-octane, quarter-star stuff and we'd probably have gone better on paraffin,' said John. The delay was not exactly soothed by reports that exceptionally heavy rains, sweeping the country weeks earlier than usual, had created atrocious conditions on the roads north of Iringa. The alternative route, eastwards towards Dar es Salaam, involved an extra 500 miles and was too long to merit serious consideration. Fingers crossed, the couple set course for the badlands.

The rain reports were right. The dirt road between Iringa and Dodoma was a nightmare of deep mud, boulders and brutal, torrent-carved gullies. The Range Rover growled on like a hippo, ploughing past abandoned trucks, buses and tractors. But the ignition problem became increasingly serious. Worried about damaging the engine, John stopped to take another look at the system while Lucy brewed soup. The trouble was traced to wiring in the steering column and solved on a temporary basis by wedging everything into place with a sandal. 'All frightfully technical,' John chuckled.

Indicated by Michelin's cartographers as 'likely to be impracticable in bad weather', the road over the plain to Dodoma was submerged beneath what amounted to a vast lake dotted with trees. 'I should really have walked ahead, checking the depth, but we pushed on and inevitably paid the penalty,' John confessed. 'We chugged her out on the starter, dried everything as best we could, then tackled another really bad section. The rear suspension took a particularly terrible pounding and we spent a lot of time slithering sideways on wet clay. It was essentially a case of trying to keep going at a fair speed while watching for hazards like knee-deep ruts running right across the track. We tried to slide her, because going in at an angle reduces the impact a little. Lucy drove for most of the night and did a wonderful job in extremely demanding conditions.'

Swift reactions and quick-wittedness are clearly no problem for a woman who pilots light aircraft, is a free-fall parachutist and a doctor of archaeology to boot.

The service crew at Arusha, some 60 miles south of the Kenyan border, were all smiles and enthusiasm despite having spent six chilly hours waiting on the roadside. Petrol? Their 20-litre can, the only fuel available in a town of some 75,000 people, provided a slender reserve for the run to Nairobi. A special permit took care of the officially closed frontier, but there was no sign of the Kenyan customs man: 'He was sleeping in a hotel a few miles up the road and we were eventually given permission to go there. In fact we just slowed down and headed for Nairobi,' John revealed. 'From there on it was a super drive, apart from killing a goat. It jumped up and would have demolished the radiator if we hadn't insisted on Tom Walkinshaw's chaps fitting that crash bar. But animals in general were less of a worry at night than unlit lorries.'

Davinder Singh, general service manager for the Cooper Motor Corporation of Kenya, escorted the Range Rover into Nairobi, where his mechanics were waiting. Rapping out orders in Swahili and English, he organised a thorough service which included a new shock absorber and replacing the rear suspension's self-levelling unit. Both had given up the ghost in Tanzania. John and Lucy were whisked off to the Fairview Hotel for breakfast and their first real sleep since leaving Cape Town.

Seven hours later, at 4pm, they were back on their feet and racing through another meal before embarking on a brief shopping expedition. John bought a long, broad-bladed *panga* for cutting brushwood while Lucy filled a bag with dried fruit, tins of spaghetti and four bottles of Lucozade. 'Splendid stuff. Instant energy. We always use it on the Safari Rally,' Davinder enthused. By 6pm I was riding shotgun as his white VW Passat estate guided the Range Rover out of the city and onto the road for Khartoum, nearly 2,000 miles away. He sighed as he waved farewell. 'They need all the luck in the world. The roads up there are bloody awful – and there are places where just *finding* the road can be very difficult.'

Too true. One stretch was better than expected – it had been built to serve President Moi's country retreat – but there were many miles of rib-rattling boulder-to-boulder stuff. The stretch from Lodwar to Lokichokio, just before the Sudanese border, was bad news. Constantly changing from second to third to second to third, they battled onwards through the wilderness west of Lake Turkana. 'What we were following had never been a road in the European sense of the word,' Lucy explained. 'It was just a track that generations of travellers had decided was the best way to cross the desert.'

Two days earlier Lokichokio had been raided by a band of

Kalashnikov-toting guerillas. John and Lucy were greeted by nothing more extraordinary than a small party of British soldiers – members of the 5th Light Infantry Battalion who 'just happened' to be on an adventure-training exercise a few miles south-east of their depot in the heart of Shropshire. They provided food, fuel and what was probably the first bottle of champagne ever opened in that remote cluster of mud huts. The meeting, planned months earlier over a post-prandial whisky, underlined the 24-carat value of John's military contacts.

Up at the border they met the two-man crew of a G-wagen who had spent more than three weeks slogging their way southwards from Khartoum to Juba, and nearly four days getting from Juba to the frontier. 'Hell, we've got to reach Juba in 12 hours,' John spluttered. 'They didn't speak to us after that. We were obviously crazy.'

Getting the exit papers stamped was no problem, but the Kenyan customs official proved awkward. Working on the basis that his counterpart on the southern border had been side-stepped, John decided to make a run for it. 'Lucy was dying to go behind a bush, but I went like stink for about 20 miles, one eye on the mirror and not daring to stop until I was sure we weren't being chased.'

It was a classic case of exchanging the frying pan for the fire. After sprinting through what amounted to no man's land the Hemsleys were held up for three hours by bloody-minded Sudanese officials in Kapoeta, about 160 miles east of Juba. From there they went as fast as conditions permitted, picking their way between rocks, thumping in and out of gullies and passing what John knew were ambush sites. They had been warned to expect bandits.

A soldier tried to prevent them crossing the White Nile to enter Juba at 2am on the Wednesday, but his defences were battered down by a barrage of verbal artillery. Sue Farmer, the local consul, provided scrambled eggs, hot drinks and precious fuel.

The 1,000 miles from Juba to Khartoum, where I was waiting, were squeezed into 27 dusty hours, many of them spent crossing a vast plain, devoid of landmarks, where they navigated by their compass and the stars. Lucy kept the needle on 90mph for three hours while hurtling along the bank of a vast canal being dug to short-cut one of the Blue Nile's biggest meanders. Kosti, less than an hour south of Khartoum, eventually put tarmac under the Michelins for the first time in nearly 1,700 miles.

Colonel David Fanshawe of the Grenadier Guards, Her Britannic Majesty's Defence and Military Attaché in the Sudan, was one of the rocks on which the adventure had been built. But even his brisk manner and peerless organisational ability failed to overcome the easy-going attitude of the smiling Sudanese. It was a Friday, the Muslim day of rest, but the local Land Rover agent had promised to have his mechanics on parade at noon. They rolled up at 2.30pm – 'That's pretty good for this part of the world,' said the colonel – and the service manager arrived an hour or so later. No electricity was available, because Khartoum's supply falls about 75 per cent short of demand. From my viewpoint it was wonderful to watch a very British officer trying to come to terms with a culture so far removed from the Grenadier Guards. I was also fascinated to meet Mrs Fanshawe's mother, a splendid old lady whose father-in-law, Angus McNeill of the Seaforth Highlanders, had fought in the Battle of Omdurman, close to Khartoum, in 1898. His comrades included young Winston Churchill, and McNeill's paintings illustrated the future Prime Minister's book about the campaign. Mrs McNeill formed an evocative bridge with the past when David Fanshawe's driver chauffeured us to Omdurman in the official Ford Cortina. This was where Sudanese warriors dressed in medieval-style chain-mail and colourful surcoats suffered 26,000 casualties in a few hours. The British toll was 430.

John lost valuable sleeping time supervising the service. He had to make do with barely three hours' rest before returning to the garage, now lit by a solitary inspection lamp, where fuel from two-gallon drums was siphoned into the tanks amid much coughing and spluttering. Champagne accompanied a fine meal in the Fanshawe residence while

John and Lucy were briefed on the route towards Egypt by John and Jenny Aylen, experienced desert travellers who had driven from Cairo to Khartoum a few months earlier. 'You will have to hire a guide at Wadi Haifa,' they said, 'because from there to Aswan it's about 430 miles through trackless desert east of Lake Nasser. The route's used by maybe a couple of dozen vehicles a year. There will be times when you find yourself going south when you *know* you should be heading due north, but you must believe the guide unless you are absolutely certain he's gone wrong.'

It was 11pm when the Range Rover, complete with a new set of shock absorbers, sped out of Khartoum and covered a few miles on tarmac before getting back to the rough stuff. Four hours later came the second of the trip's six punctures. The airbag jack's valve failed, spitting up a stone which nearly blinded Lucy. They had to dig a hole under the wheel. At one point John swept at high speed into a huge area of wet sand, which threatened to swallow them. He thought it was the end of the road – the sand was up to the tops of the front wheels – but the differential lock and low-range reverse gear did the trick.

Early morning found them in Atbara where two of David Fanshawe's invaluable contacts, senior Sudanese officers, provided fuel and food. It was a good start to an anxious day, with lots of deep sand and many nail-biting hours of navigating by compass across a pitiless desert with no landmarks. 'We were often hitting patches of axle-deep sand at 60mph and coming out at a walking pace if we were lucky,' John recalled. 'Once or twice we only *just* chugged through and emerged giving thanks for that big V8's wonderful torque.'

Heading towards them near Abu Hamed came two VW Kombis kitted out for desert travel. Bogging down 45 times between them, they had taken more than three days to fight their way from Wadi Haifa at the head of Lake Nasser. John and Lucy clipped that down to just seven hours by abandoning the 'official' route and following the railway built by Kitchener's army in 1898. The narrow-gauge track forced them to run with one set of wheels rumbling over the sleepers while the other bounced through the sand, but the ride was reasonably smooth at a steady 50–55mph. 'We were going great guns until we hit the points for a passing loop and popped a front tyre,' said John. 'But using the railway saved a lot of time and we reached Wadi Haifa just before 12am. We knew it was Wadi Haifa because the track just vanished into the lake.'

Two digital watches were exchanged for beds in the local doctor's combined surgery and operating theatre, a room notable for the dirtiest sheets Lucy had ever seen. A guide was found, but he went off to get his kit and never returned. The problem was compounded by border officials who refused to let the travellers push on into Egypt. 'We kicked our heels until noon, then just sneaked out of town,' said John. 'We didn't dare risk the desert east of Lake Nasser without a guide, but by that stage I'd discovered that a new road was being built on the western side. Reaching it would involve crossing the Nile by boat and covering about 180 miles of very desolate country south of Aswan.'

They made their way to a point opposite Abu Simbel, but could not cross without permission from an Egyptian army captain who was elsewhere, cavorting with a lady. Next morning he sent an armed escort over with the pint-sized ferry. The skipper was a magnificent old character, but shipping a vehicle was obviously a novel experience. 'When we reached the far side I realised there was nothing in the way of a ramp or even a rough track – just bloody great rocks,' John said. 'All we could do was wedge boulders under the gangplank – it was just about the same width as a tyre – and borrow the boat's engine cover to support the other wheels. They just spanned the gap when the old chap kept his engine running hard. I honestly thought we were going to lose everything in the lake, but shot off in reverse amid great applause and ghastly cracking noises.

'The army captain offered us lunch, but made it quite clear that he was very, very angry with us. Getting into Egypt this way just wasn't the done thing and we were under military arrest. However, he sent us off to Aswan with a guard-cum-guide, Sergeant Ahmed, who was clearly terrified by the prospect of travelling through the desert with a couple of lunatics. The route was marked by dead camels, but we went very fast. There were no problems as long as you didn't charge into a dune.'

Although the officials in Aswan were polite, friendly and helpful, sorting out the paperwork involved five different offices and 19 hours. Free at last, running on tarmac and mingling with the first open-road traffic encountered since Kenya, the Range Rover raced northwards beside the Nile before bearing right at Qena to reach the Red Sea and avoid Cairo. The road over the mountains was officially closed to non-military traffic, but Lucy just smiled and waved at bewildered soldiers as they stumbled from their sentry boxes. 'The technique is to keep going fast as long as there's no barrier right across the road,' John explained. 'The private or lance corporal knows he'll get into trouble if he reports the incident. With luck, if he fails to report it, nobody will know where the vehicle's come from, and someone else will be on duty if and when it's stopped. So he goes back to sleep and does nothing. From our angle it was worth taking the chance. If you play everything by the book you never get anywhere.'

A road pitted with huge potholes followed the coast to Ismailia where they slept in the Range Rover before catching the morning's first ferry over the Suez Canal. Then it was through the Sinai Desert, littered with abandoned T-62 tanks and other war debris, to Gaza and the Israeli border. Suddenly, out of a roadside tent, popped a British sergeant-major serving with the multi-national peace-keeping force. 'Brigadier Hemsley? We've been waiting for you, sir. Just follow me.'

His help enabled the potentially tricky frontier to be crossed in less than an hour, opening the gate for a dash to Jerusalem and the all-important Allenby Bridge. The only official route between Israel and Jordan, it was the one point singled out by many experts as almost certain to bring the trip to a halt. The alternative involved trying to get through the bloody chaos that is Lebanon. Time was tight, because the bridge closes at 2pm and travellers must arrive no later than midday. It was 1.55pm when the Range Rover appeared, but a French girl in army uniform flagged it down, grabbed the passports, made a quick phone call and jumped aboard. Minutes later, bewildered but delighted, John and Lucy were in Jordan. 'We were the first civilian vehicle to cross the bridge in five years.'

A military escort whisked them straight through Jordan, but soaring morale was shot down in flames by the Syrian immigration man at Deraa. For diplomatic reasons, no mention of the Allenby Bridge appeared in their passports. How had they entered Jordan? Had they taken a ferry from Egypt to Aqaba? It seemed like a good idea, but the man was far from convinced and ordered them to wait. David Fanshawe had been right when he predicted political problems in the Middle East.

Eighteen hours passed, punctuated by questions, telephone calls and a night of troubled sleep in the Range Rover. Light appeared at the end of the bureaucratic tunnel midway through the Thursday morning, but John waited until all the documents had been stamped and handed over before firing a volley at the immigration man. 'I think you're the worst bloody advertisement your country could possibly have. You're rude, arrogant and downright bloody incompetent,' he said. High-level communications having made it clear that this was no run-of-the-mill traveller, the Syrian clutched John's sleeve and made forgive-and-forget noises. 'Let go of me! I'm a British citizen!' barked the brigadier.

'It sounded splendid,' said Lucy. 'But our departure was hardly *Land of Hope and Glory*. The dust-clogged engine wouldn't start, just when we wanted to make a really quick getaway, and John had to give me a push. It fired at the foot of the last hill.'

John got rid of his tensions by doing the 90-minute drive to Damascus in less than an hour. They were met by Tony Whitehorn, Land Rover's resident engineer, who tackled a roadside service while people from the British embassy provided baths, steaks and sausages. Two hours later, after inspecting the most solid air filters Tony had ever seen, the Hemsleys were racing northwards up the excellent road from Damascus to Bab al Hawa and the Turkish border.

It is 2,800 miles from Damascus to London. The route through Turkey involves poor roads, high mountains, heavy snowfalls and locals who drive as if there is no tomorrow, which is often the case. Burial grounds are wall-to-wall with accident victims. The drifts were deep in places – even the snowploughs were struggling – but the hard-charging Hemsleys raced from the Syrian capital to Marble Arch in 60 hours. Lucy averaged 80mph along the motorways of Austria, West Germany and Belgium, and hit an indicated 110 on one downhill swoop. Villach to Calais, 850 miles, was covered with just one brief stop to make a call from the border at Aachen.

My wife and I were on the dock at 4am on a cold Sunday morning when Sealink's ferry delivered the Hemsleys to Dover. Exactly 86 minutes later the travel-stained Range Rover was clocked home at Marble Arch, 14 days 19 hours and 26 minutes after leaving Cape Town. 'A wonderful holiday,' John beamed. 'My only regret is that we missed some super scenery by covering so many miles at night.'

Can that time be beaten? Probably. But it will take a great deal of punctilious planning, an exceptionally fine vehicle, lots of luck, superb contacts in critical places and the sort of know-how that John Hemsley has acquired over many years. But the most essential factor could well be a slim, blonde and indomitable Australian wife.

15

A BREEZY TRIBUTE

TO THE BOY KING

1990

This is the life. Your reporter is in Aswan, Egypt. Abdul, the Nile Ritz's barman, has just handed me a tall glass of cold Stella beer to wash away dust accumulated while hurtling across the Nubian Desert. His slightly conspiratorial smile is a reminder that a slightly squiffy guest provided last night's post-prandial entertainment. Llewellin sported a turban, fashioned from a bath towel, while keeping tropical ailments at bay with doses of Old Parr whisky. Colleagues were informed that the eponymous Thomas Parr, who is buried in Westminster Abbey, was born only 12 miles from where I first saw the light of day. According to local lore, Parr lived from 1483 until 1635 and fathered the last of umpteen children when he was 120.

Right now, the most benevolent of zephyrs is whispering across the broad, fast-flowing River Nile, whose waters glow like rose-tinted gold beneath the westering sun. A tall-masted felucca glides by, its sail as graceful as a swallow's wing. I sip my beer while recalling how one of the most mind-blowing drives of a lifetime was made additionally memorable by an incident worthy of *The Guinness Book of Records*.

Peugeot has a reputation for taking the Worshipful Company of Typewriter Tappers to places that few other manufacturers would even consider. This time around, sun-baked southern Egypt, where camshafts and carburettors are heavily outnumbered by camels, was deemed suitable for a get-together with several variations on the lion-badged marque's 605 theme. I was itching to drive the 3.0-litre SV24, which delivers 200bhp at 6,000rpm. Gallic grunt is optimised by the excellent aerodynamics of a body shaped in Pininfarina's studio. But wind-cheating efficiency isn't synonymous with character. By the same token, discreet styling is an asset if you prefer 'stealth bomber' cars to the extrovert variety.

'The automobile is a means of transportation,' we were told during the first of Peugeot's notoriously narcoleptic press briefings. That sensational news kicked-off a fascinating 300-mile day spent driving downstream to Luxor and back. Luxor, probably the most important archaeological centre in a country renowned for such things, was called Thebes by the ancient Egyptians. There were awful puns about Ali Baba and the Forty Thebes as we explored the vast, spellbinding Temple of Amen-Re in Karnak. The most amazing of the temple complex's many links with the Egypt of the Pharaohs is the hypostyle hall, where 134 pillars of carved stone, each 75 feet high, have stood in silent majesty for 3,300 years. My ancestors were living in caves when architects and artists, supported by legions of labourers, toiled to create this wonder of the ancient world.

As for the drive, I partnered another hack, Matthew Carter, as we shared one of Egypt's busiest highways with just about everything from venerable Peugeot 504 taxis to camels, donkeys laden with sugar cane and seriously dead dogs. Ruts and potholes were big enough to be mistaken for bomb craters.

Had today's road and traffic conditions been like yesterday's, the 400-mile flog from Aswan to Abu Simbel and back might have become a little tedious. But the road built in the 1960s, after the Nile was dammed to form Lake Nasser, could have been created specifically for the benefit of fast cars. Apart from gentle undulations, a few long, sweeping curves, and the biggest herd of camels I've ever seen, it was flat, straight, and virtually devoid of other travellers. Carter took the SV24's wheel for the first stint. He grinned, floored the accelerator pedal, glanced westward across the shimmering Nubian Desert's miraged immensity, and said 'If a tyre blows, there's 2,500 miles of sand to slow us down before we reach the Atlantic.'

We didn't have to raise our voices as the 605 went faster and faster. The needle reached the end of its scale, but didn't stop until it was indicating the metric equivalent of 162mph. Despite three brief stops, we averaged just over 100mph all the way to Abu Simbel. Chatting over lunch, nobody could recall ever driving so far so fast.

Abu Simbel witnessed an archaealogical miracle when Lake Nasser was being created. Two great temples, carved into solid rock, were carefully cut into blocks – the total weight was 400,000 tons – then reassembled on higher ground. The biggest had been built for King Ramses II, a world-class egomaniac who ruled the roost about 3,200 years ago. Four statues of the king, each 67 feet high, despite depicting him seated, flank the entrance.

The Guinness Book of Records incident took place when Carter, bowling along at 150mph, overtook George Bishop, a legend in his own lunchtime and one of our profession's most senior citizens. Llewellin, unable to resist a challenge, poked his posterior out the window. This wasn't just a land-speed-record moon. It was a beautifully orchestrated tribute to the most famous of all ancient Egypt's rulers. Carter beeped the 605's horn as the deed was done. 'Toot-and-car-moon!' we hooted.

16

HIGH JINKS IN
THE SAHARA

1991

'You will encounter sand,' we were warned by Corrado Provera, Automobile Peugeot's chain-smoking director of public relations. Sand? Your most intrepid of reporters, a swashbuckling blend of Indiana Jones and Crocodile Dundee, declared his flabber to be well and truly gasted. You must be joking, mon brave. Who would expect to encounter sand while driving across the Sahara, which accounts for approximately 3.5 million square miles of the planet's surface – we're talking about an area roughly 13 times bigger than Texas – and includes the world's most immense dunes among its superlatives?

Having fired an arrow tipped with sarcasm, it behoves me to maintain the British penchant for fair play. This is done without hesitation or reservation, because Corrado's reputation for stating the obvious is nothing to his ability for achieving the impossible. In this case, he talked Peugeot's top brass into letting him mount an expedition the scale and severity of which might well have daunted the likes of Jeep and Land Rover.

The original idea was to mark the end of Peugeot's centenary year, and emphasise the company's long-standing reputation in Third World markets, by inviting a multi-national assortment of automotive scribblers to battle from Morocco to Jordan by way of Algeria, Tunisia, Libya and

Egypt. Iraq's rape of Kuwait put the stopper on that one, if only because the crisis turned poor little Jordan into a front-line state. But the alternative version of *La Piste des Lions* – The Lions' Track – posed an even tougher challenge by delving deeper into the Sahara. Starting in Taroudant, Morocco, and finishing in Nefta, Tunisia, the route covered 5,100 miles, about 2,200 of which were off-road.

The first and last of the expedition's five stages accounted for most of the on-road motoring. True to form, Llewellin was volunteered for what promised to be the hardest slog. It totalled 937 miles. All but 276 of them concentrated right at the end of the fourth and last day, were on desert tracks stippled with the bleached bones of camels. After flying to Djanet, near the point where Algeria, Libya and Niger meet, right on the Tropic of Cancer, we passed just one small, scattered settlement while driving 700 dusty, bone-jarring miles.

We went adventuring in remarkably standard versions of the front-wheel-drive 205, 309, 405 and 605. Peugeot has been active in this part of the world since 1892, so all the *Piste des Lions* cars had been given the standard 'Africanisation' treatment. This consists of beefed-up and slightly raised suspension, ten per cent more body welds, and filters compatible with dirt-laden fuel. Extras deemed prudent for this caper included a two-way radio, an auxiliary fuel tank, steel bash plates at front and rear, and a competition-type ceramic clutch designed to survive an awful lot of wheelspin. Personal luggage had to share stowage space with camping equipment, because even the sybaritic French couldn't make five-star hotels materialise in the middle of the Sahara.

The cars were supported by four-wheel-drive Peugeot P4s – France's version of the Mercedes G-wagen – plus three big, powerful, four-wheel-drive trucks. Typical of back-up vehicles evolved for the Paris–Dakar Rally, the trucks carried spares and tools, food, drink and a mind-boggling array of communications equipment by which my keener colleagues could communicate with the outside world by satellite. Llewellin relied on nothing more sci-fi than a notebook and pen. Here's a digest of what I jotted down.

Monday: Paris to Algiers. Tick the 56th country off my bingo card, then gaze down as Air Algeria's ancient Boeing 737 drones over a sun-baked eternity of desert. Oceans of rippled, puckered sand give way to equally vast expanses of black rock riven by deep, dark chasms from which jagged pinnacles rise like the spears of giants who roamed and ruled in the time before time began. Today's traveller struggles to imagine how bold and determined the first Europeans to cross this awesome void must have been.

Djanet airport's runway is just a pencil mark flanked by one small building. Djanet itself, a remote and attractive little oasis town, is sheltered by the cliffs of the Tassili N'Ajjer, a sandstone massif whose highest point stands over 7,000 feet above sea level. These brutal yet beautiful mountains cover some 50,000 square miles, but few people have ever heard of them. The name is Arabic for Plateau of Rivers. This is not a flight of fancy. Rock paintings, some of which are more than 8,000 years old, make it clear that this wilderness, where sun and rock are now hammer and anvil, was once a place of hunters and herders, farmer and homesteads, elephants, antelopes and domesticated cattle.

We spend the night in Djanet's finest hotel. Fat City! The room shared with Andrew *Road & Track* Bornhop measures four paces by three, has two beds, almost at floor level, one chair, a small chest of drawers, and, more likely than not, hot and cold running scorpions. Time to take a *shufti* at my *Fodor's North Africa* guidebook: 'In the absence of imported entertainment, the Djaneti are keen on local festivities, religious and private,' it reveals. 'Music and dancing are common . . . masked warriors sing, dance and beat the drums while the Djaneti, their long black *haik* leaving the face uncovered, wave garishly coloured bits of muslin.'

Sure enough, after-dinner entertainment not suitable for those of a nervous disposition is provided by yelling, leaping Touareg nomads who clash shields and *just* manage not to give one another the salami-and-kebab treatment with swords and spears. Traditional music, provided by an orchestra of equally enthusiastic twangers and puffers, is amplified by devices handed down from father to son since whenever the most justifiably optimistic of Yamaha salesmen rode into town.

Tuesday: With whom is the only Brit destined to drive? On a mission such as this, a top-notch companion is no less essential than a parachute when sky diving. Bornhop has all the right qualifications. These range from laughing a lot to having desert driving experience. My first-hand knowledge of the subject is zero. He's also young and big enough to push the car while yours truly makes encouraging noises from behind the steering wheel. Unfortunately – for me, not him – he's assigned to partner Kim Derderian, Peugeot Motors of North America's enchanting public relations manager.

One of Corrado Provera's henchmen explains, a little diffidently, that I've been teamed with a German, Peter Hellgut. He looks like a bear with a sore head, but is actually a freelance writer with a sore hand. This will prevent his driving for at least a day. Hellgut takes all of three minutes to announce himself as a diamond in the Star of Africa class. He's the same age as I, has driven across the Sahara twice, speaks excellent English and – bless all the saints – has the most rumbustious and resilient sense of humour. We're going to have a *lot* of fun.

We bid the blacktop farewell in our 1.6-litre 309 within five minutes of leaving the hotel. The surface for the first few miles is washboard, with corrugations that make the eyes rattle like dice in a shaker. Then we plunge into an immense sea of soft, shimmering sand through which the Peugeot snarls, slithers, bucks and roars at what feels like 1,000mph.

'Jeeee-zuss! Off-roading in Wales was never like this!' I yell.

'Bugger Wales!' Hellgut hollers from the depths of his Touareg headdress. 'Power! More power! Slow! Watch out! Bugger that Belgian wanker! Powerpowerpower! Slow! Power! Careful! Aaargh!'

Keeping the right foot hard down is the name of the game in sand with grains that provide no more grip than iced ball bearings dipped in oil. Hellgut delivers a non-stop barrage of jokes, anecdotes, observations and quintessentially Anglo-

Saxon expletives while I hammer the 309 along at 5,000 revs in second. I've never concentrated so hard for so long while driving. The alternative, as more than a few of our Belgian, Spanish, French, Swiss and Portuguese friends have discovered, is a heart-stopping ride on the end of a P4's tow rope.

Djanet is only two hours behind us when the floor begins to smoke. Hellgut says his chauffeur's socks must be on fire, the smell's so awful, then agrees that the clutch is the more likely culprit. In fact, heat from the exhaust is melting the carpet's plastic backing. Dropping to 4,500rpm prevents us from becoming a mobile barbecue. We reach a pass where little imagination is needed to picture naturally sculpted rock formations as the ruins of a colossal fortress. At the start of the climb, a notice in French warns that the track is dangerous for the next 125 miles. To the sign has been added 'Not if we can cycle it. Rog and Tony – 7/2/87'.

When we pitch our tents, amid scrub indicative of water, flies arrive to feast on infidel flesh and blood. As we wait for food, my broad-brimmed Australian hat attracts 'Crocodeel Dondy' plaudits from our Algerian guides. Their equipment spans the ages from new Toyota Land Cruisers to goatskins filled with water. Hellgut goes crazy when he realises that the French have provided gallons of wine, but not a drop of beer, which is what you need after a hard day in the desert. He also jokes about the expedition's female doctor who, in all honesty, could not be mistaken for Brigitte Bardot in her pert and pouting prime. 'By the end of the trip even she will look beautiful,' he asserts, then guffaws something unprintable about ostriches and head-in-the-sand sex.

Wednesday: Hellgut's right hand has recovered, so we now have a fully fledged Sahara specialist to drive the 1.9-litre 405. He's *very* good. We rarely run anything other than first when the burly Berliner is doing his stuff. I quote from my notebook: 'Fast, safe, inspires total confidence. Reads the desert like a strike aircraft's radar. Reacts like lightning to soft sand, hard sand, boulders, washboard, gullies. Fires broadsides in basic Anglo-Saxon when Belgians, time after time, sneak up alongside while the convoy's halted. Then he moves into the lead and bawls "Suck my dust!" while storming along in a full-blooded power slide. What a star!'

We lose an hour or more, waiting for stick-in-the-sand colleagues to catch up, then race across an eternity of flat, firm desert. Hellgut's right hand is beginning to hurt, so I shift gears while he gives 'Up!' or 'Down!' orders and operates the pedals. We call this secret weapon the Voice Controlled Transmission.

Night falls, but there's no sign of the support vehicles. The cars attempt to reach them, but blunder off into a great confusion of dunes. Making progress is no easier than getting out of a maze with your head in a black bag full of talcum powder. We decide to go without food rather than spend the rest of the night getting stuck every five minutes. Beyond the point of wanting to struggle with the tent, we sleep beneath the Sahara's immense canopy of stars. As the temperature drops, almost to freezing point, Hellgut calls for the doctor to warm him up, and suggests ways in which this could be achieved. Fifi does not respond.

Thursday: A night of chattering teeth is followed by a breakfast of orange juice, stale bread and toothpaste. Then we board a 605 with the 3.0-litre V6 engine and 170bhp on tap. Intoxicated by such power, Llewellin loses points for hitting a rock hard enough to puncture one of Monsieur Michelin's tyres. Although incapable of withstanding such shameful abuse, the tyres in general have astonished us all by romping across surfaces that look bad enough to reduce them to shreds. The 605 is big and comfortable, but lacks the extra measure of agility that made the 405 so much fun during yesterday's long drive. Today, eastward views are dominated for hour after hour by dramatic, flat-topped mountains of naked rock. They look like settings for a *Lost World* adventure. Late in the afternoon, fuel tanks that together hold about 40 gallons are refilled in the middle of nowhere, Peugeot having organised a rendezvous with an air-cooled, six-wheel-drive Magirus-Deutz truck. Locals joke and smoke while petrol gushes in all directions from a pump old enough to have lifted water from the bilges of Noah's ark.

The world's biggest sand dunes are in this part of the Sahara. We camp in the lee of one that must be all of sixty miles long and about 1,000 feet high. The sunset is splendid enough to render even Hellgut speechless for 37.89 seconds.

Friday: The P4s start the day by hauling our 1.4-litre 205, and every other car, through exceptionally soft sand. After that, the going's quite easy for 120 miles, despite the threat of a sandstorm. A proper road, albeit with stretches that appear to have been cratered by bombs, then takes us all the way to the remote oilfield settlement of In Amenas. There, watched by locals who think we're crazy, and are right, we pitch our tents beneath a dusty soccer pitch's floodlights. We're back in civilisation, if only by Saharan standards.

By the end of the expedition, as opposed to the end of the leg tackled by your dust-caked chronicler, the overall damage report was impressive by virtue of its brevity. The most significant items, in addition to such trifles as 39 shock absorbers, included a clutch for a 605, a gearbox for a 405, seven driveshafts and one radiator. The delightful Ms Derderian enabled me to add an equally delightful new euphemism to my repertoire. She reported 'changing the oil' in her 309, the engine having been drained by smiting a rock.

17

BRITISH ISLES

OYSTERS AND GUINNESS IN GALWAY

1986

Dicky Walsh, cox'n of the Rosslare lifeboat for many a storm-tossed year – like his father before him – looked as if he had come straight from Central Casting in Hollywood. Built like a barrel, weatherbeaten and genial, eyes twinkling under the peak of an old seaman's cap, he could have been hired to preside over the superb collection of model ships, navigation lights, old photographs and newspaper cuttings, enamel signs and turn-of-the-century posters that make the Hotel Rosslare's bar more fascinating than many a maritime museum. Dicky contemplated the thick, smooth, creamy head of his tenth Guinness, then raised the pint as gently and affectionately as a mother lifting her new baby. 'Wonderful stuff,' he chuckled. 'What a pity there's not eight nights in the week to enjoy it.'

It was easy to agree. No matter how long they may be, visits to Ireland are always too short. You need at least all the time in the world, and then another few days. Time to chat over a glass of stout with the likes of Dicky Walsh; time to wonder what tales could be told by any one of 10,000 ivy-clad ruins; time to walk in St Patrick's footsteps, to explore the lakes and mountains immortalised by William Butler Yeats; time to synchronise the mental gears with a more relaxed way of life; and, more likely than not, time to recover from late nights and laughter.

We had just three days to drive an Audi Coupé GT from Rosslare to Galway, enjoy ourselves at the city's annual Oyster Festival, then travel homewards by way of the Dublin–Holyhead ferry. A true grand tourer – swift and comfortable, sure-footed and remarkably economical – the Audi could have covered the 180 miles between Rosslare and Galway in a morning. But that would have been like wolfing the *menu gastronomique* in a five-star restaurant. Our route, as interesting as it was illogical, spread the journey over 12 easy-going hours. When my wife joked about Irish miles, I gently reminded her that the old unit of measurement was indeed 27 per cent longer than its English counterpart.

Armed with a Michelin map and *The Companion Guide to Ireland* by Brendan Lehane, we went to Wexford and New Ross, which is very old, and then to Kilkenny before looping back toward Cashel. Granted more time, we could have combined having a drink with choosing a coffin in Johnstown, where a sign typical of the details that help make Ireland so memorable proclaimed 'Bar-Lounge-Undertaker'.

Photographer Tim Wren, like countless travellers before him, gasped when he saw the Rock of Cashel, a great fist of limestone rising from the greenest of fields. Fortified long before the dawn of recorded history, it is now crowned with a cluster of evocative buildings. They include a slender and perfectly preserved round tower nearly 900 years old, the chapel built by Cormac Mac Carthaigh, King of Munster, in the first half of the 12th century, and the great cathedral, now open to the sky, that was completed in 1270. Brian Boru, who defeated the Vikings in 1014, was King of Cashel *and* High King of all Ireland.

Five hundred years earlier, St Patrick visited Cashel after being told that King Corc of Munster had decided to become a Christian. The road was long, and the saint old, but Corc wanted to be baptised without delay. When the ceremony was over, the horrified saint realised that his pointed staff had pierced the king's foot. Corc was puzzled by the apology. Knowing how Christ had suffered on the cross, he thought it was an essential part of the ritual.

Cashel is richly endowed with such stories. Henry VII's viceroy, Sir Edward Poynings, burned the cathedral when the Irish rebelled in 1495. His explanation – 'I thought the archbishop was in residence' – was perfectly acceptable to the king. The locals will also tell you that the cathedral was abandoned in the 18th century, because Archbishop Agar was 'a fat, lazy old fellow' and too indolent to walk up the hill. Sunrise on St Patrick's Day is *said* to be framed by the cathedral's east window, we were told. 'But nobody in Cashel has ever got out of bed early enough to see if that's true.'

Why did I hop round St Patrick's Cross three times without stopping? Because the reward, according to a lady who didn't look or sound like a practical joker, was a lifetime free from aching teeth.

It would have been a short way to Tipperary had we not detoured to the Glen of Aherlow. The extra miles were made memorable by southward views across the vale to the steep, whalebacked Galty Mountains. Rising to 3,018 feet, they were a reminder that Ireland is not as flat as a snooker table from coast to coast, despite its reputation for interminable peat bogs. Limerick's crowded streets were an unwelcome reminder that we hadn't wandered out of the 20th century. There was plenty of time to compose a five-liner appropriate in more ways than one:

> *The fleet-footed Audi Coupé,*
> *Makes driving a joy, day by day;*
> *But this traffic's so thick,*
> *That like Sean, Pat and Mick,*
> *All we can do now is pray.*

Bunratty Castle, eight miles beyond Limerick, was a stronghold of the O'Briens who ruled this part of Ireland in the Middle Ages. The fact that they were notorious poisoners is revealed when guests assemble for medieval banquets. Blue-rinsed matrons from Chicago, determined to trace their Irish roots, tackle traditional fare with ring-twinkling fingers while maidens warble 'Danny Boy' to the plangent music of a harp, and wine gushes from earthenware jugs. My passengers had to take my word for all this, because it was mid-afternoon and we wanted to see the Cliffs of Moher before pushing on to Galway.

Roads quiet even by Irish standards took the Audi westwards to the coast at Liscannor, where John Holland was born in 1841. Holland was a Fenian who designed submersibles intended to sink British warships in the struggle for home rule. Ironically, his design was later adopted by the Royal Navy, whose first sub was launched in 1901. Atlantic waves were pounding the majestic Cliffs of Moher, where we braved a stiff, salty breeze to admire stunning views across the Aran Islands to Connemara's distant peaks. These are *real* cliffs, nearly 700 feet high, that rise as vertically as the walls of a stupendous fortress. They are patrolled by wheeling, plunging squadrons of gannets, fulmars, guillemots and bright-billed puffins.

The sun was on its way to the New World when we reached The Burren, an extraordinary plateau of naked limestone formed beneath the sea, then pushed up about 260 million years ago. Huge 'pavements' of smooth rock added to the impression that we were in a region fashioned not by nature, but by legendary heroes who walked the misty world in seven-league boots. A report quilled in Cromwell's time described The Burren as 'savage land yielding neither water enough to drown a man, nor a tree to hang him, nor soil enough to bury'. But rare flowers flourish in the limestone's crevices, and birds of prey share the high places with wild, shaggy, long-horned goats.

The Audi followed the narrow road that ducks and dives, flicks and twists along the coast from The Burren to Galway Bay. The day's first *serious* driving had everything to do with a table booked at Moran's Oyster Cottage, a thatched and whitewashed haven on a peaceful estuary where swans glide like stately galleons. Moran's seafood has been delighting travellers since the 1760s, we were told by 80-year-old Michael Moran, the genial patriach whose son, Willie, now runs the business. Why are the oysters so good? Because they are fresh, said Willie, and the nearby beds are natural, not cultivated. We devoured a dozen, accompanied by Guinness, home-baked brown bread, smoked salmon, prawns and succulent crab claws. All of which made me wonder why tomorrow's festivities in Galway included Mayor Mulholland being presented with the season's first oyster. I put the question to Willie Moran. 'They've been in season for nearly a month,' he grinned, 'since the beginning of September. But this is Ireland.'

The Great Southern Hotel is the place to stay for the Galway Oyster Festival. It hosts the social shindigs and overlooks Eyre Square, where the parade starts. The bar was packed with fun-loving folk from Ireland and overseas. America's hope for the World Oyster Opening Championship had travelled 6,000 miles from Washington State. Norway's contender was a Japanese gentleman who explained that he ran a seafood restaurant in Oslo. We dubbed him Magnus Kamikaze, Last of the Samurai Vikings.

We awoke to what the Irish call a soft day. Rain drifted from a sky the colour of old pewter, giving revellers every excuse to chase breakfast down with large measures of Irish whiskey potent enough to fuel a spacecraft. Outside, oysters were being given away by old ladies in traditional bonnets and shawls when Eyre Square suddenly erupted to the stirring music of the Friendship Band from Belfast. Clad in fishermen's smocks and caps, marching behind a leader whose smile made up for the sun's absence, they bounced through *Tiger Rag* and other jaunty, toe-tapping favourites before launching into *The New Colonial March* when the parade started.

Old Galway's narrow streets echoed to the sound of cornets and trombones, drums and cymbals, as the Pearl of the Oyster – a serene, dark-haired beauty with eyes like polished ebony – made her way to the 16th-century Spanish Arch in an open carriage. There she made a speech of welcome, in English and lilting Gaelic, before presenting the ceremonial mollusc to Mayor Mulholland. Then the world and his wife poured into a marquee erected where wine and brandy used to be unloaded from Spanish galleons. Chowder, oysters, smoked salmon and other seafood abounded, and Guinness flowed freely enough to suggest a pipeline running across Ireland from the 58-acre brewery in Dublin. None of us could recall ever seeing such an amazing assortment of people having such a good time together. Nuggety little men, who almost certainly earned their daily bread the hard way, joked and clinked glasses with Sloane O'Ranger types. Red-faced farmers in tweeds thick enough to conceal several badgers stood shoulder to shoulder with tall, elegant and quite sensationally beautiful blonde twins straight from the realms of fantasy. Ulstermen raised their glasses to drink the health of staunch Republicans while contestants from six nations steeled themselves for the World Oyster Opening Championship.

They were watched with professional interest by Willie Moran. He retired, to give the others a chance, after setting a new world record by opening and neatly presenting 30 oysters in 91 seconds during the 1984 festival. Peter Manzi from Green's Champagne and Oyster Bar in Duke Street, St James's, London, needed just over two minutes to retain the title won in '85. His most impressive rival, the extrovert Patrick Gaborit from France, was built like Mont Blanc. Patrick's idea of a light snack is probably a horse sandwiched between two breadvans. Magnus Kamikaze finished last, despite tremendous vocal support from a crowd that thought there was something wonderfully Irish about an oyster-loving Nipponese Norseman. Due to finish at 3pm, the oyster luncheon was roaring along at peak revs in top gear when we left just before five – 'The bar closes in November,' the master of ceremonies had announced – and made our way back to the Great Southern past street entertainers and pubs filled with music and laughter. My intake had been limited to one small glass of Guinness, because we were due to meet Willie Moran's brother at the oysterbeds, 12 miles from Galway. Wading thigh-deep, armed with a basket, and a huge rake, John Moran needed little more than ten minutes to fill a small trailer whose contents represented a great deal of money. He grinned when asked why the family's oysters were held in such high esteem. 'There are several reasons, but their quality has a lot to do with these beds, here on the estuary, having just the right blend of fresh and salt water. But I prefer a good steak, myself.'

Moran's renown is rivalled by that of Paddy Burke's pub in nearby Clarinbridge, so we stopped for a dozen on our way back to Galway. They were excellent, we agreed, but not in *quite* the same class as Moran's. Tim Wren said they were more like 'ordinary' oysters, but that didn't deter him from ordering another platter.

The Galway Oyster Festival's social climax is a banquet and ball in the Great Southern. Guests in dinner jackets and magnificent full-length, off-the-shoulder dresses worthy of a Buck House binge sipped pre-prandial drinks to the music of the indefatigable Friendship Band, now supplemented by a mighty sousaphone. The bar did actually close at midnight . . . but for only an hour. Next morning, a red-eyed waiter reported that the last revellers had departed shortly after 7am. Later, much later, they would be giving serious consideration to founding a society dedicated to the prohibition of noisy breakfast cereals. It was reasonable to suppose that the most dedicated dancers and drinkers had covered far fewer miles per gallon than the Audi.

Sunday's deserted roads made the going quick and easy as we headed for Dublin by way of Ballinasloe and Athlone, a town whose castle defied 25,000 attackers after the Battle of the Boyne in 1690. Why were there were no regrets about not having time to explore the mountains, lakes and rugged coasts of Connemara and Donegal? Because that gave us the best possible reason for planning another jaunt to the Galway Oyster Festival. Knowing the Irish, Cox'n Dicky Walsh's eight-day week will have been adopted by then.

THE LITTLE MAN
WITH THE BIG HAT

1987

We all need heroes. On the wall by my desk is a photograph taken in 1857. The background is a mass of immense chains, forged to help launch an ill-fated leviathan whose length and tonnage would not be exceeded for the better part of half a century. In the middle of the picture stands a man sporting a hat like a steamboat's funnel. Dark eyes glint in a strong, confident face framed by black sideburns, neatly trimmed. A cigar juts from a corner of his mouth. He is wearing a lapelled waistcoat embellished with watch and chain, and a loose-fitting jacket that reaches almost to his knees. Hands are thrust into the pockets of mud-caked trousers. This famous photograph is a portrait of Isambard Kingdom Brunel, the indefatigable engineer whose genius helped make Britain the first great industrial nation. He designed railways, bridges, the world's longest tunnel, the world's biggest ships, a prefabricated hospital for the Crimean War, and a floating siege gun propelled by steam. The 'island' bar characteristic of many Victorian pubs was his idea. It provided swifter service for the Great Western Railway's multitude of passengers. When a coin lodged in his windpipe, and the operation performed by London's most eminent surgeon failed to remove it, the indomitable engineer devised the apparatus that did the trick.

Born in Portsmouth in 1806, Sir Marc and Sophia Brunel's

only son soon made it clear that he had inherited his father's gift for civil and mechanical engineering. Both needed to take little more than a glance to detect fundamental design errors. Isambard was still a schoolboy when he predicted, correctly, the imminent collapse of one of Hove's proud new buildings. His teachers included Louis Breguet, the famous maker of watches and scientific instruments, but IKB's formal education ended at 16, when he became his father's assistant.

Two years later, the Brunels set about driving the world's first underwater tunnel beneath the River Thames in London. The revolutionary tunnelling shield perfected by Sir Marc would have worked well had the geologists been correct when they predicted a thick layer of clay between Wapping and Rotherhithe. But the ground was weak. Objects as big as a shovel fell through from the riverbed. Isambard directed this titanic struggle after his father became seriously ill, spending up to four days and nights underground without a break. Early in 1828, he was lucky to escape with his life when the Thames flooded the workings, killing six men. The project was abandoned, but work started again in 1835. Today, the tunnel is part of the London Underground network's Metropolitan Line.

Brunel was elected a Fellow of the Royal Society at the ripe old age of 24. A year later, competing with such established talents as Thomas Telford, he was appointed to design and build a bridge across the Avon Gorge at Bristol. But constant shortages of money made this one of several projects that failed to reach fruition during the years of frustration that followed the tunnel disaster.

Brunel's luck then changed dramatically. On 7 March, 1833, the young man was appointed to engineer what became the Great Western Railway from London to Bristol. Enthralled by what many would have considered an awesome burden of responsibility – the task involved planning and supervising the building of the line – he worked for eight years at a pace hectic enough to ruin the average mortal's health in eight months. Brunel often started at 5am and kept going until the early hours of the next day. In addition to engineering the line, he had to negotiate with landowners, and fight many of the GWR's battles in the House of Commons.

This human whirlwind covered distances far greater than many a modern motorist, but had to rely on coaches and hired horses before the railway opened. They lacked speed, reliability and flexibility, so Brunel designed himself a black carriage, dubbed the *Flying Hearse*. Horse-powered, fast and comfortable, it carried everything from plans and engineering instruments to a large supply of his favourite cigars. The seat folded down to form a bed when he treated himself to the luxury of sleep.

What car would Brunel have chosen had he been able to send a time machine on a shopping trip into the closing years of the 20th century's penultimate decade? That question merited careful consideration when I decided to trace his tracks from London to Cornwall. Described as 'an artist and a visionary' by his biographer, L T C Rolt, Brunel was given the GWR's top job a few weeks before celebrating his 27th birthday and was being paid £2,000 a year at a time when farm labourers were being deported for having the temerity to claim the equivalent of 75p for a six-day week. The best choice, I decided, would be a Bentley. Brunel would have appreciated the combination of adequate power, leather-trimmed luxury and suspension firm enough for a reasonable rate of progress to be maintained on minor West Country roads.

God's Wonderful Railway starts from Paddington Station, where Brunel's three great ribbed arches of wrought iron still soar above the platforms. The adjoining Great Western Royal Hotel was the biggest in Britain when the doors opened in 1854. Brunel was the first chairman of the board. A small bedroom on the fourth floor of this chateau-like edifice then cost the same as half a pint of port. Figures symbolising Peace, Plenty, Industry and Science looked down on the Bentley from the hotel's elaborate pediment. Paddington Station and the Great Western Royal combined to form the starting point of an international transport system typical of Brunel's vision. You could spend a night at the hotel, plough through a vast breakfast, walk a few paces to your train, travel to Bristol, and from there sail to New York on a ship also designed by the GWR's resident genius.

The little man in the stovepipe hat was an acid-tongued perfectionist when provoked. One luckless assistant was sent a letter describing him as 'a cursed, lazy, inattentive, apathetic vagabond'. Withering sarcasm was another IKB speciality. The manager of the railway refreshment rooms at Swindon penned a peevish epistle after hearing from a certain Mr Player that the engineer had complained about the coffee. Brunel's reply was a classic. 'Dear Sir:' he hissed. 'I assure you Mr Player was wrong in supposing I thought you purchased inferior coffee. I thought I said to him I was surprised you should buy such bad roasted corn. I did not believe you had such a thing as coffee in the place. I am certain I never tasted any. I have long ceased to make complaints at Swindon. I avoid taking anything there when I can help it.'

Swindon now serves a fair cup of coffee, but a glass of North Star beer would have been appropriate. Why? Because *North Star* was the locomotive that hauled the first train when the line from London to Maidenhead was opened, in the summer of 1838. Built at Robert Stephenson's works in Newcastle-on-Tyne, and originally intended for the New Orleans Railway, *North Star* pulled 200 passengers at 36mph. The veteran was scrapped in 1906, but a superb replica is the focal point of the Great Western Museum in Swindon. The Brunel Room's exhibits include wonderfully detailed and very artistic drawings for the suspension bridge across the Avon Gorge, a model of one of the long, lofty timber viaducts designed for the Cornwall Railway, and a fine portrait painted by the engineer's brother-in-law. The Gooch Gallery commemorates Sir Daniel Gooch, the GWR's first locomotive superintendent. Gooch was an MP for two decades, but never made a speech. 'It would be a great advantage to business if there were a greater number who followed my example,' he said.

The museum is part of the new town that became the GWR's technical nerve centre. Brunel designed its terraced limestone cottages in association with Matthew Digby Wyatt, the architect who later helped him create Paddington Station.

To quote Matthew Derrick, whose *Brunel's Britain* is no less commendable than Rolt's classic biography, the 'railway village is yet another example of Brunel's desire to provide reasonable living conditions for the work force'.

The most astonishing fact about the line from London to Bristol is that it was the work of a young man with no previous experience of railways. There was very little reference material available, because Brunel was appointed only eight years after the opening of the line between Stockton and Darlington heralded the dawn of a new age. Casting aside all but a few of the most fundamental precedents, Brunel built a track with rails 7ft 0.5in apart instead of accepting the 4ft 8.5in standard gauge favoured by George Stephenson. The decision caused a furore in engineering circles, but the young man stuck to his guns, as always. Calculations and experiments had convinced him that the broad gauge would mean bigger engines, more power and greater comfort. Gooch's mighty locos lived up to expectations, eventually thundering between London and Exeter in well under five hours. But conservatism held sway elsewhere, and the last broad-gauge train reached the end of the line in 1892.

The Bentley wafted westwards at a sedate 55–60mph, giving me plenty of time to reflect on the fact that Brunel's astonishing portfolio of talents included the ability to focus on details without losing sight of his grand, long-term objectives. For instance, he filled his notebooks with local rainfall statistics, jotted down the best types of grass to bind soil, and sketched small architectural features to enhance the GWR's buildings.

Brunel was also a fearless, inspirational leader of men. His courage had been proved beyond all doubt during those battles beneath the Thames. He now supervised the immense and extremely dangerous drive to complete the Box Tunnel between Swindon and Bath. It was he who took command when storms of tropical ferocity flooded the Thames valley, reducing the great cutting east of Reading to little more than two miles of steep-sided swamp. The tunnel, whose elegant western portal we admired from the A4 in the Wiltshire village of Box, was the biggest single challenge faced by Brunel on the way to Bristol. Before work started, one of his most persistent and vociferous opponents, Dr Dionysius Lardner, 'proved' that westbound trains would accelerate to 120mph if their brakes failed. All passengers would perish, he declared. Nobody could survive such a speed. Lardner later proved, beyond all doubt, that it was impossible for a coal-fired ship to cross the Atlantic.

Nearly two miles long, by far the greatest project of its kind ever undertaken anywhere in the world at that time, the tunnel through the limestone hill behind Box called for the excavation of almost 250,000 tons of rock and soil. Water poured in after winter storms, a ton of candles were burned every week, 30 million bricks were needed to line the walls and vaulted roof. Accidents claimed more than 100 lives during the five-year struggle. The rising sun is said to send a shaft of light right through the tunnel on 9 April. There are no prizes for guessing the date of Isambard Kingdom Brunel's birthday.

It was early afternoon when we reached Bristol, where tangible links with the engineer are thick on the ground. Here his first ship, the *Great Western*, was completed in 1837. His second, *Great Britain*, was launched by Prince Albert, six years later. The *Great Britain* was the first ocean-going iron ship to be driven by a propeller. Power came from four single-cylinder engines, which formed an inverted 'V'. Each piston was just over seven feet across, punched a two-yard stroke and produced about 300 horsepower from 7,200 litres. Brunel's epochal ship was strong enough to survive for almost a year after running aground on the storm-lashed coast of County Down and to defy Cape Horn's wrath on many voyages to Australia and San Francisco.

In 1886, long after Brunel's death, she left South Wales with a cargo of coal, which shifted during a storm in the South Atlantic. Badly damaged, the *Great Britain* limped to the safety of the Falkland Islands. A survey concluded that she was too far gone for repair, so one of the most important vessels in the history of seafaring spent the next half-century as a hulk in which wool was stored. In 1937 she was towed the few miles from Port Stanley to Sparrow Cove. Holes were smashed in the hull, and what Brunel had called 'the finest ship in the world' settled down, fortunately in shallow water.

Thirty years later, Dr Ewan Corlett, a marine architect with vision, audacity and confidence worthy of Brunel himself, launched a campaign that eventually succeeded in bringing the *Great Britain* back to Bristol, back to the dry dock where she was built. Admiring her graceful lines from the depth of that dock, we could appreciate the awe and pride she must have inspired when new. The *Great Britain* was then the world's biggest ship, 322 feet long from graceful bow to ornate stern. Restoration work watched by more than 100,000 visitors a year has been going on since 1970.

We threaded our way across the city to Clifton, a suburb of steep hills climbed by terrace upon terrace of elegant houses, Georgian and Regency, with what could well be Britain's finest collection of ornate, cast-iron balconies. Walter Owen 'WO' Bentley and his brothers were educated at Clifton College, a short stroll from the gorge-spanning suspension bridge that was completed in 1864, five years after the engineer's death. Rolt points out that the original plans had to be altered, but adds: 'The broad principles of the grand design were still Brunel's and today . . . in a world satiated with engineering marvels, the grandeur of it all can still uplift the heart. More surely than any lineaments in stone or pigment, the aspiring flight of its single splendid span has immortalised the spirit of the man who conceived it.'

The next morning's first destination was the River Tamar, on the outskirts of Plymouth, where Brunel spanned 1,100ft with a bridge combining beams, suspension chains and huge arches in the form of two elliptical, wrought-iron tubes, each weighing more than 1,000 tons. The central pier rises from water 70 feet deep at high tide. Built to carry the railway into Cornwall, the Royal Albert Bridge was formally opened by the Prince Consort in 1859.

The Bentley then nosed through a tangled skein of narrow lanes to Starcross, on the broad estuary between Exeter and

Dawlish. The village's main street is dominated by a big building that could have been transplanted from a *piazza* in the heart of Italy and is the only significant memorial to Brunel's one great failure. The engineer decided to use 'atmospheric power' rather than conventional steam locomotives on the South Devon Railway. The driving force was air pressure acting on a torpedo-like piston running in a knee-high iron pipe between the rails. The piston was connected to the train through a continuous 'flap valve' made of leather kept pliable by whale and seal oil. Pumping stations like the one at Starcross evacuated air from the pipe ahead of the train. Nature's dislike of even a partial vacuum did the rest.

A great deal of money was invested, and there were days when trains whooshed along at 70mph, but even Brunel eventually had to admit defeat. The main problem was the leather valve. Under constant attack from salt-laden air and voracious rodents, it was plagued by leaks that greatly reduced the system's efficiency.

What became of Isambard Kingdom Brunel? He had terrible problems building the *Great Eastern* whose enormous launching chains are the backdrop for the photograph on my office wall. She gradually took shape on the muddy shore of the Isle of Dogs, downstream from central London, and was designed to carry enough coal to sail from England to Australia and back without refuelling. Nearly 700ft long and displacing 32,000 tons, she was destined to be the world's longest ship for 41 years. Another seven passed before her tonnage was exceeded. This in an age when technology was accelerating faster than ever before.

But progress was intolerably slow as Brunel and his colleagues wrestled to construct and launch a vessel of unprecedented size. Photographs show how the jaunty figure of 1857 became the haggard old man of 1859. Isambard Kingdom Brunel died in September of that year, while the *Great Eastern* was on her maiden voyage.

19

WIZARDS OF OOZE

1988

Heavy rain had turned the track over the Welsh mountains into a ribbon of deep, stinking mud that sloshed, squelched, sucked and slurped like a voracious giant squid in a sea of spaghetti. I was concentrating hard, this not being the best of places for an unscheduled stop, but the corner of my left eye detected a sudden movement, deep in the valley. I turned just in time to glimpse a dark, sinister, sharp-edged shape trailing a wake of rolling thunder. Our little convoy – Land Rover County, Mitsubishi Shogun, Isuzu Trooper – had indeed climbed high enough for us to glance *down* into the cockpit of a hurtling RAF jet. No wonder we felt on top of the world.

That brief encounter with the Tornado was not typical of the two days spent zig-zagging through Wales, from Swansea Bay to the Snowdonia National Park. Following ancient tracks little used since the 19th century, we saw more sheep than people, more crows than cottages, more fords than Fords. Getting away from civilisation is the great pleasure of off-road driving. There were towns, of course. But the biggest dotted along the 300-mile route – Llandovery, Tregaron, Rhayader, Machynlleth, Bala – were quiet enough, out of season, to be advertised as insomnia cures by the Wales Tourist Board.

We crossed Offa's Dyke to find out if the Shogun and Trooper were worthy rivals for what Solihull's drum-beaters describe as the 'comfort and style' Land Rover. We also wondered if any of the trio would emerge as a serious, cost-cutting alternative to the superb, fashionable, but brutally expensive Range Rover. All three contenders were powered by turbo-boosted diesels.

Good companions are more important than four-wheel drive, coil springs, differential locks and low-range gears, because life's not worth living if you can't have a few laughs over the alfresco beer and butties. The team assembled for this expedition rated top marks under that heading. Richard Bremner, deputy editor of *Car* magazine, shared the M4 from London with group art director Adam Stinson and photographer Tim Wren. Determined to avoid *Car* being accused of male chauvinist piggery, I enlisted two lady drivers – Mrs Llewellin and Dr Kate Keohane. Keohane's a great traveller whose experiences include camel-trekking in north-west India, but this was to be her first crack at off-roading on four wheels, rather than four legs. Her medical expertise would be most welcome, if only to suggest hangover cures.

We joined forces at the Seabank Hotel in Porthcawl. Next morning was crisp and clear, and Exmoor's distant hills looked close enough to touch. Mrs Llewellin, the daughter of a tough old livestock dealer from the Welsh Marches, celebrated by haggling the price of two flasks of the hotel's coffee down from £4.50 to £2.

Thirty miles separated us from Sarn Helen and our first attempt at anything rougher than the previous night's post-prandial port. We nose-to-tailed north, leaving Swansea Bay to climb a deep, wooded valley punctuated by platoons of terraced cottages, abandoned coal mines and other reminders of the Industrial Revolution.

Sarn Helen is said to be named after the Welsh princess who married Magnus Maximus, a thruster ambitious enough to proclaim himself Emperor of Britain in the good old days, when all you needed were a strong arm and a sharp sword. The southern section crosses Fforest Fawr's high moorland before petering out near a well-preserved fort on the River Usk, between Brecon and Sennybridge. It was the main road through Wales in Roman times, but precious little maintenance work has been done since the legions hurried home to fight Alaric and his Visigoths. That was about 1,600 years ago.

Fforest Fawr was beautiful that morning, a wilderness of wind-rippled browns and greens, of moss, fern and lichen, of rowans and hawthorns steaming gently as the sun soothed boughs diamond-bright from the previous night's heavy rain. Fast-flowing water sluiced the tyre tops as we forded the River Neath, where shapes lurking a few inches beneath the surface turned out to be slabs of limestone, not Celtic crocodiles. Sarn Helen's landmarks include Maen Madoc, a slender monolith carved with ancient, weathered writing, a meeting place for the hobbits and elves of Middle Earth. At its base were offerings left by travellers who must have passed this way a day or two earlier – plastic bags and cartons, sharp-edged cans, wrappers, a broken bottle. The latterday orcs who leave their rubbish behind should be staked out, naked, and left to the mercy of carrion crows. They don't deserve the leniency of a public flogging.

It was Keyhole Kate's turn to drive the County when we reached the first tricky stretch. Like the rest of us, at one time or another, she had difficulty with the stubby lever that has to be moved sideways to engage low range and lock the differential. Bremner later had a nasty moment when it jumped out, leaving him in neutral when he needed the lowest of low gears to crawl down a very steep slope. Keohane also discovered what can happen when you lose track of where the front wheels are pointing while struggling to get out of deep, muddy ruts. When the tyres bit, she suddenly found herself heading more due west than north-east.

Vehicles were switched again before the longish road run that took us to Llandovery, then north to the Llyn Brianne reservoir. Llandovery is where the Welsh drovers – hardy souls who herded cattle, sheep, pigs and even geese to markets in far-off England – established their own Bank of the Black Ox.

The Trooper set a cracking pace on the road that loops and roller-coasters above Llyn Brianne for many a mile, then we paused to picnic at Soar-y-Mynydd, a tiny chapel remote almost beyond belief. The assembled multitude were treated to the rare delight of your reporter playing the opening notes of the *Skye Boat Song* with one finger on the foot-powered organ. That exhausted my repertoire, so we tackled the trail over the mountain to Llanddewi Brefi. The track starts with a formidably steep slab of crumbling rock followed by a long pull up deep ruts. The Shogun impressed by getting up in high-range-first while the County and Trooper relied on stump-tugging low. The Shogun's driver, Mrs Llewellin, later admitted that she had clean forgotten to juggle the range-change lever.

An hour later, fingers were crossed tight enough for our medical adviser to worry about circulation problems. The convoy was heading due north again, this time on a route pioneered by medieval monks on their way from Llandovery to Strata Florida Abbey. They must have been able to walk on water, because the track is forever dipping into the River Tywi. It was deep enough to wash bonnet tops. This route by-passed Tregaron, where I once spent a seriously convivial night drinking Old Sheep Dip whisky in the Talbot Hotel with P J O'Rourke, one of America's finest writers.

There's always a hint of the Wild West about Tregaron on a Saturday night. Sure enough, a wedding party degenerated into a colossal punch-up while O'Rourke and the Llewellins talked the hind legs of several donkeys. His award-winning account of the trip included the following: 'Our tab outran the wedding's within an hour, and by midnight we were as drunk as any leek-wearing Taffy you could find in a day's ride by sheepback . . . How do you tell the bride at a Welsh ceremony? It's important, because she's the one you're not supposed to punch in the face. In the morning Llewellin looked as if he'd been on the losing side, but he couldn't remember whether he'd gotten into a fight or just finished the bottle of Old Sheep Dip.'

Our target for the night was the Elan Valley Hotel, near Rhayader. Getting there the hard way took us due east along a track. In my experience, this continuation of the Monks' Way has always been rough and muddy in places, but not too difficult. However, I knew that a few yards of relatively good going had been washed away, leaving an apparently bottomless bog little more solid than oxtail soup. The light was fading fast when we reached that lonely spot. Most of the gap had been plugged with logs and rocks, but a vehicle's length looked distinctly iffy. Stinson reckoned the Range Rover could make it. Range Rover? I should have mentioned that art director and snapper were lording it over the peasants in Land Rover's luxurious flagship.

Gung-ho Stinson's heart was in the right place – but the Range Rover was in the mire until its stablemate came to the rescue. Reluctant to make a lengthy detour – 'Never waste good drinking time!' was Wren's battle cry – we embarked on a DIY road-building exercise. Softly-softly is generally the name of the off-road game, but there are times when a judicious use of welly is just what the doctor ordered. This was one of them – and the prescription worked. All four vehicles bucked through without a split-second's hesitation. We crossed the soggy wilderness under driving rain, skirted the Claerwen reservoir, reached a proper road and sped through tunnels of trees where every leaf danced like a whirling dervish in the headlights.

Alan Lewis and his staff made us welcome at the Elan Valley, just as his predecessor had greeted Queen Elizabeth and the Duke of Edinburgh when the Claerwen was officially opened – if that's what you do with a reservoir – exactly a quarter of a century earlier. Three of the team tip-toed off to bed after a good meal, but Keohane joined the Llewellins for a nightcap in the public bar, where the domino team were celebrating a victory fit to be ranked alongside Trafalgar and Waterloo. One character identified Doc Kate as just what was needed to make life sweeter on his lonely farm, high in the hills. Negotiations were entrusted to our Haggler-in-Chief, Mrs Llewellin. She was close to agreeing a price when mine host called it a day. We asked Keohane's suitor how he was going to get home. 'With great difficulty,' he laughed.

Bulging with breakfast, we hurried in the general direction of Aberystwyth before striking due north towards where Plynlimon, source of Wye and Severn, looms above the Nant-y-Moch reservoir's dam. On to Machynlleth for fish and chips, down the A493 and a minor road, then over the hills on a wonderful track that ends near Tywyn. This one climbs through ravines too narrow for a king-sized American off-roader, snakes along a near-vertical slope with little more than a tyre's width between you and eternity, and eventually reaches one of the finest vantage points in Wales. On a clear day, which this was, you can see the whole of Cardigan Bay – an immense crescent that sweeps the eye from Bardsey Island to Pembrokeshire to Snowdonia's peaks and, in the south, high hills that roll away towards the Brecon Beacons. The main hazard on the way down was a wicked gradient of saturated turf. Even *thinking* about the brakes would have been tantamount to suicide.

Inland by way of Dolgellau and Bala, then back to the rough stuff for a crossing of the Berwyns. Part of the climb was muddy, but good tyres and take-it-easy tactics chugged us to the top at about 1,000rpm in high range's lowest gear. It was dark when we reached Llanarmon Dyffryn Ceiriog, and there was more off-roading ahead, but the native guide was now on home ground, near Oswestry. Despite that, I nearly fell off my perch when the headlights picked out a sodden figure pushing a racing bicycle across the moor.

Votes were cast when we reached Castell Llewellin. The Shogun came out on top. All placed it first for road work, and all but one rated it second only to the Land Rover, which scored maximum points for off-road ability, when the going got tough. But my memories kept flashing back to that brief encounter with the RAF. The best way to off-road across the Welsh mountains has to be in the cockpit of a low-flying Tornado.

20

THE COLOSSUS OF ROADS

1989

Take a deep breath, because Thomas Telford's story is indeed breathtaking. Born on 9 August, 1757, this son of a Scottish shepherd was destined to become Britain's greatest builder of roads and bridges since Roman times. Robert Southey, Poet Laureate, nicknamed him 'Pontifex Maximus' and 'The Colossus of Roads'. He was elected a Fellow of the Royal Societies of London and Edinburgh, and became the Institution of Civil Engineers' first president. Sweden, grateful for Telford's work on the Gotha Canal, dubbed him a Knight of the Royal Order of Vasa. All this was a far cry from childhood, when 'Laughing Tam' earned five shillings a year, and a pair of socks, for herding livestock and running errands.

He lived in the age of four-legged horsepower, but packed more miles into year after year than the average modern motorist. The roads, apart from those he built himself, were atrocious. Projects in which the indefatigable Scot was involved, to a greater or lesser extent, included the London–Holyhead road, the world's biggest bridge, the Caledonian Canal, docks and harbours scattered as far afield as Dover and the Hebrides, drainage schemes in East Anglia, a church or two, the highway from Warsaw to Russia, a bridge over the Danube at Budapest, and the soaring 'Stream in the Sky' aqueduct on the Llangollen Canal.

Telford's life was so nomadic that his temporary lodgings in the Salopian Coffee House in Charing Cross, London, were temporary from 1800 until 1821. When he bought his own home at 24 Abingdon Street, Westminster, the Salopian's new owner was horrified. He had just paid an extra £750 – a very substantial sum – for the honour of having such a famous man as a resident.

It is difficult to picture Telford working less than eight round-the-clock days a week, five weeks a month, but he found time to write poetry, translate Latin verse into English, teach himself French and German . . . and darn his own socks.

When he died, a few weeks after his 77th birthday, the engineer was laid to rest in Westminster Abbey, near another of the Industrial Revolution's greatest heroes, Robert Stephenson. Time passed. Technology accelerated at an unprecedented rate, powered by the hissing, smoking majesty of steam. Thomas Telford's reputation was eclipsed by that of Isambard Kingdom Brunel, the charismatic genius born almost half a century later into a very different world whose foundations Telford had striven so long and hard to lay. But fate was eventually to reward the shepherd's son with a tribute given to no other engineer. In 1968, the huge town that now straddles the London–Holyhead road, east of Shrewsbury, was named in honour of Thomas Telford's achievements.

Having decided to spend a few days following in his footsteps, venturing as far north as the Pentland Firth, all I had to do was select the most appropriate vehicle. Reaching that decision took all of a minute, because one contender towered above the rest, literally and metaphorically. Telford, an eminently practical and understandably frugal man, would have been delighted by the diesel-drinking Range Rover's unique blend of space and pace, by its modest thirst and lack of ostentation, by its lofty build – useful when out on surveys – and its ability to keep right on *beyond* the end of the road.

Armed with maps and books – including L T C Rolt's superb *Thomas Telford*, Derrick Beckett's invaluable *Telford's Britain* and Samuel Smiles's *Lives of the Engineers*, first published in 1862 – I left home one Friday afternoon, heading for Langholm, on the A7 north of Carlisle. My night in the Eskdale Hotel, right opposite the library partially endowed by Telford, would have been peaceful had it not been for trucks thundering along the little town's narrow main street, a clock that chimed loud enough to be heard in Tierra del Fuego, and a gang of pre-Neanderthal drunks who bellowed like wild animals until halfway between midnight and breakfast.

Early next morning, I followed the deserted B907 up Eskdale to the old Westerkirk parish burial ground at Bentpath. Tall, lichen-mottled headstones stood sentinel in a landscape speckled with sheep and a great strutting of pheasants. No sound was louder than the clear, swift, pebble-bedded river's cheerful babble as I searched for, and eventually found, the stone carved in memory of 'John Telford who after living thirty three years as an unblameable shepherd' died on 12 November, 1757. That simple tribute was cut by his son, Thomas, who was born nearby, three months before his father's death, in the remote valley of the Meggat Water. A clump of trees now marks the site of the hillside cottage.

Back on the B907, a simple memorial to the engineer faces the school he attended before being apprenticed to a stonemason in Langholm. He worked on the bridge that still spans the Esk, gradually mastered his craft, then walked to Edinburgh, where an elegant new city was growing to the north of the castle.

Two years later, in 1782, Telford went to London, and was employed in the building of Somerset House. By chance, his burgeoning talents attracted the attention of William Pulteney, Member of Parliament for Shrewsbury, who was said to be the richest commoner in the land. Blessed with an income of £50,000 a year – several million in today's money – he invited the young man from Westerkirk to turn Shrewsbury's medieval castle, perched on a sandstone bluff high above the meandering Severn, into a suitably palatial residence. Pulteney also pulled all the strings to get his protégé appointed Surveyor of Public Works for the County of Salop. Telford retained the title until the end of his long life.

He had hoped to become an architect, but was steered into civil engineering by the County of Salop appointment. Between 1790 and 1796 he was responsible for about 40 bridges in Shropshire alone. His career total was more than 1,000. The first, built of sandstone at a cost of £5,800, still spans the Severn at Montford Bridge, five miles north-west of Shrewsbury. It was designed to cope with nothing more weighty than horse-drawn carts, but has stood the test of time just as resolutely as the majority of Telford's works. Unlike their modern counterparts, the men of the Industrial Revolution built structures in the pious hope and expectation that they would endure until Judgement Day.

High hills crossed by narrow, serpentine roads rise between Eskdale and the main road to Glasgow. Sensible folk were still savouring the last of their haggis and marmalade when the Range Rover reached the A74 that links Carlisle and Glasgow. Telford knew this route well, because, to quote Samuel Smiles, it was in 'so ruinous a state as often seriously to delay the mail and endanger the lives of travellers' before an Act of Parliament authorised Telford to do his stuff. 'Probably the finest piece of road which up to that time had been made,' was Samuel Smiles's opinion.

I detoured to Lanark, where Telford's superb Cartland Crags Bridge – three stone arches spanning a wooded chasm – sweeps traffic almost 130 feet above the Mouse Water, then crossed Glasgow and headed for the Highlands up the western side of Loch Lomond.

Telford devoted an immense amount of time and energy to improving communications in the Highlands, and also to punctuating the region's formidable coast with safe harbours built under the auspices of the British Fisheries Society. Samuel Smiles makes it perfectly clear just how isolated and primitive this part of Britain was before another Act of Parliament gave Telford the go-ahead. 'The country lying on the west of the Great Glen' – which extends from Fort William to Inverness – 'was absolutely without a road . . . It even began to be feared that the country would become entirely depopulated, and it became a matter of national concern to devise methods of opening up the district so as to develop its industry and afford improved means of sustenance for its population. There being no roads, there was little use for carts. In the whole county of Caithness there was scarcely a farmer who owned a wheel-cart. Burdens were conveyed usually on the backs of ponies, but quite often on the backs of women. The interior of the county of Sutherland being almost inaccessible, the only track lay along the shore, amongst rocks and sand, covered by the sea at every tide. The people . . . lived in family with their pigs and cattle . . . and spent the whole of their time in indolence and sloth.'

Telford alleviated the problem by driving mile after mile of road along lonely glens, across rivers, over moorland and mountain pass. Many routes ran westward, forging links between the Great Glen, the coast and the islands of Islay, Jura, Mull and Skye. Other roads were driven northward into country that most Britons regarded as only a little less remote than the moon. One went inland to Lairg, then up to Tongue. The other pioneered what is now the A9's route to Wick, then north-westward for Thurso.

This, plus other major works in progress south of the border, should have been more than enough to keep a dozen hyperactive engineers at full stretch. But the erstwhile stone-cutter had a gargantuan appetite for work. In 1803, the year the great Highland road building programme started, he took up the challenge to build the Caledonian Canal. This would enable ships as big as His Britannic Majesty's 32-gun frigates to sail through the Great Glen, between the Atlantic and the North Sea. There were two main reasons for embarking on a project that was expected to cost £350,000 and take seven years to complete. First, Britain was at war with France, so waterways that would protect shipping from Napoleonic privateers were in favour. Second, the Pentland Firth east of Cape Wrath was 'the dread of mariners'. Once again, *Lives of the Engineers* sets the scene. 'Thus it was cited by Sir Edward Parry, in his evidence before Parliament in favour of completing the Caledonian Canal, that of two vessels despatched from Newcastle on the same day – one bound for Liverpool by the north of Scotland, and the other for Bombay by the English Channel and the Cape of Good Hope – the latter reached its destination first!'

Telford and his team were almost overwhelmed by problem after unpredictable problem as they toiled in a region not synonymous with idyllic weather. Some of the 29 locks had to be blasted from solid rock. Primitive steam dredgers, built specially for the task, smoked and clanked interminably to clear channels through the ooze of aeons. Mud as deep as a cricket pitch is long didn't prevent Telford building what was then the world's biggest lock, where the canal meets tidal water near Inverness. At the Fort William end, the flight of eight locks at Banavie was dubbed Neptune's Staircase by Southey, the poet. It was 1822 before a ship passed right through the canal, and by then the cost had risen to £912,375. The waterway was a triumph for Georgian technology, and for the human spirit, but a commercial failure. Ships became bigger – and the Pentland Firth a little less fearsome – when steam arrived to supplement sails.

Forty miles of narrow but officially first-class road were shared with just three other vehicles as the Range Rover followed Telford's route across the peat-bogged, loch-dappled, mountain-studded wilderness from Lairg to Tongue. Then I headed eastward to Thurso and Wick – vast conurbations by local standards – and there dropped anchor for the night.

'The bleakest of God's towns on the bleakest of God's bays,' is how Robert Louis Stevenson described Wick. It was here that Telford, wearing his British Fisheries Society hat, created what Smiles describes as 'the greatest fishing station in the world'. The harbour was certainly a place for penitents and masochists at 8 o'clock that Sunday morning. The wind from the North Sea sliced and stung like a scalpel dipped in acid. So I headed for home, following Telford's road down the coast to Inverness, then cutting across to see the delightful bridge – complete with castellated towers – that spans the River Spey at Craigellachie. The original ironwork was cast in far-off North Wales by William 'Merlin' Hazledine, one of Telford's most trusted associates.

In 1793, several years before the Scottish adventures started, Telford was appointed 'Sole Agent, Architect and Engineer' to the Ellesmere Canal Company, which intended linking the Mersey, Dee and Severn. Although the plans had to be modified, the project did enable Telford to create one of the 'Seven Wonders of the Waterways'. I have seen the 'Stream in the Sky' aqueduct many times. I have crossed it by boat more than once, and played cricket in its shadow, but never fail to be awed by its soaring, slender beauty.

Crossing the Vale of Dee, between Llangollen and the English border, was the greatest of the Ellesmere Canal's many challenges. Convention dictated long, time-wasting ladders of locks linked by little more than a dumpy embankment, pierced by culverts, along which the canal would run in a channel of puddled clay. Telford had a much better idea. He projected a 19-arch aqueduct, just over 1,000 feet long, that would rise 127 feet above the fast-flowing river's rocky bed. The upper part of the graceful stone piers would be internally braced with cross-walls, to combine strength with lightness. 'The navigable road', to quote Poet Laureate Southey, would run in a trough of cast iron, not puddled clay.

Such was the plan. Many considered Telford to be crazy, because nobody had ever attempted anything like this before, but Pontcysyllte was built exactly as intended, at a cost of £47,018. Sir Walter Scott, one of his compatriot's fast-growing legion of admirers, said it was the most impressive work of art he had ever seen. Legend tells that bullocks' blood added strength to the mortar while Welsh flannel, soaked in syrup, sealed the joints between Hazledine's iron plates. A similar trough, but encased in stone, takes the canal across the River Ceiriog, where it forms the Anglo-Welsh frontier.

Both aqueducts are within a stone's throw of the road to Holyhead, which Telford masterminded between 1810 and 1826. The need for a highway through Snowdonia and across Anglesey had been apparent since 1801, when the Act of Union abolished Dublin's parliament and centralised the

United Kingdom's government in London. Irish MPs, spearheaded by Sir Henry Parnell, began agitating for more civilised links with the capital. Holyhead was the most convenient ferry port, but from there on it was hard going. Samuel Smiles uses such terms as 'tedious, difficult and full of peril' and 'a miserable track, circuitous and craggy, full of terrible jolts, round bogs and over rocks'. Conditions were so atrocious that the Post Office's attempts to run a mail service between Shrewsbury and Holyhead were soon abandoned.

The route surveyed and eventually built by Telford made conditions as easy as possible for horse-powered transport, despite running through some of Britain's most rugged terrain. Even today, the almost complete absence of steep gradients is appreciated. Traffic permitting, there are very few places where a modern car needs anything lower than fifth gear. The road itself rested on a massive foundation of stone blocks, each seven inches long by four wide, with chips wedged between them. The blocks were covered with six inches of tightly packed stones, then topped with gravel. Drainage was excellent, and the road was flanked by narrower carriageways for light traffic. The most elegant of many mainland bridges crosses the River Conwy at Betws-y-Coed and is a reminder that Telford designs could be functional *and* decorative. The cast-iron spandrels are embellished with national emblems – rose, leek, thistle and shamrock – and also bear the names of Telford, Hazledine and his foreman, William Stuttle. A bank-to-bank sweep of iron letters tells the world that 'This arch was constructed in the same year the Battle of Waterloo was fought'.

Telford decided to replace the Menai Strait ferry with a tall, graceful suspension bridge whose main span of 579 feet would be the longest in the world. Thousands of excited spectators watched and marvelled as the first chain was hoisted into place. Friends who rushed to congratulate Telford 'found the engineer upon his knees engaged in prayer'. When the bridge was opened to traffic on 30 January, 1826, the journey from Holyhead to London, which had been virtually impossible, could be completed in little more than 24 hours. Telford hated ceremony, so this landmark in civil engineering history was completed without so much as a mumbled speech.

The fact that he declined to accept fees for the vast amount of work done for the British Fisheries Society is equally typical of the shepherd's son who 'had a joke for every little circumstance'. His greatest reward was always the satisfaction that stems from seeing a noble project successfully completed. Thomas Telford once said: 'I hold that the aim and end of all ought not to be a mere bag of money, but something far higher and far better.'

21

THE FINEST HOUR

1990

He was the right build for a fighter pilot, or a scrum half, and looked younger than his years. Eyes that had scanned the skies from the cockpit of a Hawker Hurricane, half a century before, glinted in Air Vice-Marshal Harold Bird-Wilson's tanned and smiling face. 'Birdy' autographed my *Battle of Britain* book and recalled being shot down by the Messerschmitt Bf109E of cigar-smoking Adolf Galland, one of the Luftwaffe's greatest aces. He introduced me to John 'Cat's Eyes' Cunningham, Britain's most famous night-fighter pilot, then asked 'Fred' to add his signature to my collection. Fred, who had also been a Hurricane pilot during the battle, remained in the Royal Air Force until 1973. By then he was Air Chief Marshal Sir Frederick Rosier, Fighter Command's last Commander-in-Chief.

Fred, Cat's Eyes and Birdy were just a few of the modest old heroes who were on parade for the opening of the special Battle of Britain exhibition at the RAF Museum in Hendon, a stone's throw from the London end of the M1. Meeting them was the *grande finale* to a five-day, 1,500-mile odyssey at the wheel of a Bentley Mulsanne S, undertaken to mark the 50th anniversary of the RAF's epoch-making clash with the Luftwaffe. There were several good reasons for choosing the Bentley. For a start, whatever car was used had to be as quintessentially British as roast beef and cricket on the village green. Bentleys are made by Rolls-Royce Motor Cars in Crewe. The factory was built in 1938–39 to manufacture Rolls-Royce Merlin engines for Spitfires and Hurricanes. The

Spitfire's designer, Reginald Joseph Mitchell, had a Rolls-Royce car. Jeffrey Quill's highly commended book, *Spitfire: A Test Pilot's Story*, contains several affectionate references to 'my old 3.0-litre Bentley'. Billy Fiske, a young fighter pilot commemorated in the crypt of St Paul's Cathedral, London, thundered along southern England's sun-baked roads in a supercharged Bentley, complete with leather bonnet straps and worthy of Bulldog Drummond. Fiske was one of several Americans who volunteered for the RAF more than a year before Uncle Sam joined in the struggle. I was also reminded, while wondering what car would be best for this once-in-a-lifetime pilgrimage, that Fighter Command's headquarters, on high ground in the London suburb of Stanmore, had been an 18th-century mansion called Bentley Priory. That was the nerve centre from which Air Chief Marshal Sir Hugh 'Stuffy' Dowding directed the prolonged aerial battle.

While waiting for the red Mulsanne to appear outside the Crewe factory's impressive new reception hall, I recalled the background to the struggle that inspired some of Churchill's most spine-tingling oratory. From the British viewpoint, the Second World War started on 3 September, 1939, two days after Germany unleashed its blitzkreig – 'lightning war' – assault on Poland. In the west, the so-called Phoney War, the lull before the storm, lasted until 10 May, 1940. Eleven days later, the first of the Panzers that had raced across northern France at astonishing speed reached the English Channel. Operation Dynamo, which plucked 338,226 British and French troops from Dunkirk's blood-stained beaches, started on 26 May.

Dowding, despite immense political pressure, eventually refused to send more fighters to France, where they would be sacrificed on the funeral pyre of a lost cause. He stated his case in what has been described as the most famous letter in the RAF's history. After reminding the Air Ministry that 52 fighter squadrons had long been considered essential to defend Britain, and pointing out that the number had tumbled to 36, he said: 'If the Home Defence Force is drained away in desperate attempts to remedy the situation in France, defeat in France will involve the final, complete and irremediable defeat of this country.'

France gave up the struggle on 21 June. Just over a week later, Hitler ordered his commanders to prepare detailed plans for the invasion of Britain, an enterprise for which control of the air was deemed essential. Britain now stood alone, in a position of unprecedented peril, awaiting the full fury of Reichsmarschall Hermann Goering's cock-a-hoop Luftwaffe.

According to Richard Hough and Denis Richards, whose *Battle of Britain: The Jubilee History* is required reading, the air fleets charged with bringing about the RAF's demise mustered about 1,260 long-range bombers – Junkers 88s, Heinkel 111s and Dornier 17s – plus 317 of the screaming Junkers 87 dive-bombers that had proved so effective over mainland Europe. Messerschmitt Bf109Es, powered by a Daimler-Benz V12 whose assets included a direct fuel-injection system, accounted for most of Germany's 1,089 fighters. Twin-engined Messerschmitt Bf110s made up the balance.

Hurricanes outnumbered Spitfires by almost two to one in the home team's line-up. Figures quoted by the RAF Museum are 347 to 199. Bristol Blenheims, Boulton Paul Defiants and a flight of Gloster Gladiator biplanes raised the total number of Dowding's fighting-fit aircraft to 640. No wonder Churchill's famous tribute – 'Never in the field of human conflict was so much owed by so many to so few' – came to mind as rather more than two tons of Bentley Mulsanne whispered away from Crewe, en route for Stoke-on-Trent. Half a century earlier, Rolls-Royce's supercharged Merlin V12 had produced 1,000bhp from 27 litres. That gave the MkI Hurricane a 324mph top speed. The early Spitfire was good for 350mph in level flight and climbed to 20,000 feet in just over nine minutes.

The myth about the power of today's Rolls-Royce and Bentley cars not being revealed is kept alive by writers who should know better. Thanks to European markets, which insist that 'adequate' does not constitute sufficient information, it should by now be common knowledge that the Mulsanne's naturally aspirated, 6.7-litre V8 develops 222bhp at a genteel 4,200rpm. Some 330lb-ft of torque is generated 2,700 revs lower down the scale. Performance figures? My stopwatch credited this heavy, square-shouldered status symbol with reaching the mile-a-minute mark in 9.7 seconds. The maximum, which I didn't check, must be a little over 120mph. The speedometer was a paragon of precision.

Why was Stoke-on-Trent my first target? Because it was here that Reginald 'Spitfire' Mitchell, a schoolmaster's son, was born in 1895. A section of the City Museum and Art Gallery in Bethesda Street is dedicated to the engineer who became Supermarine's chief designer at the age of 24, and died of cancer just 18 years later.

Photographs of Mitchell and the aircraft he masterminded overlook a Spitfire LFXVI that was delivered to 667 Squadron in 1945. Fifty-four years have passed since the prototype's maiden flight, but the Spitfire, in my judgement, remains the most graceful and beautifully proportioned of all aeroplanes. In a corner of the Spitfire Gallery stands a Merlin, parts of which have been removed to reveal such details as four valves for each 2.25-litre cylinder. An excellent power-to-weight ratio was one of the most outstanding characteristics of an engine that was eventually modified to belt out as much as 2,640bhp.

Two-level air-conditioning soothed and susurrated as the Bentley inched through narrow streets, solid with slow-moving traffic, then made up for lost time on the road to Derby. My destination was the Rolls-Royce aero-engine company's headquarters in Nightingale Road. Here, in the Merlin's birthplace, light streams through a window whose stained glass depicts a young RAF pilot. The inscription reads: 'This window commemorates the pilots of the Royal Air Force who in the Battle of Britain turned the work of our hands into the salvation of our country.'

Quiet main roads and free-flowing motorways, cruised at a discreet and theoretically fuel-efficient 80mph, took the Bentley to Southampton by way of Middle Wallop, in rural Hampshire. This most euphonious of 1940's fighter bases stands amid fields that roll gently down to thatched cottages clustered around olde worlde pubs and medieval churches. The sky above these idyllic villages was ripped apart, time and time again, when Goering's bombers attempted to defeat

Fighter Command by wiping Middle Wallop, and the rest of the front-line aerodromes, off the map.

Four o'clock found the red Bentley parked outside Southampton's Hall of Aviation, which is close to the Supermarine factory's site. Links with Mitchell include a Spitfire MkXXIV powered by Rolls-Royce's 36.7-litre, 2,350bhp Griffon. But the collection's most remarkable aircraft is one of the two Supermarine S6 seaplanes designed to contest, successfully, the very prestigious Schneider Trophy in 1929. Two years later, a development of that astonishingly sleek aircraft raised the world air speed record to almost 410mph. Lessons learned from the seaplanes were applied to the Spitfire.

The first of almost 23,000 Spitfires and Seafires flew from what is now Southampton's airport at Eastleigh. In the passenger terminal, a plaque unveiled by Mitchell's son gives the date as 5 March, 1936. Jeffrey Quill is convinced that the maiden flight took place a day later. Such quibbles concerned me less than the fact that the Bentley's fuel warning light was on after only 266 quite sedate miles. Just over 18 gallons were needed to brim the tank before visiting Tangmere. No fewer than 124 gallons had sloshed into the Mulsanne by the end of the trip.

A small aviation museum occupies one corner of Tangmere, an airfield that was bombed on 16 August, 1940, by Ju87s that dived almost vertically from 12,000 feet. Anti-aircraft guns held their fire rather than risk hitting the Hurricanes that were taking off as the Stukas came down, sirens wailing. Billy Fiske, the Bentley man, died that day. Watching the sun set from what remains of Tangmere's control tower, I said a prayer for all the foreign pilots who contributed so much to the RAF's strength. They included 145 Poles and 87 Czechs.

Early next morning, another link between automobiles and aircraft was forged during a brief stop at Brooklands, between the Surrey towns of Byfleet and Weybridge. Opened in 1907, and now the home of a motoring and aviation museum, Brooklands was the world's first made-to-measure track for car racing. In 1935, Oliver Bertram and the Barnato Hassan Special, based on an 8.0-litre Bentley, lapped the circuit at 142.6mph. It was from Brooklands, which incorporated an airfield, that the first Hurricane made its maiden flight on 6 November, 1935. Designed by Sydney Camm, the eldest of a carpenter's dozen children, the Hurricane shared the Spitfire's armament as well as its engine. Each wing concealed four Browning 0.303in machine guns fed by a total of 2,600 shells. The guns were generally set for their fire to converge at 250 yards. Accurate shooting was essential, because there was rarely time for more than a two-second burst. But the pressure on Fighter Command became so great that many pilots had never fired a shot until they went into action for the first time.

Biggin Hill, only 15 miles south-east of London's heart, played a key role in the capital's defence. Today, Hurricane and Spitfire replicas flank the entrance to the airfield's Chapel of Remembrance, which is open to visitors. The White Hart, down the road in Brasted, was a great favourite with this famous fighter station's pilots. Many signed the blackboard, which is now in the RAF Museum at Hendon.

Standing on Dover's white cliffs, I tried to picture the scene on 10 July, 1940, when German attacks on a big convoy of merchant ships sparked off a series of furious dogfights. This was eventually deemed to be the day the Battle of Britain started. Two months later, Goering and his staff enjoyed a picnic on Cap Gris Nez, 21 miles from Dover, while 1,000 aircraft assembled to attack London. The assault's scale and ferocity were unprecedented. Among those who flew to smite the Luftwaffe's armada that Saturday were three squadrons from Duxford. Their leader, Douglas Bader, had rejoined the RAF in 1939, eight years after losing both legs when his Bristol Bulldog crashed.

Duxford, on the M11 near Cambridge, was the Mulsanne's next touchdown point. The airfield where the first squadron to fly Spitfires was based is now part of the Imperial War Museum. I spent a long afternoon that wasn't half long enough admiring one of the world's finest collections of military and civil aircraft. The room from which operations in the Duxford sector were controlled during the Battle of Britain has been restored, down to such details as a 'Careless talk costs lives' poster.

A top-secret chain of coastal radar stations made a priceless contribution to the efficiency of such 'ops' rooms. That's why the Bentley headed due east from Duxford to Orford, a delightful little Suffolk village whose main street ends at a quay. Four men travelling in two cars, an Armstrong Siddeley and an MG, reached this isolated spot on 13 May, 1935. Accompanied by two RAF trucks laden with equipment, the scientists were there to build Britain's first experimental radar station. The full story is told in *Radar Days* by Dr E G 'Taffy' Bowen. He recalls relaxing in the Jolly Sailor, where I lingered over an excellent pint before taking a room at the Crown and Castle, where Robert Watson Watt and his colleagues spent many a long night talking about what was then called Radio Direction Finding.

Next morning, Squadron Leader Colin Patterson welcomed me to the RAF's Battle of Britain Memorial Flight at Coningsby, between Boston and Lincoln. He flies the four-engined Lancaster bomber. We struck a light-hearted deal, letting him drive the Bentley while I sat, spellbound, in the narrow cockpit of a Spitfire Mark IIA that flew in the Battle of Britain.

I drove as far north as Flamborough Head, because Yorkshire's answer to the white cliffs of Dover witnessed an almighty dogfight on 15 August, 1940, then spent a night near Lincoln before wafting down the A1 to meet yesterday's heroes at Hendon. The RAF Museum in general reduced me to a gaping, gasping, wide-eyed schoolboy. I could have spent two or three days there, but wanted to visit Bentley Priory before returning the Mulsanne to its home in Cheshire.

The last name on my itinerary was Tern Hill, 15 miles south-west of Crewe, which had been a training and operational base in 1940. On 18 July, a pupil pilot who had just celebrated his 23rd birthday, and was about to be posted to Biggin Hill, took off in a two-seater Harvard, which crashed near Nantwich at 3.15pm. He left a pregnant widow. Her son was born on 23 October, 11 days after Hitler, thwarted by Fighter Command's resolution, rolled up his invasion plans. Fifty years later, the Pilot Officer's son was commissioned to roam far and wide across England, gathering material for a story about the Battle of Britain. He drove a red Bentley Mulsanne.

22

GIRALDUS CAMBRENSIS
AND THE GT40

1993

The question was predictable. 'Is it a kit car?' they asked when we pit-stopped in Pontrhydfendigaid, Llancynfelyn, Machynlleth and Penrhyndeudraeth. Do-it-yourselfers inspired by the mighty Ford GT40 are ten-a-penny, but photographer Martyn Goddard and I were devouring the Celtic miles in a lookalike built by Ray Mallock's *very* professional engineers. Suffice it to say that Mallock and his colleagues have a rock-solid reputation for designing, building and running the sort of cars that contest Le Mans. The team's expertise has been enlisted by such respected marques as Aston Martin and Nissan.

The RML GT40 project dates from July 1990. The first car was completed just seven months later. Powered by a 300bhp version of Ford's 5-litre, small-block V8, it proved good for 0–60mph in 4.7 seconds, with driver and passenger on board. The top speed of about 180mph looks impressive until you remember how the fastest of the originals, with seven litres of bellowing Detroit iron bolted behind the cockpit, claimed to have reached 230mph on the Mulsanne straight at Le Mans.

The keys to the second RML GT40 were handed over early one spring morning. Bearing in mind the philosophy behind the car's creation – 'We were determined to build a racing car that would be able to travel on public roads,' says Ray Mallock – lesser mortals would have settled for a conventional day of driving and snapping. We decided to take the 'travel on public roads' bit to heart by retracing a famous journey undertaken in AD 1188 and recorded, in delightful detail, by the son of a Norman knight and a Welsh princess. His name was Gerald de Barri. He became archdeacon of Saint David's and is now remembered as Giraldus Cambrensis or Gerald of Wales.

The many impressions recorded by this tall, opinionated priest in the *Journey through Wales* and the *Description of Wales* were distilled from material gathered over about 700 miles. The going was never easy. What roads existed in Wales had been neglected since the Romans abandoned this far-flung province. That was already 800 years in the past when Gerald's party set off from Hereford at the start of an odyssey that would take almost two months. Llewellin and Goddard had two days. Fortunately, we hadn't been ordered to emulate our predecessors by stopping here, there and everywhere to preach spellbinding sermons. Rallying support for the Third Crusade to the Holy Land was the reason for the great trek on which Gerald's exalted companion was Baldwin, Archbishop of Canterbury.

The good Ford had blessed us with far more horsepower than the medieval monks, but their saddlebags would have been welcome. Space for Louis Vuitton cabin trunks wasn't a priority in 1963, when Ford Advanced Vehicles launched the GT40 programme. My luggage was pared down to an ultra-compact toothbrush – provided years ago by the Fini Hotel in Modena, Italy – a squeeze of toothpaste, a comb, a tiny Braun shaver and a notebook. A clean shirt, socks and underpants were stuffed behind my seat. Goddard's small bag of personal and professional kit was wedged between his knees.

Gerald's description of the Welsh people as 'light and agile' came to mind while lowering myself into a car that stands just 40 inches above the road. That's low enough for the roof to be a target when any dog bigger than a corgi cocks its leg. But the race-type seats are snug and visibility's not *too* bad, except over the shoulder. Air conditioning prevents the cabin from becoming an oven that would give a new meaning to fast food. Goddard looked a little apprehensive as the doors slammed, the V8 rumbled to life, inches behind our ears, and I selected the lowest of the authentic five-speed ZF DS25 gearbox's cogs. It was time to inform the quivering wretch that I claim descent, on my mother's side, from an eighth-century Welsh warrior, Brohcmail, Prince of Powys. He who casts aspersions on such a man's courage and ability does so at his peril, I said. In the words of Giraldus Cambrensis: 'The Welsh value distinguished birth and noble descent more than anything else in the world . . . they avenge with great ferocity any wrong or insult . . . They are vindictive by nature, blood-thirsty, and violent.'

Doubts about the wisdom of living with RML's GT40 for two days had evaporated long before we reached Saint David's, where the Welsh patron saint was born about 1,500 years ago. As expected, the surprisingly flexible V8's power and torque enabled challengers to be dismissed with another inch of throttle and, maybe, a lower gear to rub salt into the wounded pride. The inevitable downside, for a road car, is steering with a glued-to-the-ground feeling at *very* low speeds. This is exacerbated by a lock that requires six or seven bites to complete what would normally be an easy three-point turn.

Voices don't have to be raised all that much to converse at up to about 90mph. Goddard cursed this, because it encouraged me to keep peppering him with Geraldian quotes. For instance, realising that the steering wheel can be removed, to foil all but the most resolute thief, prompted the following: 'It is the habit of the Welsh to steal anything they can lay their hands on and to live on plunder, theft, and robbery, not only from foreigners and people hostile to them, but also from each other.'

Nothing surprised the Englishman's guide and chauffeur more than the quality of the latterday GT40's ride. The carefully compromised suspension works wonders for traction – and, therefore, stability – on surfaces where small vertical movements might otherwise make the huge tyres lose a percentage of their grip. The main drawback, noted as we looped northward on switchbacks flanked by stone walls and hedges, is that your eyes are slightly less than three feet from the road. One is also aware of minimal ground clearance.

Castell Llewellin, literally within a stone's throw of Gerald's route across Shropshire from between Whitchurch to Oswestry, was a convenient place for lunch. But will Goddard reciprocate when I'm next in London? Not if he noticed what Giraldus Cambrensis said about the Welsh as guests: 'If they come to a house where there is any sign of affluence and they are in a position to take what they want, there is no limit to their demands. They lose all control of themselves, and insist on being served with vast quantities of food and, more especially, intoxicating drink,' he warned.

23

THE ROAD TO
MUCKLE FLUGGA

1994

This is unlike any midnight I have experienced before. June is exactly three weeks old and we've reached the end of the road. A line drawn straight ahead from here crosses the North Pole and thereafter encounters nothing more solid than ice before it reaches an island off the coast of Siberia, some 3,500 miles away. There's a strip of fretted cloud along the horizon, and the wind blows strong and cold at this latitude, but the sky is a lambent, luminescent palette of soft blues and pinks. Check the time. Tuesday turned into Wednesday two minutes ago, but I am reading the *Shetland Times* without straining my 53-year-old eyes. You don't need to travel to Lapland or Baffin Island to watch the sun reach its northern solstice. Punctuated by three ferry crossings, the road to Muckle Flugga is a reminder of how close Britain gets to the Arctic Circle. The Shetland island of Unst is as far from London as London is from Prague, for example.

The longest day of the year is a good time to drive north. Such a journey is also a useful test of a vehicle with a dash of adventure in its character, such as the Ford Maverick. The route to Aberdeen and the ferry to Lerwick, Shetland's capital, is motorway or dual carriageway all the way. The only conditions that could have suited the Maverick better would have been 400 downhill miles supplemented by a benevolent wind. Cruising in fifth gear, preferably with a light load, is what this 2.4-litre Tonka Toy does best. Less flattering circumstances focus attention on the rather dismal power-to-weight ratio. My left arm and both legs have developed bigger muscles from ripping up and down the gearbox and repeatedly flooring the accelerator in an attempt to maintain an acceptable rate of progress.

Aberdeen is a focal point for exploiting the North Sea's oil and gas. As the Maverick reaches the harbour, overlooked by a robustly Victorian skyline of clock towers, turrets, pinnacles, finials and steeples, the smell of fish is a reminder that the sea's more traditional harvest still plays an important role in the city's life. Ice clinks in pre-dinner drinks as P&O's ferry *St Clair* clears the breakwaters and starts her 14-hour voyage through the night.

Light filtering through our cabin's curtains fools me into thinking it's breakfast time at only 2.25am. A few hours later it's much darker as rain driven by a strong, cold wind hammers down. In the Viking Restaurant, we eat porridge and kippers amid thoughts almost as black as the sky. Taking 'available light' photographs at midnight is an important part of the expedition's brief. At this rate, a flash will be needed at noon.

Conditions haven't improved by the time the Maverick lands. A quick prayer to the Viking gods is appropriate, because Shetland's culture is much more Norse than Scottish. The sea-wolves whose dragon-prowed longships crossed the Atlantic long before Columbus reached the New World discovered these islands about 1,100 years ago. Norway, Sweden and Denmark were united in 1469, when Shetland and Orkney were pledged as part of the dowry on the occasion of the Danish king's daughter's marriage to the prince who became King James III of Scotland. The islands should have eventually reverted to Norse rule, but have remained Scottish and British for 525 years. Place-names such as Hjaltasteyn and Hamnavoe are evidence of how deep the Norse roots run.

Road atlases generally use a different scale for Shetland, masking the fact that the archipelago's southernmost point Sumburgh Head, is almost 100 miles from Muckle Flugga.

ABOVE LEFT *England 1957: Aboard the Dover–Calais ferry on his first foreign journey, Llewellin shares the deck with his stepfather, Clenyg Llewellin, and his sister, Adrienne.* (Muriel Llewellin)

Big wheels rolling. *America 1985:* ABOVE RIGHT *Paul Hughes's V8 Cat-powered Peterbilt hauls very expensive cars for very rich people.*
BELOW *Delivering an immaculate 1936 Rolls-Royce to its new owner in Fort Lauderdale.* (Phil Llewellin)

Meeting the legends. ABOVE *America 1988: Chevrolet Corvette in Wyoming, en route for the Devil's Tower where the alien spaceship landed in* Close Encounters of the Third Kind. BELOW *Driving for miles without seeing another car in Montana, heading for the spot where George Armstrong Custer and his soldiers fought to the last man in 1876.* (Phil Llewellin)

Laxative Ridge. RIGHT *America 1993: This extraordinary rock formation near Moab, Utah, is officially known as the Lion's Back. Llewellin, pictured starting the climb in a Range Rover, renamed it Laxative Ridge.* (Beth Llewellin)

Inverness to Chester in seven minutes. ABOVE *America 1997: Jaguar's sleek XK8 pauses by a reminder that humans aren't at the top of the food chain in the snow-capped Rocky Mountains.* (Phil Llewellin)

Hunting ghosts in Nevada. BELOW *America 1999: Deep in Nevada, Llewellin takes the wheel of what used to be Belmont's fire truck. One building revealed timesheets from 1944, a 1961 calendar and a 1974 copy of the* Reader's Digest. RIGHT *Nevada's long dusty roads and empty spaces contrast with the surreal experience that is Las Vegas, not a million miles from where this picture was taken.* (Martyn Goddard)

Ticking them off in a Packard. *America 1999: Bud and Thelma Lyon's magnificent Packard Club Sedan enabled Llewellin to complete his set of US mainland states in vintage style.* (Phil Llewellin)

Into the far north's freezer. *Canada 1982: Other vehicles are few and far between on the Dempster Highway in the middle of winter.* (Phil Llewellin)

Canada 1982: It's cold enough for flesh to freeze in seconds when Ken Kirby's indomitable Kenworth stops at Eagle Plains, a stone's throw from the Arctic Circle. (Phil Llewellin)

High jinks in the Sahara. *Algeria 1991:* BELOW *Lessons learned during many years of selling cars in Africa stood Peugeot in good stead during the* Piste des Lions *journey through the Sahara.* OVERLEAF *Time for a little exercise as the sand claims yet another victim.* (Phil Llewellin)

The little man with the big hat. ABOVE LEFT *England 1987: The nineteenth century engineering genius Isambard Kingdom Brunel, pictured by the* Great Eastern's *launching chains, would have been fascinated by the Bentley's turbocharged, 6.7-litre V8 engine.* ABOVE RIGHT *Bentley in Paddington Station, London, where intrepid Victorians could start their journey to New York via Bristol.* BELOW *Clifton suspension bridge was built after Brunel died. It spans the deep Avon gorge at Bristol.* (Martyn Goddard)

***Wizards of ooze**. LEFT Wales 1988: Checking the way ahead on foot,
Llewellin wonders if the time has come to be winched out of a quagmire.
(Tim Wren)*

***The Colossus of Roads**. ABOVE Wales 1989: The graceful Waterloo Bridge
over the River Conwy at Betws-y-Coed is one of Thomas Telford's more
flamboyant masterpieces. BELOW Scotland 1989: Snow brings winter magic to
the old A9 near Bonar Bridge. Thomas Telford would have appreciated the
diesel-engined Range Rover. (Phil Llewellin)*

The finest hour. ABOVE *England 1990: Bentley and Spitfire form a quintessentially British scene at RAF Coningsby, home of the Battle of Britain Memorial Flight.* (Phil Llewellin)

LEFT *England 1940: Pilot Officer Philip Crush, the father he never knew, inspired Llewellin to commemorate the Battle of Britain. The 23-year-old pilot served in the Royal Warwickshires before transferring to the RAF.*

Giraldus Cambrensis and the GT40. *Wales 1993: Seeing over hedges was a problem while following a medieval priest's route around Wales in Ray Mallock's beautifully crafted replica of the Ford GT40.* (Martyn Goddard)

The road to Muckle Flugga. *Scotland 1994: Llewellin looks towards Britain's northernmost outcrop – and on the longest day of the year the sky is still so bright at midnight that he can read the* Shetland Times. RIGHT *Over hills and sea to reach Muckle Flugga.* (Tim Wren)

All in good time. *Britain 1999:* ABOVE *Brian Parry at JB Joyce of Whitchurch, Shropshire, the world's oldest clockmaker.* BELOW *Big Ben, ringing out over London's Houses of Parliament, is the most famous timepiece in the world.* (Ian Dawson)

Great Britain's greatest drive. ABOVE *Scotland 2001: The remains of Carn Liath broch, a prehistoric stone tower situated on a rocky terrace overlooking the Sutherland coast.* BELOW LEFT *A piper plays for the tourists.* BELOW RIGHT *The Summer Isles Hotel at Achiltibuie has the world's northernmost Michelin-starred restaurant.* OVERLEAF *A motorist's view of Eilean Donan Castle.* (Ian Dawson)

Cooke's tour to Abadan. ABOVE *Turkey 1976: Traditional transport contrasts with European trucks in eastern Turkey, not far from Mount Ararat.* BELOW *Turkish boys on the hunt for cigarettes. Failing to hand over a packet can result in getting a rock through the windscreen.* (Phil Llewellin)

Kamikazes and Kalashnikovs on the road to Pakistan. RIGHT *Turkey 1978: Llewellin was riding shotgun and nearly lost his left arm when the Leyland Sherpa was hit by a truck en route for Pakistan.* (Phil Llewellin)

Driving to the end of the world.
ABOVE *Argentina 1999: Lapataia Bay in Tierra del Fuego, almost 2,000 miles from Buenos Aires, is the end of the world's southernmost road.* LEFT *Far from the land of her fathers, Marta Rees serves traditional afternoon tea at her home in the Chubut Valley's old-established Welsh colony.* (Phil Llewellin)

Racing goats and scalp-lifting rum. RIGHT *Tobago 2003: Pampered grand prix drivers could learn a few lessons from the annual Buccoo Goat Race Festival.* (Dave Allen)

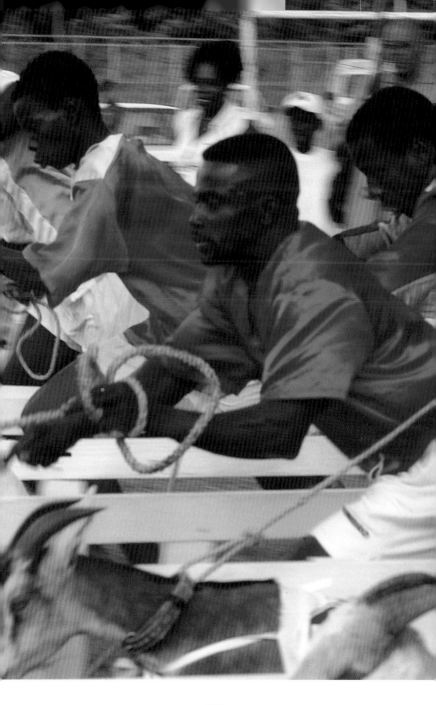

Battling through Borneo. ABOVE *Indonesia 1985: Mile after mile of mud was one reason for the Camel Trophy convoy's progress being much slower than planned.* BELOW *Whoops! Locals in two-wheel-drive Toyota Hilux pickups must have wondered why the visitors were such incompetent drivers.* RIGHT *Heavily-laden Land Rovers had to cope with some seriously gung-ho driving techniques.* (Phil Llewellin)

China with western half-devil Clarkson. LEFT *China 1988: Citroën's massive Operation Dragon drive across China recalled epic journeys undertaken by the company in the 1920s and 1930s. The Chinese know all about their own dragons, but were fascinated by Llewellin's Welsh version. One asked: 'Is this dragon more important than your king?'* RIGHT *Travelling companion Jeremy Clarkson, before he became a media star, contemplates breakfast on the overnight train from Beijing to Zhengzhou.* (Phil Llewellin)

Old cars and good times on the equator. BELOW *Malaysia 1993: Dancers welcome the Louis Vuitton Vintage Equator Run to Johore Bahru, a five-minute drive across the causeway from Singapore.* (Phil Llewellin)

Back to the bloody beaches. LEFT *France 1984: Landing troops by glider at Pegasus Bridge, during the last hour before D-Day, called for steel nerves and incredibly precise flying. It was one of the Allies' most remarkable feats during the Second World War. This plaque, on a café near the bridge, marks the first house in France to be liberated on 5 June 1944.* (Phil Llewellin)

The Bentley boys. BELOW *France 1986: Bill Woodward at the wheel of his 1929 Bentley, dressed as if for a mid-winter expedition to the South Pole.* (Phil Llewellin)

France's spaceship on wheels. RIGHT *France 1990: Andrew Brodie (left) and Llewellin wonder where to go, while Brodie's long-striding Citroën DS19 takes a break.* BELOW RIGHT *At the end of the day, Llewellin concentrates on a bottle of fermented grape juice.* (Martyn Goddard)

DE PARIS
À
GENÈVE

ENTRE SENS
ET
St FLORENTIN

And the wall came tumbling down. ABOVE
*Germany 1990: When Germany was divided, the
Trabant epitomised the gulf between East and West. This
one is pictured by part of the Wall that divided Berlin
from 1961 until 1989.* BELOW LEFT *Berlin's
Checkpoint Charlie was the most famous – or infamous
– point where pass-holders could move between the two
German states.* BELOW RIGHT *After unification, mind-
boggling posters, paintings and graffiti covered the wall.*
(Phil Llewellin)

When the gates of hell opened. ABOVE LEFT *France 1986: Seventy years after the Battle of the Somme, one of the bloodiest campaigns of the Great War, Tom Stephens, a 91-year-old veteran, gave this photograph of himself to the author after they met in Albert.* ABOVE RIGHT *Memorial to the Glasgow Highlanders at High Wood. Each of the 192 stones came from Scotland – and each one represents a dead soldier.* (Phil Llewellin)

Taking the high road. BELOW *France 1997: Passes climbing to more than 9,000 feet provided spectacular views while driving an Aston Martin DB7 Volante over the Alps from Lake Geneva to Nice.* (Martyn Goddard)

A tribute to yesterday's heroes. *Austria 2002: Neo-vintage Morgan Aero 8 following the route taken by the Paris–Vienna racers in 1902. Vienna's Prater Park is where the 1902 city-to-city race ended. Cinema buffs will recognise the Ferris wheel from* The Third Man. (Richard Newton)

The great quote. *France 2002: Robert Louis Stevenson's account of his French adventures with a donkey called Modestine still inspires walkers.* (Beth Llewellin)

And that's as the fulmar flies, not as the Maverick motors. Traffic is unlikely to be a problem, because the islands are home to only 22,000 people, a third of whom live in Lerwick. But we wonder how the Ford's suspension will cope with roads built on peat, which might be a convenient source of fuel, but does not get the civil engineer's vote as the best of all foundations. But our dentures remain intact. The excellence of Shetland's roads is a tribute to how well the islanders have managed income from Sullom Voe, the deep-water anchorage where Europe's biggest oil and gas terminal has been operating since 1978. Fuel costs are much higher than on the mainland, but broad ribbons of smooth blacktop snake and spear across landscapes that have changed only in detail since the first Norsemen ventured ashore, exploring the beautiful wilderness of hills, cliffs, heather, lakes and, here and there, relatively sheltered areas suitable for farming.

Our prayers are answered when the downpour ceases and the Maverick cruises northward beneath clear skies. After a memorable drive along Dales Voe – 'voe' being the Norse word for what would be a sea loch in mainland Scotland – the Ford zigs and zags down to where the ferry sails from Mainland to Yell. I haven't a clue what the inter-island crossings will cost, so we travel with wads of cash rather than risk being made to swab the decks in lieu of an acceptable form of payment. Small but powerful, to cope with ferocious tides and currents, the ferry resembles a D-Day landing craft and leaves the jetty like rally driver Colin McRae at full throttle. The charge for one vehicle, three people and 20 minutes of travel is only £3.60.

Time is not a problem, so I point the Maverick's smooth snout along the road that runs eastward to Hanmavoe and Burravoe, where the white-washed Haa of Burravoe dates from 1672 and is the island's oldest building. The propeller blade that stands outside is a memorial to the Catalina flying boat that crashed near here in 1942. A few miles up the coast, a tall stone in the graveyard at Mid Yell commemorates nine Norwegian sailors who died in 1941. Geographical and historical factors gave Shetland a key role to play during the war, when fishing boats shipped refugees over from Norway – occupied by the Germans since 1940 – then went home laden with weapons, ammunition, explosives and saboteurs. The story is told in *The Shetland Bus* by David Howarth.

Photographer Tim Wren wants to photograph the Shetland ponies that are as much a part of the islands' culture as the distinctive knitwear. Mrs Llewellin, a farmer's daughter, charms several to an appropriate location within seconds, then attempts to make friends by using the technique demonstrated years ago on television by Barbara Woodhouse. This involves winning the animal's confidence by breathing up its nose. The pony responds by farting. Wren says: 'You must have blown too hard.'

Yell to Unst is another £3.60 crossing and we have the ferry to ourselves. Unst is an island of rolling hills, high cliffs and sandy beaches pounded by the Atlantic. It is early evening when the Maverick reaches Buness House, on the shore of Balta Sound, where as many as 600 herring boats rode at anchor during the decades of plenty that spanned the end of the last century. Buness House has been in David Edmondston's family since 1775 – almost 300 years after his ancestors sailed to Orkney from mainland Scotland. When we booked, several weeks earlier, Jenny Edmonston warned that her home was being restored after years of neglect. We were welcome to be the first paying guests on a take-us-as-you-find-us understanding.

Visions of eating from tins of corned beef while cowering beneath a tarpaulin give way to the reality of peerless hospitality. The guest rooms are wonderful. Wren's, which used to be the nursery, is papered from floor to ceiling with posters and pages from magazines that span the years from the end of Queen Victoria's reign to the 1940s. A six-course dinner is seasoned with advice, information and anecdotes, few of which are less than hilarious. David Edmondston used to fly Meteors, Hunters and Harriers for the RAF before he became a pilot with Loganair. He recalls flying to the Shetland island of Foula with a Civil Aviation Authority official who asked to have a taxi meet him at the terminal.

David laughs: 'I told him that Foula has about two miles of unclassified road, so there's no great demand for taxis, and that the terminal is a wooden hut, about the size of a cupboard, where he might find a fire extinguisher.'

There's no need to use the Maverick's lights at 11pm, when we start the last, short part of our long drive. This really is the road to Muckle Flugga. A slight element of compromise is essential, however. No vehicle has ever turned a wheel on Muckle Flugga, because our theoretical destination is a rocky islet whose lighthouse is Britain's last building. The road along the high headland due south of the Flugga peters out into a footpath, which crosses the Hermaness National Nature Reserve, inhabited by more than 100,000 puffins, gannets, guillemots, shags, razorbills and kittiwakes.

Saxa Vord, a headland a few hundred yards east of Hermaness, has great views of Muckle Flugga and the rock called Out Stack, which David Edmondston owns. Any concerns we might have had about the road to the RAF's hilltop radar station not being the northernmost in Britain evaporate when we realise that a rough track, built quite recently for the benefit of peat diggers, takes us as near to the North Pole as it is possible to drive in Britain. Nearby, two wonderfully incongruous sets of tall, white posts and an equally surreal scattering of little flags mark the realm's northernmost rugby pitch and golf course. It must be fun kicking a penalty or going for a big drive when the wind's gusting to more than 150mph. Wren has difficulty concentrating on his camera, because Saxa Vord is inhabited by fearless, dive-bombing skuas big enough to make off with a fully grown photographer – even one that has just eaten a six-course banquet.

How long does the sun set for? That is the question nobody can answer with a shred of authority until I contact the coastguard in Lerwick. The answer comes wrapped in a package of jargon about conditions known as civil, astronomical and nautical twilight. On 21 June, the sun is swallowed by the sea at 10.33pm and appears again at 3.38am on 22 June. This is longer than expected, but does not take into account the fact that it skims a mere 18 degrees below the horizon, so the official condition is 'twilight all night'. Sure enough, at 1pm it's possible to drive the Maverick back to Buness House with the lights off.

A five-star breakfast sets us up for the start of the two-day, three-ferry journey home. But first we nip back up the road to Haroldswick and send postcards from Britain's northernmost post office. Back on the main island we explore Jarlshof, Shetland's greatest archaeological site, where dwellings dating back to the Iron Age have been fully excavated since being exposed by storms.

My only regret, as we cruise down Bressay Sound, into the open sea and past Fair Isle, is not having had time to visit Mousa. The little island is famous for having the finest of all Iron Age circular stone towers. Known as a broch, it has a spiral staircase contained within its double-skinned outer wall. I mention this to my wife. She smiles and repeats the words that have become a mantra after so many journeys: 'What we've done is give ourselves a good reason to return.'

24

ALL IN GOOD TIME

1999

My left wrist sports a Casio Data Bank that does just about everything but make the tea. It tells the time in umpteen different countries, remembers telephone numbers, beeps loud enough to wake me up and calculates what $87.54 represents in real money. This multi-function plastic marvel cost only £35, weighs next to nothing and is not much bigger than the simple, conventional gold watch that has been ticking on my right wrist since 23 October, 1961, when I celebrated my 21st birthday. At the other extreme, our astonishingly clever and determined prehistoric ancestors marked time's passage with monuments that combined precise astronomy with mind-boggling feats of civil engineering. For instance, constructing Stonehenge, which is aligned to celebrate the year's longest day, involved transporting dozens of four-ton stones about 220 miles from Pembrokeshire in south-west Wales to Salisbury Plain. Across the Irish Sea, the winter solstice was critically important to whoever built the magnificent 200,000-ton burial mound at Newgrange.

Stonehenge and Newgrange were visited during a journey for which Audi's mile-shrinking A6 4.2 quattro played the role of a delectably smooth, swift, luxurious and sure-footed time machine. The story really started a few weeks earlier, when conversation at a dinner party zeroed-in on the moment when 31 December, 1999, becomes 1 January, 2000. Someone wondered if there was a neutral nanosecond between the old millennium and the new, the instant between the tick and the tock, but what really fascinated us was how time has been measured since technology advanced from sundials and hour-glasses to the atomic clock that is accurate to within one second in three million years.

Luxurious seats took the sting out of a 6am start as the Audi A6 whispered through awakening London, its suspension soaking up punishment from roads overdue for repair. Suburbia suddenly gave way to an illusion of open country where the line that is the basis of the world's time zone system crosses Greenwich Park. Greenwich's status dates from 1884, when the International Meridien Conference was held in America. Newspapers have run stories about Pacific islands being the first places to greet 1 January 2000, but the Royal Observatory at Greenwich is unequivocal. The resolutions passed in 1884 make the Prime Meridien passing through Greenwich the point at which the new Millennium will begin, I noted.

I can picture a man pushing one of those old-fashioned contraptions that paint white lines on the road, but the Prime Meridien is invisible, of course. Well, almost invisible, because the words 'East Longitude' and 'West Longitude' flank a brass strip set into a stone on the Royal Observatory's north-facing outer wall. As a bonus for time travellers, the observatory's main gate is flanked by one of the earliest public clocks powered by electricity. Made in 1852, it is always on GMT. On a nearby tower, a red 'time ball' installed in 1833 is raised at 12.55pm and dropped precisely five minutes later, so that ships in the Thames can check their chronometers.

The A6's next stop was in London SE1, where a visit to The Oval, Surrey County Cricket Club's headquarters, time-warped me back to 1956 and a day spent watching England's heroes – Cowdrey, Richardson, Sheppard, May, Compton, Washbrook, Evans, Lock, Laker, Tyson and Statham – doing battle with an Australian team whose stars included Miller, Lindwall and Benaud. I can still see Frank 'Typhoon' Tyson being leg-glanced by Colin McDonald. The crowd applauds the graceful shot . . . then realises that Lock has caught the bullet-fast ball inches from the ground.

The reason for this pilgrimage was the clock by the

members' entrance to the pavilion. Approximately ten feet high by eight feet wide, it has a cricket bat for a minute hand and depicts the ground in Queen Victoria's reign, complete with players whose actions mark the passing of time. One bowls, the batsman plays forward, the wicket-keeper raises his arms and the fielder moves from side to side. Presented by an exceptionally loyal supporter to commemorate Surrey's 150th anniversary in 1995, this unique clock was made by Sinclair & Harding in Cheltenham.

There is no prize for guessing that the A6 wafted us across Westminster Bridge, where the Palace of Westminster was bathed in sunlight as Britain's most famous timepiece looked down from its ornate tower. Big Ben is actually the bell that chimes, not the clock that ticks, and its name recalls portly Sir Benjamin Hall. He was Minister of Works between 1855 and 1858, when the 13.5-ton bell was cast.

Photographer Ian Dawson could get across London with his eyes shut, but he let this country bumpkin rely on Audi's optional navigational system. Sure enough, instructions based on signals from orbiting satellites guided us to the M3 and, in due course, to a street within a short stroll of Salisbury Cathedral, where we had the Dean and Chapter's permission to photograph a machine that could have inspired Heath Robinson. Near the north-west end of the nave, a frame of hand-wrought iron, about four feet high, contains the wheels, barrels, levers, ropes and other components that form what is believed to be the world's oldest working clock. Identifying it as a clock without knowing what you are looking at would be quite a feat in the absence of a dial or hands. Believed to date from 1386, and powered by stone weights that operate the driving barrel and the strike barrel, it was built to make a bell sound the hours. What appears to be an enormous key is the air-brake that prevents the striking side from running too fast.

The script called for an overnight stop in a setting of timeless tranquillity, so we were delighted when Michelin's guidebook steered the Audi from Salisbury to Howard's House in Teffont Evias, a hamlet that could have been created to epitomise rural England at its most traditional and idyllic. Our rooms were as welcoming as the staff, and the service was as excellent as the food. In short, Howard's House, with its two-acre garden, is the sort of effortlessly stylish hotel that travellers dream of finding at the end of a long day.

A breakfast notable for the best porridge I have ever tasted set us up for the short drive to Stonehenge, where rain added a dash of glistening mystery to the monoliths and trilithons that brood over Salisbury Plain like a convocation of sombre giants. The approach to this World Heritage Site is disappointing, and visitors are not allowed to walk among the stones, but these drawbacks failed to quench my excitement. The earliest feature at Stonehenge is a circular bank and ditch that date from about 3000 BC. The relatively recent part developed between 4,500 and 3,500 years ago, when the bluestones were transported from Pembrokeshire's remote Preseli Mountains, probably by using rollers and rafts. The great sarsen stones, weighing as much as 45 tons came from the Marlborough Downs. Nobody can be sure why Stonehenge was built, but we do know that on 21 June, the longest day of the year, the sun rises over the Heel Stone and spears directly through the centre of the circle. Stonehenge asks more questions than it answers. One that kept the conversation flowing as we switchbacked across Wiltshire under menacing clouds was how long it took our distant ancestors to realise that sunrise and sunset were predictable, day after day, year after year. And we agreed that 'Why?' is far more intriguing than 'How?' when talk turned to bringing the bluestones from Pembrokeshire.

Our next destination was Whitchurch, the Shropshire town whose businesses include J B Joyce, the world's oldest clockmaker. Founded in 1690, the company has made clocks for literally hundreds of churches and several cathedrals, for stately homes, town halls, railway stations and universities, for a palace in Afghanistan and a dockyard in India, for the Customs House in Shanghai, the Post Office in Adelaide and the City Hall in Cape Town. Brian Parry was working on the clock from the municipal buildings in Liverpool. The city had decided to mark the millennium by restoring chimes that were silenced during the Second World War, he explained, posing for Dawson's camera amid machinery that to my eye looked more like a medieval printing press than a clock.

Next morning we scampered over the rain-lashed Pennines to visit Bob Gardner at his home near Doncaster. He joked about buying, selling and restoring antique clocks being a little more sedate than his career as a Royal Corps of Transport officer whose duties included throwing vehicles out of high-flying aircraft. He restored and rallied cars before clocks came into his life by chance, a few years ago, when 'Hey! This is a wizard wheeze!' was his reaction to buying one for £200 in Yorkshire and selling it for £700 in London. Old clocks are as interesting as old cars, he enthused, the main difference being that you can restore a clock in three months while a car takes more like five years. How did he acquire so much knowledge in such a short time? He chuckled. 'One thing the Army does is teach you how to learn about things. If you're put in charge of anything from drains to guided missiles – subjects about which you know nothing whatsoever – you'll be a world expert within six months.'

He showed us an elegant Regency clock, worth about £3,500, before uncovering a £50,000 replica of John Harrison's first marine chronometer, made by the Sinclair & Harding craftsmen whose work we admired at The Oval. Coincidentally, our route to the westbound M62 passed through Foulby, where Harrison lived as a boy at the end of the 17th century. His determination to overcome the immense problems involved in making a clock that would remain accurate at sea – the key to navigating beyond the sight of land – inspired the best-selling book, *Longitude* by Dava Sobel.

Britain's biggest clock is in Liverpool, where each of the Royal Liver Building's four dials is 25 feet in diameter. The Royal Liver Friendly Society decided to build a new head office overlooking the River Mersey in 1907. Inside, where the south tower's blend of art deco and stark modernism reminded us of Buck Rogers and King Kong, we examined the clock that was started just as King George V was crowned on 22 June, 1911. Glyn Morris, our guide, rattled out statistics. The minute hands are 14 feet long and three feet across at their widest; the mechanism weighs four tons; and the four dials incorporate 15 tons of ironwork plus a ton of opal glass, which can withstand wind pressures of up to 11 tons per square inch. Everything appeared to be on a heroic scale until opening a small box revealed short, slender lengths of metal. The gentle noises they make when struck are amplified to sound the hours. Usually turned off at night, the chimes were to ring out to tell Liverpool when 1999 became 2000.

We admired spectacular Welsh scenery as the A6 carried us from Liverpool to Chester to Bangor and over the Menai Strait to Anglesey for a good meal in the Treaddur Bay Hotel, ten minutes from Holyhead. Next morning, plump, succulent kippers fortified us for the dash to Ireland aboard Stena Line's HSS catamaran. Powered by huge jet engines, *Stena Explorer* covers the 52 miles between Holyhead and Dun Laoghaire in 99 minutes, which makes the traditional ferry seem like a galley propelled by sails and slaves.

North-west of Dublin, the River Boyne flows through a lush valley in a landscape stippled with passage-grave mounds in which cremated remains were buried long ago. Newgrange, the greatest of these wonders, was built between 3500 BC and 2700 BC, covers almost an acre and is faced with quartz and granite boulders from as far afield as the Wicklow Hills, south of Dublin, and Dundalk Bay, in what is now Northern Ireland. Experts reckon that dragging a four-ton stone two miles from the nearest quarry took 80 men four days. But it may have been easier. According to legend, the stones were dropped by a sorceress as she flew over County Meath. Coins reveal that Romans visited Newgrange, which features prominently in mythology as the tomb of gods and kings, and as the place where Cuchulainn, Ireland's greatest folk hero, was conceived.

A bewitching aura of ancient magic made the spine tingle as I stooped and squeezed along the narrow passage that opens out into a lofty chamber whose corbelled roof has remained completely waterproof for 5,000 years. The passage climbs just enough to prevent any light from the entrance reaching the chamber, but above the entrance is the 'roof box'. This apparently insignificant slot's purpose was revealed when our guide switched off the light and plunged the chamber into darkness that could not have been blacker had I immersed my head in a bucket of pitch. When she pressed another switch, to simulate sunrise on the shortest day of the year, we gasped as a finger of light entered the chamber. The first person to witness this in thousands of years was an archaeologist who decided to concentrate on the winter solstice while excavating Newgrange in 1967. He noted how the first pencil of direct sunlight lanced through the roof box at 08.58 and the beam was cut off from the tomb exactly 17 minutes later. The educated guess is that Newgrange's builders aligned the mound to mark the day when winter begins to recede and the world is reborn.

Newgrange was the sole reason for visiting Ireland, so the time-shrinking HSS whooshed us back to our Welsh hotel just in time for a nightcap. In view of this journey's theme, nothing could have been more appropriate than hearing the barman call: 'Time, gentlemen, please!'

25

GREAT BRITAIN'S GREATEST DRIVE

2001

The almost surreal juxtaposition of land and sea became even more spectacular as the blood-red Porsche Boxster S climbed the Pass of the Cattle, prompting the almost heretical thought that Scotland's north-west coast makes even California's famous Highway 1 appear no more beautiful than a Siberian city's industrial wasteland in midwinter. Photographer Ian Dawson and I have visited more than 50 countries scattered across six continents, but we agreed that this day's views surpassed anything we had ever seen before.

Scenery was not the only attraction. Scotland's northland is blessed with roads that could have been created just to delight anyone who enjoys driving, particularly in a car as swift and sure-footed as the Boxster S. Traffic is spread thinner than butter on a pauper's crust, except at the height of the holiday season, because very few people live beyond the Great Glen that extends between Inverness in the east and Fort William on the west coast. Wick and Thurso, by far the biggest communities encountered between the start and finish of our 600-mile journey, muster fewer than 10,000 inhabitants each. Third place goes to Gairloch, with just over 2,000. A region where human beings are heavily outnumbered by sheep contrasts with Britain's image as one of the most over-crowded places on the planet.

The Boxster's qualifications were established en route to

Inverness, a long day's trot from London. At the emotional and aesthetic end of the scale, Porsche's compact roadster looked terrific with red warpaint and smart alloys wrapped in Pirelli's meaty P-Zero tyres. From the practical viewpoint, we appreciated front and rear stowage compartments with more than enough room for luggage and photographic equipment. The 3.2-litre Boxster's competence as a powerful, torquey, smooth-riding and reasonably economical cruiser impressed us as we loped northward to Inverness, brimmed the tank, dropped the top and launched into the sun-blessed afternoon.

We left the busy main A9 road and dashed over Struie Hill for wide-ranging views up the coast, where heather-clad mountains stand sentinel above the North Sea. The peaks have Gaelic names such as Beinn a'Bhragaidh and Meall Dheirgidh, which are best pronounced while standing on your head and gargling malt whisky. The A9 is a well-used road by local standards – we encountered another vehicle every five minutes or so – but traffic wasn't a problem when Carn Liath was built about 2,000 years ago. Standing in a field and devoid of any commercialisation whatsoever, Carn Liath is the remains of a tower, known hereabouts as a broch, whose lichen-mottled stones provided shelter and protection for several families when this part of Scotland was populated by the Iron Age ancestors of folk called Picts.

Eyes popped and jaws dropped as we motored into Helmsdale, a tiny fishing port whose crabs and lobsters are trucked as far as Spain. Keith Parkes, the silver-bearded skipper of a boat that's available for everything from fishing to whale-watching trips, assured us that no visit to Helmsdale was complete without nipping into La Mirage and meeting its proprietor, Nancy Sinclair. And he was right. Sinclair and her restaurant take their cues from television's old *Dynasty* soap, which is the last source of inspiration you'd expect to encounter in sleepy, back-of-beyond Helmsdale. A tongue-in-cheek character with dazzling blonde hair, a heart-shaped beauty spot, fancy sunglasses, fingers clustered with huge rings, and a pink leather bomber jacket, Sinclair posed with the Porsche while I studied photographs of her ladyship shooting the breeze with all manner of celebrities.

Helmsdale is where the landscape changes as the A9 suddenly snakes from sea level to 750 feet. Unlike its crew, who were digesting their breakfast, the Boxster flexed its muscles and ran hard across gently undulating Caithness, the so-called Lowlands beyond the Highlands. Whaligoe is typical of place-names that date from when Vikings crossed the North Sea from Scandinavia. Wick, another link with that era, was nearly deserted as the Boxster tiptoed through in a couple of minutes, early on a Sunday morning.

We side-stepped John o'Groats, which is little more than a name, and pushed on to Dunnet Head, which really is the British mainland's last gasp. A lighthouse built by Robert Louis Stevenson's grandfather is perched on the edge of a 340-feet-high cliff, but its windows have been shattered by stones hurled up during storms of apocalyptic ferocity.

We eased the Porsche through Thurso, then along the increasingly spectacular coast. To our left, relatively flat Caithness gave way to jagged, Tolkienesque mountains whose height is accentuated by their steepness and their proximity to the Atlantic Ocean. Much of the way westward used to be a narrow squiggle of single-track road with car-sized passing places every few hundred yards. Many of those miles are now covered by smooth, two-lane blacktop over which excellent visibility and an almost complete absence of traffic let us drive the Boxster hard without upsetting anyone. These thrilling sprints illustrated the split personality that makes the Porsche ideal for a trip like this. On the one hand, its power, grip, brakes, six-speed gearbox and exquisite steering combine to thrill anyone who enjoys driving fast in safety. At the other end of the scale, plenty of torque makes it delightful when you are just loafing along with the top down, enjoying the scenery.

'Two of our cars have been wrecked in accidents involving deer since we moved up here from England,' said the lady at the tourist information office in Durness, where driving over a cliff and into the Atlantic was the only alternative to turning south. Besides deer, this land of peat, heather, rock and loch also provides a little grazing for sheep and long-haired, long-horned Highland cattle. Fences are few and far between, so there's always a chance that an animal will suddenly decide that ambling across the road in front of a hard-charging Boxster is more fun than chewing grass. It is equally important to realise that maps can be misleading. God alone knows how many travellers have planned to eat, fuel up or spend the night in Laxford Bridge, 19 miles down the A838 from Durness. What appears on the map to be a place of some significance, by local standards, is nothing more than the point where a bridge crosses over the River Laxford.

The direct, 50-mile route from there to Ullapool, with its population of 1,200 hardy souls, involves one of the best driving roads I know. The alternative is a coastal loop over exceptionally narrow, sinuous and switchbacking single-tracks. There are at least two compelling reasons for taking the longer, slower route. First, it runs through the heart of Assynt, a geological wonderland where rocks that were formed nearly three billion years ago are overlooked by mountains that take your breath away. The finest of them all is Suilven. Second, a very short detour leads to Achiltibuie, where the cuisine at the Summer Isles Hotel rates a coveted star in Michelin's guide to Britain's hotels and restaurants. Run with immense charm and style by the Irvine family, it comes close to being my very favourite hotel.

Anyone with an atom of sense would spend a couple of nights here – granted sufficient funds, because it's not cheap – but time was at a premium, so we sighed and moved on after an early breakfast. Glorious weather made this decision easier to accept as the Porsche headed for Ullapool along a road huddled beneath the almost vertical southern flank of Stac Pollaidh, another wondrous mountain. Ullapool is a delightful little fishing and ferry port whose neat, whitewashed buildings overlook the shimmering waters of Loch Broom. Housed in what used to be a chapel, the town's small museum has a fascinating audio-visual exhibit about 'one of the great wilderness areas of Europe' where wildlife includes eagle and sparrowhawk, otter, wildcat and red deer, salmon, mackerel and herring. There's also a model of the *Hector*, a little three-master that sailed from here in 1773 with about 200 emigrants on board. Most of them reached the Canadian province of Nova Scotia – New Scotland – three months later.

Complemented by perfect weather, the scenery became more and more memorable after the Porsche started looping through Wester Ross. Scotland's eastern and northern coasts are relatively straight, but this one looks as if it were shaped by a hyper-active maniac with a hacksaw and a blunt axe. The tidal lochs that plunge deep into the landscape also make nonsense of conventional ways of measuring distances. For instance, at one point, we were only ten straight-line miles from Achiltibuie, but had driven about 60 miles since leaving the Summer Isles Hotel. This can be an advantage. A friend of mine was drinking long after the official closing time in an isolated pub. He eventually asked a weather-beaten local what the situation was with regard to the police. The old man chuckled, sipped his whisky, thought for a moment and said: 'The policeman lives on the other side of the loch. That's 40 long, hard miles away by road or five minutes by ferry . . . And I'm the ferryman.'

This coast's biggest surprise is Inverewe Gardens, where exotic trees, shrubs and flowers from all over the world flourish in a location that's about as far north as Juneau, Alaska. This is thanks to the soothing Gulf Stream, which brings relatively warm water from the Gulf of Mexico. The mild climate encouraged one dauntless landowner, Osgood Mackenzie, to create a garden after acquiring the 12,000-acre estate in 1862. When he started, there was just one small tree growing on the Inverewe peninsula. Despite being so far off the beaten track, the garden now attracts more than 130,000 visitors a year.

Loch Ewe itself is a reminder that remote places may have witnessed great events, even if you assume nothing significant to have happened since the dawn of time. Now stippled with a few small boats, this sheltered anchorage was an important naval base during the First and Second World Wars. This is where HMS *Nelson*, a 36,000-ton British battleship armed with nine 16-inch guns, was holed by a mine laid by a German submarine in October 1939. One month earlier, *Nelson* had taken Winston Churchill from Orkney to Loch Ewe.

The last loop of this dream drive started 40 miles beyond Gairloch. A mountain like a legendary ruined city steepled above the Porsche as we ran down Glen Torridon before creeping along the single-track road to Applecross, a tiny village on a snug, sandy bay. We ate a late lunch there before experiencing the stupendous views all over again while climbing the Pass of the Cattle – *Bealach-Na-Ba* in Gaelic – and then plunging back to sea level at Loch Kishorn. Tackled in the opposite direction, the pass is reckoned to be Britain's longest steep climb as it rises from sea level to 2,054 feet in six miles. This understates the situation, because most of the ascent is squeezed into about a mile of narrow zigzags. Approaching from the west, we peered into the deep, stygian ravine and wondered whether we would have to send the Porsche down by parachute.

Another 90 miles unfurled between Loch Kishorn and Fort William. The scenery was superb and the road enabled the snarling Boxster to stretch its legs again. Landmarks included Eilean Donan, the most romantic of Scotland's many castles. But even the sight of Buckingham Palace and the Statue of Liberty floating across the cerulean sky on clouds pulled by a host of angels would have been an anti-climax after what we had already experienced.

26

MIDDLE EAST

Cooke's Tour to Abadan

1976

Martin Lyon is the cheerful, energetic and efficient boss of Abadan Services, a Fareham-based company, founded a year ago, that has plunged enthusiastically and successfully into the now almost legendary business of hauling freight from Britain to the Middle East. He runs six orange-and-white Mercedes 1924 trucks and his drivers include 42-year-old Bill Cooke, a nuggety little native of County Kildare who has lived in Swindon since he was a boy. I'm proud to call him my friend, because it was Bill who drove me precisely 4,071 miles from England to Iran, from rainy Hampshire to the blistering heat of Abadan, at the top of the Persian Gulf. We were pulling a Rentco trailer, lightly laden with builders' moulds and tools. It was Bill's sixth Middle East run, but his first through the Eastern Bloc countries. The traditional route to Turkey had been ruled out by the acute shortage of Austrian and Yugoslavian transit permits.

Day One: We hit London at the wrong time, with the morning rush hour at its thickest, but the sight of all those bowlers, brollies and briefcases made us feel pretty good, despite the traffic. Imagine plodding to yet another grey, predictable, paper-shuffling day behind a desk when you could be up there in the cab of a Merc, heading for the Persian Gulf.

Harwich is a friendly, hassle-free port and the 21-hour Prins Line ferry crossing to Hamburg is definitely a good thing. The food is excellent, drivers get special duty-free rates and there's a disco until some unearthly hour in the morning. Bill was soon renewing old friendships and forging new ones as the beer flowed and the tales grew taller. A few of the lads had done the Eastern Bloc run before and there was no shortage of advice. 'Mind you,' said Bill, 'I tend to treat everything I hear with a pinch of salt until I've seen things for myself. Everything can change completely from one trip to the next.'

Day Two: There was no time to linger in Hamburg's notorious Reeperbahn district – the ferry docks within a stone's throw of the nearest red light – but we did spot one blousy whore dressed as a nun. Another, old enough to be Queen Victoria's granny, leered from her window. 'She's different,' joked John 'Robbo' Robbins, the owner-driver of an F86 Volvo. 'She pays you.'

The atmosphere was very grim at the East German frontier, 30 miles away. Granite-faced guards indicated that we must not leave the cab, and any attempts at matey humour were cut short by laser-like glances. Equally chilling was the realisation that we had just passed through a vast network of fortifications sealing us off from Western Europe. We were behind the Iron Curtain and must not stray from the official transit route that runs round Berlin to Dresden and the Czech border. East Gemany is as mountainous as the average bowling green and it was easy to maintain a crisp average. The miles slipped by as the Merc's mercifully quiet engine soothed away the last traces of my king-sized hangover. Bill, infinitely more sensible, responsible and abstemious than his passenger, was as chirpy as a sparrow.

In Dresden we saw our first set of traffic lights since leaving West Germany, then ran through hilly country to the border. It was dark and bitterly cold, but the East German dog handler turfed us out of the cab for half an hour. It was sheer bloody-mindedness, because the snarling alsatian completed its sniffing routine in less than five minutes. We eventually slunk back to our seats after balancing the risk of a bullet against the near certainty of our feet freezing to the windswept tarmac.

Unlike their neighbours, the Czechs actually smiled as they stamped our passports and processed paperwork that included the bulky TIR carnet. We felt a good deal more relaxed while easing down the wickedly long, steep hill towards Teplice for a sleep. The 1924's cab is none too

243

spacious, but the top bunk was more welcome than the best bed in the world's most luxurious hotel.

Day Three: We awoke to warm sunshine and the announcement that Robbo's kettle was on the boil. Good news indeed, because Bill's gas bottle is empty and there doesn't seem to be much chance of replacing it this side of Istanbul. Running through attractive country, with blossom flanking the roads and hares going crazy in the fields, we skirted Prague before stopping for food. A few British trucks roared by, hooting happily, homeward bound and reminding us that we had hardly started. But the weather was still good, traffic was light and it would be easy to reach the Hungarian border beyond Bratislava by early evening. Or so it seemed.

We had just passed mile after mile of multilingual signs proclaiming 'Peace' when a traffic cop materialised from a ditch and flagged us down. After 10 minutes of shrugging, grimacing, sign language and Bill's marvellous Irish-German, we realised it was a public holiday. All trucks had to be off the road between 3pm and 9pm. We hadn't been told at the border? Too bad. The fine worked out at roughly £7 – a small fortune in Czechoslovakia – but Bill made it very clear that the Merc would stay put and crumble to rusty dust before he put his hand in his pocket. The lawman eventually settled for a packet of cigarettes, but only after we had promised to park in the next town. Robbo cursed the Czech police in general. 'Last time I was here I fancied a drink with my food and bought one of those cartons of beer. I'd had a couple of swigs when this copper strolls up and fines me for drinking and driving. So I chucked the carton into the gutter and the bugger fined me again, for dropping litter!'

Bang on the dot of nine we moved off, following the motorway to Brno and finally stopping on the outskirts of Bratislava. Night driving in Czechoslovakia is made easy by the almost total lack of traffic and pedestrians. Everyone seems to be in bed with the lights off by 10pm. Maybe it's something to do with the country having more beautiful, dark-eyed, mini-skirted girls per square mile than any other I have ever visited.

Day Four: An eyeball-to-eyeball confrontation with a

zebra got us off to an unusual start. It took a few bleary seconds to cotton on to the fact that we had parked alongside a zoo. The animals were being fed, but we forgot about breakfast in our haste to reach the border. Yesterday's copper had warned that all trucks had to be off the road again by 7am. We hit the frontier with minutes to spare.

The map showed a motorway about 60 miles down the road. It would have been a great help if the Hungarians had got round to building it. At a place called something like Tattybanana we brimmed the 85-gallon tank and enjoyed a snack served by a bosomy blonde who looked like Zsa Zsa Gabor, Hungary's most famous export, in her younger days.

Budapest was a disaster. We took a wrong turning immediately after crossing the Danube – which is no more blue than a mug of coffee, Mr Strauss – and lost a couple of hours exploring lanes to the south of the city. Judging by the way they reared up and bolted into the fields, dragging their carts behind them, the local nags had never before been treated to the sight of a big truck. Back on the right road at last, we hurried eastwards over a vast plain. The big cheese on the Romanian frontier could have been the late and unlamented Herman Goering's twin brother. Like most of his colleagues, notably the guy in the bureau de change, he had obviously been gargling heavily during the evening. He had already knocked Robbo for 200 cigarettes and his glazed, porcine eyes lit up at the sight of another UK truck waiting to be plundered. 'You have drugs? Dirty pictures?' he bellowed hopefully, hand resting on the howitzer-sized pistol hanging from a belt big enough to strap a howdah to an elephant. 'You have weapons' – he made a grossly obscene gesture – 'Only for the wife, eh? You have whisky?'

'Yes,' we said, and Bill was promptly marched back to the cab where the bloated old bandit sunk almost a third of a bottle of Johnnie Walker in two vast, bubbling gulps. By the time we left he seemed to be on the brink of a richly deserved heart attack. Fatal, we hoped, because he had done nothing to speed us on our way. Cigs and swigs are all part of the game, but you do expect a little help in return, not just a volley of belches.

Day Five: Yesterday's breakfast consisted of a stick of

chewing gum. Today's five-star spread was chocolate fingers and cream crackers washed down by smoke from the first of countless cigarettes. I'll soon be as fat as that slob on the frontier if I don't cut down on rich, nourishing toothpaste. Such were the thoughts that cruised through my mind as we headed from Arad to Sibiu, ignoring the AA's recommended route because it involves lots of hard slogging in the mountains around Cluj, which sounds more like a disease than a town. Romanian roads are not too bad, although some urban stretches resemble opencast mines. Drunks were the biggest problem. By mid-afternoon they were so thick on the ground we came to the conclusion that it must be an extremely serious offence to stay sober on a Sunday. One guy fell off his bike and landed so close to our wheels that he must have been treated to the world's fastest haircut.

Night had fallen by the time we reached the first stretch of motorway since Czechoslovakia. Leaving the flickering orange flares of Pitesti's oil refineries behind us we sped towards Bucharest, the Merc humming along at 55mph or so with quite a bit held in reserve. We stopped on the far side of Bucharest and Bill looked pleased as he puffed the day's last cigarette. 'The Bulgarian border's only an hour down the road, so you can say we've knocked off five countries in five days. Not bad going, but the really hard grafting doesn't start until we turn left in Ankara. And that's another 700 or so miles.'

Day Six: Clattering hoofs and the jingle of harness act as a non-stop alarm clock, for this is a part of the world where horsepower still means precisely that. Women toil in the fields while their husbands smoke and snooze by the roadside. The more productive men nod at the reins of sedately jogging carts, occasionally mustering enough energy for a good scratch. But it was all action at the frontier. The paperwork was finished in 30 minutes and all we needed before crossing the Danube into Bulgaria was a rubber stamp in the passports. It was too good to last. We reached the desk seconds behind a coachload of tourists and kicked our heels for three hours. Bill's natural good humour wilted in the hot sun. 'At this rate,' he growled, 'we'll have to apply for citizenship, not exit visas.'

It was mid-afternoon before we started reeling in the Bulgarian miles, but even then our run south was slowed by long stretches of rough cobbles beyond Byala. By this stage the road signs were causing some concern, because the Bulgarian alphabet differs from our own. Words like Zp3ddo7zov, with most of the letters looking as if they have been accidentally printed back to front, do precious little to help the man with the map. The notice you just passed could mean anything from 'Drink more milk' to 'The road ahead has been swept away by an avalanche'. The mountain beyond Gabrovo seemed to climb for ever, but at last, almost 1,800 miles from Fareham, we saw the first sign for Istanbul.

Day Seven: Kapikule must be one of the world's busiest borders, but paperwork on the Bulgarian side is handled by two men – one for passports, one for carnets – who operate from a pair of offices no bigger than ice cream kiosks. You wait endlessly, frying in summer and freezing in winter. We just got wet. The only laugh throughout the entire grey, miserable morning came when a truck stopped suddenly and its trailer's canvas roof decanted gallons of rainwater all over the customs man waiting to search the cab. After seven hours we crossed into Turkey – a run of maybe 300 yards – and the wretched process started all over again. Tempers were not soothed by the tax levied for the extremely dubious privilege of using Turkish roads. We escaped with £127, thanks to having so little weight in the trailer, but Robbo was hit for more than £200 while others had to fork out almost twice as much.

It can take literally days to get away from this ghastly place, but we escaped after a total of 12 hours, celebrating with a few slugs of lunatic's broth before bed. It would be nice to report that the night air was filled with exotic oriental sounds, but we were lulled to sleep by the shouts and howls of a group of drunken Bulgarians beating merry hell out of each other at the far end of the lay-by.

Day Eight: It is Robbo's birthday and he enlivened breakfast with a Jimmy Young impression. 'What's the recipe today, Jim? A Middle East driver's daily diet, would you believe. One cream cracker, 200 smokes and 700 effing kilometres!' At noon we reached the Londra Mocamp, on the western outskirts of Istanbul, and managed to grab the motel's last vacant room. The world looked better after a shower, a shave, a whirlwind tour of the city, several drinks, steak, chips and the sight of a belly dancer doing navel exercises.

Day Nine: Running through Ankara, Sivas, Erzincan and Erzurum, the 1,050-mile road from Istanbul to the Iranian border is a brutal test of trucks and drivers. Rarely dropping below 4,000 feet and climbing to more than twice that height, it gets so cold in winter that diesel turns to a waxy jelly. When the snows melt, torrents raging down from the mountains frequently take sections of road with them, and the plains become inland seas. In summer you are choked by swirling dust. Some surfaces are good, but most of the route is little smoother than the crater-pocked face of the moon. Nine out of ten Turkish drivers seem hellbent on suicide, which gears you up for their Iranian counterparts, who are even worse. That's why Bill deemed it prudent to rest for 24 hours before the really hard grafting started, a mere 1,981 miles after leaving home.

Although it includes a couple of stiff climbs, the road from Istanbul to Ankara is just about the best in Turkey. It would be an easy 280-mile punch if traffic was restricted to TIR trucks. As it is, you have to contend with the dreaded tonkas and kamikazes. Tonkas, named after Tonka Toys, are the small trucks that infest Turkey's roads. Many carry scrap metal and it is often difficult to tell where the load ends and the truck starts. Most emit fumes so black and dense that it is impossible to avoid the conclusion that they run on a mixture of rancid mutton fat and camel's urine. The two-lane road to Ankara is very busy, even by UK standards, but that does not prevent tonkas overtaking four abreast. Drivers do not use mirrors or signals, but are very good at sounding the horn.

Kamikazes are the long-distance buses, inevitably made by Mercedes and therefore not lacking in power. They are driven as if there is no tomorrow, which is frequently the case, and specialise in passing you at 90mph on blind corners. When a kamikaze brakes – a phenomenon observed as often as the second coming of Christ – you know there must be *real* trouble ahead. According to Bill, they go so fast because their schedules demand the sort of average speeds that Niki Lauda would be proud to maintain in his Grand Prix Ferrari. The conditions of employment are simple, he said: 'Arrive late more than once and you lose your job. Run to time and, later if not sooner, you lose your life.'

Nerves jangling like a ragtime piano, we reached the Ankara Mocamp and were charged £1 for parking overnight in an ocean of mud. Other facilities worthy of mention included open, unlit inspection pits waiting to cripple the unwary walker.

Day Ten: On the outskirts of Ankara there's a soul-stirring signpost with fingers pointing to Iran, Iraq and Europe. We turned left and eventually reached Yozgat, where a roadside hoarding extolled the merits of the Zumrut Hotel. There were also zum ruts in zer dual-carriageway running through zer town. To be more precise, the road appeared to have been heavily bombed, then flooded. With a bit of imagination the local tourist board could advertise the town as Turkey's answer to Venice. Conditions became worse and worse, with potholes ranging from shallow, saucer-sized babies to chassis-shattering monsters, almost as big a barn doors and up to a foot deep. Another Turkish trick involves building the edges of the road up so sharply that straying from the straight and narrow is almost as fatal as dropping a wheel over the rim of the Grand Canyon.

Wrestling with the wheel and keeping one eye open for oncoming traffic, Bill fell in with the local custom of driving on the right . . . and the left . . . and up the centre. Anything goes when you're trying to avoid the really wicked craters, and the rule of the road boils down to being bigger or smaller than whatever happens to be coming towards you. Given even a half-decent surface this would be a fast road, because traffic is not heavy and the mountains are joined by endless straights. But with things as they are you just grit your teeth, hang on tight and give thanks for a really well-engineered truck.

We stopped for the night in Zara. The grubby garage charged us £1.60 to park and the young bandit who took the money had the cheek to say that he would keep an eye on the truck for a 20-cigarette bonus.

Day Eleven: The Rafahiye Pass climbs to 5,085 feet between

Sivas and Erzincan, and it was here that Bill almost diverted to the Pearly Gates during the winter. The Merc's front wheels started tramlining along deep ruts in the iron-hard ice and he juddered to a halt within inches of an immense vertical drop with not so much as a rusty strand of barbed wire between him and eternity. He reckons it was only the build-up of snow in front of the truck that saved him. Last winter was said to have been the most hellish for 35 years. In places the drifts were higher than the top of a trailer and some drivers got through four sets of chains on a single trip.

At Erzincan, set in a vast natural bowl rimmed by snow-clad mountains, it took only two hours to get a call through to Martin Lyon in England. Delays like that drive you mad in the UK, but out here, where lost time can be counted in days, or even weeks, you have to accept that everything depends on the will of Allah. We stopped for the night just before Horosan, paying to park on yet another muddy patch. 'Things are looking up,' said Bill. 'They've put in a cold-water tap since I was last here. Real five-star facilities.'

Day Twelve: I have been forced to revise my opinion of the Turkish roads encountered so far. After today's 150-mile nightmare, from Horosan to the border at Gorbulak, they now seem like the smoothest and most benign motorways ever built by the greatest of all civil engineers. This stretch, down to a single track in places, was infinitely more punishing than anything I had experienced before, including the instrument of torture that runs through Jordan from Maffraq to a place called H4. The sole exception to that carefully considered judgement is the 65 miles of desert between H4 and the Saudi frontier. And that lacks even the faintest hint of any road whatsoever.

The Merc has excellent suspension and superbly comfortable seats, but only a hovercraft riding on its cushion of air could have travelled this road in anything approaching comfort. It should be graded according to the Richter Scale. The panel of warning lights fell out of the facia, the top bunk's retaining bolts were ripped clean out of the frame, the screenwasher bottle broke loose and was never seen again. Sleeping bags, tinned food, saucepans, torches – anything capable of moving crashed onto the floor. Only a fool would have tried to replace them while on the move, because the bumps were so severe that releasing your grip on something solid could easily have resulted in a nasty injury. The really bad bits lay beyond the notorious Tahir Pass that climbs to 8,122 feet and can be a killer in winter. It is not too bad in good weather – Sherlock Holmes might have detected faint traces of tarmac in a couple of places – but the thought of tackling those bends and gradients in ice and snow made me shudder.

About 15 miles before Dogubayazit – known to the cognoscenti as Doggybiscuit – we spotted a UK-registered Fiat 619TI in distress. The driver, Mike Lambe, a newcomer to the Middle East, had spluttered to a halt with fuel-feed problems 48 hours earlier. After a lonely night he managed to get a fitter out from the town, but by then the batteries were flat and it was clear he would have to spend another night in the wilds. Pointing to the nearby hills and drawing a blood-curdling finger across his throat, the fitter urged Mike to seek refuge in Dogubayazit, but he was determined not to leave the truck to be ransacked.

We brewed tea and listened to the story of the previous night. 'At about 11pm I heard voices outside and kept very quiet, hoping they'd go away. Then someone banged on the cab. I don't mind admitting I was bloody terrified. I put the light on and looked out to see a group of bandits with shovels and God knows what else in their hands. The leader said that if I didn't give them money and cigarettes he might not be able to prevent his mates getting a bit violent. I didn't fancy losing the load and being beaten to death into the bargain, so I gave them 400 lira' – just over £13 and a small fortune in eastern Turkey – 'plus 200 cigarettes. I told a copper about it this morning, but he just shrugged his shoulders.'

We soon got the Fiat running again and escorted Mike into Dogubayazit. The fitter tried to charge him £50, but Bill's formidable haggling talents cut him down by a tenner. Meanwhile, a local entrepreneur asked Mike if he would like to earn some money by taking a load of jeans to Teheran. 'Don't touch it, no matter how much he offers,' Bill warned.

'You can bet your life he's smuggling drugs. If you get caught in Iran they'll lock you up and throw away the key.'

The last few miles to the border, where we waited for seven hours, was nose-to-tail trucks and flanked by reminders that a lot of people spend a lot of time here, inching eastward. I'm talking about acres of litter and gut-churning evidence that facilities don't include toilets. The clouds suddenly lifted to reveal graceful Mount Ararat, an extinct volcano all of 16,945 feet high. The sight revived my flagging spirits, but Bill was unimpressed. 'Every time I see it I remember the story of the ark and wonder what poor old Noah did to deserve ending up here,' he groaned. Incidentally, the neighbouring corner of the USSR is inhabited by Armenians, who are said to be very light-fingered. The traditional recipe for Armenian omelette starts with 'First steal six eggs'.

Clearing the last border before Abadan was as welcome as a glass of cold water in the desert. It was our eighth frontier since leaving England and the delays totted up to more than 30 hours. Even more welcome was the knowledge that we had at last reached a country with really good roads.

Day Thirteen: Iran's long, blissfully smooth straights gave the 11.6-litre Merc a chance to exercise its 240 horses as we sped through the sunny morning. Somewhere beyond Tabriz we were flagged down by an oncoming British truck. 'One of the lads has had a spot of bother a few miles down the road,' the driver told us. 'The drainplug on one of his tanks came adrift and he lost about 100 gallons of diesel before realising what had happened. He's getting it mended, so keep your eyes open.'

Bill and I exchanged glances. No, it couldn't be. But it was. There on the roadside was the bearded figure of Mike Lambe, getting the tank welded in surroundings that made Steptoe's yard look as tidy as the forecourt of Buckingham Palace. The owner obviously lived on the premises. His shack, piled high with scrap metal, boasted a bed. We noted the cockerel perched on the pillow and hoped the bloke would one day be able to afford a proper alarm clock. We helped Mike replace the tank, then parted company for the last time. He was heading for Teheran, we turned right at Takistan, starting the last leg to our destination at the top of the Persian Gulf.

Night driving in Iran is quite an experience, because the locals are not too fussy about such optional extras as lights. Some, presumably blessed with X-ray eyes, manage with none at all, not even rear reflectors. Others trundle along with a pair of red lights picking out the road ahead, so there's a risk of pulling out to overtake what is in fact an oncoming vehicle. One truck's tailboard was illuminated by a flickering oil lamp that fell off and burst into flames.

Day Fourteen: The road from Khorramabad to Abadan runs through a vast gorge and crosses some rugged, parched mountains scarred with landslides. The scenery is spectacular, but seems to bring out the worst in the Iranian truckers. They drive every bit as badly as their Turkish counterparts, but there is an all-too-obvious difference in size – and, therefore, in killing power – which makes you hope you remembered to keep up your life insurance payments. Unlike poverty-stricken Turkey, Iran is a wealthy country and can afford good machinery. So instead of being pestered by pint-sized tonkas you have to contend with huge Macks, 1632 Mercs and F89 Volvos driven by characters who wouldn't be safe pushing Dinky Toys across the kitchen floor. I lost count of the number of times we were overtaken on completely blind bends by two, three and even four or five locals hurtling along at 55–60mph with little more than the thickness of a cigarette paper between tailboard and front bumper. Only Bill's experience and skill kept us off the mortuary's cold marble slab.

We gradually dropped to the sea-level plain leading to Abadan. Travelling by truck should give you plenty of time to get acclimatised, but we had spent several days at around 6,000 feet and the lowland heat suddenly hit us like a molten hammer. Even after dark, running at 50mph with every window open, the wind rushing through the cab was no more refreshing than the suffocating breath of a blast-furnace. When we reached the Abadan International Hotel, at the end of the most eye-opening 4,071 miles of my life, the doors leading to the air-conditioned interior seemed like the Gates of Paradise.

27

Kamikazes and Kalashnikovs on the road to Pakistan

1978

The truck that nearly killed us was a beefy old DeSoto AS600 with a massive front bumper that was right-angled by the bowel-watering impact. That was in Turkey. The menacing monsters that threatened to blast us off the road were Russian-built T-52 tanks. That was the blood-soaked *coup d'état* in Afghanistan. The cops who thought we were spies were a couple of fat, bored clodhoppers with nothing better to do on a Sunday afternoon. That was Yugoslavia. It was impossible to identify the car that came racing towards us at night, down the wrong side of a dual carriageway. But that was Pakistan. We were fined in Bulgaria, stopped by a sandstorm in Iran and had our fair share of mechanical maladies. Had our luck not changed, after more than 5,000 nail-biting miles, we would probably have been gunned down by Pathan tribesmen in the Khyber Pass, where it is always open season for travellers. There were times when a bullet between the eyes would have been welcomed as a merciful release.

The object of the exercise was to transport several tons of equipment from England to Pakistan for the British K2 team under Chris Bonington. Despite its computer-like name, K2 is the world's second highest mountain and stands close to the Chinese border, roughly 1,000 miles north-west of Everest. Bonington's eight-man squad includes six tigers who were involved in the conquest of Everest's toughest route a couple of years ago. They are attempting K2's awe-inspiring West Ridge, a knife-edge of wind-blasted snow, ice and naked rock on which no man has ever set foot before. The problems may well prove even greater than those encountered while climbing Everest the hard way, and this time there are no high-altitude porters to carry supplies for the sahibs.

LRC International is the expedition's main sponsor. The company's £25,000 accounts for roughly half the budget. If LRC fails to ring a bell, their products include Durex contraceptives, Duraplug electrical goods, Halex toothbrushes and Woodwards gripe water. The latter is made in Pakistan, so it's nice to know that the sun never sets on the British burp. BL Cars provided 2.5 Sherpa vans for the overland trek, the odd half being the nether parts of a minibus that a bit of inspired cutting and welding had transformed into a trailer. I got involved when a BL contact rang early one Monday morning. 'I know you do daft things,' he said, 'so how about a run to Pakistan?'

Day One: Fame at last. According to *The Times*, *Daily Telegraph* and *Guardian*, across whose pages our smiling faces were plastered, we hit the road 48 hours ago, after a reception at the Pakistan embassy in London. Never believe what you see in the papers. In fact, we spent two days chasing after such last-minute details as a carnet to get us through Turkey. The overland team consists of yours truly and bossman Tony Riley pulling the trailer, plus Allen Jewhurst and Chris Lister in the solo Sherpa. Tony is travelling out the hard way – the other seven climbers follow by air – and is on his third trip to the Karakoram mountains. Two years ago he and another climber went from North Wales to Islamabad, Pakistan, in (a) six days and nights, and (b) a Ford Transit bought second-hand in Manchester. He assures us that this run will be a lot more restful. Tony is also the expedition's ace cameraman and the film he shoots on the mountain will be put together by Chris and Allen. It should be networked sometime around Christmas.

The 1.8-litre Sherpas have overdrive on third and top gears, low-compression petrol engines to cope with lousy fuel, massive air filters to keep out desert dust, stone guards for radiators and sumps, eyeball-searing Cibie Bi-Oscar spotlights to illuminate wandering camels, towing gear at both ends, and a few extra instruments. Being a diplomatic soul, I will not reveal precise details of payloads and gross weights, although they were checked before we left London for Dover and the Zeebrugge ferry. We are, however, carrying 50 per cent more than Tony had bargained for. Despite the burden, Leyland's man had reckoned we should get 16–18mpg gallon from the trailer rig and maybe 18–20mpg from the solo. A check at Dover suggested he was right about the latter, but Tony and I were struggling to reach 14. At this rate we will be forced to stop every three hours or so. An extra tank would have been worth its weight in diamond-encrusted gold.

Day Two: Sure enough, we spluttered to a halt near Liege, cursing the pitiful range while giving thanks for six five-gallon jerricians. A few hours later I was nibbling away at the autobahn miles when the overdrive failed. We need it on the climbs, where it helps to keep the engine revving hard, and also on the faster bits where flat-out motoring in direct top sounds far too frantic. A quick search failed to reveal the fault, so we let the other van take the trailer and pressed on to a service area. There, thanks be, a more thorough investigation revealed the blown fuse I had overlooked. Lacking a spare of the right strength, we used silver paper and motored on, alert for the acrid smell of smouldering circuits.

We stopped for the night near Nuremburg, having covered 450 miles since leaving Zeebrugge, cooked in a picnic area beside the autobahn and pitched a two-man tent for Allen and Chris. Tony and I tried the Sherpa's bunks, which run across the vans immediately behind and above the seats. Just the job for midgets, contortionists or masochists who enjoy getting the cramps.

Day Three: The morning put Germany behind us, but

thanks to one thing and another it took almost four hours to cover the first 115 miles. Nothing untoward happened, but this little convoy seems to lack the hard-punching, keep-rolling spirit that has become second nature to me after so many long hauls with the professionals. Austria was slow going, although the spectacular, snow-clad scenery provided a rich measure of compensation. But the mountains echoed to Anglo-Saxon curses when Allen pulled up and peered under the bonnet. Petrol was gushing from the carburettor. There was obviously something very wrong with the SU's float chamber, but the nature of the ailment baffled us all. We pushed on towards the next town – and there, on the outskirts, was a Leyland dealer. The boss tackled the job himself, muttering something about a casting flaw, unearthing a spare and sending us on our way rejoicing in just 20 minutes.

Searing lasers of Cibie light, seemingly bright enough to melt concrete half a continent away, paved the road into Yugoslavia. We called it a day just beyond Zagreb, having put 500 miles under our wheels since morning, then settled down on the Sherpas' bunks and seats, with thick strips of foam for mattresses. The gentle music of passing trucks lulled us to sleep.

Day Four: There's no tent to be dismantled and stowed away, but we still manage to spend more than an hour getting the show on the road, heading towards Belgrade down a busy highway flanked by wrecks and wreaths. A strong wind is blowing right on the port bow, tugging at the lofty roof racks and keeping Tony and I down to 55mph, no matter how hard the accelerator is pressed. Belgrade, according to the RAC map we bought in Dover, marks the start of a motorway that runs right down to Nis, within an hour or two of the Bulgarian border. But the autoput, as the Yugos call it, putters out after a few miles for which conned travellers are charged a hefty toll. So we stopped for a hard-earned meal, chuckling over a menu featuring such translations as fried cheat fish, beef teak and stewed different.

Sixty miles from Nis we were treated to a spectacular sunset, and decided it must be a good omen. Ten minutes later the ignition warning light flashed and we stopped in a cloud of steam. Nothing more serious than a broken fanbelt? No such luck, the pulley that drives the fan had disintegrated. Chris and Allen towed us to a café where beers were sipped while Daffy Duck jabbered away in Serbo-Croat on the TV. The only answer, we decided, was to pull the sick Sherpa to Nis and contact one or other of the two Leyland dealers listed in the company's guide to overseas service. Tomorrow being a Sunday, the chance of finding a mechanic on duty is probably about the same as the risk of encountering a polar bear in the Sahara. Fingers crossed, praying for nothing much in the way of hills, we hobbled on.

Day Five: 'What a way to run a bloody expedition,' Tony groaned. He had slept with his feet stuck out of a window and was as wet as the unfortunates who failed to get tickets aboard Noah's ark. We were towed to Deligrad, on the outskirts of Nis, but there was no trace of the Leyland garage mentioned in the booklet. Nor could we find the alternative address, although a policeman assured Tony and Allen it was a private house. Then a strolling mechanic, a sort of Serbo-Croatian AA man, appeared as if by magic, took the mangled pulley and vanished in search of a replacement. Our luck was changing.

Tony decided to pass the time checking through a crate of photographic gear while I strolled down the road to snap something that had caught my eye. It was a cutout figure of a policeman with arms extended to warn drivers of a sharp bend. The shutter had just clicked when a VW braked hard and out jumped a couple of real live Yugocops. Cameras and passports were confiscated and we were ordered to follow the Beetle to police headquarters in the city centre. I had visions of being put up against a wall and offered the traditional last cigarette, but the chief had rather more sense than his underlings and we were allowed to go after an uneasy hour. Meanwhile, back at the Sherpa, the strolling spannerman had returned with a genuine Unipart spare and we were back in business. He charged the thick end of £100 for his time and trouble, but even that was better than rotting by the roadside.

And so to Bulgaria, every inch of which was traversed in the dark. Rain lashed down as we sped along avenues of blossom-laden trees, crashing and splashing through sleeping villages paved with spring-crunching cobbles. Unfortunately, local laws do not permit cars or vans to run with auxiliary lights, or so we were told by the keen young copper who stopped us just before midnight as we were plodding towards Plovdiv. This seemed strange in a country where lights in general appeared to be optional extras. The fine worked out at roughly £5 per vehicle, but we had the last laugh. The law fell into a ditch while striding back to his car.

Day Six: We reached the Turkish border at Kapikule at 3am and didn't escape until midway through the morning. At one stage they seemed all set to strip the vans and check every single packet of biscuits, roll of film and cylinder of oxygen. As we drove off, Tony sighed with all the gusto of a whale surfacing after a long spell under water. 'I feel about ten years younger,' he grinned. 'Getting through that lot has been worrying me for months.'

At the Londra Mocamp, on the outskirts of Istanbul, we washed, ate and telexed England before mixing it with heart-stopping Turkish traffic en route for the great suspension bridge over the Bosphorus. We still had more than 3,500 miles to go, but you do get one almighty boost when you realise you have crossed an entire continent and will henceforth be driving through Asia. However, motoring between Istanbul and Ankara is like playing Russian roulette with all but one chamber loaded at the best of times. After dark the road is a murderous nightmare of multi-coloured lights with the local Tonka Toy trucks and kamikaze coaches overtaking three abreast unless they can possibly find space for more. Needing sleep more than anything else, we pulled onto a campsite beside the Gulf of Izmir, grabbed a meal and were out like lights.

Day Seven: I awoke just before 6am, remembering last

night's gallant talk of making a dawn start and striking deep into Anatolian Turkey by nightfall. The others were called, but 40 frustrating minutes ticked by before the first bleary-eyed figure crawled from the tent. It was Chris. 'Why didn't you pull the bloody thing down on top of us,' he said. 'You should know us well enough by now.'

It had rained hard during the night, leaving pools of water on the grass. Chris and Allen were out onto solid ground in a matter of seconds, but it took two precious hours of cussing, sweating and mud-splattered heaving to extricate the trailer-towing Sherpa. By that time the site looked like a First World War battlefield. A dreadful stench from the van that did all the donkey work made us realise that only a miracle of Lazarus-raising stature would enable its tortured clutch to complete the journey. Rightly or wrongly, we decided to jump that fence when we came to it.

Kazan is not much of a place – just a scruffy little village straddling the main road some 30 miles before Ankara. The road is straight and flat, so there are no visibility problems, and we were bowling through at around 35mph when this big-nosed DeSoto eased away from the cluster of buildings on the far side of the highway. It started chugging across the road, heading for a filling station where a small crowd was standing to watch the world go by. He must have seen us. He must ease off to let us through. He keeeps moving. Slow and lethal. Like a river of lava. The unthinkable is happening.

Helpless in the passenger seat, I could do nothing but pray. Tony hurled the van to the right. A stomach-turning, metal-tearing crunch that seemed to last forever. With all that weight on the roof we must roll. Visions of slaughtered pedestrians. We stopped, upright and alive. People were milling around. A little kid ran up with a glass of water. An old man hobbled up and handed me the door handle while I realised that my left elbow was bleeding from a small cut. I'd been within an inch of losing the arm, which was poking out of the window. Don't worry, the locals gestured. We saw it all. Not your fault. Fingers tapped heads, then pointed to the truck driver. The man's crazy. Don't worry. Uniformed men appeared from nowhere, standing guard, posing for pictures, scrounging cigarettes. We had been lucky: a split-second either way could have rung down the curtain. As it was, the Sherpa and trailer had extensive but superficial damage. We were not even bruised.

DeSoto Dan was not insured, the police said, but was offering the equivalent of £20 to square the account. We accepted – it seemed better than nothing – but if the cash was ever produced it must have gone straight into the Turkish law's ever-open pocket. You just shrug and give thanks for being alive. We must proceed to Ankara, they explained, and get an accident report made out. Without it we would certainly get stopped elsewhere and be accused of a hit-and-run offence. So we drove to the British embassy, where we had a contact, parked the battered Sherpa in the grounds and got justifiably plastered in the staff club. Beds were arranged for the night, but precise details got lost in the haze of expatriate alcohol. By the time Tony and I emerged the other crew had vanished, so I collapsed into the van while Tony snored peacefully beneath the stars on Her Britannic Majesty's immaculately trimmed lawn.

Day Eight: Bonington's name opens all manner of official doors and it was the consul himself who took us under his wing. He confirmed that we would be in trouble without a proper accident report. He could provide the appropriate document – the man who hit us had admitted guilt – but it had to be stamped and signed by the police chief in Kazan. Tony and Allen drove to the village after visiting the local Leyland dealer to seek his opinion about the clutch, and were told it should see us through to journey's end.

The little convoy left Ankara in late afternoon, complete with the precious document. Sure enough we were soon stopped by the first of several policemen who asked to see evidence of our innocence. Yesterday we had been tempted to press on, but gave thanks for playing it by the book. Then came the first section of really bad road – mile after bruising mile of holes, ruts and ridges surfaced with nothing more substantial than muddy gravel. We stopped for a roadside brew, watching the sun go down and making plans. A night in Yozgat, we decided, and then a long day that would take us to Horasan, or even the Iran border.

An hour later, Tony and I realised it was some miles since we had seen the other Sherpa's lights in our mirrors. We paused and then went back, hearts sinking at the sight of hazard lights flashing their amber warning. The clutch had died just 136 miles after we had been assured it would last for another 3,000. Allen managed to crunch into third, blessing the overdrive, and limped into Yozgat at midnight. We got rooms in the Yilmaz Hotel, then joked about it all over several beers. At times like this, a sense of humour is the most blessed of gifts.

Day Nine: British truckers who follow the TIR trail through Turkey tend to have an opinion of the natives that is not so much low as subterranean. I used to share that view, but now wonder if it has developed because Middle Easters see too much of the officials and too little of the ordinary folk. In our case, everyone was keen to help and concerned to get us mobile again as soon as possible. For instance, two characters in the bank across the road took Tony to what was indeed the best garage in town, then contacted the only citizen who was fluent in Turkish and English. In the evening, while I stayed by the phone, Chris and Allen went out for a meal with young Abdullah, the mechanic who had removed the clutch, and a couple of his mates. And the locals insisted on paying.

Tony had taken his life in his hands and boarded a kamikaze coach for Ankara, where communications with home should be a little easier. Making international calls from the mighty metropolis of Yozgat is like trying to swim the Channel in diving boots while pushing a laden supertanker with your nose. But we do have staunch allies in the capital and the RAF lads we had met in the embassy club promised to pull out all the stops. 'Bring the clutch plates over tomorrow,' they said, 'and we'll get them fixed right away.'

Day Ten: With luck we could have been in Islamabad by now. As it was we have covered only 2,350 miles and almost half of them were knocked off in the first 48 hours. But things are looking up. The RAF organised a car, shortly after dawn, and it sped back to Ankara laden with Allen, Chris and the clutch plates. I sat in the lounge reading, sipping endless small glasses of tea, trying not to think ahead. Planning had become pointless. We were living from minute to minute. Bonington rang in the afternoon, miraculously getting through from England. Could we make it to Teheran? If we could, Leyland was flying a couple of mechanics out to meet us. John Bull's answer to the US 7th Cavalry was on its way.

Comrades and clutch plates returned in the evening, but just too late to catch the garage before it closed. Past caring, we went out in search of a meal and bumped into none other than Abdullah the Spannerman, who promptly offered to do the job there and then. He worked for almost five hours, shivering in the sub-zero night on a pavement illuminated only by headlights. It was a magnificent effort at no extra charge. We gave the lad a handsome tip, a K2 expedition T-shirt and, most appreciated of all, English cigarettes.

Day Eleven: Daylight is precious when crossing eastern Turkey. With that in mind we were called at five o'frosty clock, but early morning lethargy and an almost immediate petrol stop saw two hours slip away before we were well and truly rolling. There was every reason to keep on trucking, because our Afghan visas stated quite clearly that the borders would be closed for a fortnight. The reason was unknown, but we had only eight days to reach Pakistan.

This was Chris and Allen's first drive outside Europe and we had been telling them travellers' tales about the terrible roads beyond Ankara. The brutal stretch to Yozgat seemed to confirm our stories, but things had improved out of all recognition since Bill Cooke and I passed this way in the Mercedes in 1976. There were still holes that could shatter suspensions and dislodge your dentures, but it was more like tackling a really bad minor road in rural France than battling along a neglected farm track. In other words, sheer bliss by Turkish highway standards. The one really bad section involved 50 miles somewhere in the wilderness between Sivas and Erzincan. It was a new road and would have been delightful had it been surfaced. We ploughed and crunched through mud, gravel, fist-sized stones and huge craters, blessing the rugged Michelin tyres and the laminated windscreens as bullet-like pebbles were fired by lumbering trucks.

It was hard going in more ways than one. Even the smoothest surface could do nothing to alleviate the power-sapping effect that altitude has on engines. Our 1.8-litre Sherpas had only about 64bhp on tap at sea level, but most of central Turkey is as high as the summit of Ben Nevis, and there are passes of up to 7,000 feet and more to be climbed. Indeed, we would now be above 6,000 for most of the time before plunging down the Khyber Pass to the plains of Pakistan. The other van took the climbs in its stride, but Tony and I had 50 per cent more weight to pull, thanks to the trailer. Worries about blazing brakes ruled out making up for lost time on the serpentine descents.

We growled on, much of the time in first and second gears, passing mud huts and dusky toddlers whose apparently friendly waves almost invariably turned out to be gestured requests for cigarettes. Imranli, where £3 bought four good lunches, seethed with excited, rain-soaked youngsters who went crazy with delight when cameras appeared. On over passes littered with tumbled boulders the size of armchairs. It started snowing, making it impossible to see where the land ended and sky began. We crept through swirling clouds, cursing the damn fools for driving without lights. Down to Erzincan, where tractors and horse-drawn carts sloshed along a main street surfaced from kerb to kerb with inches of black, sticky mud.

From there the Asian Highway climbs again, very slowly but steadily, following the headwaters of the Euphrates before clawing its way up the last pass before Erzurum. It was dark before we reached the top, and raining hard enough on the far side to make visibility a major problem. To hell with pitching tents or sleeping in vans. We found a good city-centre hotel at £4.25 per double room, paddled the streets for a decent meal, then slept like the proverbial logs after a 400-mile slog.

Day Twelve: Electronically amplified chanting of a religious nature awoke us long before the promised 5am call that never came. Breakfast was straight from the Old Testament – unleavened bread, honey, olives, and tasty cheese made from goats' milk. We ate while discussing the day's major decision. Should we follow the traditional TIR route over the formidable Tahir Pass, where a gravel road corkscrews to more than 8,000 feet, or go left in Horasan and use the northern alternative? By all accounts the latter had a good surface, but involved maybe 50 extra miles. It seemed like cheating to side-step Tahir's legendary perils, but local advice and fresh snow on the slopes at little more than 6,000 feet left us with few doubts. We forked left. Any lingering regrets about taking the easy way were soon forgotten as we cruised over smooth, traffic-free roads and marvelled at the splendour of our surroundings. Racing down from the mountains, the Tigris foamed and thundered through gorge after spectacular gorge, washing the feet of immense cliffs of multi-coloured rock. Then we entered a broad valley, cradled by lofty mountains, and even the trailer-towing Sherpa was able to hold 60–65mph through a suddenly lush landscape of green pastures, fertile fields, slender trees with silver bark, and avenues of fresh, delicate blossom. To the left, beyond the river, little more than a stone's throw away, was Russia.

We clambered over the steep western shoulder of Mount Ararat, its snowy peak wreathed in stubborn clouds, hit an incredible 80mph on the long downhill straight to Dogubayazit and reached the border just before 3pm. There were very few trucks of any nationality. Indeed, we had seen only one on British plates since leaving Yozgat, 630 miles and almost 36 hours earlier. Despite our status as private vehicles with faultless paperwork there was a sickeningly predictable problem. True to form, the Turkish customs bandit made us turn out a couple of the carefully packed boxes and started going through their contents – jam, condensed milk, biscuits, sugar – while muttering about guns and drugs. After ten minutes he made it clear that every single item would have to be checked unless we cared to change his mind with a little baksheesh. He suggested what amounted to almost £50, but settled for nearer £15. Tony shrugged and paid. Time meant more than money on this trip.

Getting into Iran was relatively easy, but it still took nearly three hours before a faultlessly polite young man with excellent English let us through without so much as glancing at the Sherpas. Good roads, no traffic and the heady prospect of spending tomorrow night in Teheran provided the spur to keep us driving in shifts until an hour or two before dawn.

Day Thirteen: We greeted the morning in the highest of spirits, despite sleeping for only four hours in the cramped confines of the Sherpas. Morale soared higher than ever after spotting and photographing our first camel. We even escaped with a stern caution when a hawk-eyed young policeman stopped Tony for passing a truck on a solid white line. 'No take-by-take,' he explained. In the afternoon, with a brisk breeze blowing from the west, we were able to pull the trailer at 65mph for hour after hour over the endless, mountain-flanked plain towards Teheran. But there was no sign of Chris and Allen. We waited and waited, then decided to push on to the capital. They were almost certainly shooting off a mile or two of film and would soon be back in our mirrors. No such luck. Should we go back? That could cause even bigger headaches if they had taken a different route through one of the towns and were, in fact, ahead of us. If they were in trouble, we told ourselves, it would make sense to organise things from Teheran with the help of LRC's man on the spot.

The road became a lethal, fast-moving nightmare of cars and trucks. I felt like a man on a fraying tightrope without a safety net as Macks by the hundred thundered past two abreast while smaller vehicles tried to edge through on the inside. Life was not made any easier by the lusty wind that was now sending sand across the road in clouds thick enough to zero visibility in a split second. Tony took over for the final couple of hours, eventually running down the country's only motorway, where sheep grazed on the verges and suicidal locals strolled.

Teheran was even worse – a chaotic hell of revving engines,

flashing lights, blaring horns, maniacal speed, crunching metal, shattering glass and motorbikes rasping the wrong way down broad, traffic-choked avenues. I wish I could forget the moment when a guy emerged from a house, dragged a goat to the gutter and slit its throat. We were drained by the time Tony contacted LRC and was told that the Leyland lads were already in the city. The sponsor's man turned up trumps, booking us into the Royal Hilton, no less, but even the prospect of buckshee luxury failed to banish thoughts of Chris and Allen. 'Worried sick,' says the notebook. 'They are somewhere back down the road with no cash, apart from dollars, no documents for the van and no details of contacts in Teheran. Have rarely felt so low and have serious doubts about the rest of this doom-laden journey.'

Day Fourteen: Tony, a phlegmatic character on his third expedition to the Himalayas, called the British embassy first thing to ask if they had any news. There was none. 'I suggest you contact us again, later in the day, if you want, to make it official,' said the lady. I had visions of the pair festering in a cell, arrested after unintentionally filming something of military importance. Worse still, they could have been killed in one of Iran's innumerable road accidents. It was not difficult to picture the Sherpa's burned-out hulk being examined for clues to the identity of two charred corpses. Breakfast was a gloomy meal made memorable by an immaculate and elderly Japanese gentleman who carefully added rashers of bacon to a bowl of grapefruit segments.

BL Cars had sent two mechanics to Teheran to check the Sherpas before we left to tackle the last 1,900 miles to Islamabad. Mike Davies was to fly home immediately, but Stuart Hall – big, bearded and cheerful – is coming with us. They examined our van with clinical care, cleaning off thick layers of caked Turkish mud to discover cracks in both arms of the trailer's A-frame. It could have gone at any moment, sending the precious load careering over a precipice or into a roadside crowd. Apart from that, the van was in excellent condition even though it has been driven extremely hard. The engine hadn't used a drop of oil and fuel consumption had improved steadily, despite the going getting harder. The overall average of 16mpg was fair enough in view of the terrain and the fact that with the trailer we were grossing 4.5 tons. Even the solo van tipped the scale at three tons.

We were just about to call the embassy again when Allen and Chris arrived, more than 24 hours after they had vanished from our mirrors. We had taken different routes through Zanjan and they had got their rear wheels stuck in a huge rut on the town's outskirts. That delayed them long enough to be caught in a dust storm that we just missed. Conditions became so bad that they checked into a motel for the night. They had been unable to contact LRC, because the company is not listed as such in the directory. But they made it in the end, cheerful as ever, and the reunion was toasted with remarkably good Persian wine while a belly dancer wiggled her hips. Stuart and Mike worked late to replace the clutch fitted by Abdullah.

Day Fifteen: We now have four days to get through Afghanistan before the borders close for a fortnight. Despite the urgency, it took a long time to get the show on the road. Stuart and I sat in the foyer, checking our watches every few minutes. 'What you seem to need is someone to say "We move out at nine o'clock sharp" or whatever,' said our new recruit. We finally got rolling just before noon, two hours late, and headed north towards the Caspian Sea. It was a drive of breathtaking splendour, for the route climbs under the shadow of Mount Damavand, Iran's highest peak at 18,500 feet. You reach what appears to be the top of the interminable pass, clear a crest and wonder if your eyes are playing tricks. The road goes on and on, reaching maybe 10,000 feet before plunging down, down, down through hairpin after hairpin. The engine roars in second and third. You worry about brakes, bumps and buses.

We stopped for a meal – 'Dog's leg and rice,' Stuart diagnosed, cautiously prodding the dish he had selected after the customary tour of the kitchen. It took four hours of hard, maximum-concentration driving to cover 100 miles, but the vivid change in scenery made it seem as if we had traversed an entire continent. The land around Teheran had been brown and dusty, but the Caspian coast was a fertile paradise of rich greens and browns, of rice fields, neat hedges and busy little towns with statues, fountains and broad, tree-lined avenues. We followed the road eastwards, eating again after dark and deciding to press on through the night. It made more sense to reach that vital border 24 hours early than five minutes too late. Lightning flashed over the sea. Or was it the nearby Russians launching a nuclear attack? Knowing our luck, we seemed certain to run into at least a small war before the world was very much older. The coastal plain gave way to wooded, rainswept mountains where bears still roam wild and probably devour travellers foolish enough to stop for a wayside leak. Driving in shifts, making use of the Sherpa's tiny bunks, we were at last mounting the all-out effort that had not been seen since 1,000 miles were knocked off in the first 48 hours from London.

Day Sixteen: In the small hours of the morning the terrain started to level out as we skirted the desolate fringes of the Dasht-i-Kavir, Iran's northern desert. Good roads, no traffic and the laser-like auxiliary lamps enabled us to cruise flat out as we headed for Mashad, a holy city much visited by pilgrims. Our non-stop drive was rewarded by a splendid sunrise over the Russian peaks to our left. Breakfast in the city – tea, bread, honey and cheese – then off again over the endless, shimmering plain with its huddles of mud huts and peasants toiling under the pitiless sun. Teheran's plush hotels, gleaming limousines and tower blocks seem 10,000 years away, and you wonder how Iran's immense oil-derived wealth is shared.

Speeding down straights that vanished into a pinpoint of haze, Stuart and I wondered what had happened to the others. Inexplicably, they had shot past us in Mashad's traffic. But could we be sure they were up ahead, somewhere in the wilderness of sand, huge lizards and tumbling, wind-driven balls of scrub? At noon, when 720 miles had been packed into 24 red-eyed hours, we stopped for petrol and were immediately mobbed by excited children. Had they seen another van like this? The dark heads shook. A breakdown, maybe. Should we go back and look, risking the loss of precious, hard-won hours? We decided to continue, eventually spotting the other Sherpa at a garage, close to the border. Chris had somehow failed to see our vehicle in Mashad and thought he was chasing us.

We took a wrong turning – quite a feat in this almost roadless part of the world – and sped several miles before being turned back at a mud-walled fort straight from *Beau Geste*. The frontier itself boasted what appeared to be a smart restaurant, but the food was terrible. The chips were stone cold and Stuart, fast emerging as the team's gastronomic wit, reckoned the alleged chicken must have died of thirst.

Western Afghanistan's main point of contact with the world looked just like the semi-derelict Mexican villages you see in Wild West films. Painted mud, baked by the sun, had cracked and fallen from the walls to reveal crumbling bricks with fist-sized holes gaping between them. Dusty fragments of net curtains were draped across broken windows. Flies by the thousand buzzed and swooped over an ancient leather sofa, its rickety base supported by stones. A very old man was sloshing muddy water over the concrete floor of the health office where another cloud of flies swarmed over a hypodermic needle that must have been plunged into countless arms. The compound, watched over by a sleepy soldier, was a tumult of battered coaches, travel-stained cars and Russian-built trucks painted in every colour and pattern imaginable. Hawk-faced men in turbans, flowing robes and baggy trousers stuffed into high boots mingled with veiled women and angelic-faced children begging in the dust. A young man came over, dressed in a jacket of great antiquity and a pair of faded jeans with more patches than original material. He held out his hand – 'Welcome to Afghanistan' – and we stood dumbfounded by the shock of hearing English in such an outlandish setting. He looked a little hurt and repeated the greeting. We shook hands, slowly realising he was an immigration official. Although very polite and friendly, he and his colleagues took more than three hours to process our paperwork, carefully noting such details as spare wheels, cassette players and anything else that could be sold.

Customs formalities were handled by a character in a greasy, oil-soaked boilersuit with 'Tourist Office' on the left breast. He muttered hopefully about whisky, but eventually settled for a pot of strawberry jam, squatting on the ground and devouring it with the aid of a ballpoint pen. Meanwhile, the smiling youth who had greeted us was waving towards the sofa's pile-driving springs and delving into the pockets of his venerable jacket. He handed us currants and almonds, cracked on the floor with the handle of a big screwdriver, but we declined politely when faced with a glass of soupy water that would probably have proved as beneficial as drinking battery acid. No doubt about it, the Afghans are proving every bit as delightful as Tony said they would. 'Most of the time they're bombed out on hash and just stand around laughing,' he said

Seventy miles later we reached Herat and got rooms in the Mowafaq Hotel. The desk clerk jotted down details in the register before pushing it towards us, upside down, for signatures. 'Sign it that way,' he shrugged. 'Everything in Afghanistan is upside down. One hour ago Kabul Radio say we have revolution.' Allen shook his hand. 'We're on your side!' he asserted. We went to the dining room and spent almost £10 on what turned out to be the hotel's last five bottles of good German beer. Herat seemed peaceful enough, but would our sleep be shattered by the sullen thunder of artillery? Chris chuckled: 'You realise, of course, that this sort of death is specifically excluded from life insurance.'

Day Seventeen: Despite our fears we slept soundly until 6am when an amplified radio started blaring in the street. Stuart padded out across the floor, carpeted wall to wall with smooth concrete, and returned with news of the president's death. It took the familiar eternity to rouse Chris and Allen, so I walked to the nearby tourist office. The man behind the desk, ear glued to the radio, said coaches were running to Kabul as usual and there was no reason why we should not proceed.

Afghanistan is about five times bigger than England with way under half as many people. The average life expectancy is 37, according to one source checked before leaving home, and 92 per cent of the people are illiterate. Most of them inhabit the arid wilderness and live in mud huts or tents, fighting an age-old battle against summer temperatures of 50 degrees C and less rain than falls on Old Trafford during the average cricket match. The country entered the railway age in 1976, when a line was built linking Kabul to Iran. America and Russia, keenly aware of Afghanistan's strategic importance, have endowed the country with 1,550 miles of paved roads. Wales, by way of comparison, has 20,000 miles. Kabul lies 400 miles east of Herat in a straight line, but the highway swings south and is twice as long.

Driving down that incredible, interminable road, flanked by blistering desert and gauntly majestic peaks of naked rock, you feel no more significant than a grain of sand. The sun beats down like a golden hammer. Distant mountains appear to be floating on vast, shimmering lakes, but a glimpse of water is an occasion for excited comment. Wild camels shamble across the road, but you can drive for hours without seeing another living creature. It makes the Tapline road through northern Saudi Arabia seem like the M1 on a busy Friday evening. The villagers, this searing day, had news of the revolution when we stopped for fuel at pumps guarded by local militia with fixed bayonets. It is good, they say, because the new military government will be for all the people. The radio says so. It must be true.

A dark blob appears on the late-afternoon horizon, slowly revealing itself as a small forest of healthy trees with rich, dark-green foliage. This is Kandahar, the country's second city. We drive unhindered through the bustling streets and keep going until midnight, narrowly avoiding a dead camel and the battered remains of a vast bird.

Day Eighteen: Getting up at 4am is a grim way to start what you realise might just possibly be your last day this side of the Pearly Gates. I was at the wheel when we reached the outskirts of Kabul and were confronted by tanks and troops with machine guns at the ready. They waved us through, into streets thronged with people who seemed to be going about their business as usual. But there were more tanks and more soldiers at every junction as we found our way to the road for Jelalabad and the border, now just 130 tantalising miles away. On the far side of the city was yet another tank. 'The road is closed. Very dangerous,' said the troops manning the checkpoint. 'You must go back.'

So we turned round and joined a group of British travellers in a nearby field. Many had been in the city when the attack started and had fled to the British embassy as rebel tanks slaughtered the loyalists, artillery thundered and MiGs howled down to pour rockets into the bloody holocaust. Tony and Allen went off in search of bread, promising to be back in ten minutes, while we started preparing breakfast. They had been gone less than a minute when someone came rushing into the field. The road was open! An hour later there was still no sign of the other Sherpa. Another hour, and then another. Suddenly, the drone of passing traffic was cut by the blood-chilling scream of jets. Two flights of MiGs were hurtling in low from the north. Upper lip far from stiff, I wondered if the ditch and stone wall would be sufficient protection if the fighters' wings started flickering with lethal fire. But the planes banked away over the city and vanished without firing. Just a show of strength. But still no sign of Tony and Allen.

Chris took it all with enviable calm, but I was cursing and almost weeping with anger, frustration and worry. Had they risked taking pictures and been shot? After exactly four hours they appeared, having spent the morning visiting a bank, the British embassy . . . and a restaurant. And we had flung our breakfast into a ditch, wanting to be ready the instant they returned.

We passed the solitary tank, thinking the way ahead would be clear, then rounded the foot of a low hill for an encounter I will never forget. Tanks lined the dusty verge, squat and brutal against a backcloth of soaring, snowclad peaks burning with white fire in the blistering noonday sun. Their heavy machine guns were trained on the gravel road by lean, hard-eyed Afghan troops, hunched with concentration as they fingered triggers and swept the sinister muzzles in slow, menacing arcs. More soldiers stood between the tanks, all in full battle kit, all poised to fire. These were the men who had fought a battle in the heart of Kabul, less than 48 hours earlier, storming the presidential palace, gunning down the country's leader, Mohammed Daoud, his family, bodyguards and staff. Avenging forces were rumoured to be marching on the capital. You could smell fear, see it etched on every face.

Nervously, urgently, a soldier flagged us down with his Kalashnikov AK-47, bayonet gleaming. He peered into the Sherpa, the polished blade inches from my nose, then grunted as I fumbled, ever so carefully, for one of the illustrated leaflets that explained we were carrying supplies to Pakistan for a British climbing expedition. An officer in the bulky black headgear of a tank commander appeared at the driver's window. He leaned across Tony and jabbed the 5mph mark on the speedometer. The officer, like so many Afghans, spoke a little English: 'Go faster,' he warned, 'and they shoot you.'

'That sounds like the ultimate penalty for speeding,' I muttered as Tony started easing down the road. Dark hands waved sternly – 'Slow down' – and the gunners on the tanks followed our dusty path over open sights. I traced the outline of the Celtic cross hanging on its chain over my heart – 'Go easy, for Christ's sake go easy' – but no matter how slowly Tony drove the hands still waved us down. Was it all going to end here, in sunlit surroundings of peerless beauty beside the surging, foam-flecked waters of the Kabul River? Such thoughts seem absurdly melodramatic now, in the comfort and safety of home, but were horribly appropriate that morning as we inched towards the Kabul Gorge, under the Afghan guns.

Clear at last, the Sherpas plunged into the awe-inspiring ravine with its raging river, vast walls of vertical rock and road so tightly corkscrewed you could lean out and drop something on the vehicle below. It makes any other pass I have seen look no more dramatic than the verdant acres of Hyde Park. A laughing, waving Afghan was riding down on the roof of an ancient bus. Who cares about politics, revolutions and dead presidents?

Through the sweltering afternoon to Jelalabad – tanks at every bridge and junction – and so, at last, to the frontier at the foot of the Khyber Pass. The Pakistanis quizzed us about the coup for the benefit of army officers who sat in the passport control office, trying to pretend they were just resting their legs. I wandered among amazingly decorated trucks and looked up at little forts perched on the crags. The Khyber may not equal the Kabul Gorge for scenic majesty, but it must have more atmosphere than all the rest of the world's passes put together. It was towards this cleft in the mountains that 4,500 British and Indian troops struggled with 12,000 camp followers in 1842, at the end of the first Afghan War. Few made it back.

Standard dress for local men still includes rifles and crossed bandoliers of cartridges. Travellers are still shot, which is why the pass is normally closed well before nightfall. But this was not a normal day and we were allowed over. Tony opened a couple of cans of Guinness to celebrate, then went like a maniac, defying every law of gravity, centrifugal force and mechanical engineering as he hurled our cumbersome, trailer-towing Sherpa up the pass. How we failed to turn over, smash the suspension, fracture the chassis or hit any one of several local trucks and coaches will remain one of my life's great mysteries. But I could understand his wild enthusiasm. We were less than 140 miles from Islamabad, where old friends in the British embassy could be relied on for stiff drinks, hot baths and comfy beds.

Our breakneck descent came to a brief halt just below a huge and immensely evocative 19th-century fortress with 'Khyber Rifles' picked out on the ground in white stones. The view was too good to miss, so we scrambled up a rocky outcrop and looked down to the plains of north-west Pakistan, slowly fading into the twilight. It was a magical sight, but we suddenly realised that a truck had stopped and deposited a Pathan tribesman, complete with rifle. We hurried back towards the vans, muttering what we hoped would sound like greetings and remembering the warning not to stop on the pass. The man looked wicked enough to cut his own mother's throat for the price of a drink, but a huge grin suddenly cracked his leathery face. He held out a hand in friendship, said 'Hello, Johnny' and vanished into the rocks like a lean, colourful ghost.

Pakistan's berserk traffic gave us some final nasty moments, notably when a car came racing down the wrong side of a dual carriageway beyond Peshawar. The way they drive in those rainbow-hued trucks and psychedelic 'jungly buses' makes even Teheran's traffic seem like the Institute of Advanced Motorists on their best behaviour. We reached our destination exactly 408 hours and 5,422 miles after leaving London. There was a definite end-of-term atmosphere after we met Tony's friends and poured strong celebratory drinks into stomachs that had not been given a meal for more than 48 hours. Tony treated himself to a rare smile: 'Having survived that lot,' he said, 'climbing the bloody mountain may not seem quite so difficult after all.'

Postscript: The K2 expedition came to a tragic and premature end when Nick Estcourt, one of the world's finest climbers, was swept to his death by an avalanche at 21,000 feet. Two other members of the team were already suffering from altitude sickness, so the attempt was abandoned.

28

CARIBBEAN AND SOUTH AMERICA

DRIVING TO THE END OF THE WORLD

1998

The Llewellins and their fly-splattered Ford Ranger were not quite alone on the primitive road that threaded its way through the immensity of south-west Patagonia, overlooked by the snowy mountains that form South America's spine. Dominated by the granite monolith of Mount Fitz Roy, the distant Andes' glacier-sculpted splendour contrasted with the view to our right, where flat, scrubby desert, inhabited by such strange creatures as the armadillo and the strutting, ostrich-like rhea, sprawled all the way to the Atlantic Ocean. The Ranger had been cantering along the gravel for about ten minutes when we passed a tanker. Believe it or not, the big rig with its cargo of petrol and diesel was the only vehicle we encountered heading in the same direction during the one and a half days that it took to cover 600 dirt-road miles while en route from Calafate to Bariloche. Six of the 18 vehicles that came towards us in that time appeared to be running in a loose-knit convoy, for mutual support in a wilderness where it was foolish to assume that a name on the map was anything more than a name on the map. One place was just a bullet-holed sign.

Nothing mattered more than scanning the endless ribbon of gravel for hazards while keeping an eye on the fuel gauge, in case a stone punctured the tank. But there were visions of Eva Herzigova, the model whose Wonderbra adverts gave new life to the old saying about cups that runneth over. The lady made one of my dreams come true during last summer's Festival of Speed party at Goodwood House, far away in England, when she smiled, puckered her lips, leaned forward and . . . plucked my name from the hat. The raffle's star prize was a brace of business-class tickets to anywhere in the world served by Lufthansa.

Several months later we landed in Buenos Aires, slung our bags into the back of the four-wheel-drive Ranger's *doble cabina* and headed for Patagonia, which accounts for most of southern Argentina. Reasons for choosing such an unfashionable destination included a long-standing determination to visit the Welsh colony that dates from 1865, when 153 pioneers staggered ashore at what is now Puerto Madryn, 900 miles down the inhospitable coast from Buenos Aires.

Apart from that, our plans were vague and unambitious. Although my curriculum vitae includes a few hazardous drives, the *Lonely Planet* guide to Argentina gave the impression that being injected with bubonic plague was the sensible alternative to driving in the world's eighth biggest country. In fact, the allegedly blood-stained RN-2 was almost deserted as the Ranger headed for Balcarce, Juan Manuel Fangio's birthplace. The great racer's life is commemorated in a fine museum where sleek Mercedes and Maseratis contrast with the maestro's pre-war Chevrolets and Fords. Spending a night in what used to be his bedroom kicked this three-week adventure off to a terrific start.

The RN-3, eastern Argentina's generally excellent main road, became quieter and quieter as we approached Puerto Madryn. This almost eerie absence of traffic prompted Mrs Llewellin to suggest going all the way to Ushuaia, the southernmost town on the planet. So that's what we did. When the wind blew hard from Antarctica, 2.5 litres and

116bhp of turbocharged diesel struggled to flog the Ranger along at 65mph. When it relented, we galloped at 80–85.

We spent three nights in Puerto Madryn, in an apartment overlooking the bay where Ferdinand Magellan anchored in 1519. He was killed later in the voyage, but his crew became the first men ever to circumnavigate the world. The Ranger had its first taste of rough-stuff motoring when we explored the nearby Valdes peninsula whose bays and beaches attract right whales, elephant seals and Magellanic penguins, which also breed in vast numbers down the coast at Punto Tomba.

Sunday being Sunday, we went to a Welsh chapel in Trelew, the main town in the Chubut valley, which the Welsh irrigated and cultivated after starvation had taken its toll. From there the Ranger bowled inland to Dolavon, where many of the cemetery's headstones were engraved in Welsh. At least one of the people buried in this remote place had been born a few miles from our home on the Welsh Marches. Best of all, in the afternoon we lingered over a traditional Welsh tea served by Marta Rees at her spotless home in Gaiman, a tiny town that is now the focal point of Patagonia's Welsh culture. Marta's grandfather was 15 when he sailed to Patagonia in 1865. Her eyes glistened with tears, and so did ours, as she remembered her beloved 'Nain' – Welsh for grandmother – talking about the old country.

The Ranger won its spurs during the 650-mile day that took us down to San Julien, a small town on one of the coast's few sheltered havens. Magellan anchored here. So did swashbuckling Sir Francis Drake, 57 years later, on his way to becoming the first Englishman to circle the globe. Both captains stopped to execute mutineers.

An early start put us into Rio Gallegos midway through the next morning. Aware that we would have to transit Chile to reach Argentina's slice of Tierra del Fuego, and too well travelled in outlandish places to risk pressing on without the correct paperwork, we sought advice from a very helpful lady in Rio Gallegos's tourist information bureau. Most of the day dribbled away before the powers that be decided not to grant permission. The lady apologised: 'This has happened before, many times. We are so far away that people in Buenos Aires are unaware that getting from here to Tierra del Fuego by land involves passing through another country.'

During an otherwise frustrating day we bought a photograph of a bank that used to stand a few blocks from the tourist bureau. Bruce Chatwin's fine book, *In Patagonia*, took us back to 1909 when the bank's manager was impressed by two charming Americans, and their female companion, who had expressed an interest in buying land. The strangers accepted his invitation to lunch, then tied-up him and his staff, stuffed every note and coin they could find into their saddlebags, and galloped out of town. The audacious *pistoleros* were Robert Leroy Parker and Harry Longbaugh – Butch Cassidy and the Sundance Kid – and their sharp-shooting moll, Etta Place. We crossed their trail again, far away to the north, where a derelict cabin near Cholila recalls the brief period when they switched from robbing to ranching.

Determined to reach the last town on the planet, we sky-hopped southward aboard a twin-engined Saab 340. When it landed at Ushuaia, where snowy mountains sweep down to the Beagle Channel, we were greeted by a band, a lot of very excited people and umpteen vehicles bedecked with bunting. The taxi driver, who spoke fluent English, roared with laughter when I said: 'How did you know we were coming?'

The visiting VIP was Fernando de la Rua, who was destined to become Argentina's next president. Ten minutes later we were in downtown Ushuaia, renting a funny little Daewoo Chico with a 796cc engine, when he breezed into the office, accompanied by a media mob, and gave us the flesh-pressing politician's big hello as cameras recorded the moment for posterity. Mrs Llewellin smiled sweetly while muttering: 'Don't mention the Falklands.'

'That's the garage at the end of the world,' I commented while passing a cluster of pumps on the Avenida Malvinas Argentinas. The road soon became a gravel track that snaked past a narrow-gauge railway – built by convicts, when Ushuaia was a penal colony that made Alcatraz seem like the Ritz – and went on to where RN-3 ends at the head of one of the Beagle Channel's many bays. To all intents and purposes, this is as far south in the world as you can get a car without chartering a ship or a helicopter. We celebrated with a good dinner – Ushuaia has a lot of restaurants and several very fancy shops – slept with Antarctica's wind rattling our bedroom's window, then flew back to Rio Gallegos and the Ranger.

Why tackle a marathon journey in a four-wheel-drive pickup? The slightly tongue-in-cheek choice was prompted by the possibility of encountering a few miles of ruts and potholes. In fact, we were in Ushuaia when yours truly took a really close look at the map and gasped an expletive. We were into that night's second bottle of wine before I risked breaking the news that getting back to Buenos Aires through western Patagonia was going to involve rather a lot of dirt-road motoring. And then some. The rough stuff eventually accounted for about 1,000 of our 5,000 miles. The most rewarding of them took us from Calafate to where the Perito Moreno glacier's 150-feet-high wall of blue-and-white ice meets Lake Argentina, and vast towers collapse into the water. The sight was hypnotic enough to hold us spellbound for a couple of hours as the glacier, moving at about six feet a day, made noises that ranged from the sharp, startling crack of a single rifle-shot to the awesome rumbling thunder of distant howitzers.

Aware that we were venturing into really remote country, we kept a careful count of traffic encountered while heading north from Calafate. I say that to reduce the risk of being accused of exaggerating, because this is the astonishingly lonesome road on which we passed the tanker. We were not trying to be adventurous by taking the gung-ho alternative to a properly paved and serviced highway. Route 40 being the only south-to-north road in that part of the world, the Ranger was earning its corn on Patagonia's answer to England's M6 or California's I-5. Bajo Caracoles, one of four tiny communities scattered along the way, had the only fuel for 300 miles.

But being alone in the world did not make driving as easy as sipping a beer. The realisation that a slight lapse or mistake could have extremely serious consequences explains why I have never concentrated harder for longer. Fortunately, Argentina's variation on the Ranger theme felt as strong as an ox despite every nut, bolt, screw, washer, weld, seal, filter, bearing, spring, grommet, clip, bulb, bracket, fuse, wire, widget and throstle sprocket being pulled, pushed, twisted and shaken for every inch of the way. Remarkably little dust got into the cabin, the seats kept us comfortable and noise levels were mercifully low, despite stones attacking the underbody like non-stop machine-gun fire for hour after hour.

It rode better than expected for most of the time, enabling 70–75mph to be maintained when the gravel ran arrow-straight from horizon to horizon, but patches of sun-baked washboard agitated the leaf-sprung back axle enough to make the rear wheels skip out of the 'tramlines' and slither sideways in the gravel. More often than not, this fishtailing was exacerbated by ferocious blasts of wind broadsiding down from the Andes.

The big surprise when we reached a remote little town, nine hours after leaving Calafate, was a hotel with a bath. I was stretched out on the bed, reflecting on our journey while waiting my turn, when Mrs Llewellin pulled the plug and squealed for help as water swirled from the tub and gushed back up through a hole in the floor. This drama wrenched my thoughts away from Tierra del Fuego, where the sign at the end of the road had revealed us to be 1,903 miles from Buenos Aires and, as I observed, as casually as possible, a mere 11,092 miles from Port Barrow, Alaska. Not for the first time, my wife said: 'Don't even *think* about thinking about it.'

29

RACING GOATS AND SCALP-LIFTING RUM

2003

I knew we had reached a fun place when hazards encountered on the road between the airport and the capital included chickens, goats, cattle and the guy who zig-zagged towards us at the wheel of a 1969-ish Chevrolet Impala. Had he been titillating his tonsils with something stronger than coconut water? That's a strong possibility on Tobago, a Caribbean island where supermarkets sell rum that's labelled as being at least 75 per cent alcohol by volume. Your jetlagged reporter was in self-preservation mode, considering which way to weave, when I realised that the old Yank tank's driver was actually being very careful. He was using local knowledge to avoid potholes big enough to be mistaken for the crater made by the comet that did for the dinosaurs. Remembering the whereabouts of each and every rib-rattler is not such a big deal when you live on an island that accounts for only 116 square miles of the planet's surface. Texans have bigger swimming pools.

First impressions were confirmed when we reached our rented villa and I sipped a therapeutic rum punch sundowner while studying tips for visiting drivers. They included the following:

Drive on the left: Thanks to our British heritage most of us observe this basic rule, though a few local drivers prefer the centre-of-the-road approach, usually on blind corners.

When is a hand signal not a hand signal? Chances are, when you're following a Tobago driver. Most of us tend to emphasise our conversational points with lots of gesticulating, even when driving. Hence, an arm waving furiously out of a car window might possibly be (a) a signal that the driver intends to stop or turn; (b) a signal that you should pass him; or (c) the punctuation of a violent in-car argument over politics or cricket.

Should I rely on indicators? In general, yes. But you should be aware that some of our larger trucks do not have either functioning indicators or brake lights.

Driving at night: Bear in mind that a single headlight speeding towards you through the darkness does not necessarily indicate a two-wheeled vehicle. Some local drivers consider that one headlight is quite sufficient to their needs.

Wet roads and rainy weather: Many local motorists, and many rental cars, make do with very smooth tyres, and are liable to skid in wet conditions.

What do I do if I have an accident? If conscious, keep cool.

Exploring this unspoiled island in a toy-like Suzuki Samurai became less nerve-wracking as we came to terms with local driving habits. The first outing made it clear that most of the potholed roads are very narrow, very steep and have countless corners per mile. Hazards include pedestrians who may have been swigging *babash*, the illicitly distilled white rum that makes the 75-per-cent firewater seem like a breakfast drink for babies.

That first drive's highlights included a truck laden with gas cylinders, which stormed past us on a blind corner. Minutes later we were given the same treatment by a Nissan Sunny Super Saloon, complete with a huge exhaust pipe, which appeared to have at least seven people on board. The driver obviously believed that anything coming the other way would dematerialise if he parped the horn. Seconds later, we rounded a corner and there he was, stopped in a place of maximum danger to disgorge a passenger amid much waving and shaking of hands. Tobagonians regard a narrow road's blind corners as the best place to stop, the theory being that you slow down for corners, and slowing is only one step away from stopping. How's that for logic?

Then a small motor cycle buzzed past like a demented hornet. The rider was wearing one of those Rastafarian hats that are big enough to be mistaken for a multi-coloured version of the Taj Mahal's dome. This happy-go-lucky dude was so close he could have bitten my ear off had he not been swigging a Carib beer while zig-zagging down a vertiginous hill towards idyllic Englishman's Bay.

Our six-year-old Samurai had clocked 55,000 miles. The interior looked as if it had housed a pack of wild dogs, but the important bits worked perfectly. I take my battered straw hat off to any vehicle that's tough enough to survive that distance on Tobago's roads. However, you can bet your last glass of *babash* that the people who gave us such wondrously named runabouts as the Mighty Boy and the Jimny Fishing Master didn't have this island in mind when they designed the Samurai. The 1.3-litre engine lacks the torque you need for tackling climbs that would daunt an F-18 with the afterburners blasting flame. On the credit side of the balance, more gearshifts than a supercomputer could count explain why my left arm and leg – this being a right-hand-drive model – have never been more muscular.

The pace of life is so relaxed that fast food can mean fasting for a couple of hours before the first course arrives. By the same token – well, almost – the island has a 30mph speed limit. This must have escaped the notice of driver of the surface-skimming missile that crossed the lights on the outskirts of Scarborough, the main town. The dark-green coupé was unidentified because it was going far too fast for my senses to register anything other than a noisy blur passing one of Tobago's many ancient Land Rovers. The hypersonic hero must have been using his island's unique fuel additive. This consists of one bottle of the aforementioned rum to one teaspoon of the manifold-melting, supernova-hot sauce made by a Winnie Neptune, an old lady with a stall in Scarborough market.

The annual Buccoo Goat Race Festival is Tobago's hilarious answer to Royal Ascot and the Kentucky Derby. The commentator chortled about winners living like pampered sultans, surrounded by concubines, while losers are served alongside curry crab and dumplings. Bernie Ecclestone should take a tip from Buccoo next time Formula One's drivers need an incentive to try harder.

30

FAR EAST

Battling Through Borneo

1985

One thousand miles through the jungles of Borneo. That was what Camel Trophy '85 was all about according to the advance publicity. Indeed, that was what Camel Trophy '85 was all about according to full-page colour adverts placed in leading European publications the week after the event ended. Accompanied by a facsimile telex with a 'Base Camp Borneo' dateline, they talked of 500 miles being covered and depicted two macho males paddling a Land Rover 90 down a tropical river on a rubber raft. The truth was just a little different. After nine days, with only three left before the 26 vehicles and 85 men returned to civilisation, only 42 off-road miles had been covered. The final off-road total, flattered by wheels spinning in mud, was a paltry 164 miles. The dramatic river crossing? That did happen – but the stills and the movie footage were bagged several months earlier to get the shots safely in the can long before the multi-national assortment of competitors, officials, scribblers and camp followers arrived in East Kalimantan, the Indonesian part of Borneo.

The organisers toughed it out in public, talking about 'this unique and wonderful event' while describing the Borneo fiasco as the best since R J Reynolds Tobacco International set the Camel Trophy ball rolling in 1980. That was odd, because previous capers in Sumatra, Brazil, Papua New

Guinea and Zaire had more or less achieved their objectives, covering big distances in grim conditions. In private, however, the men behind what was billed as 'the great adventure' revealed a distinct lack of gruntle. They muttered about bad decisions and, most serious of all, bad publicity.

Ironically, the stinkweed manufacturers from Winston Salem, North Carolina, had made a rod for their corporate back. In addition to writers and photographers travelling in the convoy, they had mustered another posse of 35 media men who were based at Mission Control in Balikpapan, one of only two places of any size in East Kalimantan. Each day, small groups were wrenched away from bar, pool and prostitute, bundled into a helicopter and whisked a few farcical miles to where it should all have been happening. Apart from returning with news of precious little progress, the daily shuttle service was a constant reminder that the jungle-bashers, apparently way out in the boondocks, were in fact within a few flying minutes of civilisation. In addition, the sight of crisp, clean visitors fresh from showers and air-conditioned rooms did nothing to boost the morale of the sweat-soaked, mud-caked heroes battling with horrific heat and humidity.

Selected from more than 600,000 applicants and coming from all walks of life – doctor, architect, garage mechanic, fighter pilot, forestry engineer, pizza tycoon, accountant, policeman, you name it – the 32 finalists were jetted to Borneo from Brazil, Holland, Belgium, Germany, Switzerland, Spain, Italy and Japan. Each nation was represented by a couple of two-man teams, all driving Land Rover 90s with very comprehensive equipment. Like its predecessors, Camel Trophy '85 set out to be a long, off-road rally whose outcome depended on the results of 'special tasks' masterminded by the competitions manager, Graham Fazakarley, a long-serving Land Rover engineer and a veteran of two previous Camel capers. He was assisted by George Richman, a former Land Rover employee, and two mechanics, Roy Mullet and Gordon Vickers, who performed major miracles to keep the vehicles running after they had been brutalised by gung-ho drivers with kamikaze instincts.

Camel Trophy '85 had its moments, of course. How often, for instance, have you driven along a snake-infested river with water swirling well above your waist? Or been guided inch by inch across a bridge that was more daylight than rotten logs? Or emerged, bruised but not broken, from a vehicle that bounced off a jungle track and rolled five times before being catch-fenced by dense foliage? But the highlights could not gloss over the fact that in terms of a 1,000-mile adventure, Camel Trophy '85 was a joke. In off-road terms, it was about what Land Rover engineers cover in a typical day's testing at Eastnor Castle. Here's what happened.

Day One: Big crowds, including many of East Kalimantan's top people, line the route as police escort the convoy out of Balikpapan at sweltering 6pm. High spirits mingle with apprehension. It's great to be rolling after months of anticipation, but all wonder about what perils await us in the jungle. After 20 miles we leave the bitumen and start low-gearing along a logging trail that's all axle-deep mud and ruts vicious enough to send you slithering over crumbling cliffs. The diesels roar and grumble, but not loud enough to mask non-stop cries from countless invisible creatures. Blood-curdling shrieks, frantic twitters, noises like a finger running down the teeth of a comb. The only time you don't hear the teeming wildlife is when torrential rain lashes the jungle like machine-gun fire. Graham Fazakarley starts his first special task – down then back up a wicked hill with a fast-flowing river at its foot to cool hot-headed competitors with more bravado than brains.

By 4am, when the last crew has finished the course, the rest of the party is snatching sleep in Land Rover seats or on the sodden ground. The scene recalls pictures of exhausted British and American soldiers littering lanes during the Battle of Normandy in 1944. On through what's left of the steaming, stygian night. On to the site of an old logging camp where the enterprising and ever-cheerful Brazilians, destined to win the Team Spirit Award, waste no time moving into the ramshackle remains of a hut. We are tired, very tired, but fatigue is mixed with a masochistic feeling that pushing yourself brutally hard is all part of the great game. It does a flabby, soft-living scribe good to lock horns with Mother Nature for the thick end of a fortnight.

Day Two: One hour in the Land of Nod, then at 6am we're reactivated by Andreas Bender, the expedition's leader. Lean, bronzed, bearded, cool as a cucumber, a noted mountaineer and explorer, he jokes about nights being short in the eastern hemisphere, gentlemen. Another special task is started – six miles of mud-plugging with a 45-minute time limit – but crew after crew flounder in the filth. Morale wilts as the sledgehammer temperature climbs to well over 38 degrees C accompanied by suffocating humidity. Insects the size of corgis launch sortie after sortie as bored, frustrated men curse, snarl and swig flat, warm mineral water from plastic bottles. Time to get on good terms with the expedition's burly Austrian doctor. The fridge fitted to his Land Rover 110 has cans of local Bintang beer stored with the snake serum, and there's a lot more of the former than the latter. Doc's done this sort of thing before. He gets his first taste of action when one of the officials, dropped about a mile short of the task's turning point, staggers past his destination, walks through the crippling heat for an hour or two, drinks all his water and is eventually found in a semi-collapsed state. Back at the camp the ashen victim lies in a precious patch of shade, drinking enough water to float an aircraft carrier. At this rate our 12-day supply will soon be gone.

Six o'clock and only four vehicles have completed the course in 11 hours. Midnight comes and goes, hoisting the total to eight finishers before Graham admits defeat. One of the Swiss Land Rovers has left the track and landed on its roof. A German crew toppled over at the same spot.

Time to rest. Some crews have hammocks and campbeds, the meticulous Japanese have tents big enough to house a three-ring circus. Others, including us, stretch out on groundsheets sheltered by flimsy awnings, trying to sleep as thunder booms overhead and rain hammers down. We have not advanced one inch today.

Day Three: None of the eight completed the course within the time limit, so Graham and Andreas decide to scrap the task. 'We'll have difficulty just making progress through that lot,' is the verdict. Roof rack laden with scribblers and snappers, another Land Rover capsizes on its way to recover the Swiss and German crews.

Another special task – fast down a hill, then pedal-to-metal through mud – sends one of the Brazilians over the edge. Thirty men and three Land Rovers drag it back up the near-vertical slopes, ripped by thorns, sweating buckets in the awesome heat. Yesterday, newcomers to the jungle, we teased each other with visions of cold beer served by beautiful barmaids. Today we would welcome a glass of fresh water poured by Quasimodo's ugly sister. Standards and relative values are already changing.

It's late afternoon and we're creeping over a series of narrow, creaking, cross-your-fingers log bridges spanning ravines carved by racing streams. The most rickety one of all bends and splinters over a drop deep enough to swallow a church tower. An early halt is dictated by the visiting 'tourist bus' chopper. It lands on a sandy hilltop and is immediately surrounded by excited locals who appear from nowhere to clap, cheer, point and giggle. The convoy is joined by Roy and Gordon who have spent the day helping replace the clutch ruined by one of the Spanish crews. They lose points for using spares and accepting professional help. More serious by far is the realisation that yesterday's sunstroke victim has developed a brain-scrambling form of jungle fever. Normally the most stoical of men, he is firmly convinced that the competitors are plotting homosexual rape, mutilation and murder. He lies next to me, clutching a machete, and mutters about taking a few of the bastards with him.

Day Four: Time to start wondering what the hell's happening. The planned route is blocked by a landslide, so the convoy starts heading due north instead of due south. But according to one official source we are still proceeding as planned. Be that as it may, the next 15 to 20 miles, said to have been checked during a recce, are expected to keep us hard at it for two or three days. That prediction is to prove very optimistic.

After completing a spectacular special task with Land Rovers taking to the air like pterodactyls – the Swiss roll for the second time – we push on along a trail that's rapidly being recaptured by the jungle. Out come the machetes and chainsaws, hacking a path through the greenery before Andreas calls a halt at the foot of a long, steep, slippery hill. The resident crazy is still certain his life's in danger. There's talk of sending him back to Balikpapan on the next chopper, before he breaks completely.

Day Five: Once again the trail is blazed by machetes and chainsaws. Passengers plod through the heat like defeated soldiers, realising how terrible it must have been to fight the Japanese in such a hostile environment during the Second World War. It's too hot to eat. Your stomach heaves at the thought of another tin of greasy, liquefied corned beef. Sweat sears your eyes like acid. Camp followers smoke, swear and kick their heels as gangs of competitors cut their way down the side of a ravine, build a bridge and organise winching operations up the far slope. A mile or so later, long after dark, it's down another muddy, nerve-shredding ravine, hard right over a river, then slowly up the opposite bank – almost too steep for walking – hauled by three winches. The last crews snatch 15 minutes' sleep.

Day Six: Red-eyed and frustrated, we cover 400 yards before halting to greet the chopper and start a special task. Competitors see how far they can get up a hill without winching while one of the native guides confirms my belief that all is not well. 'Can't understand why we've come this way,' he says. 'The trail gets harder and harder. There are many bridges to build, big bridges, and one part has been completely washed away. The next few miles will take many, many days. I have told them that.'

Then it's on through the blistering afternoon to a big clearing semi-circled by a muddy river where we bathe our stinking bodies, rinse filthy clothes and agree it's like being in a five-star hotel. On the debit side of the balance, the river flows through a gorge that has to be spanned by a 45-foot bridge. The good news? Old Crazy, although still not 100 per cent right, has clawed his way back to the brink of sanity and evacuation plans are quietly set aside. A key decision is announced. Immediately after crossing the river, and reaching another big clearing, men and machines will be airlifted to a better track, about ten miles away, by a trio of helicopters. This incredibly expensive exercise has been planned for months – presumably because it will make great movie footage – but not for this part of the route. The vehicles could have been lifted out of the first clearing, of course, so the bridge is constructed just to provide photo opportunities.

Day Seven: Built with big logs, small logs and sand ladders, and masterminded by the Swiss architect, the bridge looks good enough to survive a direct hit by a Stuka. Watching it take shape is the only thing to do throughout another endless day of heat and flies, mitigated only by dips in the river. We cross late in the afternoon and reach a clearing littered with the rusting, rotting debris of a long-abandoned logging camp. By now I'm aware of not eating and drinking properly in this hellish climate, mainly because my pre-departure requests for advice about suitable provisions were brushed aside. The situation is getting serious, so I recall books about British prisoners-of-war in Colditz and Stalag Luft III while liberating several of the German competitors' army ration packs. They provide a great variety of delicious, nourishing, easily cooked food, plus crystals that make the water tasty while also replacing minerals lost through sweating.

Day Eight: Heavy rain and hot coffee. The bedraggled Brits bury their last bottle of Famous Grouse as the helicopters set about their business. But first the Land Rovers need to have mud carved and scraped from their bellies. Still too heavy for the big chopper, so off come the doors and spare wheels. The bigger 110s can't be lifted until their winches and seats are removed as well. About half the vehicles and personnel have been whisked over the trees when night brings the operation to a halt.

Day Nine: The last crews join the rest of the party and spend most of the day searching for components and personal equipment before rebuilding their vehicles. 'Camel Trophy!

More like Camel Garage,' growls one competitor. Two others seriously consider turning their backs on the event and walking off through the jungle. Graham, still on ground not covered by his recce, checks out two special tasks for the night. Andreas decides we must head for the river.

Day Ten: Time is running out and we have covered barely 60 miles since leaving Balikpapan. But now the Camel Trophy gets a shot in the arm. To reach the village of Rampanga – our first contact with the outside world for five days, apart from the choppers – we must navigate about a quarter-mile of river with water creaming over the bonnets. A few Land Rovers make it unaided. Others plunge into deeper water and squat there for an hour or more, diesels throbbing, exhausts bubbling, before being winched to dry land. This is something to remember.

So is the village, where we tuck into tasty food, liberally garnished with hyperactive ants, and swig every can of Bintang the friendly locals can produce. Another special task, then into the night on relatively good roads. There are mocking cheers when the group headed by Andreas goes missing and is reduced to firing distress flares. Together again, we reach a riverside village at 5am and sleep, briefly, under a blanket of rain.

Day Eleven: Another relatively good day, punctuated by special tasks, modest bridgework and a drive through the evening to Kotabangun, a small town – vast by local standards – on the River Mahakam. Welcoming banners span the dusty track, the mayor makes a speech and we watch a display of traditional dayak dancing.

Day Twelve: The trip to Kotabangun was just another photo opportunity, so it's back down the same track, build another bridge and here we go for the penultimate special task. A speed hillclimb gives one of the German crews sufficient points to join their Japanese rivals at the top of the list. Late at night, the Camel Trophy's winner is decided when the Germans come home ahead of the ever-smiling Orientals. Few people bother to sleep when we reach a huge plantation whose owner has lit an almighty bonfire and is selling Bintang by the bucket. Camel Trophy '85 is all over apart from a slow, tedious, escorted drive back to Balikpapan.

Competitors and camp followers alike make merry at Camel's expense during the prize-giving party. We have been ordered not to shave, because whiskers will look better on the photographs. Later, the local hookers make a fortune while my memory is of a disconsolate Belgian, out in the jungle: 'To think I've taken three weeks without pay to endure this farce,' he growled.

Day Thirteen: We fly to Jakarta, where I share a room with my pal Lars Dahlhof, a Swedish journalist. My clothes are so disgusting that I leave the suitcase open on the window bay's floor. During the night I hear the sound of falling water, switch the light on and see half-asleep Lars watering the wall. 'Oh no!' he gasps. 'I am thinking we were still in the jungle.' I laugh about the incident a few hours later, when it's time to start the day, and tell the Swede there's no need to be embarrassed. He says: 'But there is, Phil, because before I pee on the wall, I pee in your suitcase.'

Back in England my appearance attracts the attention of one of Her Majesty's Customs and Excise officers. When asked to open my case, I flip the latches – 'It's full of the stinking clothes I've been wearing for two weeks in the jungles of Borneo' – and invite him take a look while I observe from a safe distance. The stench makes him step backwards, then gasp and chuckle. 'I see what you mean, sir. I hope you have a *very* understanding wife with a *very* good washing machine.'

31

CHINA WITH WESTERN HALF-DEVIL CLARKSON

1988

Welsh Frankton's prodigiously perspiring answer to Marco Polo is in Peking, where an immense depiction of Chairman Mao Tse-tung gazes inscrutably down from the medieval Gate of Heavenly Peace. Flanked by slogans – 'Long live the People's Republic of China' and 'Long live the unity of the peoples of the world' – the portrait stares across a square literally bigger than many a British farm. This flagstoned vastness, a popular place for flying kites big enough to frighten Boeings, is also overlooked by the Great Hall of the People, the Monument to the People's Heroes and the People's Cultural Park. The People's Republic of China is indeed a very peopled country. It accounts for one in four of the world's population. A young man with a shy, polite smile approaches the trio of Europeans. We are known, colloquially, as 'monster faces' and 'western half-devils'. He says: 'Excuse me. Do you speak English?' and is delighted by the reply. He's a regular listener to the BBC World Service, we're told. Another smile: 'English famous for playing cricket,' he says. Llewellin, astonished and delighted, turns to one of his companions and says: 'Cricket! A flickering candle of hope in the alien darkness.'

China rates 197th on the motor industry's list of favourite destinations for journalistic freebies. It's in the same class as Chad, Siberia and Spitzbergen. Scribblers who toe the line are brimmed with champagne while executive jets whisk them to nine-star hotels in locations favoured by the world's wealthiest sybarites. At the other end of the scale, I was squeezed into a CAAC airliner's cattle-class seat for the interminable flight to China, handed the keys to nothing more exciting than a 55bhp hatchback and invited to visit People's Cotton Mill Number Three or the Han Yang Maternity and Family Planning Centre.

This opportunity to take a look behind the Bamboo Curtain came about when Citroën invited me to spend a few days with the Operation Dragon caper that gave young people from nine European countries an unprecedented chance to spend a month seeing all manner of sights while driving AXs from Hong Kong to Peking. Operation Dragon was given the go-ahead because 'Dragon Years' in the Chinese calendar have always been associated with significant events. The powers that be agreed to mark this one by granting Citroën's 108-vehicle travelling circus more freedom of movement than any western half-devil monster faces have enjoyed since 1 October, 1949, when Chairman Mao proclaimed the People's Republic of China.

This was also a massive public relations exercise. There's talk of China needing two million vehicles by the end of the century, so the doors are wide open. Operation Dragon's real *raison d'être* was to make sure that Citroën's name rang the right sort of bells in Peking. Three thousand Brits applied for places. Twenty were accepted. They included one actress, two policemen and the computer programmer without whom no latterday *Canterbury Tales* would be complete. My convivial comrade, a young motoring writer from Yorkshire, was looking forward to being screen-tested for BBC TV's *Top Gear* programme when he got home. His name was Jeremy Clarkson.

We studied Citroën's guide to China while heading for Paris to join a posse of Euroscribblers. This document had useful advice on just about every appropriate subject – apart from driving in China. Take earplugs, it suggested, because Chinese hotels tend to be very noisy. Toilets? Out in the sticks, what few facilities exist come nowhere near western notions of acceptability. Ladies interested in privacy should pack a folding screen. Avoid seeming too familiar with young Chinese women, it cautioned. There was also a note about the Chinese being in the Olympic gold medal class for spitting.

A few other snippets of information had been gathered before leaving home. For instance, China sprawls over almost four million square miles and is home to 1.1 billion people. Road transport? The vast majority of China's 300,000 cars are either taxis or official transport for VIPs. The fact that 477,305 cars were sold in Britain during last August puts that figure into some sort of perspective. Most people rely on pedal power, so national assets include some 350 million bicycles.

Chinese motoring magazines are difficult to read, or would be if there were any, so I consulted an automotive encyclopaedia before packing my chopsticks. It revealed China to be the home of such revered marques as Dong-Feng, Hong-Qi, He-Ping, Changjiang, Feng-Huan and Jingganshan. None of these names roll off the tongue quite like Ferrari or Jaguar, but they do sound much better than the Zil, Zim, Zis, Zat and Zother inflicted on Russian motorists.

Sunday night was spent at the Holiday Inn near Charles de Gaulle airport. The food and service were awful, so we investigated the contents of several bottles of wine. Clarkson had a theory that getting well and truly beveraged would help deaden the pain of our non-stop flight to Peking. I agreed, seconds before falling off a bar-stool for the third time that night.

Monday: CAAC stands for Civil Aviation Administration of China. 'China Airlines Always Cancel' and 'Chinese Airliners Always Crash' are popular alternatives. Wish I'd not read a *Daily Telegraph* report that highlighted CAAC's reputation for poor service, an apparently indifferent attitude towards safety and scant regard for timetables.

Tuesday: Flight CA934 lands on time at 7am. Having to wait for customs and immigration officials to report for duty suggests that such punctuality is indeed unusual. Outside, it looks grey enough to be England on a really cold, miserable

November day, but temperature and humidity make me feel as if I'm wearing a heavy blanket in a sauna. The air is like hot cement dust. Our minibus has speed-related air conditioning. This depends on how wide the windows can be opened, and on the position of the driver's right foot.

China's answer to the M4 between Heathrow and central London is little more than a bosky lane. Bicycles burdened with immense panniers, and trikes equipped with platforms big enough to take goods plus two or three people, account for most of the rush-hour traffic.

First impressions of Peking? It makes Blaenau Ffestiniog on an incredibly vile day look like a cross between the Garden of Eden and Shangri-la. Modern buildings completely devoid of anything other than ugliness line mile after mile of broad, straight, characterless streets. Mission Control is the Jianguo, one of several posh hotels built since China started welcoming visitors who had previously been regarded as imperialist running dogs. It's as typically Chinese as the Savoy, Claridges or Connaught, which may not be a bad thing. The contents of my room's mini-bar include Beefeater gin, Bell's whisky and small bottles of claret.

We need sleep, but lunch is served at 11am. Dishes include what look and taste like fossilised golfballs. The last course is soup. Thought for the day? If the Chinese were so clever, why didn't they invent the knife and fork? Then it's off to the Forbidden City, which was actually the imperial palace from the 15th century until 1912, when the last Manchu emperor was given the old heave-ho. This complex of huge but elegant pagoda-roofed buildings painted in greens, golds, reds and blues is described in one authoritative guidebook as the country's most imposing architectural masterpiece and, indeed, 'without a doubt the most magnificent historical structure in existence today'. But even the most magnificent of masterpieces is difficult to appreciate when fatigue and brutal, suffocating heat are exacerbated by several million people. Many of them stand by Clarkson while cameras click. Being snapped with a giant western half-devil monster face earns extra points. Just about every visitor totes a still or video camera, but the Forbidden City is just that from the Belgian television crew's viewpoint. What's the problem? They've been told that their cameras are too big.

Wednesday: The Citroëns we've travelled so far to drive are 800 miles from Peking, heading north for Zhengzhou, where we're due to join the convoy tomorrow. Today, a minibus whose driver is in no danger of exceeding the nationwide 40mph speed limit takes us to the Great Wall. We spend forever droning through drab surburbs that swelter beneath a yellow-grey sky. It's that baleful colour because pollution is mixed with dust carried eastwards at high altitude from the deserts of central Asia. Motorised vehicles are heavily outnumbered by bikes, trikes and carts powered by up to three horses. Eyes peeled for such things fail to spot any sources of petrol or diesel.

Half of China's population has chosen this day to visit the Great Wall, which is 3,750 miles long and said to be the only man-made structure visible from the moon. That's nonsense, but it's a fact that work on this otherwise mind-boggling bulwark started several centuries before the birth of Christ. The section nearest Peking dates from 1368–1644 when the Ming dynasty ruled the roost. Wide enough for five horsemen to ride side by side, it snakes and switchbacks over steep, wooded hills. This must be a magical place to visit when the world is cool, clear and quiet, not hot, hazy and seething with humanity.

The other half of China's population is at the Ming Tombs, which we visit after chopsticking a lunch whose best dish may well be spiced worms. The tomb chosen for our delectation would make an adequate underground car park or a magnificent wine cellar. The nearby Sacred Way, lined with all manner of 15th-century statues, is far more impressive. The guide asks if my country's culture includes mythological animals. She's amazed to be presented with a badge depicting the red dragon of Wales. 'Is this dragon more important than your king?' she asks.

By midnight all the Chinese who had been at the Great Wall are sleeping on the ground outside Peking's main railway station. All those who had been at the Ming Tombs are snoring on the floor inside. We board a 'soft' sleeper – these trains are reserved for monster faces and Chinese bigwigs – which departs within five seconds of the advertised time. Clarkson is awarded an extra can of Changlee beer for discovering how to switch off the six-berth compartment's source of ying-tong music punctuated by incomprehensible announcements.

Thursday: The sado-masochistic Brits torture each other with visions of home – bacon and scrambled egg, sausage and grilled tomato, toast and marmalade – while breakfasting on noodle soup, spring onions and boiled string vest. People's Train 121 heads south across a surprisingly green plain. We pass fields planted with rice, works where bricks are still made by hand, and herds of goats tended by eternally patient old men whose faces, shaded by traditional straw hats, are the colour and texture of medieval parchment. Our train shares the line with earthquaking steam locomotives, notably QJ-class 2-10-2 giants based on a Russian design from the Fifties. We cross the Yellow River – more than a mile wide at this point, despite being 400 miles from the sea – and prepare to become part of Operation Dragon at long last. Just before the train reaches Zhengzhou our carriage's cleaning lady throws all the rubbish out of the window.

'The main topic of conversation is bowels, because we've all had the trots at least once since leaving Hong Kong,' we're told by a cheerful and rather pukka English girl who appears to be smuggling a pair of melons. She is an excellent source of information. 'Chinese ladies don't have much in the way of boobs, so everyone's fascinated by the bigger variety. The Chinese students travelling with us are delightfully naïve. One of them looked very puzzled when contraception was mentioned. He said they were taught to whistle until the urge went.'

There have been one or two unfortunate accidents on the road from Hong Kong, so People's Traffic Commissioner Chow tells the new intake of monster faces how to drive before licences are issued. He talks like an AK-47 automatic rifle. 'Be careful! Be careful of cars! Be careful of trucks! Be careful of buses! Be careful of bicycles! Be careful of animals!

Be careful of people! Be careful of *anything* that can move! If you hit a person, and they are alive, discuss accident with them! If dead, discuss with other person! Stop when light red! Go when light green!'

Capitalist lackey Llewellin is tempted to ask Commissioner Chow a question – 'Shouldn't it be red for *go* in a Communist country?' – but recalls advice in the guidebook. 'Remember that if the Chinese have a sense of humour, it is certainly not the same as ours.'

The afternoon is spent visiting People's Cotton Mill Number Three, where 9,000 people are employed. Salary plus bonus averages £50 a month and they get seven days holiday a year.

Friday: Literally tens of thousands of people line Zhengzhou's streets as the half-devils hit the road for Luoyang. Out of town, going fast enough to snatch top gear for a few seconds is greeted with ironic cheers, because the heavily policed convoy's pace is glacial. Average speed to Luoyang is 22.4mpg.

Immense crowds watch us driving to the Friendship Hotel. It's out in the sticks, where locals accustomed to seeing one Dong-Feng a month are astonished by the size of Citroën's cavalcade. In addition, we are almost certainly the first westerners these people have ever glimpsed. Here, as in Zhengzhou and other towns, the cars ahead of us are greeted with nothing more than polite smiles or blank looks. Clarkson and Llewellin are greeted with great gales of laughter, because we wave through the sunroof. People point, wave, shout and almost fall off high buildings. We couldn't have attracted more attention had the AX been pulled by a dozen naked *Playboy* bunnies. Clarkson turned to me and said: 'This makes you realise what it must be like to be famous.'

The night's entertainment, a press conference, is worth attending just to hear the interpreter trying to say 'molybdenum'.

Saturday: Twelve hours are needed to drive 240 miles up the Yellow River's valley to Xian. The roads are good, apart from a few very short sections where the surface has vanished, and what other traffic there is has to stop while

Operation Dragon passes. Why so slow? Because the schedule includes no fewer than four food-and-leak stops. Because we encounter brief but ferocious downpours. Because no Chinese policeman is going to break the speed limit, even when escorting monster faces.

Xian is the end of the driving road for Clarkson and Llewellin. Tomorrow we visit the world-famous army of terracotta soldiers before starting the homeward haul. The otherwise excellent Hotel International can't provide the celebratory champagne we've been promised by Citroën's public relations lady, Dominique Morgan, but does stock Guinness Foreign Extra Stout. The extent to which the world has shrunk is underlined when I sip it while flicking through the *China Daily* newspaper, reach the sports page and am informed that Surrey's cricketers beat Glamorgan by ten wickets at The Oval.

32

OLD CARS AND GOOD TIMES ON THE EQUATOR

1993

Locals refer to Singapore as a fine city, but the visitor nods and smiles before the pun is explained. Draconian laws enable the courts to fine you for just about everything from possessing chewing gum – this is part of the state's war on litter – to failing to flush the toilet. Nothing less serious than death is the mandatory penalty for dealing in drugs. Playing safer than safe, I flushed my Alka-Seltzers down the loo before Singapore Airlines' Boeing 747-400 Megatop completed its non-stop, 6,760-mile flight from London.

Singapore is a very modern, exceptionally clean and enviably prosperous place whose assets include the world's busiest port. But its relationship with the automobile is about as relaxed as the official line on dope. That said, slapping huge taxes on new cars is generally the best way to cultivate an interesting population of oldies, particularly in a former colony where Austin, Morris and Wolseley used to share the sweltering streets with Riley, Humber and Hillman. But not in Mr Lee Kuan Yew's up-to-the-minute Singapore. 'Export or scrap after 10 years' is the rule, unless you are granted a certificate of exemption.

This extraordinary state of affairs explains why the 500-mile Louis Vuitton Vintage Equator Run from Singapore to Kuala Lumpur, billed as Asia's premier event for old motors, attracted more than its fair share of attention. The 58-car line-up included a 1914-vintage Mercer Roadster, the swashbuckling Alain de

Cadenet's 1931 Alfa Romeo 8C-2300, two vast Cadillacs – originally owned by President Sukhano of Indonesia – three Bugattis, four Bentleys, an Armstrong Siddeley Sapphire, a delectable Aston Martin DB4 convertible, several Jaguars and a BMW 503 from the manufacturer's museum in Munich. Of three Rolls-Royces, one was a pre-production Phantom II built in 1928 and driven for two years by none other than Sir Henry Royce. Seven or eight of the starters were not the sort of cars that spring to mind when contemplating a made-to-measure set of Louis Vuitton's mega-money luggage. There was a Morris Ten saloon from the 1940s, two roly-poly Austin A40 Somerset convertibles – the saloon version was the first car I ever drove – and a 42-year-old Hillman Minx ragtop known as Elsie. I predicted navigational problems for the Morris, because its road book and maps had been entrusted to a guy named Wong Wai Keong.

'I think the Louis Vuitton people have been a little surprised by some of the entries,' one of the Malaysia and Singapore Vintage Car Register's stalwarts confided. We were combating the heat and humidity by sipping chilled Moët et Chandon during one of the parties that made me wonder whether Singapore's acclaimed medical services extended to free liver transplants for visitors. 'The club is well aware that the likes of the Morris Ten and Hillman Minx wouldn't be considered for a Louis Vuitton event in Europe. But this isn't Europe. You have to be very keen to keep an old car on the road out here and they all deserve a share of the limelight,' he said, calling for another bottle of fizz before telling tales of a local driver whose escapades earned him the nickname of Nearly Dead Ted. This encounter took place in the Raffles Hotel. Named after Sir Stamford Raffles, who founded Singapore in 1819, it was a legendary watering hole in the days when the sun never set on the British Empire. Old colonial hands tell you about the tiger that was shot under the billiard table in 1902. Chinese waiters buried a hoard of silver cutlery in the garden after Britain's surrender to the Japanese in 1942 – a capitulation that was followed by 100,000 military and civilian deaths. A few years later, friends of mine were dining in the restaurant when a British army officer, whose mood could be described as whimsical and humorous, drove a Land Rover up the steps and into the foyer.

The republic of Singapore is just 80 miles north of the equator, its suffocating heat exacerbated by high humidity. Stepping out of an air-conditioned hotel or car is like being cloaked in the steaming pelt of a grizzly bear while breathing oxtail soup. Your reporter was not designed to operate in such conditions. I was melting beneath my straw hat long before James Harwood – a splendid Australian in knee-length, empire-building shorts and a white pith helmet – flagged the first car off from the Padang at 8am. Nearby, rugby players were training hard while wilting visitors from northern latitudes tried to muster enough strength to tackle the champagne breakfast. Umpteen acres of greensward have made the Padang one of the city's focal points since the Singapore Cricket Club was founded in the 1850s. This evocative starting point for the Louis Vuitton Vintage Equator Run is overlooked by St Andrew's Cathedral, which was built by Indian convicts and appears to be made of white icing sugar. The previous church was demolished after being twice struck by lightning. This convinced the locals that the site was bedevilled by evil spirits. According to legend, the Indians laboured under the impression that the Brits would need human sacrifices to appease the gods.

James Harwood was not the only participant whose attire recalled the colonial era. Kjeld Jessen, driver of the 1929 Bentley, looked just like Lofty in *It Ain't Half Hot, Mum*. Ferrari expert Antoine Prunet, at the wheel of a 1927 Bugatti Type 37, sported a hat that would not have been out of place in Lucknow during the Indian Mutiny of 1857. Another guy told a nice little tale about the days when only the right sort of chaps owned motors as classy as his 1934 Bentley. A previous owner made a note in his diary after selling the car to strangers for £525. 'They don't look like Bentley people, but that's life, I suppose,' he wrote. Indubitably the right sort of chap, His Royal Highness the Rajah Muda Tengku Idris Shah, the Sultan of Selangor's heir, had chosen to drive a 1932 Ford. Dad's full name is Duli Yang Maha Mulia Sultan Salahuddin Abdul Aziz Shah Alhaj Ibni Almarhum Sultan Hisamuddin Alam Shah Alhaj Sultan Dan Yang Dipertuan Negeri

Selangor Darul Ehsan Dan Jajahan Takluknya. I kid you not.

Another wealthy nabob must have been responsible for gold-plating the Riley Lynx whose brightwork ruptured my retinal veins. It attracted almost as much attention as the Hollywood blonde in the passenger seat of Alain de Cadenet's supercharged Alfa. Singaporeans are not yet fined for admiring old cars, so there were waves and cheers as machinery from six decades headed for the causeway that spans the Straits of Johore. The Singapore of clustered skyscrapers could be a freshly minted western city. Johore Bahru, however, the gateway to Malaysia's jungle-clad peninsula, has all the sights, sounds and smells that a traveller associates with Asia.

Thirty years ago there was a sporting chance of sharing the bustling streets with the Aston Martin DB3S that had won the 1961 Malayan Grand Prix. Its owner recalled: 'Malaya in those days had good roads with little traffic, and when the car was painted in the royal colours of Johore one could use its terrific performance to the full, and the police would salute as we went by.'

Throbbing drums welcomed us to a fortress-like building on a hill above the city. Amazingly beautiful, graceful dancers whose movements were choreographed by the cracking of a whip performed in a rippling blaze of silk on the red-carpeted steps.

Morris Minors, Ford Anglias, Land Rovers, Bedford trucks and other vehicular hangovers from colonial days make Malaysia's roads much more interesting than Singapore's. But lifeboats and hovercraft would have been more appropriate when the blackest of menacing clouds dropped rain that reduced visibility to a few feet and turned roads into swirling rivers topped with a froth of red mud. The seals on the sliding door of our Mitsubishi minibus were no match for the tropical storm's relentless fury. We could imagine what it was like in cars as old and open as the two grand prix Bugattis.

'Cheated death again!' whooped John Caves from California, as his 1940 Ford V8 reached Malacca at day's end. He was joking. Similar sentiments were voiced with 24-carat sincerity by the couple whose MG TF had plunged into a 20-feet-deep ravine, from which it was pulled by excited villagers. Pressing on regardless – that's what these events are all about – they ended up finishing a very respectable 15th in the class for cars built between 1946 and 1960. Placings depended on following the route – quite a feat on the maze of unsigned dirt roads that criss-cross Malaysia's vast rubber, oil palm and banana plantations – reaching the checkpoints on time, then combining speed with precision and agility during the decidedly tricky little driving tests.

Despite the monsoon, only two cars failed to complete the first day's route. The Morris Ten deserved a special award for running out of water while the Austin Seven managed to ignite during a deluge that would have extinguished the Great Fire of London within two minutes. 'I have never been so wet and dirty,' sighed David Bayliss, who spent many years in this part of the world before returning to England. His mud-covered Alfa was one of a very small batch of six-cylinder, 1.5-litre Mille Miglia Speciales built to contest Italy's great 1,000-mile race in 1928. The 6C-1500 was designed by Vittorio Jano, the engineer whose other masterpieces included the 8C-2300 driven by Alain de Cadenet. 'The Cad' had the taste and sense to buy and race wonderful old cars years ago, when they changed hands for next to nothing. He recalls being offered $4m for the Alfa P3 single-seater that cost him just £700.

During dinner we were entertained by dancers who made even the exquisite Johore Bahru troupe look like sumo wrestlers knee-deep in wet concrete. They helped divert your whine-and-dine correspondent's attention from the 'warm white fungus' that formed part of an eight-course ethnic feast.

Next morning, police escorted us to the heart of Malacca, a 600-year-old seaport with strong Chinese, Portuguese, Dutch and British influences. Stalls selling eggs, fruit, vegetables and huge, sullen catfish that must inspire countless mother-in-law jokes lined the bumpy, palm-shaded road up the coast. We followed the hard-charging Mercer for several miles, listening to the strident bark of its 5.2-litre engine while dodging the Suzuki, Honda and Yamaha mopeds that sound like indefatigable swarms of demented hornets. Inland, where the jungle forms a solid wall on each side of the road, azalea, hibiscus and bourgainvillea shared the lush verges with cattle, goats, sheep, geese and chickens. Dragonflies the size of Flying Fortresses patrolled deep ditches where stagnant water steamed beneath high noon's hammering sun. Each time we stopped to watch the cars go by, I remembered what had been said about the local cobras being all of seven feet long. In this part of the world, it makes sense to unleash a tame mongoose before taking an alfresco leak.

The atmosphere was best of all in the plantations – the biggest employ several thousand people – where vast naves, arcades and colonnades of trees form tall, graceful arches across roads of red dirt. It was easy to turn the clock back several decades as we cheered the bucking, clattering Model T Ford that amazed the pundits by winning its class and finishing fourth overall, behind a trio of rakish little MG TA square-riggers. Lofty Jessen deserved bonus points for nonchalantly smoking a big cigar as his Bulldog Drummond dreadnought of a Bentley crossed wooden bridges that didn't look strong enough to support a rickshaw. Any talk of this being a piece of cake, old boy, was quashed by Basil Renolds. The genial Australian drove his Bentley as fast as he dared, but was all of five minutes late on a plantation section where the permitted time was 21 minutes.

The Louis Vuitton Vintage Equator Run ended with a black-tie dinner in Kuala Lumpur, where oceans of Veuve Clicquot and dozens of prizes were dispensed. Winners and losers toasted such heroes as Cecil 'MG' Kimber, Vittorio Jano, Henry Ford, André Citroën, William Lyons, Donald Healey, Walter Owen Bentley, Ettore Bugatti and Henry Royce, the uncompromising engineer whose Phantom had been likened to the *Titanic* as its weight reduced the finishing ramp to matchwood.

A rather hoity-toity lady reporter who was covering a rally for the first time – 'I'm concentrating on the lifestyle angle' – shook her head as we recalled splashing through the plantations. 'How can a man complain about what his wife spends on clothes,' she asked, 'if he drives a valuable old car along roads not fit for a Land Rover? I still don't know if these people are very enthusiastic or just ever so slightly mad.'

My pun-loving pal from Singapore chuckled. 'It's a fine line,' he said.

33

EUROPE

BACK TO THE

BLOODY BEACHES

1984

D-Day plus 40 years found your battle-scared, bottle-scarred correspondent in the little town of Ste-Mere-Eglise, where men of the US 82nd and 101st Airborne Divisions landed a few minutes after midnight on 6 June, 1944. They arrived by parachute. My transport, marginally safer and more conventional, was a 1943 White scout car crewed by Belgians. One of them sported a Seaforth Highlander's uniform complete with kilt. Another was rigged out in the tunic and tartan trews of the King's Own Scottish Borderers. Neither had ever set foot in Scotland. They didn't even speak English. Mind-boggling inconsistencies were delightfully typical of the great D-Day anniversary operation mounted by Britain's Military Vehicle Conservation Group and its counterparts on the European mainland. You could bet your last bottle of beer that the gum-chewing guy in 1944-style US Army combat kit, with a pack of Lucky Strikes strapped to his helmet, had as much American blood as the Prince of Wales or Charles de Gaulle.

I met Sir Winston Churchill before sailing to Normandy. He died in 1965 – but there he was, plodding round the Portsmouth showground where the MVCG had mustered its men and machines before crossing the English Channel. It was a sight to make even the most avid toper switch to nothing stronger than milk. Leaning on his ebony cane, the great man growled greetings, flourished a cigar big enough to sink a battleship, raised two V-for-Victory fingers . . . and was really mine host at a pub, a few miles along the coast. After that encounter I could have coped with General Dwight D Eisenhower and King George VI setting up drinks for Field Marshal Gerd von Rundstedt and Adolf Hitler.

The vehicles were the real thing, the right Second World War stuff, and numbered nearly 800 when the British convoy was joined by contingents from France, Belgium, Holland and elsewhere. Jeep, GMC, Dodge, Chevrolet, Plymouth, Federal and Diamond T shared Normandy's narrow roads with Bedford, Hillman, Daimler, Morris, Humber, Albion and Austin. There were tanks and armoured cars, trucks and half-tracks, ambulances and weapons carriers, staff cars and a veteran bus for the 21-man military band in their scarlet tunics. General Bernard Montgomery's 1937 Phantom III Rolls-Royce towered like an anthracite sculpture above equally immaculate two-wheelers from the likes of Harley-Davidson, Norton, Villiers, Matchless and BSA.

Peter Gray, the MVCG's founder and chairman, spent his early years on Jersey, a small island that's British despite being within sight of the Normandy coast. It was occupied by the Germans from 1940 to 1944. Peter traces his interest in military vehicles back to 1950, when he bought a Jeep. It was just a cheap, reliable form of day-to-day transport. Very unfashionable, he recalls, even during that grim period of 'export or die' austerity, when personal transport rarely amounted to anything more complicated than a bicycle. Time went by and attitudes changed. He started meeting people who shared his interest in old military machinery, formed the MVCG in 1969 and organised its first visit to France five years later. The MVCG now has 1,200 members scattered all over the world. They travelled from as far afield as the USA, South Africa and Australia to take part in the 'Liberty Highway' celebrations and commemorations.

Peter Gray has more military vehicles than I've had hot dinners. He ticks them off like a hen counting her chickens.

There's the Harley-Davidson and a very rare amphibious variation on the Jeep designed by Ford in co-operation with a New York boat-builder. Dodge is represented by a four-wheel-drive weapons carrier, a command car and an ambulance. 'I've an idea that, if you were half-dead when you went into the ambulance, you'd be completely dead when you came out,' he chuckles. 'It's very claustrophobic.'

Heavier metal includes several six-wheel-drive GMC trucks – one crewed by Aussies, another entrusted to a convivial cohort from Massachusetts – and a lofty four-by-four Federal tractor, hauling a ten-ton trailer. The Federal, its cab resembling an eggcup on an elephant, was driven by Bill Tait, a British veteran of the Normandy campaign. Impressed? You ain't heard nothin' yet, because Peter's collection also includes an M-10 tank. Mere mortals might think it's a *very* big deal to own a full-size main battle tank, but that's just what the M-10 was designed to demolish. Based on the Sherman, but equipped with a much bigger and better gun, it was evolved after campaigns in North Africa and Italy had made it horribly clear that Allied tanks were no match for their German rivals. The fearsome Panzer IV, invariably known as the Tiger, had an 88mm gun whose shell could penetrate armour 120mm thick at a range of 1,000 yards. The fact that a Tiger could KO a Sherman at 4,000 yards was bad news. Even more sobering, however, was the fact that a Sherman couldn't pierce a Tiger's frontal armour no matter how short the range. Hence the M-10, whose high-velocity, three-inch gun could sling a shell nine miles.

Peter's pride and joy, rescued from a scrapyard, tips the scales at 28 tons and has a brace of 450bhp supercharged Detroit Diesels. They drive the tracks through a five-speed gearbox that shifts as sweetly as a straw cutting through concrete until the oil gets warm. Registered and taxed as a private car, the M-10 is ideal for sorties to the Pig and Whistle if your pocket can handle the 2.2mpg fuel bills.

Moving the monster to Portsmouth from Peter's home in Worthing, 35 miles along the coast, required a 14.5-litre Diamond T tank transporter whose six-cylinder Hercules engine sounded like dinosaurs mating. Driven all the way from Sweden, the transporter collected its load and wasted no time attracting a policeman's attention. His eyebrows went into orbit. The whole caboodle was over-length, over-width, overweight and over here. The canny Swedes, conveniently forgetting that they could speak fluent English, were eventually escorted by half the West Sussex Constabulary.

This representative of the Queen's Own Portable Typewriter Regiment was assigned to Dick Davidson and Chris Evans, stalwart citizens whose knowledge of the Second World War is matched only by their capacity for having a good time. They got through more liquid than the M-10. Dick, an engineer at a nuclear power station, spent two years restoring a 1942 GMC six-by-six wrecker known as *Schlachthof Funf – Slaughterhouse Five* – whose fixed boom was typically used by motor pools for lifting engines. On this trip it provided an excellent vantage for such heroic activities as drinking beer alfresco while hailing bosomy, dark-eyed, long-legged French damsels. Nitty-gritty details include a 4.5-litre engine that slurps about a gallon of petrol every 9.5 miles on a good day with a favourable wind. Top speed? There's a crisp 45mph on tap once you've worked your way through a transmission with a five-speed gearbox supplemented by a two-speed transfer case. It takes all of ten yards to make you realise why Dick travels with earplugs in addition to such essentials as a Garand semi-automatic carbine. The back of the truck is reasonably quiet, but riding in the shoulder-to-shoulder cab is like being inside the howling, throbbing engine of a Flying Fortress, running hard for home. You can sense everything from brain to bowels being relentlessly liquefied and threatening to trickle out through the lace-holes in your shoes. If the good people who run Alcoholics Anonymous want to try some really serious aversion therapy, they should invest in a fleet of Second World War trucks. After the war, the gallant old skull-splitter served with the French Army before being given an honourable discharge in 1979. Letters and numerals picked out in white paint now identify

Slaughterhouse Five as belonging to the US Army's Fifth Corps, whose troops hit Omaha Beach at 0630 hours on D-Day.

Omaha, Utah, Gold, Sword and Juno were codenames for beaches spread out along some 60 miles of the Normandy coast between Le Havre and Cherbourg, ports with defences capable of repelling any direct assault from the sea. Although the beaches were guarded by everything from big guns to barbed wire and literally millions of mines, attacking them was the best way to punch holes in the 'Atlantic Wall' built by the Germans after France surrendered in 1940. Hitler was convinced that the Allied invasion, if it ever came, would be launched far away to the north-east, where England and France face each other over just 21 miles of water. Many subtle subterfuges kept him thinking that way long after the Americans, British and Canadians, plus men of the Free French Army, started battling their bloody way through Normandy.

The invasion was called Operation Overlord. Eisenhower was the supreme commander. Ground forces were under Montgomery, a brilliant but controversial British eccentric whose 1942 victory at El Alamein had turned the tide in North Africa. Monty's character can be judged by a remark made many years later, during a debate about relaxing the law regarding homosexuals. 'This sort of thing may be tolerated by the French,' he barked, 'but we are British, thank God.'

Control of the air, the most vital of all factors, had been achieved long before D-Day. Allied bombers, raiding by day and night, forced Hitler to pull his Messerschmitt and Focke-Wulf fighters back for the defence of German cities. Relatively few remained in France to supplement the anti-aircraft guns when the four-engined Flying Fortresses and Lancasters pounded coastal defences, bridges, railroads and other key targets.

Southern England became a vast military camp where British and Canadian troops were joined by more than 950,000 Americans. No fewer than 163 new airfields were built for Operation Overlord. More than 50,000 vehicles were mustered in fields, lanes, big towns and tiny, isolated villages old enough to remember archers and pikemen leaving for France in the 14th century. The hammer was cocked. The finger was on the trigger. Ike, Monty and the other commanders at SHAEF – Supreme Headquarters Allied Expeditionary Force – could only pray for the right combination of moon, weather and tides.

Churchill double lit another cigar as the first of three MVCG convoys headed for the ferry berth amid the naval history that is Portsmouth dockyard. Tim Wren, photographer and friend, and the son of a Normandy veteran, hailed me from the deck of a DUKW as the band emerged from its bus to fill the midnight air with tunes of glory. At home on land or water, at least in theory, the DUKW was one of several vehicles developed specially for Operation Overlord by Major-General Percy Hobart's 79th Armored Division. It was evolved from the 2.5-ton truck, which Eisenhower rated among the Allies' most vital pieces of equipment, along with the bulldozer, the Jeep and the C-47 Douglas Dakota transport aircraft.

Later in the week, Wren was aboard the DUKW when its owner decided to cruise down the canal from Caen to the sea. It made a fine sight, plunging down the slipway and gathering speed. But something was not quite right.

'You *did* put the plugs in?' asked the driver, sounding like a man who hears a burglar and hopes it's the cat.

'Yessir. Front and rear.'

'Front and rear? Front and rear! What about the big bugger in the middle! Jeeeezuss Christ!'

The vehicles dubbed 'Hobart's Funnies' also included an amphibious version of the Sherman with canvas skirts and twin propellers. Other tanks were modified to 'post a letter' of high explosive into concrete fortifications at point-blank range, roll canvas roadways over soft sand, unfold bridges across exceptionally wide, deep ditches, and beat paths through minefields in a fury of flailing chains. Hobart's Mark VII Crocodile was anything but funny if you happened to be on the other side. The Crocodile, not the sort of thing you expect from a nation of cricket-playing gentlemen – 'I say, old boy, that's taking it all a bit *too* far' – hauled a 400-gallon tank of fuel to feed a hellish device capable of sluicing targets with high-pressure flames at a range of 100 yards.

Weather that was bad, but not quite thumbs-down bad, tormented the vast invasion fleet that set course for Normandy on 5 June, 1944. That greatest of all armadas totalled some 6,500 vessels of every shape and size, from battleships like floating islands of gun-bristling granite to nimble minesweepers and landing craft packed with the men picked for H-Hour. Operation Overlord was destined to put 130,000 men and 14,000 vehicles ashore before D-Day ended. Another 23,500 landed by parachute and glider.

We, on the other hand, left Portsmouth in the early hours of 4 June, 1984, and crossed to Cherbourg in conditions so placid the sea could have been frozen. The only casualty observed by your correspondent was a young Londoner, dressed as an 82nd Airborne 'Screaming Eagle', who staggered from the bar and mumbled 'Thought these ferries had stabilisers' before collapsing in a corner.

The bar later closed without warning. No problem for Dick Davidson, who launched a one-man commando raid by slinking to the freight deck – 'No entry during voyage' – and liberating a few cans from *Slaughterhouse Five*. We toasted the clear, crisp, rejuvenating beauty of a dawn whose silver-gold sky was punctuated by a few small puffs of cloud. Forty years earlier they would have been the smoke from exploding ack-ack shells.

We landed at 0630 hours. Jubilant crowds lining the streets? Well, not quite. The burghers of Cherbourg were still abed, probably cursing the noise as Peter Gray's convoy assembled for breakfast in a supermarket parking lot. I nodded off in the truck's sunny cab, awakening to that time-warp feeling when a command car's PA system started playing Glenn Miller favourites. Purdom me boy, is that the cat you knew that chewed you, Vat 69. And so forth. I clambered down and chatted with a man from the West Country of England. He had never been to France before, but held the maps his father had carried ashore on D-Day.

It was time, in the words placed in Henry V's mouth by William Shakespeare, to imitate the action of the tiger, stiffen the sinews, summon up the blood, disguise fair nature with hard-favor'd rage, then lend the eye a terrible aspect. Measuring up to the final requirement was easy enough after 24 sleepless hours with Dick, Chris and the potent products of various breweries. The peepers resembled bite-sized snacks for Count Dracula.

Cherbourg, huddled beneath high bluffs still studded with German gun emplacements, was wide awake when the MVCG convoy started rolling through at 9am. I had expected a mixture of half-hearted waves and quizzical stares. After all, Gray's Grenadiers had been doing this sort of thing since 1974, albeit on a smaller scale. What we got was platoons of ecstatic children, squealing and cheering and flourishing flags. Old people, many with tears trickling down their cheeks, clapped, shouted, blew kisses and fingered the V-for-Victory sign. Monsieur le Mayor and other bigwigs saluted from the banner-bright Town Hall's steps as we entered the main square. The band, instruments gleaming like burnished gold, was playing a jaunty old march called *Colonel Bogey*. Its unofficial lyrics, enduring relics of wartime Britain, detail the alleged testicular peculiarities of certain Nazi leaders:

Hitler, has only got one ball.
Goering, has two but only small.
Himmler, is somewhat similar;
But poor old Go-balls has no balls at all.

Before the parade it had all been one big chuckle. But passing through those crowded streets, cheered by people who had survived the four long years of terror, injected the first of many emotional moments into the trip. At least once a day I would see, hear or just think something powerful enough to bring a fist-sized lump to the throat and briefly fill the eyes with pepper-hot tears. Just take a deep breath, swallow hard and say a silent prayer for the 56 million men, women and children who died between 1939 and 1945. Normandy alone is the last resting place of 115,000 Allies and Germans. Thousands of French civilians sleep in their native soil. Inevitably and ironically, many were accidentally killed by the very men who came to liberate them.

I had sung the words to *Colonel Bogey* as we cruised past the Town Hall. Now, as the convoy rumbled out of town, thoughts turned to the heart-rending works of Wilfred Owen, perhaps the finest of all war poets. He was killed in action a few days before the First World War ended in 1918. At first I put it all down to being a romantic, sentimental Celt, then noticed supposedly stolid Anglo-Saxons going through the same swallow-and-sniff routine. But another characteristic of the 'Liberty Highway' exercise was the speed at which emotions changed. It was impossible to remain sombre as *Slaughterhouse Five* climbed the hill from Cherbourg a few yards ahead of Dick Windrow and his lively load of liberators in *King Malfunction*, an immaculate short-wheelbase Diamond T built for Uncle Sam in 1941.

Next stop was Montebourg, a village whose entire population must have been lining the main street. There had been talk of an official reception – free drinks, in other words – but that would have left nothing more than mouse droppings in the civic coffers. So we dug into our pockets, liberated a bar and experienced the primeval delights of a traditional French lavatory. Translated into Second World War terms, it's like the pilot telling the tail gunner where to aim. Apart from the obvious hazards, there's always a sporting chance of your wallet slipping from the back pocket and plummeting in the general direction of Australia. I believe there's a link between primitive toilets and illiteracy. You can't contemplate the contents of a book or a newspaper while squatting over a noisome hole in the floor.

Montebourg was the parting of the ways, if only for a couple of days. The British vehicles headed for Arromanches, Gold Beach's focal point on D-Day, while the Americans were to camp at Ravenoville, near the northern end of Utah Beach. We waved farewell as the Brits departed in a tumult of Harley-Davidson sirens. Clearly confident in Peter Gray's organisational ability, and in the discipline of his followers, the police gave the MVCG a free hand with traffic. It was difficult to imagine Britain's boys in blue taking such an easy-going attitude as big old bikes, uniformed riders grinning from ear to ear, closed crossroads and blasted up and down the convoy like hornets stuffed with steroids.

The drive from Montebourg to Ravenoville wriggled us along narrow lanes squeezed between apple orchards and small, lush, high-hedged fields bright with buttercups. As the Allies learned to their cost, this lovely landscape, as soft and gentle as an angel's smile, provided superb cover for the Germans. Snipers lurked amid the apple blossom. MG-42 machine guns, good for 1,200 rounds per minute, spat death from the ditches. Rickety, picturesque barns concealed Tiger and Panther tanks.

I pitched my hip-high tent within sound of the sea, then snoozed for an hour or two before *Slaughterhouse Five* went to Ste-Mere-Eglise. The square was seething with old men who had been young, eager-to-swoop Screaming Eagles in 1944. The human effigy hanging in a parachute from one of the spires of the ancient church recalled their comrade, Private John Steele of the 82nd Airborne, who survived despite dangling there for several hours with a footful of bullet. The paratroopers were dropped long before H-Hour to secure the invasion's northern flank, then join forces with troops thrusting inland from the sea. Sixty miles east, gliders of the British Sixth Airborne slipped through the midnight darkness, landed right on target – this was one of the war's greatest flying feats – and captured two vital bridges. The proprietor of a nearby inn, the first building in France to be liberated, rushed into his garden with a spade and excavated 98 bottles of champagne that had been buried since 1940. Good show, chaps. But could Major John Howard and his tiny force of 150 hand-picked men prevent German armour from forcing its way across the bridges to attack Sword Beach after H-Hour?

'Time to inspect the gun battery at Crisbecq,' Chris said as we left Ste-Mere-Eglise. 'But if we nip into that little bar for five minutes, I'll have time to ferret appropriate information out of the official campaign history.'

The night was blacker than a Welsh Methodist minister's hat by the time we beat a tactical retreat from tavern to camp. Driver Dick limited himself to a couple of small beers. His colleagues, I regret to report, had their good intentions dissolved by calvados, a brew distilled from cider and sufficiently potent to fuel Exocet missiles. Everything reasonably under control until the young couple running the place, delighted to be part of a great event, offered king-size shots free, gratis and for nothing. We felt obliged to reciprocate, but that effectively cancelled their hospitality, so another round was poured. It turned into a wonderfully bibulous version of tennis, with drinks, not balls, being thwacked backwards and forwards . . .

Sunlight. A child chanting, chanting, chanting outside the tent. Innocent as the dew, he lowers the zip, catches sight of Llewellin, squeaks like a startled mouse, and flees to find his mother. Dick and Chris, younger and more resilient than yours truly, greeted the new day with King Edward cigars before crawling from their sleeping bags.

'Time to inspect the gun battery at Crisbecq,' said Chris. 'But if we find a good place for lunch, I'll have time to ferret appropriate information out of the official campaign history.' It was an amazing statement. Weeks seemed to have passed since anything solid had been consumed. I perched on the Jimmy's boom, blowing away the cobwebs, as we ambled up the coast to a restaurant within grenade-lobbing distance of the waves, where we lingered over many courses. Crisbecq, on a low escarpment about two miles from the sea, is where the Germans planted one of their long-range, 210mm Skoda nasties, operated by a 297-man garrison. The massive concrete fortifications resisted ferocious attacks by land, sea and air for six days, and checked progress along the road to Cherbourg. At the battery we met Professor Charles Bondurant, from Roanoke College, Virginia. A calm, quiet man, he had served with the First Engineering Special Brigade and spent D-Day blowing exits into the sea wall on Utah Beach.

Evening found us in fine fettle for liberating the stately Château de Quinville. You paid next to nothing, then assaulted a cold buffet sluiced down with jug after jug of red wine. A touch of class? How about rubbing regal shoulders with the exiled king and queen of Romania, military vehicle buffs who had driven their Jeep all the way from Switzerland. Pity they didn't join us for the real party when *Slaughterhouse Five* and its crew returned to camp, where we decided that no wars would be fought if everyone drank enough. So we formed IUTA – International Understanding Through Alcohol – and swore eternal friendship.

Operation Overlord's mighty fleet included six battleships whose big guns, supplemented by constant attacks from the air, hammered German defences immediately before H-Hour. Dawn was a little quieter on 6 June, 1984. No guns, bombs or rockets. Just the dull thudding of hangovers as men emerged from tent and truck to face the crackling fury of cornflakes. Dick and Chris decided it was time to exercise. That's easy enough when your truck travels complete with a folding bicycle designed for paratroopers, and a non-military but pre-war tandem bike. They weren't involved in the ceremonies at Ste-Mere-Eglise, where Peter Gray laid a wreath on the war memorial, which is why I hitched a ride in the Belgians' White scout car.

Later in the day, however, I shared a table in a crowded bar with the Massachusetts Minutemen. Did those guys know their stuff. They could tell you what colour socks Joe Snurdwangler was wearing the day his wife's cousin invented the Sherman's counter-rotating widget. The bar ran out of beer, so they decided that their borrowed six-by-six GMC needed to flex its muscles on Utah Beach. We sped along the sands for a couple of miles with wonderfully evocative air cover provided by a Spitfire, a Hurricane and the Lancaster from the RAF's Battle of Britain Memorial Flight. Battle ensigns were lacking, but bottles glinted bravely in the afternoon sun.

But what's all this? Why the hell are serious types with real guns erupting from the dunes and turning us back? Ain't this a free country, buddy? Ye gods! You would have thought we were charging towards an internationally televised ceremony featuring assorted kings, queens and presidents. Which, we learned, we were. Deflected but not dejected, the Yankees switched their attack to the restaurant where we had lunched the previous day. More solids. I was savouring a post-prandial coffee and calvados when who should arrive but the MVCG's one and only unit of the legendary Tandem Light Cavalry. Stap me vitals! It made one proud to be British.

Filling them in on the day's activities made me miss my lift back to the camp. No problem, said Dick, igniting the day's umpteenth King Edward. A fine athlete like Llewellin, blessed with the balance of a tightrope walker, would find it easy to be the third member of the tandem's nocturnal crew. The concept didn't seem *too* stupid after a few more swifties, but I was eventually offered a motorised alternative. That was bad news, in a way, because I'm interested in natural history and the tandem explored several ditches as Dick and Chris illustrated Sir Isaac Newton's point about the law of gravity.

Battle fatigue made us one of the last vehicles to evacuate Ravenoville on the wet, wind-lashed morning of 7 June. By that stage we had recruited a young British semi-punk. His US combat gear couldn't be faulted, but the pink hair didn't look quite right. The black studs in the left ear? They could have been some localised skin disease, or maybe scars left by a liberated lady eager for nylons and chewing gum. The youth's name was Warwick, and his family tree sounded interesting. 'I might be the rightful king of France,' he confided as we bowled through the rain to Bayeux, flat out at 45mph.

Ancient and beautiful, miraculously spared from bombs and shells, Bayeux is famous for a 230-feet-long pictorial tapestry embroidered 900 years ago to illustrate William the Conqueror defeating King Harold of England at the Battle of Hastings in 1066. Bayeux was liberated on 7 June, 1944. We arrived just in time for the big parade. God knows how many Second World War vehicles inched through the narrow streets. Somebody tossed out an estimate of 600. It could have been 1,000. Whatever the figure, they were still arriving when we left after a couple of memorable hours. The streets were rivers of flags fluttering above shouting, cheering, waving, laughing, weeping people. V-for-Victory! Bottles and glasses were raised in salute. V-for-Victory! Excited kids scrambled for candies flung from Jeeps by Screaming Eagles or soldiers of the 'Big Red One' infantry division, which suffered heavy casualties on Omaha Beach. There were special cheers for the kilted Highlanders, at least one of whom was a genuine Scot from Aberdeen. Attracted by singing, I picked my way through the crowds to a bar where veterans of the Sixth Airborne Division were raising a chorus loud enough to endanger the foundations of Bayeux Cathedral. Grab a beer, join the party, and who gives a tinker's cuss for leaden skies. So we stood on the sidewalk and sang everything from *Kiss Me Goodnight, Sergeant Major* and *Tipperary* to *Land of Hope and Glory* followed, of course, by the French national anthem. They must have heard that one in Paris.

The civic reception was a disaster if you lacked the patience, strength, stamina, cunning and tactical expertise to reach the bar. Officially intended for MVCG members, it attracted half the freeloaders in France. We abandoned all hope and retreated in good order to our camp on the edge of town. There I was grabbed by an American who had travelled from Saudi Arabia for the celebrations: 'Mr Llewellin, sir, you have just volunteered to help our demolition team. Our target for tonight is this bottle of Johnnie Walker Black Label. The penalty for desertion is death. The penalty for not deserting is just another hangover. In the words of General Eisenhower, the free men of the world are marching together. I have full confidence in your courage, devotion to duty, and skill in battle.'

It's tough being a post-war correspondent.

Next morning it's time to cut and run, leaving Dick, Chris and the pink-haired rightful king of France to soldier bravely on for another week. My only regret, as the train clattered towards the ferry, was not meeting a D-Day legend by the name of Bill Millin. Now a hale and hearty 61, Bill was Brigadier Lord Lovat's bagpiper. He waded to Sword Beach skirling *Highland Laddie* before marching up and down the sands playing *The Road to the Isles* as shot and shell screamed and burst about him. Lovat and his commandos raced eastward to help Major John Howard's men hold what became known as Pegasus Bridge. Lovat apologised for being two minutes behind schedule. That was typical of what Cornelius Ryan in his enthralling book *The Longest Day* calls 'the studied nonchalance the British traditionally assume in moments of great emotion'.

There were other examples on D-Day, 1944. One of the launches off Sword Beach played *Roll out the Barrel* over its loudspeakers. There were bugles and hunting horns. A Royal Marine officer, swimming towards Gold Beach under intense fire from German machine guns, was heard to say 'Perhaps we're intruding, this seems to be a *private* beach.' Best of all, in my considered opinion, was the young Shakespeare buff who read his men Henry V's great speech before the Battle of Agincourt on 25 October, 1415. It was the feast of Saint Crispin:

We few, we happy few, we band of brothers;
For he today that sheds his blood with me
Shall be my brother; be he ne'er so vile
This day shall gentle his condition;
And gentlemen in England now a-bed
Shall think themselves accurs'd they were not here,
And hold their manhoods cheap whiles any speaks
That fought with us upon Saint Crispin's day.

34

THE BENTLEY BOYS

1986

Bill Woodward's four-and-a-half litre Bentley was throbbing down the London–Dover motorway at a majestic 85mph. Not bad, I chuckled. Not bad at all for a car that's been on the road since 1929. Then suddenly we were passed by what sounded like an old piston-engined Lancaster bomber with all four Merlins running at full throttle. It was hard-charging John May's Bentley, a tuned-to-perfection Speed Six with a three-inch, straight-through exhaust pipe. 'Good for just over 120,' Bill hollered.

Believe me, the Bentley Boys are alive and well and going like hell. Beautiful old cars worth a rajah's ransom are given boot-to-bulkhead treatment worthy of Woolf Barnato, Tim Birkin and the rest of yesterday's Le Mans heroes, not pussyfooted along at 50 to 55mph. This is the Bentley *Drivers'* Club, they frequently remind you, not a bunch of trophy hunters whose idea of fun is a Sunday afternoon spent polishing vintage carburettors. I joined them for the club's four-day Bollinger Rally. It was a tough assignment. Qualifications included a liver in first-rate working order, a taste for oysters and sides strong enough not to be split by prolonged laughter. First came a champagne breakfast in London. Then we had to drive across northern France to Maison Bollinger, in a small town near Reims, for a buffet lunch accompanied by enough 1979-vintage fizz to float the USS *Nimitz*.

Hilarious dinners rarely ended before midnight, because BDC types are adept at squeezing every last droplet of fun from the great sponge of life. Few can generate more mirth than Bill Woodward. You could call him a Bentley enthusiast. He has four, the most recent being a 1985 Mulsanne Turbo. His driving is exactly what you expect from a rip-roaring extrovert who spent the 1939–45 war piloting Catalinas, Beaufighters and Mosquitoes after training in open-cockpit Tiger Moth biplanes.

Getting ready for the 1,200-mile jaunt made me feel like Captain Scott dressing for his ill-fated trudge to the South Pole. Heater? Well, the exhaust pipe runs under the passenger's feet. So, umpteen sweaters were topped with a weatherproof, knee-length Barbour coat, plus an ancient college scarf thick enough to stop Halley's comet in its tracks. Flying helmet and goggles, too, because Bill almost always runs with top and windscreen down. Only the aero-screens, little bigger than your thumbnail, prevent chattering teeth being pried from gums at 90mph. All that kit, supplemented by a waist-to-ankles blanket, makes a big difference. It's the difference between being *incredibly* cold and your widow hearing the coroner announce death due to hypothermia.

But top and screens were up when we set off on the 180-mile drive from the Welsh Marches to London. April was doing a flawless impression of December, notably when a full-blooded blizzard suddenly hit the motorway. 'Should be able to climb above it,' Bill roared, recalling his RAF days. Geriatric wipers coped for all of two minutes. Valiant attempts to clear the screen by hand were rewarded only by lumps of snow vanishing up sleeves. 'There's only one thing for it,' said Bill, changing down and flooring the throttle. 'Go faster and blow the bloody stuff away.'

Despite the storm, the old-timer *averaged* a mile a minute to London. Lolloping along at a low-revving 70–80mph, we wondered how many 1986 models would still be doing their stuff in the year 2043. Steady cruising was punctuated by gung-ho sprints – 'Just to show the buggers what these old cars are made of.'

Our base was the elegant and exclusive Capitol Hotel, in a quiet street behind Harrods, London's and probably the world's most prestigious superstore. At the hotel bar, we bent late-night elbows with Ted Young, a seafaring man who bought his 1923 3-litre Bentley for just £40 some 25 years and 100,000 miles ago. Its value has increased by about 65,000 per cent since 1961.

Clothing appropriate to your Bentley's age had been requested for the Bollinger-and-bacon breakfast. There were mind-boggling plus-four suits straight from Bertie Wooster's wardrobe, ancient tweed jackets, knee breeches, deerstalker hats and monocles. Slinky dresses, beads and foot-long cigarette holders were sported by Roaring Twenties flappers, one of whom strutted her stuff in a bathing costume that revealed saucy glimpses of knee.

'Champers for brekkers! How absolutely spiffing.'

'Doesn't one *always* have champers for brekkers, old chap?'

Twenty-two immaculate Bentleys, mostly pukka vintage jobs, eventually hit the road for Dover and the 21-mile ferry crossing to France. Commuters gaped, waved, and cheered. That was amazing. The typical Londoner, blasé beyond belief, wouldn't spare Dolly Parton more than two glances if she danced naked in front of Buckingham Palace, partnered by the Archbishop of Canterbury. More happiness was spread when Bill stopped for petrol. Noting the size of the Bentley's tank, the guy taking the money suddenly decided he could afford a Caribbean holiday.

Calais to Reims is about 200 miles across an undulating landscape fertilised by the bones of countless Allied and German soldiers killed during two world wars. It was cold that April afternoon. Cold enough, as we Brits say, to freeze the testimonials off a brass monkey. After a couple of hours at serious speeds, I could sense my heart struggling to cope with ice crystals pumped from frozen extremities. 'This is the life,' said Bill, thundering past a Renault 25 whose driver looked as if he'd just seen the Four Horsemen of the Apocalypse. 'We'll make a man of you yet.'

Face was saved when the car in front stopped at a wayside tavern. It was the 1926 ragtop crewed by BDC chairma'am Ann Shoosmith and president Ray Wiltshire. You know it's a trifle chilly, old sport, when the top BDC people feel obliged to pause for coffee and shots of Dr Cognac's anti-freeze, with which we toasted the club's 50th anniversary. Chairma'am Shoosmith's 60-year-old charger is a 3-litre chassis with a four-and-a-half-litre engine. That's a quick combination, as milady proved when we followed her to the Hotel de la Paix in Reims, spearing along tree-lined straights typical of rural France, sweeping through long, flowing curves as seductive as Brigitte Bardot in her pouting prime. These old-timers with the winged 'B' badges don't just go like sherbet off a hot shovel in a straight line. They also steer, corner and handle in a way that amazed and delighted this newcomer to the joys of vintage motoring. No wonder Ettore Bugatti called these Bentleys the world's fastest trucks.

What about stopping? Would you believe ABS? That's right, but it stands for 'Anticipatory Braking System'. An ability to foresee the future became increasingly important as Bill's brakes, diagnosed as having been fitted with sub-standard linings, became less and less efficient with every application. Retardation came a poor third to noise and smell, triggering jokes about the chef's special tonight being either grilled Girling or fried Ferodo liberally garnished with white knuckles.

The hotel's underground car park, reached at dusk, was thick with vintage exhaust fumes. Why worry about carbon monoxide poisoning when you're about to die of hypothermia? I mused. But half an hour chin-deep in a near-boiling bath thawed the viscera in time for dinner.

Hamlet recalled Yorick as a fellow of infinite jest whose flashes of merriment made many a table roar. He could well have been describing what Mr President Wiltshire cheerfully calls 'the rough end' of the BDC. If laughter is indeed the best medicine, the likes of Bill Woodward, Brian Fenn, Gordon Russell and John May will still be going strong 150 years from now. Talking of strength, the *soufflé de marc de Champagne* was made with a brew potent enough to melt a Bentley's pistons. Nobody dared light a post-prandial cigar until the plates were safely back in the kitchen.

Bill handed his car over to Fenn after Bollinger's lavish

Saturday lunch. Yours truly was in charge of the maps, of which there were none, so we lost touch with the rest of the convoy after stopping to click the Kodak. All of which explains why our Reims–Brussels route was every bit as direct as driving from Saint Louis to Chicago by way of New York. Brian, looking not unlike a youthful Winston Churchill, stopped and asked a bewildered German family if they happened to know where Belgium was. Pedal adjacent to metal, monocle flashing like a heliograph, he sped us across Luxembourg in just eight-and-a-half minutes. Luxembourg, for the benefit of those readers who failed geography, is a country. Not a big country, to be honest, but one that's rarely dismissed in a mere 25,500 revs. We reached the Belgian capital just in time for a dinner organised by the British embassy. It was a formal affair, so your reporter donned a dinner jacket as old as the car in which he had now covered some 750 memorable miles. Jokes about it being on loan from the Victoria and Albert Museum in London concealed the fact that it's my *only* dinner jacket. 'Might be back in fashion by the end of the century,' said Woodward, a snappy dresser whose kit included a bow tie in BDC colours.

The Bentley Boys were on parade to help promote the British Auto Festival in Liège, about 60 miles from Brussels. We were routed along relatively minor roads, presumably to avoid the risk of venerable Bentleys, Morgans, Jaguars and other John Bull machinery being tempted to dice on the motorway. So they diced on the olde worlde roads instead, watched by cheering locals who must have thought they had been time-warped back five or six decades. John May stormed past us on a rough stretch. 'If his exhaust falls off, the police will think they've found a section of the Channel tunnel,' Bill chortled, fur-lined gloves clenching a wheel bound with whipcord.

Monday was miserable. It rained hard enough for Bill to raise the roof for the first time since leaving England. But we still needed diving suits, and inside wipers, because rain swirled round the windscreen. I used to think Woodward had an enviable tan. Now I know it's rust.

The sun was shining when we reached Dover. Tops down, chaps, then up to Canterbury for a cup of good old British tea before going our separate ways. We were 150 miles from home when I finally accepted Bill's invitation to take the wheel. 'Remember that the brake's to the right of the accelerator,' he advised, 'and it's a good idea to double-declutch between first and second as well as when you're changing down, of course.'

Driving a vintage Bentley for the first time isn't too nerve-racking, if the road is clear and dry. My debut was all about three lanes of fast-moving traffic and Mother Nature suddenly unleashing a full-scale dress rehearsal for Armageddon, complete with hail like buckshot. 'This is the life,' said Bill, promising to man the pumps if it looked as if we were sinking. But I felt like one hell of a boyo as the weather eased, confidence grew and speed increased to a level almost worthy of wing-foot Woodward. We covered 120 miles before I had to drop a gear. The moment of truth. Dip the clutch, into neutral, blip the throttle, dip the clutch again, ease that massive lever from fourth to third. Per-bloody-fection! The proverbial hot knife through soft butter. But the next attempt, a few minutes later, sounded as if King Kong was attacking the transmission with a sledgehammer. 'Just a few too many revs,' said Bill. Back home, Mrs Llewellin poured big, therapeutic whiskies. We drank a toast to Walter Owen Bentley and then, massaging life back into our frozen hands and feet, drank another to the patron saint of lunatics who drive vintage cars in rain, hail, and snow. Who else but Leopold von Sacher-Masoch, the Austrian who gave his name to self-inflicted suffering.

WHEN THE GATES
OF HELL OPENED

1986

What passing-bells for these who die as cattle?
Only the monstrous anger of the guns.
Only the stuttering rifles' rapid rattle
Can patter out their hasty orisons.
No mockeries now for them; no prayers nor bells,
Nor any voice of mourning save the choirs,
The shrill, demented choirs of wailing shells;
And bugles calling for them from sad shires.

Jaguar's XJ-SC was the same blood-red as the poppies I picked in a field near the Oswestry birthplace of Wilfred Owen, the greatest of all war poets. I took them to the Somme region of northern France, to a hamlet called Thiepval, where more than 72,000 names are carved on the biggest of all British and Commonwealth war memorials. Those names commemorate only the men whose bodies were never found after history's bloodiest battle. Thousands more lie beneath neat headstones in cemeteries within a few miles of Thiepval.

The Battle of the Somme started on 1 July, 1916, after a week-long artillery bombardment that was heard in London, 200 miles away. By 17 November, Britain and the British Empire had suffered 420,000 casualties and General Sir Douglas Haig called a halt to what had been hopefully dubbed

'The Big Push'. The greatest advance had been along the main road from Albert to Bapaume. On that line, and on that line alone, the Germans had been pushed back just 6.5 miles.

The poppies we took to France in the XJ-SC were for all who died on the Somme, for all who suffered there, and for all who came safe home. In particular, however, they commemorated the men of the 6th Battalion, King's Shropshire Light Infantry, who symbolised it all for this Shropshire-born pilgrim. They were the Shropshire Pals, friends and colleagues from all walks of life who answered Lord Kitchener's call to arms and helped create history's biggest volunteer army. In the words of one of the Great War's more bitter songs, the 6th KSLI were part of Joe Soap's Army whose 'bold commander' remained safely in the rear.

June was at its burnished best as we prepared to depart for northern France in the Jaguar whose 5.3-litre V12 engine is a massive masterpiece. The power unit was appropriate, albeit in a roundabout way, because the world's first tanks, which made their debut midway through the battle, had 105bhp Daimler engines and Daimler is, of course, part of Jaguar's family. The first tanks' theoretical top speed of 3.7mph in perfect conditions was reduced to 0.5mph over ground moonscaped by literally millions of overlapping shell craters. Temperatures inside the 28-ton monsters reached almost 50 degrees C. One officer went mad, shooting his engine to make it go faster.

Shropshire, Staffordshire, Worcestershire, Gloucestershire, Wiltshire, Berkshire, Middlesex, Surrey and Kent were all on the Jaguar's route to Dover. They were just a few of the counties whose infantry regiments had been on the Somme in 1916, fighting alongside comrades from Australia, Canada, New Zealand, South Africa and Ireland, and the doomed Deccan Horse from India, who charged High Wood's machine guns with lowered lances glinting in the July sun. Driving through those counties on a summer evening, wafting along as quickly as a First World War fighter plane, I could hear the doomed youth of Wilfred Owen's poem singing *Tipperary* and *Pack Up Your Troubles* as they headed for the Channel ports. The vast majority were not professional soldiers, although the battalions they formed became part of old-established regiments. Butchers, bakers and candlestick makers, clerks, miners, farm labourers, estate agents and railway porters, they were typical of the 2.5 million Brits who volunteered between 7 August, 1914, and the end of the following year. Britain's full-time army, just 247,432 men at the outbreak of war, had been decimated long before Haig and General Sir Henry Rawlinson launched the Somme offensive.

Photographer Graham Harrison and I crossed to Calais early in the morning of 30 June, followed the autoroute for a few miles, then headed southwards from St Omer. The Jaguar loped along quiet roads flanked by slender trees and small farms with few of the hideous modern buildings that now sully so many British landscapes. That sort of motoring is the Jaguar's forte, because its magnificent engine makes the XJ-SC a superb tourer in which 100mph feels like 65–70, even with the roof off.

There were two good reasons for not taking the autoroute all the way to Bapaume. First, we had time on our side and driving on French country roads is far more enjoyable than reeling in motorway miles. Second, this trip across what Will the Quill called 'the vasty fields of France' gave me good reason to visit the battlefield of Agincourt. It was there that Henry V and the men of the longbow, a small, hungry army ravaged by sickness and retreating to Calais, faced the French on 25 October, 1415. Ripe corn, rippled by a warm breeze, covered the fields where armoured knights, invariably and quite correctly described as the flower of French chivalry, charged to their death. Henry's army, outnumbered by more than four to one, suffered only a few hundred casualties that day. French peasants, supervised by the Bishop of Arras, buried about 6,000 of their compatriots. The 'V' sign dates from that period. Pre-battle formalities during the Hundred Years War included French heralds riding out to warn that captured archers could look forward to losing the first two fingers of the right hand. The bowmen, confident in their team's record away from home, brandished those same digits and bellowed bucolic insults.

It is also worth mentioning that the heads of Henry's soldiers were protected by leather helmets remarkably like those devised for tank crews on the Somme, half a millennium later. Unlike its medieval predecessor, the 1916 version had a chain-mail veil to provide a modest measure of protection for the eyes. Weapons worthy of the Middle Ages were also used by troops fighting hand-to-hand in the trenches. They included clubs and daggers, and an elbow-length steel gauntlet with a built-in blade. Warfare's eternal nature is characterised by an even neater coincidence. Medieval chroniclers tell us that Henry's archers unleashed 15 well-aimed arrows a minute. Five hundred years later, that was the rate of fire for a British rifleman with his .303 Lee-Enfield.

I slotted my bittersweet *Oh What A Lovely War* tape into the cassette player as the poppy-red Jaguar followed another rural by-way towards Albert, the only town on the Somme front. We could now see, away to our left, the low chalk escarpment, backed by gently rolling downland, that the British assaulted on 1 July, 1916. There, as at Agincourt, ripe corn was liquid gold in the sunlight. A skylark was singing when we paused at a deserted crossroads before taking a lane towards Thiepval. At first, no matter how hard I tried, it was difficult to picture this peaceful landscape being ripped apart by the bloody talons of war. Seventy years ago we would have been passing mile after mile of guns that between them fired 1.5 million shells during that seven-day bombardment. But, as the Jaguar slowed to little more than the KSLI's brisk marching pace, and as the tape played songs that made me swallow hard, I *could* picture endless columns of Tommies, joking and smoking as they marched to the trenches.

The Jaguar crossed the little River Ancre, which cuts through the escarpment, and climbed the short, steep hill to Thiepval, where Sir Edwin Lutyens's huge memorial catches the eye for miles around. The poppies from Shropshire had reached their destination. I had expected to be deeply moved by the sight of all those names, but just shook my head and heaved a sigh. Thiepval's significance is powerful enough to numb the emotions.

We spent a couple of hours seeking a room for the night, spurring the Jaguar along at an apparently effortless 90–110mph as it traced a rectangle bounded by Albert, Bapaume, Peronne and Amiens, where the Hotel de la Paix had a vacancy. I fretted a little, but Harrison was all smiles. 'The light's no good now,' he soothed. 'But later it will be perfect. Let's go back to Albert and get something to eat.'

We were sitting outside a small café near the railway station, relaxing in the sun, sipping cold beer and enjoying excellent omelettes, when we saw something we will never forget. Walking towards us from the station was a shortish man clutching two small suitcases and a Boots plastic carrier bag. Old, but not apparently old enough to have been in the Great War, he was asking the way to one of Albert's few hotels. We drank up and offered him a lift. His name was Tom Stephens and he had boarded the train in Swindon at 6.30 that morning. We were wrong about his age. Tom was within days of his 91st birthday. The 21st had been spent in the trenches near La Boiselle, a five-minute drive from where we met him. 'When we got there, the trench was full of Royal Fusiliers, all dead,' he recalled. 'Some of the lads said a machine gun had got them. I reckoned it was probably a shell. It didn't really matter. They were dead.'

Tom later sent me a collection of precious photographs, sepia-tinted memories of himself kitted out for France, his future wife, and his comrades in a Royal Engineers' field company attached to the Royal Warwickshires. There were more than 40 smiling men in one group. Fourteen came back from an attack launched in the third week of July, 1916. The casualty rate was tragically typical.

We said farewell to our resolute and independent old pilgrim, because it was time to explore the battlefield. The light was ideal and coaches crammed with nine-to-five tourists were heading for their hotels as the XJ-SC purred out of Albert. Just before La Boiselle we crossed the front line held by the Rawlinson's Fourth Army on 1 July, 1916. The French Sixth Army had been deployed on both sides of the sluggishly meandering River Somme while their allies attacked on a front that ran roughly northwards for some 16 miles. We stopped on the crest of a ridge near Pozieres, where Graham photographed the Tank Corps memorial while I looked back towards Albert, contemplating the start of 'The Big Push'. The success of the plan adopted by Haig and Rawlinson depended on the artillery. As they assembled in the trenches, most men of Joe Soap's Army found it easy to believe that nothing, not even rats, could survive the bombardment's fury. The infantry assault, they were told, would be like a stroll in the park on a Sunday afternoon. All they had to do was advance at a steady pace and occupy trenches that would be manned only by dead Germans. Rawlinson, safe in his chateau near Amiens, was convinced that a charge would reduce his men to a rabble.

But the great bombardment's prolonged ferocity was more apparent than real. The British actually mustered far fewer heavy guns per mile than their French allies, and had relatively few experienced officers to direct their fire with precision. About one shell in three was a dud. Others exploded on impact, sending up impressive eruptions of rubble rather than penetrating the chalk and devastating the Germans' deep, well-equipped dugouts. The great strength of those fortifications was known to Haig and his staff, because the French had captured one earlier in the year. As the Tommies soon discovered, lighter guns had failed to destroy the tangled acres of barbed wire in no man's land – the wire on which thousands were to die.

The first of July, 1916, stands out as the greatest disaster in the British Army's history. Awed by the bombardment and confident in their commanders, some 60,000 men of Kitchener's Army flooded from their trenches when the whistles blew at 7.30am. Laden with more than 60lb of equipment – relatively more than mules were expected to carry – the first wave set off across no man's land, their bayonets twinkling in the sun. Some cheered and kicked footballs towards the enemy's front line. Had they been allowed to charge, and had their burdens been lighter, the Tommies might have stood a chance. As it was, the Germans, watching through periscopes, had time to race from their dugouts and man the parapets. Machine guns firing 600 rounds a minute started traversing the slopes, slaughtering wave after wave of attackers. Many died even before they reached the *British* front line, hit by shells from unsuspected German artillery positions.

Joe Soap's Army lost 60,000 men that day, including 21,000 dead. Most fell in the first hour, when the gates of hell opened wider than ever before. Thirty-two brave battalions, each of which had numbered just under 1,000 men when they went over the top, suffered more than 500 casualties. The 1st Newfoundlanders, whose preserved trenches we visited, lost nearly 700, including all their officers. Their tragedy was matched, almost to a man, by the 10th West Yorks.

Harrison and I moved on, saying little as we pondered the enormity of it all. We went to High Wood, where clustered trees were like a dark malevolent cloud posed on the northern rim of a shallow, tranquil valley waist-deep in ripe corn. Two months of grim fighting reduced the wood to a desolation of splintered stumps and cratered mud. The trees flourish now, because their roots are in soil enriched by the bones of the 8,000 men whose bodies were not recovered. Thousands more are buried in the nearby cemetery.

The land was deserted that evening. We remarked on a solitary dog's single bark as the Jaguar whispered across the valley from High Wood to Bazentin-le-Grand, an impressive name for what proved to be a few farm buildings on the reverse slope of a south-facing ridge. In the early hours of 14 July, 1916, it was attacked by a brigade that included the 7th Battalion, King's Shropshire Light Infantry. The battalion had numbered 33 officers and 905 other ranks when it reached the Somme a few days before. Several were killed when their own artillery fell short. The rest were faced with two rows of 'exceptionally strong and quite uncut wire' up to 20 yards deep in places. None of the first wave got through. The German machine gunners had the easiest of targets when following waves closed on their comrades. Survivors of that typically doomed assault eventually took refuge in a sunken lane about 200 yards from the trenches they had been sent to capture. In a few minutes, the battalion had been reduced to six officers and about 135 other ranks. Shropshire's slain included my wife's great-uncle, whose wife was pregnant. Graham nearly stepped on a half-buried shell while taking pictures at Bazentin-le-Grand. It was a sharp reminder that people are still killed by ammunition that has been awaiting a victim since 1916, just as human bones are still uncovered by the plough.

The slaughter continued for week after week, month after month. Rats became bloated to the size of cats as they feasted on dead men roasted by the sun in no man's land. The buzzing of huge, corpse-fed flies could often be heard above the thunder of battle. When they occupied trenches opposite Serre, one of several fortified villages, the Shropshire Pals found themselves waist-deep in stinking cadavers that had been there for nearly a fortnight.

When the sun set we hurried back to Albert for a beer. In the bar, surrounded by members of his battlefield tour party, was Martin Middlebrook, the Lincolnshire farmer whose *First Day On The Somme* is a stunning narrative distilled from hundreds of interviews with veterans of 1916's disaster. I hope he will forgive me for quoting a Private Smith of Joe Soap's Army: 'It was pure bloody murder. Douglas Haig should have been hung, drawn and quartered for what he did on the Somme. The cream of British manhood was shattered in less than six hours.'

36

STRONG BEER AND DAINTY DISHES

1989

Welcome to Ingolstadt, an ancient city on the River Danube that witnessed the signing of a document noble enough to be mentioned in the same reverential breath as the Declaration of Independence, Magna Carta and the Laws of Cricket. I refer to the Pure Beer Law of 1516, which helped make Bavaria the serious froth-blower's answer to the Elysian Fields. Ingolstadt is also famous as Audi's base, which might appear to explain your fleet-footed reporter's presence. But I must be the only foreign motoring writer ever to hit town without visiting the *Vorsprung durch Technik* marque's nerve centre. There are three reasons for this.

First: I'm heading in the general direction of home after a whirlwind tour of Bavaria, and the schedule is tighter than a miser's fist. Time to join fun-loving Chairman Piech and his colleagues for coffee would have been found had I been at the helm of a BMW, Mercedes or Jaguar, but the idea of driving one of Audi's new V-8-engined flagships to the birthplace it had left a few weeks earlier did nothing for my puckish sense of humour.

Second: Time being at a premium, and this 2,000-mile trip being more concerned with travel than technology, the choice boiled down to watching robots making cars or investigating the Bavarian Army Museum. Housed in the town's medieval castle, the latter fascinated me with a collection ranging from armour, muskets, swords, pikes, halberds, uniforms and martial musical instruments to huge, lion-mouthed cannon ornate enough to be classified as 16th-century works of art.

Third: I didn't risk being invited to blast a lunchtime hole in Audi's budget for the entertainment of itinerant wordsmiths. That's because my heart's not up to the strain imposed by trying to pronounce words that are ten-a-pfennig on local menus. Bavarian specialities include such tongue-tanglers as *versoffene Jungfern* and *Nonnenfurzle*.

The Audi V8 can reel in autobahn miles in a manner worthy of the legendary strider blessed with seven-league boots. Top speed is said to be 146mph. During the past few days I've spent a lot of time feeling very relaxed and comfortable while cruising in the 125–135mph bracket and blessing West Germany for being just about the only place on the planet where good roads coincide with the legal freedom to let powerful cars flex their muscles. Breakers of Britain's 70mph limit are flogged in public and then transported to the colonies, where they must spend ten years breaking stones on a bread-and-water diet. Traffic cops in most of mainland Europe regard such treatment as benign. Being allowed to push the go-faster foot in the general direction of the antipodes – granted appropriate traffic and weather conditions, of course – is as good a reason as any for visiting West Germany. The adult view of speed also helps explain the Fatherland's enviable reputation for producing cars capable of going hard, hour after hour, without the landscape being knee-deep in pulverised pistons and corkscrewed crankshafts.

One night was spent in Coburg, where a statue commemorates Prince Albert of Saxe-Coburg-Gotha. Guys with tripartite surnames tend to get noticed. Sure enough, Albert became Mr Queen Victoria in 1840. In truth, the prince consort was far brighter than many of Britain's kings. We drank to his memory in the Hotel Goldene Traube, where the trip's first stoup of Bavarian beer tasted all the better for being served by a smiling, bright-eyed barmaid with butter-gold hair. Bavaria has more than its fair share of ladies who match up to that description. How they remain so delectable in a region renowned for immense amounts of food and drink is a mystery. The typical breakfast includes enough different cereals to feed a starving cavalry regiment, acres of cheese and cold meats, fresh-baked bread piled high enough to rival southern Bavaria's saw-toothed Alps, and pastries that would tempt the most ascetic saint who ever preached the gospel of self-denial. This rates as nothing more than a light snack.

Bavaria is also famous for an astonishing wealth of baroque and rococo architecture. Many homes, shops and taverns have scenes, or even complete fairy tales, beautifully painted on their outside walls. The building industry's most celebrated patron was King Ludwig II, who ruled Bavaria from 1864 until his mysterious death in 1886. Eccentric enough to fancy himself as just about everything from a dragon-slaying Wagnerian hero to an Indian mogul, Ludwig lavished umpteen fortunes on such fantasy castles as Neuschwanstein, which could have come straight from Walt Disney's sketchpad. His grandfather abdicated after a scandal involving Lola Montez, one of history's most colourful courtesans. Bavaria's kings were far more fun than today's po-faced politicians.

Talking of fun, I should let you know that the Bavarian specialities mentioned earlier – *versoffene Jungfern* and *Nonnenfurzle* – are translated in the German National Tourist Office's very prim and proper *Let's Go to Bavaria* brochure. I can tell you, with hand on heart, that the words mean 'drunk virgins' and 'nuns' farts'.

37

FRANCE'S SPACESHIP

ON WHEELS

1990

In 1955 a 'cheering, exuberantly enthusiastic crowd' besieged Citroën's stand at the Paris Motor Show. The future had arrived in the astonishing shape of the DS19, a shark-nosed saloon that has been rightly hailed as a major landmark in the automobile's history. Features that made its rivals look like throwbacks to the chariot-and-charger age included advanced aerodynamics – to make the most of what was essentially a pre-war engine – inboard disc brakes for the front wheels, an entirely novel self-levelling hydro-pneumatic suspension, and, of course, the front-wheel-drive layout that had been a Citroën speciality since 1934.

People who flocked to the stand didn't just goggle, gasp and gape. Citroën's reputation for delivering the avant-garde engineering goods helped account for 749 firm orders being placed within 45 minutes of the newcomer's debut. By the end of the day the total had topped 12,000 and the whole of the following year's planned production had been accounted for.

Cars for the British market were assembled at Citroën's factory in Slough until 1966. One of the last, GBL 666C, was sold by the importer's Reading dealer on 10 September, 1965. The total on-the-road price was a few coins under £1,665. What is now an amazingly low-mileage car remained with the original buyer until 1968. Twenty years later, the second owner sold it to Andrew Brodie, who regards yesterday's

Citroëns as the greatest things to come out of France since Dom Perignon invented champagne.

Brodie, whose qualifications include membership of the International Food and Wine Society, suggested giving the 'Day Ess' an opportunity to stretch its legs on French roads. How would a 25-year-old example of a 35-year-old design, propelled by an engine whose roots go right back to the *Traction Avant* of 1934, stand up to a long weekend involving a four-figure mileage? Photographer Martyn 'Jean Luc' Goddard and I accepted the offer with alacrity, Brodie's credentials as a first-class travelling companion having been proved during a previous trip to Normandy with a Citroën SM. Chris Morrow, who speaks fluent French, volunteered to be our interpreter.

Thursday: Stagger out of makeshift bed in Goddard's studio at 5am. Brodie arrives in mind-boggling DS that has clocked only 15,909 miles from new. He fills Gasthof Goddard's breakfast room with doom-laden talk of dodgy driveshafts, how incredibly complicated the gear linkage is – something about ball bearings in a holed tube – then switches to such light-hearted topics as the SM's manually tensioned secondary chains. Your reporter, looking even blanker than usual, explains that at this hour he's incapable of concentrating on anything more technical than crunching cornflakes.

Boot swallows personal luggage, plus Goddard's photographic equipment, without too much trouble. But finding room for a few cases of wine will be a problem. Brodie drives with Gallic panache while Goddard navigates us out of London. Morrow and Llewellin stretch legs and relax in the exceptionally spacious rear compartment. Wave to worker ants, crawling into the city, as blue Citroën cruises eastwards at 75–80mph.

'Top speed was 101, according to the *Autocar* road test,' says Brodie. 'But the old 1.9-litre engine has a reputation for throwing rods if you get too enthusiastic. This is the high compression version' – he interjects a mocking laugh – 'so we're talking about 8.5 to one and all of 83bhp on tap at 4,500 revs. Sounds like a middle-aged bumble bee when you put your foot down.'

Must have crossed the Dover–Calais ditch literally

hundreds of times, but this is the first trip by hovercraft. The ramp's angle gives Brodie an excuse to remind us that DS features include a body that rises or falls through umpteen inches as you move a lever inside. Cars are strapped to the deck. Goddard recalls brother-in-law who used to work for Hoverspeed and once saw a Jaguar XJ6 hit the roof during a rough crossing. Depart right on time . . . but return four minutes later, with a skirt problem. Commendably swift transfer to standby craft, but I soon realise that these crossings are too short for a proper breakfast to be served. Fortunately, the International Food and Wine Society's representative produces a package of home-made *rosbif* sandwiches as the hovercraft tackles what Admiral Sir Francis Beaufort's scale classifies as a near gale.

Back on land, interpreter and chronicler comment on excellent visibility from back seat before settling down to peruse the *Financial Times*. Brodie drives to within about 70 miles of Paris, then hands over to me as rain starts to fall. My half of the split-bench front seat lacks much in the way of shape, but feels almost armchair comfortable. Soft seats tend not to be good for the back – mine has been giving trouble for years – so wonder what the end-of-day report will be. Big, single-spoke wheel, spiral-bound in black plastic. Curved dash, flanked by large air vents and demister bleeds for side windows, has rectangular speedometer, plus water temperature and fuel gauges. Seven identical knobs would be anonymous had previous owner not applied such stick-on clues as 'WSW' for windscreen wipers. Four-speed gearbox's cogs are juggled by a lever on left of steering column. The shift pattern is easy to remember, though – first is third, second fourth, third first and fourth second if compared with a conventional four-on-the-floor shift layout.

The only place for the left foot is under the clutch, because the motor is set far enough back for Brodie to nominate the DS as the world's first mid-engined five-seater. The clutch itself travels as far as Marco Polo, but engages sweetly just before knee reaches ear. Must remember that the black rubber mushroom of a brake pedal responds to pressure, not a common-or-garden car's umpteen inches of movement.

Fast-moving traffic thickens as we start negotiating the *Boulevard Périphérique*. What its owner describes as 'the full two-bob watch' of an engine lacks mid-range muscle for battling with six lanes of big-city belligerents. Car also lacks exterior mirrors, so rely on *périphériqueal* vision, supplemented by Brodie's anguished gasps, to avoid side-swiping the locals while responding to last-gasp instructions from Martyn the Map, who can't tell left from right.

Average 64mph from Calais to mid-afternoon lunch on autoroute near Orléans. Brimming 14-gallon tank reveals DS to have averaged 30.1mpg over 349 miles. Three-course meal includes apple tart notable for pastry tough enough to protect the space shuttle's nose. Push on to tranquil little spa town of Néris-les-Bains. Hotel Mercure has splendid *fin de siècle* facade – as have many other buildings – but the interior is modern, anonymous. Amazed by complete absence of twinges after 478-mile journey. Cross road to wonderfully ornate casino's restaurant. Exceptionally effusive welcome probably linked with fact that we appear to be the night's only potential gamblers. Brodie and Morrow treat Goddard and Llewellin to £30 bottle of Margaux. Corsican casino boss adds to the merriment by offering his British guests a free bottle of champagne. 'No bad feelings about Napoleon and Waterloo!' he chortles.

Friday: Why are we right in the centre of France? To visit Pierre Bardinon, one of the galaxy's greatest Ferrari fans. He lives near Aubusson and has a two-mile race track in his back garden. Before reaching there, stop to inspect a Citroën DS19 parked on verge with 'For Sale' sign on windscreen. Turns out to be a 1961 model that has covered 60,000 miles. Alphonse is asking the equivalent of just less than £2,000. Brodie and Goddard exchange glances – the snapper is another Citroëniste – but I remind them that we have a job to do. 'Punctuality is the politeness of kings,' to quote no less appropriate an authority than King Louis XVIII of France.

Bardinon's mind-blowing collection, beautifully housed in an old farm building of almost golden granite, includes a short-wheelbase 250 GT, two 250 GTOs and four Le Mans winners. The first car he ever owned, just after the war, was nothing less than a Type 35B Bugatti. He's very anxious not to be depicted as having bought the Ferraris as investments. Most were acquired years ago, when old racers were ten-a-penny by today's crazy standards. Why collect them? Because right from childhood he had been fascinated by top-quality performance cars. He has raced and hill-climbed. Pierre Bardinon is nothing if not an enthusiast. His heart's in the right place, and he has also been blessed with a great sense of humour. Within minutes we're chatting and laughing like old friends.

Would we like to join him and his wife for a light lunch? How kind. Would we like an aperitif of some sort? How very kind. Champagne? How very, very kind. Brodie is handed the short straw – 'Guess who's driving for the rest of the day' – as corks pop from bottles of 1982 Moët et Chandon. Sit at a huge granite table, made for a great 19th-century exhibition, whose top alone weighs almost two tons. 'Apple with apple' is Bardinon's suggestion for dessert. This turns out to be the best *tarte aux pommes* I've ever tasted, accompanied by old calvados whose softness belies a kick like a mule. The light lunch ends at 4pm.

We're hoping to reach Chalon-sur-Saône, about 200 miles away on iffy roads, in time to investigate a restaurant good enough to win one of the Michelin Guide's coveted stars. Brodie determines to show how swiftly the venerable Citroën can be hustled along, even on wet roads. There's a lot of roll. Chris Morrow abandons ship in Moulins. This is not a reflection on Brodie's cavalier driving – he's catching the rattler to Paris. God willing, we'll all meet up there on Sunday. Reach hoped-for destination exactly four hours after bidding the Bardinons farewell. Chauffeur says 'Passengers are disrespectfully invited to contribute to the BBC – Brodie Beverage Collection – before leaving the bus.'

Leave luggage in pleasantly old-style Hotel St Jean, overlooking River Saône, then walk through rain to Hotel St Georges's award-winning eaterie. Excellent dinner for as little as £11, in my case, ends with marc de Bourgogne, also known as Ariane rocket fuel, distilled from skins, stalks and pips left after grapes have been pressed.

Saturday: Joseph Nicéphore Niépce, *Inventeur de la Photographie*, was born here in 1765. Superb museum dedicated to him is a two-minute walk from our hotel. Spend most of morning fascinated by vast collection of cameras spanning 150 years. Leica, Mick-a-Matic, Globuscope, Hasselblad used on the moon, amazing little turn-of-the-20th-century spy cameras, huge 1940-vintage Japanese device for air-to-ground work, Victorian box cameras big enough to prompt jokes about planning permission . . . you name it. Many wonderful 19th-century images are displayed in *salons* recalling such pioneers as Louis Daguerre – his system involved nothing less hazardous than boiling mercury – and William Henry Fox Talbot, inventor of the negative.

Niépce's first snap required an eight-hour exposure. That's almost as long as some of today's car photographers take. Goddard celebrates the visit by immortalising Citroën with a pinhole camera, a technique that eschews a very expensive lens in favour of a piece of opaque paper punctured by one small hole. First attempt thwarted when devil-may-care local takes a riverside leak, unaware that he's in shot. Volunteer as chauffeur for relaxed drive through grey afternoon. Blissful lack of traffic on Burgundy's rural roads conceals venerable four-cylinder's shortage of low-down acceleration. Citroën experimented with six-cylinder engines, but lacked funds to produce them. That's one of the DS19's few shortcomings. In most other respects – space, comfort, ride, economy, aerodynamics, overall concept – it could be modern. A bit lurchy on corners, perhaps, but yesterday's dash vividly illustrated unexpected roadholding and handling qualities.

Map looks like a wine list, but Goddard's navigation steers us clear of temptation. Brodie wonders if Bouze-les-Beaune is an invitation, rather than a place-name. Despite the weather, spend a pleasant hour in Châteauneuf, a 12th-century village perched on a steep hill, high above the Autoroute du Soleil. Café in tiny square serves delicious apple-and-plum tart. Semur-en-Auxois and cobble-stoned

Noyers delight us en route to Chablis. But the day's highlight for the Citroënistes has been the sight of a 2CV Sahara from the 1950s. Devised to cross deserts, this Doox Chevoox sports four-wheel drive courtesy of front *and* rear engines.

Chablis is another nice little town. Hotel l'Etoile charges around £12 for a room, serves a fair five-course dinner for about £14, and provides ample opportunities to sample local lubricants. Grapes for top-ranking *Grand cru* wines are limited to vineyards covering only 250 acres, on gentle slopes to east and north of Chablis.

Sunday: 'Who said these skinny little buggers don't grip in the wet?' Brodie challenged, rhetorically, as the DS sped in the general direction of Paris. Rain pelting down hard enough for prudent citizens to be noting the ark-building instructions in the sixth chapter of Genesis. Stop for lunch in Fontainebleau, where half the population of Japan is visiting the former royal palace, most of which dates from the 16th century. The town's a tourist trap, of course, but despite that we get an acceptable three-course lunch for £5.50 a head. The rain stops. On to bustling Paris by mid-afternoon. Brodie commemorates what may well be GBL 666C's first visit to its spiritual home by lapping the Arc de Triomphe at a speed worthy of Alain Prost with Senna in his sights. Drive down the Avenue des Champs-Elysées, noting such quintessentially French establishments as McDonald's and Burger King, then check into Hotel de Calais, a 60-second saunter from the Place Vendôme. This is another old-style hotel – ornate brass bedsteads, antique chairs trimmed with red velvet, marble fireplaces. Around £50 is not unreasonable for a room right in the heart of one of the world's most beautiful and vibrant cities.

Chris Morrow and friend join us for dinner at Le Procope in the Rue de l'Ancienne Comédie. The other guest, Jean Blondeau, is in the same line of business as Brodie. Founded in 1686, Le Procope claims to be the world's oldest café. The list of famous patrons looked good even before we arrived. Voltaire, Robespierre, Benjamin Franklin, Napoleon . . . Hilarious evening ends with a bill that could be mistaken for distance in inches from Paris to Peking.

Monday: Briefly visit Blondeau's establishment, packed with post-war Citroëns, then point trusty DS's snout towards Calais. Goddard drives, for the first time, and is no less impressed than I've been. He doesn't go quite fast enough to join the 100mph club, which welcomed Llewellin on a deserted stretch of autoroute near Orléans. Arrive at Calais hoverport to be told that the return ticket is from Boulogne. This gives Goddard excuse for a ten-tenths charge down coast road. Channel like a millpond, so *Prince of Wales* completes crossing in 33 minutes, then it's back to the reality of south-east England's traffic. The astonishing DS19 has covered 1,309 miles at 29mpg. Verdict? In terms of futuristic technology, if not scalding performance, yesterday's big Citroën demands and deserves a place of honour among the world's most outstanding classic cars.

38

And the Wall Came Tumbling Down

1990

Dawn could have been fashioned from wet cement by a manic depressive artist. Sullen grey light oozes into the cold, damp November sky, enabling me to identify the Russian soldiers and T-34 tanks. They guard the lofty memorial to millions of comrades who died between 1941 and 1945, when Adolf Hitler shot himself in the nearby *Führerbunker*. This is Berlin, the capital whose *götterdämmerung* at the hands of Marshal Georgi Zhukov's avenging armies was chronicled by Cornelius Ryan in *The Last Battle*. Soviet forces massed for the final assault on the inner city included almost 500,000 troops, 21,000 rocket launchers, 1,500 tanks and wheel-to-wheel artillery.

The city is no longer divided by the infamous wall, built in 1961, which epitomised the stark difference between Western democracy and die-hard socialism. But this misty apology for a dawn preserves the atmosphere beloved and exploited by a generation of writers and film directors. In spirit, if not in fact, this is still, for me, the enclaved Berlin of Len Deighton and John le Carré, of the KGB and CIA, of deception and blackmail, of spies coming in from the cold.

Traffic is nose to tail in the brightly lit western half of the city, beyond the 630-acre Tiergarten Park. But the area near the Brandenburg Gate and the Reichstag building, which Marshal Zhukov regarded as the very heart of

Hitler's depraved Nazi empire, is virtually deserted. Where the best-known section of the wall ran remains in something of a limbo, while the city adjusts to its new-found unity. So we park where we want to park, despite these locations being comparable to Marble Arch and Whitehall in the middle of rush-hour London.

The car is significant. Photographer Tim Andrew and I have travelled to Berlin in a BMW 850i. Sleek, expensive and powerful, the new coupé is a symbol of what West Germany achieved, after emerging from the blackened rubble of war, and of what the future holds for those who lived on the other side of the Iron Curtain. The 850i is greeted with gasps and gapes by wide-eyed folk whose previous status symbols have been Trabants and Wartburgs. Their reaction is predictable. But the 850i also commands attention while cruising along the Kurfürstendamm, western Berlin's answer to Oxford Street and Broadway.

We had caught a pre-dawn ferry from Dover to Calais, then tackled the 600-mile slog to Berlin on a route that skirted Lille, Cologne, Hanover and Magdeburg. Driving on German autobahns, where high speeds are permitted, should have been an immense delight in a car with a 5-litre V12 engine, but we were teased and tormented by heavy traffic, rain and roadworks. Despite wasting no time at all – lunch was nothing more elaborate than an on-the-move snack – the Bavarian *Wunderwagen* averaged a modest 52mph. The more stoical side of my character said that making slow progress in leather-upholstered luxury was just a tad preferable to travelling even slower in a 20-year-old Trabant made from recycled toilet paper.

Night had fallen long before we reached the site of what Winston Churchill dubbed the Iron Curtain. I recalled entering East Germany in 1976, when steel gates thick with barbed wire clanged shut behind us before sullen soldiers and snarling dogs searched the truck and its two-man crew. This time, the contrast consisted of nothing more depressing than a down-at-heel filling station. Women queued for the loo, just as they had queued for everything else in the DDR days, but the guy who brimmed the BMW was all smiles, possibly because pumping 70 litres into one tank was still a new and uplifting experience.

It would be wrong to wheel out the cliché about feeling as fresh as a dew-dropped daisy on arrival. No car, in my experience, could have compensated for such a short night's sleep followed by such a long drive in relentlessly miserable conditions. However, we mustered sufficient energy to explore streets at the eastern end of the bustling Kurfürstendamm, where the ruined Kaiser Wilhelm church appeared to be the only building of merit in a glittering sea of glass, steel and neon. I asked a clerk on the Berlin Penta's reception desk if unity had made much of a difference to the city. He nodded and said, almost apologetically: 'Berlin was a nicer place before, as an island. Now it's far too busy for my liking.'

By the end of the following day, we had breakfasted in the Checkpoint Charlie Bistro – the actual checkpoint is now thronged with souvenir stalls – watched dawn break over the Brandenburg Gate and paused by the plywood crosses that commemorate those who died trying to reach freedom by swimming the River Spree. We had also come to the conclusion that the heart of eastern Berlin, where a number of splendid old buildings have survived, appealed to us far more than its western counterpart. Late in the afternoon we chanced on a section of the wall that is now described as the world's largest art gallery. Murals painted within the past year extend for a mile or more. They provided cheerful, hopeful memories of Berlin as the BMW headed due south for Dresden. Bruised by our Berlin Penta night, the budget was now soothed by the Waldpark Hotel's tariff. A little less than £30 was exchanged for a room with two single beds and a washbasin. We searched in vain for a bath or shower, but found only a loo whose porcelain perch threatened to fall over when sat on. This was more like the East Germany of the mind's eye.

Germany, Poland and Czechoslovakia meet within an hour's drive of Dresden, but the temptation to tick two more names off the list of dramatically changed nations was resisted. Instead, we looped south-westwards along rural roads that crossed rolling hills patchworked with huge fields, extensive forests and pleasant little towns. We shared this attractive landscape with the inevitable Trabants, most of which produce more smoke than power. At its pathetic best, the little car's 594cc two-stroke engine sounds no more mettlesome than a gnat farting in a thimble. One of the day's most vivid memories is of a hill on which two Trabants were overtaken, majestically, by a Volvo F12 truck hauling what looked like a fully loaded trailer.

Nothing more than serendipity took the BMW to Zwickau – 'Home of the Trabant' – where Auto Union's fearsome, rear-engined grand prix cars were built in the 1930s. Admiring locals besieged the 850i while Tim Andrew snapped the Trabant sign against a backdrop of a hill made beautiful by silver birches. This was the second 'last shot' of the day. By the time the third was in the bag, well after sunset, we had devoted ten hours to covering 135 miles. However, Tim's steely determination to return home with outstanding photos was matched by his companion's desire to give the 850i a really good gallop. Until then, circumstances had conspired to mask its true potential. Not having worked with the marathon man before, Tim thought my 'Now we're going home' assertion was a joke.

Ten hours and 656 miles later we were awaiting the ferry. Running on almost deserted autoroutes, we had crossed northern France in little more than three hours, but would have been even quicker had strong, rain-laden winds not been encountered between Arras and Calais. The homeward sprint didn't end when the snapper was dropped off in London. I romped the remainder of the drive's 906 miles and reached Castell Llewellin in time for a late breakfast. Later, when Tim called to check that all was well, he said: 'They told me you're mad. And they were right.'

39

Anthem for Doomed Youth

1993

This book is not about heroes.
English poetry is not yet fit to speak of them.
Nor is it about deeds, or lands, nor anything about glory, honour,
*   might, majesty, dominion, or power, except War.*
Above all I am not concerned with Poetry. My subject is War, and the
*   pity of War. The Poetry is in the pity.*

Wilfred Edward Salter Owen wrote this preface to his poetry in the summer of 1918, a few months before Germany's surrender ended the four years of madness that had claimed almost ten million soldiers, sailors and airmen. Many were impressed by the young infantry officer's talent, including such influential judges as Robert Graves and Siegfried Sassoon. Time has confirmed their opinions. Owen is now regarded as a great poet and probably the greatest of all war poets. He was born in Plas Wilmot, Oswestry, Shropshire, on 18 March, 1893. Plas Wilmot is less than a mile from the hospital where I first saw the light of day in 1940. We soon became neighbours, in a strange but influential sense, because my home from 1948 to 1965 looked across Oswestry Cricket Club's ground to the poet's birthplace.

Owen's grandfather, Alderman Shaw, was a paragon of Victorian rectitude. His son, Edward, was a cricketer, a Welsh amateur international footballer and a hard-drinking gambler who became the family's black sheep. But it was Edward who introduced his sister, Susan, to a keen young cricketer by the name of Tom Owen. He was a sober, hard-working, £75-a-year clerk with the Great Western Railway. Tom and Susan, the poet's parents, married in 1891.

I owe Wilfred Owen a debt. He opened my eyes, replacing juvenile emotions with compassion, and made me realise, at an early age, that war was a far cry from the gung-ho films watched in the Regal Cinema. Poems that etched themselves into my soul included one that describes the victim of a gas attack before ending with what was then a popular Latin quote 'Dulce et decorum est pro patria mori'. This means 'It is sweet and meet to die for your country' and is used to devastating effect after describing a soldier's agony as blood froths from his lungs.

Gentlemen honour their debts. I became determined to mark the soldier-poet's centenary by visiting just a few of the places associated with his life. The car chosen for this 1,000-mile tribute in foggy February was a Mercedes-Benz 320CE cabriolet whose 3.2-litre, six-cylinder, 24-valve engine puts 220bhp at its driver's disposal. Lieutenant Owen, whose personal transport amounted to nothing more potent than a single horse, would have appreciated the decision to treat a German car as a symbol of reconciliation.

Blasted by a leg-blistering heater, we trickled through Oswestry to Plas Wilmot. Now a doctor's home, the house built by Owen's great-grandfather has a garden whose huge Wellingtonia tree overlooks the bedroom where Tom and Susan Owen's first child was born. A blue plaque records the event. We were welcomed by Mr Youens. He has been Plas Wilmot's gardener for almost 40 years. Blankets on which sleeping dogs lie were hanging from a line in the stableyard, where Susan's rip-roaring brother used to fire his shotgun at the stars after staggering home from the pub. Plas Wilmot flattered the family's social and financial status. Owen's biographer, Jon Stallworthy, tells how Alderman Shaw left only the house, its contents and £132 when he died in 1897.

Plas Wilmot was sold and the Owens lived in Birkenhead before Tom's work took them to Shrewsbury.

There was a 'For Sale' sign outside the semi-detached house in Monkmoor Road when the Mercedes paused in Shrewsbury on its way to Dover. Boards covered the window of the attic bedroom where Wilfred started writing poetry in his early teens. Keats was his hero. He considered careers in teaching and journalism before becoming the Reverend Herbert Wigan's pupil and assistant in the Oxfordshire parish of Dunsden. Our route to Dunsden avoided motorways. We followed old roads, trickling through little towns and villages that have changed less than most since Owen left home. Riding on acceptably firm suspension, the agile Mercedes pattered past what used to be Dunsden Vicarage before stopping at the church. A slab of flaking sandstone is carved with the names and dates of Owen's parents and sister, Mary.

The young man eventually accepted an offer to teach English at the Berlitz School in Bordeaux. He had been in love with France since 1908, a year whose highlights included spending a week in Brittany as well as watching Wolverhampton Wanderers beat Newcastle United in the Cup Final at Crystal Palace.

The war to end all wars had been raging for just over a year before he decided to enlist in the Artists' Rifles. Letters reveal marked changes of mind about his attitude to the conflict. He told his mother: 'I don't want the bore of training, I don't want to wear khaki: nor yet to save my honour before inquisitive grand-children fifty years hence. But I do now most intensely want to fight.'

Honour, duty and ambivalence surfaced again, a few weeks later: 'I don't imagine the German War will be affected by my joining in, but I know my own future Peace will be. I wonder that you don't ply me with this argument: that Keats remained absolutely indifferent to Waterloo and all that commotion.'

Owen trained with the Artists' Rifles before becoming a 2nd Lieutenant in the Manchester Regiment and joining his battalion at a camp in Surrey. The immaculate young infantry officer with dark, glossy hair and a crisp moustache loved 'marching home over the wild country at the head of my platoon, with a flourish of trumpets and an everlasting roll of drums' before he sailed to France at the end of 1916.

Fog was draped over northern France like a filthy tablecloth as we headed for Doullens, between Arras and Amiens, after a night in Calais. I had raised a glass to celebrate the Welsh rugby team's thrilling defeat of England at Cardiff Arms Park that afternoon. Owen was with me in spirit. He was as proud of his Welsh blood as I am of mine. Muddy roads running over Picardy's softly rolling farmland linked sleepy Sunday villages as we followed in the poet's footsteps. It was near Doullens that he heard 'the monstrous anger of the guns' for the first time on 6 January, 1917, as the Manchesters neared the frontline that had remained virtually static for six months, despite the first Battle of the Somme that had claimed 420,000 British casualties, including 20,000 dead in a single day. Owen struggled through two feet of freezing water while inspecting the trench near Beaumont Hamel that his platoon was to occupy a few days later. He said: 'There is nothing in all this inferno but mud and thunder.'

Birds were making the only sounds to be heard when we reached the trenches and craters that have survived at Beaumont Hamel. We arrived warm and dry, then cursed a few millimetres of sticky soil. Owen and his platoon, under fire, reached the frontline after trudging along three miles of shelled road and another three miles of flooded trench. The ground was 'an octopus of sucking clay, three, four and five feet deep, relieved only by craters full of water' in which men drowned amid the exploding artillery shells and tackatacktacking machine guns. Owen spent half an hour crawling across 150 yards of noman's land to visit one of his platoon's forward positions in a landscape that made Hieronymus Bosch's visions of hell look like the Garden of Eden. The man whose brief maturity as a great poet dates from this period called it 'the abode of madness'.

We climbed the steep slope to Thiepval, where more than 72,000 names are carved on a huge monument. They are the

Somme dead whose remains were never found. Soldiers of the Manchester Regiment account for 2,000 of them.

Most of the French places associated with Owen are impossible to pin-point, because trees, buildings and other landmarks fell to the scythe of war. But Le Quesnoy is almost certainly where he was concussed after falling into a ruined building's cellar while struggling through darkness to reach an exhausted comrade. He became ill enough to be sent to hospital, but soon returned to the front. The Manchesters had advanced to near St Quentin. Owen rejoined them in time to attack Savy Wood. Going over the top was 'about as exhilarating as those dreams of falling over a precipice, when you see the rocks at the bottom surging up at you', he wrote. 'Then we were caught in a Tornado of Shells. The various "waves" were all broken up . . . When I looked back and saw the ground all crawling and wormy with wounded bodies, I felt no horror at all but only an immense exultation at having got through the Barrage.'

I walked along the disused railway line where Owen sheltered in a cutting during the battle. Twelve days without washing, removing his boots or sleeping properly were punctuated by an explosion that blew him across the track. This incident almost certainly triggered the shell-shock that caused him to spend four months in Craiglockhart War Hospital, Edinburgh. Now part of the Napier University campus, this is where he worked on such immensely powerful poems as *Anthem For Doomed Youth* and was greatly encouraged by another patient, Siegfried 'Mad Jack' Sassoon.

British war cemeteries stippled the rolling, misty fields as the Mercedes nosed along narrow roads to the north of St Quentin. It was here that Owen went back into action with the Manchesters as they attacked a formidable, in-depth system of defences known as the Hindenburg Line. A book by Dominic Hibberd tells how Owen, drenched in blood, won the Military Cross for capturing a German machine gun and turning it on the enemy. He later accepted the surrender of 200 soldiers.

The Mercedes looked as if it was made of clay by the time

we reached Bois l'Evêque, between Le Cateau and Landrecies. Le Cateau is where the British, retreating from Mons, turned to fight General von Kluck's army in August 1914. The fact that the war was still being fought in that part of France, more than four years later, says it all.

We stopped by the shuttered Maison Forestière de l'Ermitage that Hibberd identifies as the building in whose cellar Owen and his comrades spent the night of 31 October, 1918. The 25-year-old officer who could now call himself a poet – four of his works had been published – wrote a cheerful letter to his mother. Three days passed before the Manchesters advanced less than a mile, to attempt a crossing of the heavily defended Sambre Canal near Ors. The war was destined to end one week later.

German machine guns, supported by artillery, fired from the eastern bank of the waterway. It is about as wide as a cricket pitch is long. Jon Stallworthy describes the scene: 'Through this hurricane the small figure of Owen walked backwards and forwards between his men, patting them on the shoulder, saying "Well done,"and "You're doing very well, my boy."He was at the water's edge, giving a hand with some duckboards, when he was hit and killed.'

A memorial erected by the Western Front Association stands on the canal in Ors. On the outskirts of the village is the cemetery where Owen shares an immaculate rectangle of ground with 62 compatriots, all but four of whom died on the same day. I stood there for a while, silent, tearful and bare-headed in the gathering gloom, trying to think of a few appropriate and original words. But all that came to mind, while contemplating life's short road from Oswestry to Ors, were lines from *Anthem For Doomed Youth* about 'bugles calling for them from sad shires'.

40

TAKING THE HIGH ROAD

1997

'Pass the oxygen mask and keep your eyes peeled for angels,' I muttered as the Aston Martin DB7 Volante kept climbing, climbing, climbing through wind-lashed clouds in which tiny snowflakes danced like demented demons. Little more than four paces wide, the writhing serpent of glistening blacktop eventually reached the Col de la Bonette, where an engraved stone informed us that we were the metric equivalent of 9,193 literally breathtaking feet above sea level. Photographer Martyn Goddard and I were not alone. A young French couple, dressed as if for mid-winter at the South Pole, emerged from a Renault Clio. The lady gasped when she realised that the Volante's top was down. Her companion laughed, tapped his skull and said 'British'.

Mustering my best French, I explained that we were following the Great Alpine Road that links 25 passes while snaking and switchbacking southward from Lake Geneva to the Mediterranean. I think they missed my point about God creating spectacular scenery for the benefit of travellers in open cars.

But a joke-with-gestures about 'topless motoring' went down well, France being a country where bare-breasted beach babes are as common as chopsticks in China.

Had my French or their English been good enough, we might have moved on to discuss the Volante. Throughout this 2,000-mile journey, the inner voice kept nagging me about the difference between price and value, style and substance. On one hand, I have yet to meet anyone who rates designer Ian Callum's masterpiece as anything less than exceptionally beautiful. I love the way it evokes the DB4. But how much is a great shape worth? That question has become even more pertinent since Jaguar launched the XK8. Coventry's contender is not in quite the same looks league as the Aston Martin, but is more attractive than its corporate cousin in other respects. For instance, the XK8 boasts a new 4-litre V8 while the DB7's 335bhp comes from what is, in essence, an old 3.2-litre Jaguar straight-six with a supercharger.

Niggles about this and the pitifully small boot were temporarily forgotten as the Volante traced a long, graceful curve across northern and eastern France. Cantering along at 90mph virtually eliminated the risk of fines big enough to finance a bid for General Motors.

How you feel at the end of a long haul is a good measure of a car. In this case, the 650-mile drive from London to Lake Geneva's southern shore confirmed the Volante's claim to be a gentleman's express whose pace and refinement, combined with the warm feeling that flows from travelling in such an exclusive and classy creation, make each mile seem much shorter than the conventional measure. How would the Aston fare on sporting roads? That was the question as we started nosing into the mountains that arc eastward from France to Italy, Switzerland and Austria. Soon after breakfast we negotiated a few relatively minor cols – *col* being the French for a pass – but more time was spent deep down in cool, wooded gorges, where we noted a sign to a village that rejoices in the name of Urine.

Roads important enough to be coloured red on the map eventually gave way to what the short-sighted Mister Magoo would mistake for the aftermath of an explosion in a spaghetti factory. It would be stretching the imagination to describe the DB7's exhaust note as inspirational, but the sound of the supercharger – more of a discreet whistle than a spine-tingling banshee wail – bounced off great slabs of rock as the Aston was spurred from hairpin to hairpin in second and third. However, this was not one of those cars that encourage skipping and blipping from gear to gear just because shifting is fun.

Picturesque alpine houses and flower-bright meadows grazed by cattle with bells dangling from their necks gave way to stark, dramatic landscapes as the passes became higher and the road surfaces more testing. Jokes about teeth rattling like castanets were not appropriate, however, because the DB7 emphasised its *gran turismo* qualifications by riding remarkably well. The compromise between comfort and agility was difficult to fault, because today's Aston maintains the marque's reputation for building cars that handle well. The DB7 lacks pin-sharp precision, but provides enormous reserves of grip and is wonderfully agile for such a big, heavy machine.

Midway through the day, there was a nasty moment when a sign informed us that the 9,088-feet-high Col d'Iseran was closed. While I twittered about our Great Plan being thwarted by early snowfalls, Goddard convinced himself that the road was shut for repairs during the few weeks that separate summer holidays from the first blizzard. He was right. After a brisk detour westward we zigged and zagged up to 6,540 feet on the Col de la Madelaine. We chomped cheese and ham sandwiches while admiring a spectacular panorama that embraced the eternally white summit of Mont Blanc, Europe's highest mountain, 40 miles away. Spirits soared, because there was not a trace of snow at the altitudes we were contemplating.

Late afternoon saw us back en route, sharing the beautiful yet daunting road to the Col de Galibier with two bearded ecstatics who looked like middle-aged hippies and were having an enormous amount of fun in an ancient but surrealistically fast Simca 1100. Stops for photography enabled them to pass us several times, laughing, waving, tooting the horn. Was the Col de Galibier the only thing they were high on? At the top, almost 9,000 feet above sea level, where the air is dry and thin, Goddard set up yet another shot while I worried about whimpering, gurgling noises from the fuel tank and cursed the engine for declining to idle at that lung-rasping altitude. This was important, because what

Goddard modestly described as 'great art' involved yours truly driving to the brink of an abyss. Jabbing the throttle to cries of 'Come on! Another inch! Come on! Come on!' is not good for the nerves when you know there's an awful lot of nothing solid under the car's nose.

Night blanketed the mountains long before we swooped down to Briancon, which is said to be the highest town in Europe at almost 4,500 feet above sea level. Fortified in the 17th century by the Marquis de Vauban, probably the greatest of all military architects, it guards an important route through the Alps and is little more than a cannonball's trajectory from France's frontier with Italy.

Early next morning, we encountered the first of several roadside references to the Bonaparte who became Napoleon III in 1852. If my translations are not too wide of the mark, he was responsible for the *Route Imperiale* between Briancon and the port of Nice, which also marks the end of the Great Alpine Road. Later, the DB7 paused by a monument to another French monarch, Francis I, who in 1515, while at war with the Swiss, marched his army over the Col de Vars into what is now Italy. Elsewhere, the magnificently crag-perched medieval fortress at Château Queyras contrasted with structures that make ski resorts so offensive to the eye.

The Great Alpine Road reaches the coast by way of the Col de la Cayolle, a few miles west of the Col de la Bonette. Missing the second highest road in Europe would have been like visiting Niagara without seeing the falls, so the DB7 did a 125-mile loop that embraced both passes. Starting and finishing in the attractive little medieval town of Barcelonette, this circuit involved so many tight corners that my arms resembled copulating corkscrews. Not for the first time, I blessed the precise, high-geared steering – notably when darting through twisty tunnels little wider than the car – and knew I could rely on powerful, progressive brakes should we encounter vast trucks laden with timber. Which we did.

After spending so long on mountain roads it was difficult to hold the steering wheel straight for mile after mile during the fourth day's fifth-gear flog back to Calais and the ferry.

There should have been more than enough time to reach rock-solid conclusions about the drop-top DB7, but this is a car that defies logic. You buy a Volante because you want a Volante, because you are an Aston Martin person and, almost certainly, because you are enchanted by its appearance. This I can appreciate. But at the boring, rational, quantifiable end of the spectrum, I defy anyone to put forward a case for the DB7 being significantly better than Jaguar's XK8.

41

A TRIBUTE TO
YESTERDAY'S HEROES

2002

Today's *crème-de-la-crème* racing drivers keep their hands clean while armies of highly qualified engineers focus on the minutiae of suspension settings, tyre compounds, fuel levels, gearbox ratios and the subtle aerodynamic tweaks that can provide the ideal balance between downforce and straight-line speed. In sharp contrast, hitting the time machine's reverse button zaps us back to what *The Automotor Journal* hailed as 'the greatest sporting event the automobile world has yet known' – the race that crossed Europe from Paris to Vienna in 1902.

It's the night of 26 June in the Austrian town of Bregenz, about halfway along the route, and Charles Jarrott has a very serious problem. His four-cylinder, 13.7-litre Panhard's wooden chassis is disintegrating, the roughest, toughest sections of the four-day race lie ahead and the cars are locked away for the night, in keeping with the regulations. Jarrott checks into a hotel, resigned to losing hours rather than minutes when the contest restarts at dawn. And then: 'The bedroom given to me was fitted up with very solid-looking furniture, but I paid very little attention as to whether it was solid or not, as I was worrying over one thing only – how I could obtain suitable material to repair my car. I was just getting into bed and had turned to put out the light, when my eye fell upon a stand used for carrying a tray, and in a second I perceived that the four legs of that stand were exactly what I wanted.'

Visions of a wealthy English sportsman dismantling furniture at dead of night, and shedding buckets of blood in the process, illustrate just how wonderfully mad racing could be when the automobile was in its infancy. Fascinated by such stories, photographer Richard Newton and I drove from Paris to Vienna in a Morgan Aero 8, the roadster whose controversial, neo-vintage styling belies state-of-the-art chassis engineering, BMW's 4.4-litre V8 engine and a six-speed gearbox. Jarrott and his rivals clocked about 800 miles, including crossing Switzerland, where no racing was allowed, but our there-and-back journey packed almost 2,500 miles into five days.

The race attracted 137 entries and started in Champigny, south-east of Paris, at 3.30am. The departure time was anti-social, but thousands of spectators lined the road, here and elsewhere, to cheer their heroes. The entry list illustrates how many manufacturers have gone to the wall since that day of unprecedented spectacle and excitement. Mercedes, Peugeot and Renault are the only survivors from a line-up that included Mors, Napier, Panhard, Serpollet, Darracq, Delahaye and Gobron-Brillie.

The 6.4-litre Napier was driven by Selwyn F Edge. Known in France as 'an intrepid chauffeur with nerves of steel and muscles of whipcord', the Englishman was determined to bag the Gordon Bennett Cup by winning the race-within-race that finished at Innsbruck, Austria. The trophy came from James Gordon Bennett, the flamboyant American newspaper tycoon whose father founded the *New York Herald*. Edge reached the start red-eyed after struggling with engine and gearbox problems while driving from London to Paris. Describing the race in *My Motoring Reminiscences*, he recalled the frantic hours immediately before the start. 'Off came our coats once again and, for the second time in twenty-four hours, the gearbox was taken down and re-erected. For three nights we had no sleep with the exception of an hour or so sitting in an uncomfortable bucket seat or lying on the stable floor.'

The cars were barking, bellowing, comfortless monsters with wooden wheels and frames, antediluvian suspensions and tyres, heavy steering, crude gearboxes, rudimentary clutches and, this being the heroic age, almost nothing to protect the driver and his riding mechanic from dust, stones and whatever the weather gods decided to unleash. Push-and-pray brakes had to contend with colossal engines that enabled the fastest Panhard to average more than 60mph for the first day's 253-mile gallop from Paris to Belfort.

Photographs show cars leaving the start at two-minute intervals, then charging along a dusty road flanked by trees and meadows. The long-striding Morgan was soon emulating the earthquaking racers by making good time and passing the spot where Charles Rolls escaped with minor cuts and bruises after his Mors hit a tree. This was two years before he first shook hands with Henry Royce.

'The countryside was peppered with peasantry who had turned out en masse to see the giants tear by,' *The Automotor Journal* told its readers. Although today's onlookers take cars for granted, we were flabbergasted by how much attention the Aero 8 attracted throughout our drive across three countries. Critics lambast the Morgan for its cross-eyed headlights and kit-car tail, but mainland Europe's reaction was rarely less than ecstatic. For instance, we were driving through Vienna when a pedestrian hollered 'Like your style, man!' and a very *chic* young lady rushed out and said 'Eet ees a vairy beautiful car' when we stopped for fuel on a French motorway. When it needed a wash, the fire brigade in Rozay-en-Brie provided everything from a hosepipe to a bucket of hot water, then photographed each other posing with the car.

Great tracts of rural France have changed only in detail since 1902. Notable additions to the landscape include the huge Cross of Lorraine at Colombey-les-deux-Eglises, where Charles de Gaulle lived, died and is buried. He was the never-say-die general who led the Free French during the Second World War and later became President of France. We paid our respects before driving on to Belfort, a few miles from the Swiss border.

Getting a room for the night may not be a problem for the Michael Schumachers of this world, but Selwyn Edge and his exhausted mechanic walked the streets of Belfort before being offered an attic over a back-street grocery store. 'It was obviously not ordinarily used as a bedroom,' he later recalled. 'From every inch of the ceiling hung hams.'

Switzerland's ban on competitive motoring reduced the race's second day to a sedate saunter from Belfort to Bregenz. Pushing on towards Austria, we were assaulted by storms more ferocious than I have encountered anywhere else in the world, the tropics not excluded. At times it was almost impossible to see the end of the Morgan's bonnet, but stopping would have been even more dangerous than going. There were visions of being pancaked by a giant truck or of aquaplaning into eternity if Pirelli's P-Zero tyres failed to cope with so much water. The Morgan's specification does not include such wimpish comforts as airbags, ABS or traction control. When the top leaked, Newton used the Michelin road atlas's plastic cover to keep his leg dry.

A glass or three of wine restored morale and steadied the nerves after we dropped anchor in Bregenz and recalled Charles Jarrott's nocturnal adventures in the lakeside town. They started when he managed to buy a large auger and eight bolts that would, he hoped, enable the Panhard's shattered frame to be repaired at crack of dawn, when competitors were allowed to work on their cars. But he failed to find suitable timber until fate took him to the hotel with sturdy furniture. Midnight was approaching as Jarrott and George Du Cros, his friend and riding mechanic, started boring holes in what proved to be astonishingly hard wood. Holding it against the bedroom wall provided more purchase . . . and brought down masses of plaster when the auger broke through the timber.

What happened next was revealed when Jarrott wrote *Ten Years Of Motors And Motor Racing*: 'Then I had an original idea, in the execution of which I bored a hole through my arm instead of through the wood, and for the next half-hour we were devising tourniquets and tearing up bed-linen to make bandages. In fact, there was nothing in the room we did not utilize for something or other . . . I hate to think what must have been the expression on the proprietor's face on the following morning when he discovered what had taken place. There was a great rush the next morning, and we had no opportunity of getting hold of him to explain.'

Clouds heavy with rain clung to the trees as we left Bregenz and headed for the Arlberg Pass. Our concern was seeing nothing on the most scenic part of the journey, but 1902's racers feared for their lives after hearing 'the most terror-inspiring reports' from drivers who had reconnoitred the route. According to *The Automotor Journal*: 'There were gutters you could bury a man in, hundreds of them, crossing the road at right angles: it would be a trial of springs as much as of motors. Ridges, too, that lent more than a suggestion of the steeplechase, reared their crests across the way. For scores of miles, particularly in the high Arlberg country, 6,000 feet above sea level, the road hung on the brink of fearsome precipices. Ruts and loose stones abounded in the Austrian sections of the course, and the danger from these was increased by a fall of snow in the highlands.'

The road has been improved beyond recognition since 1902, but anyone with a shred of imagination can visualise how difficult it must have been to cross the mountains between Bregenz and Innsbruck. One of the Darracqs had to climb the pass in reverse, which was lower than first. Another crew removed every scrap of equipment – tools, spares, cans of oil, parts of the body – then trudged back down the pass to collect them while their car simmered at the summit. A big Panhard was hauled up the mountain by a team of horses.

Edge had this to say about the Arlberg Pass, which was the last great challenge encountered during his successful quest for the Gordon Bennett Cup: 'If the ascent was rather terrifying, it was nothing to the descent, with its never-ending twists and corners, and the thought that an instant's inattention would mean a horrible death for both of us . . . To enable horse-drawn vehicles coming in the opposite direction to reach the top, every fifty yards or so the road had been flattened out in order that the horses might have a rest on level ground: this meant that the descent somewhat resembled coming down a flight of stairs.'

A century later, even the muscular Morgan was reduced to tackling the tightest, steepest corners in second and third gears. The cogs must have wondered what was happening, because they had been idle for most of the trip. Sixth can handle just about any situation when you bolt BMW's smooth, torquey V8 into a two-seater that weighs less than a new Mini. Indeed, the only real quibble about the Aero 8's performance concerned its absurdly optimistic speedometer. My stopwatch and Newton's GPS gizmo agreed that an indicated 120mph was actually 102mph. That said, the almost magical way that exhaust-sniffers vanish when the right foot goes down confirms that the Mog' is vividly fast. It's also surprisingly comfortable, despite the narrow cockpit and seats with non-adjustable backrests. Storming home from Vienna, we clocked 700 twinge-free miles in a day.

The racers spent a night in Salzburg, then made for Vienna by way of the Danube valley, where historic landmarks include the enormous baroque abbey at Melk. Austria's dreadful roads must have seemed exceptionally awful to Jarrott's gallant companion, George Du Cros, because he covered many perilous miles lying full-length on the Panhard's bonnet, holding a towel around a leaking radiator pipe. Jarrott's adventures continued when the gearbox disintegrated and the clutch jammed just three miles from the finish. Determined to find help, he borrowed a bicycle, was briefly arrested for knocking over a burly policeman, then decided to start the Panhard's engine and crunch his way into first gear after being pushed by excited spectators. The exhaust pipe dropped off almost immediately, so our heroes crawled and crackled to the finish amid smoke, flames and vast clouds of dust. They were greeted by officials whose silk toppers and gold-braided military uniforms made the finish look more like one of the Emperor Franz-Joseph's formal garden parties than the end of a car race. At the other extreme, Jarrott and Du Cros were so filthy that 'no cabman would allow us to get into his vehicle'.

Jarrott blithely credits Henry Farman with winning the 'race of races' at the wheel of his 70hp Panhard, then adds, almost as a dismissive after-thought: 'The fastest time was actually accomplished by Marcel Renault . . . But as he was driving one of the light cars, although first in general classification, the real racing interest lay between the cars in the heavy class.'

That was a big-car driver's patronising reaction to one of racing's greatest David-and-Goliath victories. Louis Renault's brother had slain the giants by averaging almost 40mph aboard his steel-framed Type K Renault with its 3.1-litre, 24bhp engine, three-speed gearbox and steel chassis. But the top-hatted officials were at first convinced that the bearded Frenchman was a gate-crasher when he drove into the crowded Prater park long before the first car was expected to reach the finish. Disbelief turned to astonished delight when he said: 'I am Marcel Renault. I have come from Paris.'

The great Ferris wheel that starred with Orson Welles in the classic *Third Man* movie towered above the Aero 8 when we reached the Prater. A car-mad youngster who spoke fluent English, and knew all about Morgans, was mightily surprised to learn that our teeth hadn't been shaken from their sockets by Vienna's cobbled streets. The bonded aluminium frame makes this just about the most solid, rattle-free ragtop I have ever driven, and that outstanding integrity enables the race-bred suspension to be a paragon of efficiency. The ride is very firm, of course, but beautifully damped and far, far smoother than you would expect in view of the marque's reputation and the mere smears of rubber that encase the OZ Racing wheels.

But nothing impressed us more than how fast those primitive racers travelled in 1902. Factors that included excellent roads, a wickedly swift car and no need to cross Switzerland at 15mph enabled us to get from Paris to Vienna in two very long days. All things being relative, completing the course in four days, a century earlier, was a stupendous feat of strength, stamina, skill and determination. Fate decreed that Paris–Vienna should be the last of the heroic age's city-to-city races that were run from start to finish. The following year's Paris–Madrid epic was stopped after several fatalities. The dead included Marcel Renault, whose fleeting fame recalls a line from America's homespun philosopher, Will Rogers: 'Being a hero is about the shortest-lived profession on Earth,' he commented.

42

THE GREAT QUOTE

2002

The sleepy little French town of Le Monastier-sur-Gazeille, about 150 miles south-west of Lyon, is where Robert Louis Stevenson started the journey that made him famous. The young Scotsman and his four-legged companion walked southward through a remote, beautiful, legend-laced region where mountains clad with chestnut trees whaleback above stupendous river-washed gorges. The 12-day journey that inspired *Travels with a Donkey in the Cévennes* was undertaken in 1878. RLS is one of my favourite writers – his peerless legacy includes *Treasure Island*, *Kidnapped* and the greatest of all travel quotes – so his adventure's impending 125th anniversary prompted a pilgrimage in the wordsmith's footsteps.

Stevenson exchanged a few coins and a glass of brandy for his recalcitrant donkey, Modestine, which he described as being not much bigger than a dog and the colour of a mouse. There was nothing small or rodent-like about our Range Rover, which tipped the scales at well over two tons when loaded with two Llewellins, the luggage required for a couple of weeks and, after we spent a night at our convivial friend Jean Berthelot's vineyard in Quincie-en-Beaujolais, enough red wine to swim in.

It was my first drive in the latest Range Rover, so the long haul from the Welsh Marches to southern France was an opportunity to consider various facets of this soothingly luxurious and eye-wateringly expensive status symbol's character. The shape is controversial – the original's timeless, rugged, styling remains the best, in my opinion – but all manner of gourmet goodies are concealed by that lofty body. They include BMW's 4.4-litre V8 engine, a wondrously smooth, responsive, five-speed automatic transmission with low-range gears for when the going gets really tough, electronic air suspension and a very sophisticated form of permanent four-wheel drive.

Although the exterior may not have made us contemplate robbing a bank to finance a purchase, the stylish, spacious cabin earned high marks for comfort and convenience. The driving position provided peerless visibility while making me feel as important as a maharajah on an elephant.

The propagandists would have you believe that the Range Rover blends top-notch saloon handling with what it takes to keep motoring long after the paved highway has become a nightmare of mud, sand, slush and vertiginous gradients. But you don't have to be a professor of physics to realise that Mount Everest will be reduced to a molehill before a heavy, six-feet-high vehicle responds to the steering like an S-class Mercedes. Today's grippy Range Rover is vastly better than its predecessors, because it doesn't lurch into corners, but our drive to and along the tortuous *Chemin de Stevenson* spotlighted its understandable lack of truly twinkle-toed agility.

That said, selecting the transmission's manual mode makes 282bhp and 324lb-ft of torque available as easily as flicking a switch. All that grunt encouraged me to adopt a slow-in, fast-out cornering strategy that hustled the Range Rover along those tight, twisty mountain roads at surprisingly high speeds without prompting terse references to seasickness from Mrs Llewellin. It was like pointing and squirting a giant aerosol. The downside was that big boots of acceleration made the creamy V8 drink like Dubliners on St Patrick's Day. The fuel bills for our two-week, 2,800-mile journey amounted to as much as I earned in my first full year out of school, way back in 1958. I kid you not. One small town's *garagiste* joked about retiring earlier than planned when the Range Rover docked alongside his pumps and glugged enough unleaded to keep a Citroën 2CV motoring until a year next Christmas.

Running dry and having to walk in search of motion lotion was something we preferred not to do in a region haunted by memories of the Beast of Gevaudan, which roamed the land in the 1760s, features in Stevenson's book and is depicted on a wall-painting in the village of Luc. The beast 'ate women, children and shepherdesses celebrated for their beauty' before a hunter dispatched from Paris by Louis XV killed it with a silver bullet. Warnings about wolves and robbers explain why Stevenson's luggage included a revolver as well a lantern, a leg of mutton, an egg-whisk, tins of sausage and 'a great bar of black bread'.

We climbed to just over 5,000 feet while following RLS's trail and hoped to glimpse the distant Mediterranean from Mont Lozère. Reality was cloud so low and thick that my rheumy old peepers struggled to see the end of the Range Rover's bonnet. But spirits were soaring at that stage, because – miracle of miracles – we had encountered a smiling, long-striding French couple who were tracing our hero's route on foot . . . with a donkey.

Completing our tribute to Stevenson in a day was far more difficult than expected, mainly because most of the roads are very narrow and writhe over the endless mountains like hyperactive serpents. I can say with hand on recently refurbished heart that I have never, ever, tackled anything like so many corners between an early breakfast and a late dinner. There must have been at least a dozen per mile, on average, and we clocked 140 miles from start to finish. The Range Rover's gadgets include a push-button heater for the steering wheel's rim. What I needed was something to keep my hands cool as we approached journey's end in Saint-Jean-du-Gard, a few miles over the mountains from our rented farmhouse.

Stevenson's account of his adventures with Modestine has been in print ever since it was published. For me, the highlight was the drive over the lonesome hills from Cheylard-l'Evêque to Luc. Back in 1878, this part of the journey inspired RLS to pen the lines that embrace one of the all-time great quotes: 'Why anyone should desire to visit either Luc or Cheylard is more than my much-inventing spirit can suppose,' he mused. 'For my part, I travel not to go anywhere, but to go. I travel for travel's sake. The great affair is to move.'

Appendix

Maps

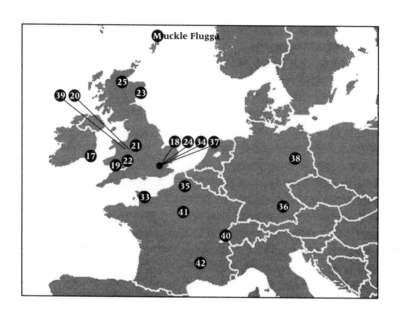

Departure points – for full listing see contents page

17	Rosslare	**33**	Ste Mere-Eglise
18 24 34 37	LONDON	**35**	Thiepval
19	Swansea	**36**	Ingolstadt
20	Ellesmere	**38**	BERLIN
21	Stoke On Trent	**39**	Oswestry
22	Hereford	**40**	Geneva
23	Aberdeen	**41**	PARIS
25	Inverness	**42**	Le Monastier-Sur-Gazeille

❶❹	Detroit	❿	Rhode Island
❷	Dallas	⓫	Hawaii
❸	Milwaukee	⓬	St John's
❺	New York (Manhatten)	⓭	White Horse
❻	Sacramento	⓮	Nairobi
❼	Salt Lake City	⓯	Aswan
❽	Montana	⓰	Djanet
❾	Nevada	26	Harwich

27 LONDON

28 BUENOS AIRES

29 Scarborough – Tobago

30 Borneo

31 Peking (BEIJING)

32 SINGAPORE

SELECTIVE INDEX

Figures in *italics* refer
to illustrations.

General

Abadan Services 242
Aircraft 30-2, 43, 73, 76, 84,
  91, 115, 145, 165, 170,
  180-6, 204, 226, 233, 273,
  280, 297, 298-9, 304,
  314-15, 321, 326
Aksarlian, Tomas 17
American Civil War 36, 82
Andrew, Tim 351, 353
Andrews, John 108
Antarctica 94, 278, 281
Arctic Circle 15, 104, 115,
  119-20, 171, 199
Arfons, Art 54
Arnold Brothers Transport
  96-7, 100, 105-6
Atlantic Ocean 32, 96-8,
  101, 153, 162, 175, 238
Automobile Magazine 57-8, 87
Aylen, John & Jenny 135
Bardinon, Pierre 345-6
Barnato, Woolf 325
Bayliss, David 308
BBC 296-7
Bell, Kurt 94
Bender, Andreas 290
Bentley, Walter Owen 163,
  309, 330
Berthelot, Jean 372
Billings, Fred 96
Bird-Wilson, Air Vice-
  Marshal Harold 180
Birkin, Tim 325
Bishop, George 142
Blondeau, Jean 348-9
Bollinger Rally 325
Bondurant, Prof Charles 320
Bonneville, Captain B. L. 49
Bonnington, Chris 254-5,
  261, 263

Bong, Richard 74
Borglum, Gutzon 50
Bornhop, Andrew 145
Breedlove, Craig 54
Bremner, Richard 166-7
Brewer, Fred 100
Brodie, Andrew *220*,
  342-6, 348
Brunel, Isambard Kingdom
  157-64, 172, 201
Bugatti, Ettore 309
Burke, Martha 'Calamity
  Jane' 51
Callum, Ian 361
Camel Trophy *216*, 287,
  293-4
Campbell, Sir Malcolm &
  Donald 54
Carter, Matthew 141-2
Caspian Sea 268
Caves, John 307
Central Time Zone 42
Chambers, Ken 127-8
Chartier, Gilles 101-4
Churchill, Sir Winston 134,
  181-2, 241, 310
Citizens' Band radio 14, 31,
  33, 43, 109, 121
Citroën, Andre 309
Clark, Bob 36, 38
Clarkson, Jeremy *219*,
  297-8, 299, 301-3
Cobb, John 54
Collins, Tom 66-9, 70-1
Cook, Capt James 94
Cooke, Bill 242, 251-2, 263
Corlett, Dr Ewan 163
Crush, Philip 204
Cunningham, John 180
Custer, Lt-Col George
  Armstrong 49-51, 194
Dahlhof, Lars 295
Dahlquist, Scott 89
Davidson, Dick 313, 316

Davies, Mike 267-8
Davis, David E, Jr 57,
  69, 77
Davis, Jeannie 69, 77
Dawson, Ian 18, 232, 236
D-Day 310, 314, 316,
  319, 323
de Cadenet, Alain 307, 308
de la Rua, Fernando 280
Derderian, Kim 146, 149
Desjarlais, Michelle 108
Dubé, Richard 95, 102-5
Dyer, Sandra 65
Eason-Gibson, Neil 128
Edge, Selwyn F. 366-9
Edison, Thomas 21
Edmonston family 226-7
Eisenhower, President
  Dwight D. 59, 311,
  314-15, 323
Elliott, Bob 40
English Channel 128, 176,
  181, 310, 332, 349
Estcourt, Nick 276
Evans, Chris 313, 319-21
Eyston, George 54
Fangio, Juan Manuel 278
Fanshawe, Col David
  134, 138
Farman, Henry 370
Farmer, Sue 133
Fay, Heather & Pat 75
Fazakarley, Graham 288-91
Ferrari, Enzo 83
Ferrari, Fred 129
Festival of Speed,
  Goodwood 278
FIA 128
Firestone, Harvey 21
Fisher, Carl Graham 59
Ford, Henry 20-1, 309
Fox, Terry 105
Frizzell, Don 116-17, 124
Gabelich, Gary 54

Gaborit, Patrick 155
Gardner, Bob 233
Gillies, Mark 77
Goat Race Festival *214*, 286
Goddard, Martyn 18, 78-9,
187-90, 343, 349, 360-3
Gold rushes 62-3, 64, 114,
115-16
Goodweiler, Mickey 79
Gordon Bennett Cup
366, 369
Grant, President Ulysses S.
50, 65
Gray, Peter 311-12, 316,
317, 318-19, 321
Gulf of Mexico 32, 240
Haddon, Larry 117
Hall, Stuart 267-70, 271
Hamilton, Bill 96-101
Harding, Warren 83-4
Harrison, Graham
333, 335-8
Harwood, James 306
Healey, Donald 54, 309
Heiler, Fred 92
Hellgut, Peter 146-8
Hemsley, John & Lucy 18,
126-39
Henry Ford Museum 21
Herzigova, Eva 278
Hill, Phil 54
Hobbs, David 43
Hogan, Ben 127, 130
Hokanson, Drake 59
Holland, John 153
Hughes, Diane 38-9, 45, 47
Hughes, Paul 34-48, 193
Irish Sea 229
J. B. Joyce, clockmakers
208, 232--3
Jackson, Eric 127-8
Jano, Vittorio 308-9
Jarem, Greg 60
Jarrott, Charles 365-6, 3
68, 370
Jefferson, Thomas 50
Jenkins, Ab 54
Jessen, Kjeld 306, 309
Jewhurst, Allen 255-62,
263, 268, 271-3
Jones, Ken 108-9, 112
Joy, Henry B. 59
Keohane, Dr Kate 87, 91,
166-7, 169
Kerik, Steve 113
Kettle, Al 109
Kimber, Cecil 309

Kirby, Ken 115-17, 118-19,
122-3, *199*
Lambe, Mike 251-3
Le Mans 24hr race 21, 187,
325, 346
Lee, Gen Robert E. 61
Lewis, Alan 169
Lincoln, Abraham 49-50,
56, 61
Lister, Chris 255-62, 263,
268-9, 271-3
Llewellin, Adrienne 193
Llewellin, Beth 7, 12,
49-50, 54, 60, 66-7, 72-5,
84, 166-70, 226, 228-9,
282, 330
Llewellin, Clenyg 193
London to Sydney
Marathon 126
Louis Vuitton Vintage
Equator Run *219*,
304-5, 309
LRC International 255,
266-8
Lyon, Bud & Thelma 84,
86, 198
Lyon, Martin 242, 250
Lyons, William 309
Malayan GP 307
Mallock, Ray 187-8, 204
Manzi, Peter 155
Marshall, James Wilson
62-5
Martin, Steve 90, 92, 94
Masterson, Bat 55
May, John 325, 328-9
McCarty, Mac 79
McGrane, Tim 73
McKay, Pat 119
McNeill, Angus 134
Mediterranean 128,
360, 374
Moran, John, Michael &
Willie 153-6
Morgan, Dominique 303
Mormons (Latterday
Saints) 28, 53
Morris, Glyn 234
Morrow, Chris 343,
345-6, 348
Moss, Stirling 54
Mullet, Roy 288
Neptune, Winnie 280
Newton, Richard 18,
366, 368
North Pole 191, 227
North Sea 175-6, 192, 237-8

Northern Lights 120
Operation Dragon *219*, 297,
301-3
Owen, Wilfred Edward
Salter 318, 331-2, 354-9
Owner-Operator Magazine
33, 36, 44
Oyster Festival 151, 154-6
Pacific Ocean 32, 73, 75,
88-9, 108, 230
Packard, James Ward 83
Paris-Dakar Rally 144
Parkes, Keith 237
Parr, Thomas 140
Parry, Brian 208
Patterson, Sq Ldr Colin 186
Persian Gulf 242, 252
Piech, Ferdinand 339
Points North Transportation
117-18
Pony Express 60
Powell, Maj John Wesley 67
Price, Bob 112-13
Prime Meridien 230
Provera, Corado 143, 146
Prunet, Antoine 306
RAC 128, 257
RAF 165, 170, 180-6, 203,
226, 262, 263, 321
Railways/railroads 84,
157-64, 300-1, 355
Rajneesh, Bhagwan Shre 31
Ramsey, Jim 68
Red Indians 49-52
Red Sea 128
Rees, Marta *214*, 279
Renault, Louis & Marcel
370-1
Renolds, Basil 309
Reynolds, Burt 31
Richardson, Brent 96, 100
Richman, George 288
Riley, Tony 255-61,
266, 274
Robbins, John 'Robbo'
243, 245
Rolls, Charles 367
Roosevelt, Theodore 50
Royce, Sir Henry 305,
309, 367
Russell, Gordon 328
Safari Rally 132
Sea Quest 94
Service, Robert 114,
117, 124
Shah, HRH the Rajah
Muda Tengku Idris 306

Ships 162-4, 192, 201, 234, 240-2, 349
Shoosmith, Ann 327
Sinclair, Nancy 237
Sinclair & Harding 231, 233
Singh, Davinder 126, 132
Smith, Kevin 61
Smith, Larry 73
Stephens, Tom *223*
Stephenson, Robert 160, 172
Stevenson, Robert Louis 176, 224, 238, 372-5
Stinson, Adam 166, 169
Stolhand, Russel 28
Subaru telescope 93
Summers, Bob 54
Tait, Bill 312
Tanks 137, 254, 273-4, 312-13, 315, 319, 350
Telford, Thomas 158, 171-9, 203
Thomas, Joe 106
TIR routes 243, 248, 262, 265
Trailways 24-5, 28
Tropic of Cancer 144
Truck magazine 14
Truckstops 34-5, 37-8, 43-5, 98, 104, 107, 118, 122
Turner, Charlie 36
Turrentine, Tom 28-9
Twiggy 41
Vanderbilt Cup races 86
Vantage Motor Works 40
Vickers, Gordon 288
Walkinshaw Racing 127
Walkinshaw, Tom 132
Walsh, Dicky 17, 150
Walt Disney World 41-2
Washington, George 49-50
Wayne Tucker Enterprises 41
Wells Fargo 64, 80
White Pass Transportation 96, 108, 116
Whitehorn, Tony 138
Wild West 16, 26, 52, 59, 168, 270
Wiltshire, Ray 327-8
Windrow, Dick 318
Woods, Tiger 89
Woodward, Bill *220*, 326, 328-30
World Cup Rally, 1970 126
Woywod, Bert 79

Wren, Tim 18, 151, 156, 166, 169, 226-7, 315
Wycliffe College 12
Yew, Kuan 304
Young, Brigham 28
Young, Ted 327
Yukon Freight Lines 123
Ziolkowski, Korczak 50

Motor vehicles, motorcycles and engines
Albion 311
Alfa Romeo
  P3 308
  6C-1500 308
  8C-2300 305, 308
  8C-2900B 77
Armstrong Siddeley 186, 305
Aston Martin 31, 36, 38, 77, 187
  DB3S 307
  DB4 305, 361
  DB7 Volante *223*, 360-4
Auburn Speedster 56, 84
Audi 340
  A6 quattro 229-31, 234
  Coupé GT 151
  V8 340
Austin 304, 312
  America 50
  A40 Somerset 12-13, 305
  Seven 73
Auto Union 353
Bantam 73
Bedford trucks 307, 311
Bentley 31, 56, 160-1, 163-4, 185-6, 201, 305, 306, 309, 325-30
  Mulsanne S 180-7
  Mulsanne Turbo 326
  R-type Continental 84
  Speed Six 325
BL Cars/Leyland 127, 255-8, 262, 263, 267
  Sherpa 255-62, 263, 266, 269, 273-6
BMW 31, 37
  V8 engine 366, 370, 373
  503 305
  633 CSi 43
  750iL 58, 60
  850i 351-3
Bridgestone tyres 118-19
Brush 21
BSA 311
Bugatti 21, 305, 309

Type 35B 346
Type 37 306
Buick 54
Cadillac 12-13, 56, 83-4, 109, 305
Carter 21
Caterpillar engines 31-3
Changjiang 298
Chevrolet 31, 41, 44, 278, 311
  Blazer K1500 Silverado 67-9, 71
  Corvette 49-58, 61, 73, 194
  Impala 283
  pickups 25, 85
Citroën *219*, 297-8, 300, 303, 349
  AX *219*, 297, 302
  DS19 *220*, 342-9
  SM 343
  2CV 348, 373
Cooper Motor Corp 132
Cord 21, 56
Cummins engines 96, 100, 102-3, 106, 108, 118, 122-3
Daimler 311, 332
Daewoo Chico 280
Darracq 366, 369
Delahaye 366
Detroit Diesels 25, 312
DeSoto AS600 25, 260
Diamond T 311, 312-13, 318
Dodge 73, 311-12
Dong-Feng 298, 302
Double Eagle sleeper 33, 42, 45, 47
Duesenberg 31, 56, 77
  Model J 73
DUKW 315
Economy Motor Buggy 56
ERA 77
Essex 21
Excalibur 32, 39
Federal 311-12
Feng-Huan 298
Ferrari 31, 44, 84, 298, 306, 345
  Testarossa 58-61
  246 GTS Dino 44
  250 GT 346
  250 GTO 346
  308 GTB 32, 39, 41
  365 GTB/4 Daytona 39-40
Fiat
  Uno 60S 50
  619TI 251

Figoni & Falaschi 77
Ford, Rouge River Plant 20
Ford 38, 42, 278, 307
  Anglia 307
  Corsair 2000E 127-8
  Cortina 134
  GT40 204, 187-90
  Mark IV 21
  Maverick 191-2, 226-8
  Model T 59, 309
  Mustang 58-61
  pickups 25
  Probe 58, 60
  Ranger 277-9, 281-2
  Taurus 58, 61
  Transit 255
  V-8 83, 187-8, 307
  350 van 97, 100
Franklin 21
Fuller transmissions 32-3,
  42, 100, 102, 106, 118
Gasmobile 56
General Motors (GMC)
  311-13, 321
  Suburban station
    wagon 118
  V8 engine 67
Gobron-Brillie 366
Goodyear tyres 33
Harley-Davidson 311-12, 318
Haynes-Apperson 21
He-Ping 298
Hillman 304, 311
  Minx 305
Honda 308
  Aero 80 scooter 40
  Civic CRX 58, 60
Hong-Qi 298
Humber 304, 311
Hupmobile 21
International
  Transtar 100, 106
  4300 109
Isuzu Trooper 165, 167-8
Jaguar 31, 298, 305,
  329, 332
  D-type 84
  XJS 75
  XJ-SC 331-3, 335
  XJ6 344
  XK8 16, 72--7, 196,
    361, 364
Jeep Grand Cherokee
  Laredo 67-9
Jingganshan 298
Kelsey 21
Kenworth 27, 31-2, 35, 37,

  95, 102-5, 108-9, 113,
  115, 117-24, 199
Kiblinger 56
Lamborghini Countach
  40-1
Land Rover 128, 134, 169-
  70, 285, 305
  County 165-6
  Range Rover 18, 58, 60-1,
    126-32, 135, 137-9, 166,
    169, 172, 174, 176, 372-4
  Range Rover County LWB
    66-8, 71
  90 288-91
  110 290, 293
Lincoln Continental 42,
  58, 60
Mack 96-100, 123, 253
  B61 Theodyne 105
Magirus-Deutz 148
Maserati 31, 278
Matchless 311
Maxwell 21
Mazda RX-7 63-4
Maybach Zeppelin 73
Mercedes-Benz 31-2, 37,
  42, 48, 92, 242-6, 248-51,
  263, 278, 309, 366
  G-wagen 127, 133, 144
  ML430 87-93
  SL500 89
  220S 41, 45
  280 SL 36, 39
  320 CE 355
  500 SEL 40
  540K 84
  560SEC 58-60
  1632 253
Mercury 31
MG 186
  TA 309
  TF 307-8
Michelin tyres 69, 109,
  118-19, 127, 131, 134,
  148, 264
Mitsubishi
  minibus 307
  Shogun 165, 168, 170
Morgan 329
  Aero 8 224, 365-71
Morris 304, 311
  Eight 11
  Minor 307
  Ten 305, 308
Mors 86, 366
Napier 366
Nissan 187

  Sunny Super Saloon 284
Norton 311
Oakland 21
Oldsmobile 73
  Toronado 45
Packard 56, 59
  Twelve Club Sedan
    83-6, 198
Panhard 365-70
Peterbilt 31-8, 40, 41-2, 44,
  45, 48, 193
Peugeot 140-1, 143-4, 146,
  148, 194, 366
  P4 144, 147, 149
  205 144, 149
  309 144, 146-7, 149
  405 144, 147-9
  504 141
  605 141-2, 144, 148-9
Pierce-Arrow 66-A 86
Pininfarina 141
Pirelli tyres 237, 368
Plymouth 311
Pontiac Bonneville 35-6
Porsche 31, 42, 84
  Boxster S 236-41
  Speedster 34
  Turbo 40, 48
  Regal 21
Renault 366
  25 327
  Clio 360
  Type K 371
  Riley 304
  Lynx 307
RML GT40 187-90, 204
Rolls-Royce 21, 31, 38,
  42-4, 56, 180, 182-3,
  193, 305
  Phantom II 305, 309
  Phantom III 85, 311
  Silver Seraph 83
  Silver Shadow 41
  20/25 34
Serpollet 366
Silver Eagle 25, 29
Simca 1100 362
Spicer transmission 108-9
Stoddard 21
Subaru 127
Suzuki 308
  Grand Vitara 78-82
  Jimney Fishing
    Master 285
  Mighty Boy 285
  Samurai 285
Talbot-Lago coupé 77

Thomas 21
Touring of Milan 77
Toyota pick-up 119
  Hilux *216*
Trabant *222*, 351, 353
Tucker 21
Villers 311
Volkswagen 126
  Beetle 258
  Kombi 135
  Passat 132
Volvo
  F12 353
  F86 243
  F89 14, 253
Wartburg 351
Weber carburettors 40
White Western Star 101
Willys Jeep 311-12, 315,
  321, 323
Winton 83
Wolseley 304
Yamaha 308
ZF transmission 189
Zil 298
Zimmer 38-9

Africa

Abu Simbel 136, 141-2
Algeria 143-5, 199
Aswan 135-7, 140-1
Cairo 135, 137
Cape Town 18, 126-9, 132,
  139, 232
Dar es Salaam 130-1
Egypt 128, 135-6, 138, 140-
  2, 144
Harare 129
Johannesburg 129
Kenya 126, 128, 131-3
Khartoum 18, 132-5
Libya 143-4
Luxor 141
Morocco 143-4
Mount Kilimanjaro 126
Mozambique 129
Nairobi 18, 126, 131-2
Niger 144
Nile 133-4, 136-7, 140-1
Nubian Desert 140
Pretoria 129
Sahara Desert 128,
  143-9, 199
Sinai Desert 137
South Africa 129
Sudan 128, 132-3, 134-5
Suez Canal 137

Tanzania 126, 128, 130
Tunisia 143-4
Zimbabwe 129

America (USA) 14, 17, 24
Alabama 42-3
Alaska 62, 83, 88, 94-5,
  119-20, 282
Alburquerque Balloon
  Fiesta 45-6
American River 62-3
Arches National
  Monument 27
Arizona 47, 55, 63, 81
Atlanta 35-6
Auburn 56, 64
  Auburn-Cord Duesenberg
  Museum 56
Austin 42-3
Baton Rouge 43
Big Rock Candy
  Mountain 54
Black Hills 50
Bonneville
  Salt Flats 60
  Speedway Museum 54
Boot Hill Museum 55-6
Bryce Canyon National
  Park 49, 54-5
California 32, 36, 38, 40,
  43, 48, 53, 58, 62-4, 76,
  83, 236
Cascade Mountains 29
Chicago 13, 32, 34, 50
Colorado 26, 55, 63, 68
Colorado River 27, 55
Columbia River 29, 75
Connecticut 83
Dallas 24-5, 29-30, 44
Daytona Beach 37
Deadwood 51
Deerfield 85-6
Denver 13, 26-7
Detroit 20-3, 49, 57-8
  Renaissance Centre 22
Devil's Tower 49, 51, 194
Dodge City 49, 55
Florida 32, 36-8, 40, 43,
  83, 88
Gettysburg 56, 59-60, 61
Glacier National Park 74-5
Golden Gate Bridge 76
Grand Canyon 27, 47, 52
Grand Teton National
  Park 53
Great Lakes 32, 54
Greenfield Village 21-2

Hawaii 62, 86, 88-9, 93-5
Hoover Dam 47
Houston 43-4
Idaho 28, 41, 53
Illinois 56
Indiana 33, 35
Indianapolis 34-5
  Motor Speedway 59
Iowa 58-9
Kentucky 35
Laguna Seca 72-3, 77
Lake Superior 74, 105
Las Vegas 40, 45, 47, 79,
  82, 196
Lincoln Highway 58-61
Lion's Back 66, 194
Little Bighorn 51-2
Long Beach 29
Los Angeles 32, 40-8
Louisiana 43
Louisville 35
Malakoff Diggins State
  Historic Park 65
Manhattan 59
Massachusetts 85-6
Mauna Kea 88-94
Mexican Hat 55
Miama 32, 37, 39, 59
Michigan 58, 73
Milwaukee 32-3, 39
Minnesota 50, 74
Mississippi River 43, 74
Missouri River 16, 74
Montana 51-2, 72, 74, 194
Monument Valley 49, 55
Mount Rushmore 49
Nebraska 13, 58, 60
Nevada 47-8, 53, 58, 60,
  62-3, 78-82, 196
New England 84-5
New Jersey 58-9, 62
New Mexico 43, 45, 63
New Orleans 43
New York 43, 58, 80, 160
North Dakota 16, 72, 74
North Wales 59
Ohio 58, 83, 90
Oklahoma 31, 42, 43-5
Oregon 28-30, 75-6
Orlando 41-2
Painted Cliffs 47
Palm Beach 40-1
Parker Ranch 90
Pebble Beach 72-3, 77
Pennsylvania 58-9
Phoenix 29
Pittsburgh 60

Pompano Beach 38
Portland 29
Red River 44
Rhode Island 83-6
Rio Grande 46
Rocky Mountains 26-7, 52, 55, 196
Route 66 (Interstate 40) 46
Sacramento 62
St Louis 32, 42
Salt Lake City 28-9, 54, 60, 70
San Francisco 58-62, 76, 162
Seattle 24, 29-30
Sierra Nevada 60, 62, 65
Snake River 28
South Dakota 50
Tennessee 36, 125
Texas 24, 25-6, 29, 42-3, 44, 63, 95
Tonopah 78-9
Utah 27-8, 29, 53-4, 58, 66-7, 194
Vermont 85
Virginia City 79
Washington 59
White House, The 56
Wichita Falls 25-6
Wisconsin 35-6, 74
Wyoming 49, 58, 63, 194
Yellowstone National Park 49, 52-3

Australia 162, 164, 232

British Isles
Aberystwyth 11, 169
Anglesey 177-8, 234
Betws-y-Coed 178, 203
Big Ben 208, 231
Bristol 158-61, 201
Brooklands 184-5
Carlisle 173-4
Clifton Suspension Bridge 201
Cornwall 159-60, 163
Cotswolds 22
County Meath 234
Devon 164
Dover 12, 139, 171, 185-6, 256-7, 325-7, 332, 343-4, 356
Dublin 151, 155-6, 177-8, 234
Fort William 174, 176, 236, 241

Galway 150-6
Glasgow 174
Gloucestershire 12, 22, 332
Holyhead 151, 171-2, 177-8, 234
Inverness 174, 176
John o'Groats 238
Land's End 12
Lerwick 191, 225, 227
Limerick 152-3
Liverpool 232-4
London 18, 128, 139, 155, 157-61, 164, 171-3, 178, 181, 185, 208, 230-1, 242, 255-6, 276, 299, 308, 325-7, 329, 351, 366
Muckle Flugga 191, 206, 227
Northern Ireland 234
Orkney 192, 226, 241
Oswestry 90, 331, 354-5
Oval, The 230, 233, 303
Paddington station 160, 201
Pembrokeshire 12, 170, 229, 232
Ridgeway, The 59
Scotland 174, 191-2, 203, 206, 209, 223, 225-8, 236-41
Shetland Islands 191-2, 206, 225-8
Shropshire 12, 124, 133, 174, 190, 232, 332-3, 334, 337-8
Slough 342
Snowdonia National Park 165, 170, 177
Stonehenge 229, 232
Sutherland 175, 209
Wales 165-70, 176-7, 187-8, 203-4, 300
Welsh Marches 63, 74, 90, 279, 326, 372
Wick and Thurso 236

Canada 14, 18, 24, 73, 75, 95-6, 110-11, 115, 119, 122-4
Alaska Highway 15, 96, 108-12, 118
Alberta 107
British Columbia 73, 75
Dawson City 115-16, 118-19
Dempster Highway 15, 115-23, 198
Edmonton 15, 106-9, 113, 120

Gander 98
Manitoba 97, 103, 107
Montreal 96, 100-2, 106
New Brunswick 99-100
Newfoundland 15, 96-8, 105, 116
North West Territories 110-11, 121
Nova Scotia 99, 240
Ontario 95, 104, 106
Ottawa 103, 105
Quebec 95, 97-104
Rocky Mountains 75, 110
St John's 96-7, 103, 105
St Lawrence Seaway 101
Saskatchewan 107
Trans-Canada Highway 96, 103
Truth Mountains 112
Vancouver 73-5, 116
Whistler Mountain 75
Whitehorse 15, 96, 108-9, 111, 114, 116-19, 121-2, 124
Winnipeg 95-6, 101-2, 105-8
Yukon 96, 107, 113-15, 117, 123

Caribbean, Central and South America
Andes 17, 277, 282
Argentina 16-17, 214, 278-81
Buenos Aires 17, 214, 278-9, 280-2
Falkland Islands 162
Mexico 63, 126
Patagonia 17, 277-81
Tierra del Fuego 16, 214, 279-80, 282
Tobago 214, 283-6
Ushuaia 16-17, 278-81

Europe
Alps 223, 362-3
Austria 139, 224, 257, 361, 365-70
Bavaria 339-41
Belgium 16, 139
Berlin 222, 243, 350-2
Brussels 329
Budapest 245
Bulgaria 246-7, 254, 257, 259
Burgundy 347
Calais 12, 139, 193, 327,

333, 343-5, 348-9, 351, 357, 363
Czechoslovakia 14, 243-4, 352
Denmark 192
Dresden 243, 352
France 16, 175, 181-2, 220, 223-4, 311, 314-16, 319, 322-3, 325, 327-8, 331-3, 360-3, 372-4
Germany 13-14, 139, 222, 243, 256-7, 340, 351-2, 354
Hamburg 242-3
Hungary 245
Ingolstadt 339
Innsbruck 366, 369
Italy 361-2
Luxembourg 329
Mont Blanc 55, 362
Nice *223*, 363
Normandy 312-18, 343
Norway 192
Paris 12, 144-5, 297, 342, 348, 365-6, 371
Pegasus Bridge *220*, 324
Poland 181, 352
Prague 244
Reims 325, 327-8
Romania 245-6
Russia 265, 272

Salsburg 370
Somme 331-8, 358
Sweden 99, 171, 192
Switzerland 321, 361, 366, 368, 371
Vienna *224*, 365-6, 370-1
Yugoslavia 13, 242, 254, 257
Zeebrugge 256
Zwickau 353

Far East
Beijing (Peking) *219*, 296-300
Borneo *216*, 288-9, 295
China *219*, 296, 298-9
Great Wall of China 90, 300
Himalayas 267
Hong Kong 297, 301
Indonesia *216*
Jakarta 295
Kuala Lumpur 304, 309
Malacca 307-8
Malaysia *219*, 307
Singapore *219*, 304-9
Straits of Johore 307
Xian 302-3

Middle East
Afghanistan 13, 232, 254, 268, 270-5

Ankara 246, 248-9, 259-63
Damascus 14, 17-18, 138-9
Gaza 137
India 166, 232
Iran 242, 248-9, 252-4, 262, 266-9, 272
Iraq 144
Israel 127-9, 137
Istanbul 244, 247-8, 259
Jerusalem 137
Jordan 127-8, 137-8, 143-4, 250
Kabul 271-5
Kandahar 272
Khyber Pass 254, 264, 275
Kuwait 14, 144
K2 254-5, 263, 276
Lebanon 137-8
Mount Ararat *212*, 252, 265
Mount Everest 88, 255
Pakistan *212*, 254-5, 263, 275
Saudi Arabia 272, 323
Syria 128, 138-9
Teheran 266-9
Turkey 13, 128, 139, 212, 242, 247-9, 251, 253-5, 260, 262-4